W9-CMH-961

PRIVACY

THE PASTORAL PSYCHOLOGY SERIES,
Number 10

PRIVACY:
A VANISHING VALUE?

Edited by
WILLIAM C. BIER, S.J.

FORDHAM UNIVERSITY PRESS · NEW YORK

LC 79–56138
ISBN 0–8232–1044–8

THE PASTORAL PSYCHOLOGY SERIES
ISSN 0079–0141

Personality and Sexual Problems in Pastoral Psychology
Problems in Addiction: Alcohol and Drug Addiction
The Adolescent: His Search for Understanding
Marriage: A Psychological and Moral Approach
Woman in Modern Life
Conscience: Its Freedom and Limitations
Alienation: Plight of Modern Man?
Aging: Its Challenge to the Individual and to Society
Human Life: Problems of Birth, of Living, and of Dying
Privacy: A Vanishing Value?

Printed in the United States of America

IN
MEMORIAM

WILLIAM CHRISTIAN BIER, S.J.

1 May 1911–6 March 1980

For the quarter-century of their existence, the Pastoral Psychology Institutes were managed under the sure hand of their founder. He proved equally adept as the sensitive editor of the published proceedings, and his painstaking care extended to this final volume, the proofs of which he finished two days before his death. May the volumes of this Series stand as a monument worthy of their originator.

Table of Contents

Preface

A series of Pastoral Psychology Institutes, under the sponsorship of the Psychology Department at Fordham University, was begun in 1955. With the single exception of 1967 when no Institute was offered, they have been presented on alternate years since their inception. The volumes in the Pastoral Psychology Series are an outgrowth of the Institutes, with the current volume containing the papers from the most recent Institute: namely, the one scheduled for 1977.

These Institutes, intended originally for the clergy and initially open only to them, began with a series of topics in which the behavioral sciences were able to make a contribution to clergymen in their attempt to deal with problems encountered in pastoral work. In more recent years the Institutes have been opened to other professionally qualified and interested persons, in addition to clergymen, and the topics selected for treatment have been broadened accordingly.

The first two Institutes, those of 1955 and 1957, dealt rather briefly with a series of topics which were combined for publication into a single volume, the first in the Pastoral Psychology Series, entitled: *Personality and sexual problems in pastoral psychology*. Subsequent Institutes were devoted to single topics which received more extensive treatment. The topics of the successive Institutes and the titles of the volumes emerging from them are listed at the beginning of this volume.

A consistent feature of the Institutes has been their interdisciplinary character. From the beginning of the series there has been an invariable emphasis on the contributions of the behavioral sciences, including, after psychology, particularly psychiatry and sociology. Frequent contributions have also come from such disciplines as theology, philosophy, political science, and social work. More limited contributions, depending usually upon the particular topic under consideration, have been made to the Institute series by anthropology, economics, the legal profession, and the judiciary. Because legal considerations enter so extensively into any modern discussion of privacy, lawyers have made a greater contribution to the present volume than to any of its predecessors.

The topics chosen for the Institute series have combined an attention to the perennial—as, for instance, personality and sexual problems and marriage—and to the contemporary. With the continuation of the series, more attention has been given to immediately current problems. Thus it can be said that the topics chosen for the more recent Institutes have been not only timely, in a period of rapidly changing times, but even occasionally ahead of the time, as, for instance, the choice of addiction for the 1959 Institute and of the role of woman in the modern world for the 1965 Institute. It has been the aim of the planners of the Institute series to select topics not only which are current, but which lend themselves to, and indeed require, the kind of multidisciplinary approach which the Institute series is in a position to provide. In selecting *Privacy* as the topic for the 1977 Institute, the planning Committee considered that it was achieving both the above-mentioned objectives.

There can be little doubt that privacy emerges as one of the central problems of our times, particularly so in the countries of the Western world. In some primitive cultures the opportunities for escaping almost continuous surveillance are very limited, but such is the resilience of human nature that the people in such societies seem able to adjust to this situation and not to be disturbed by it. The role of privacy in ancient civilizations aside, there is a long history of the esteem for the reality of privacy, even though the term itself may not have been used, in the religious traditions of both East and West, where withdrawal from the world into solitude has consistently been viewed as the most efficacious route to union with the Divine. With increasing attention to, and recognition of, human dignity in Western society in recent centuries and particularly in recent years, there has come a parallel emphasis on human rights, and central to the cluster of human rights is the right to privacy. It is doubtful whether individual privacy has ever been more highly esteemed than it is today in the democracies of the Western world.

To those interested in vindicating the legal basis for privacy, it is something of an embarrassment, as several of our contributors note, that there is no mention of the right of privacy, as such, in the United States Constitution. Similarly, it comes as something of a surprise to learn that as recent a set of documents as those of Vatican Council II contains no explicit reference to privacy. But in both cases, as our contributors suggest, the omission is verbal rather than substantive, and the reality of privacy is acknowledged in both sets of documents, though the term itself is not employed.

The modern *problem* of privacy consists in the achieving of an appropriate balance between the genuine right to individual privacy, on the one hand, and the equally legitimate need of society to know, on the other. Here is a genuine tension, which was surely existent in earlier times, but which has become enormously aggravated in our own, by reason of the advances of a technological society, particularly the remarkable advances in electronic, optical, acoustic, and other sensing devices. The problems created for Western democracies by these developments received attention in two previously published volumes to which reference is made sufficiently often by the contributors to this volume to deserve mention here. They are: *Privacy and freedom* by Alan F. Westin, and *The Assault on privacy* by Arthur R. Miller.

Privacy is a very broad topic, and I should like to employ the opportunity offered by the preface to orient the reader, somewhat at least, to the development to be provided in this volume. A glance at the table of contents reveals that there are eight sections. Section I attempts to provide some background: historically, by a consideration of the tradition of privacy in the Western world, and conceptually, by a consideration of various meanings of privacy.

It is because we recognize both the individual's right to privacy and society's right to know that we have the conflict of rights which is at the heart of the problem of privacy in our time. The development provided in this volume considers both poles of the privacy antinomy, but it starts where every consideration of privacy must start: namely, with the privacy of the individual.

Here, Section II points to the individual's *need* for privacy, for adequate psychological and spiritual development, and for proper functioning as a member of society. Section III then moves to a consideration, growing out of these basic human needs, of the *right* to privacy, as a citizen, as a counselee, and as a religionist. Admittedly, the development here is selective, but selection would be imposed in any treatment of so broad a topic, and our selection reflects the overall aim of the Institute series, which is that of pastoral psychology; hence, the special consideration of the counselee and the religionist.

Next, the focus shifts to society, the other pole of the privacy antinomy, and its intrusion on the privacy of the individual. Some limitation on individual privacy would be recognized by all as necessary to the common good. Thus, search warrants are sometimes needed and justified, as are certain restrictions on individual privacy in the name of national security. These are seen as *legitimate* limitations on personal privacy, and are treated in Section IV, although even here our contributors caution against the ever-present threat of excess. Quite different are the *non-legitimate* intrusions on personal privacy, which, following the designation provided by the title of Miller's book, we have called the assault on privacy. This is treated in Section V, where special attention is given to three such instances: namely, the intrusions provided by modern surveillance techniques, the communications media, and the agencies of government.

The next general portion of the volume is devoted to selected contemporary problems in the area of privacy. Quite evidently, there would have been many such illustrations, for that is what they were, of contemporary privacy problems. Those chosen for development clustered around two areas pertinent to the overall aim of the Institute series. The first group, consituting Section VI, dealt with problems which were of *pastoral* concern: homosexuality, abortion, and dying. In each case the question was asked: Is this a purely private issue? Section VII considered a cluster of problems broadly *psychological* in nature. They were: privacy on campus (student and faculty rights), privacy and research, and privacy and psychological testing. The final Section (VIII) looks to the future and attempts to suggest new approaches to privacy on the part of government, business, and the Church.

It needs to be noted that the papers presented in this volume represent a new departure as far as the series of Pastoral Psychology Institutes is concerned. The 1977 Institute from which these papers come was scheduled for a week in June, as was the case with all the previous Institutes in the series. In this instance, however, the Institute was canceled by reason of insufficient registration. In hindsight, it seems that the topic of privacy was perhaps less appropriate to a pastoral psychology series than any of its predecessors. While the topic is of general interest and concern, it does not appear to be a specifically *pastoral* problem; all the previous ones were. Its limitation in this respect, however, may be an advantage in terms of publication by reason of its appeal to a wide variety of persons who are concerned with the problem of privacy in our day.

As editor of the Proceedings and Chairman of the Institute Committee, I am pleased to pay grateful tribute to my fellow Committee members, all of whom are connected with Fordham University, and all of whom shared with me the responsibility of planning for the Institute out of which these papers came. They are: Dr. Stephen M. David, Professor of Political Science; Mr. H. George Fletcher, Director of the Fordham University Press; Dr. John J. Heaney, Associate Professor of Theology; Rev. Joseph G. Keegan, S.J., Associate Professor Emeritus of Psychology; Dr. Charles A. Kelbley, Associate Professor of Philosophy; and Rev. Charles Serei, S.J., Associate Professor of Anthropology.

The delay of the better part of a year in the publication of the proceedings is the result of unexpected duties at the University falling to the lot of the Editor, which substantially delayed work on the manuscript. That this volume is available now is due to the extensive and most generous editorial assistance provided by Father Joseph Keegan to whom I express my gratitude and appreciation.

November, 1979 WILLIAM C. BIER, S.J.

PRIVACY

I
PRIVACY IN CULTURAL AND PHILOSOPHICAL CONTEXT

Privacy in the Tradition of the Western World

MORTON H. LEVINE

Morton H. Levine is an anthropologist who received his A.B. degree from the University of California (Los Angeles) in 1953, and his M.A. in 1957 and his Ph.D. in 1962 from Harvard University. After earlier faculty appointments at Vassar College (1963–1968) and the Graduate Center of The City University of New York (1968–1971), he joined the faculty of Fordham University in 1971. He is currently Professor of Anthropology and head of the anthropology section of the Department of Sociology and Anthropology. Dr. Levine, who has done extensive work in the study of Basque isolation, is a Fellow of the American Anthropological Association, and a member of the American Association of Physical Anthropologists and the American Ethnological Society. He has contributed to such journals as the American Journal of Physical Anthropology, Natural History, American Anthropologist, *and the* Annals of the New York Academy of Sciences.

The human animal has a dual nature. On the one hand, man is social—so much so that the acquisition of social competence is a measure of his attainment of humanity. On the other, every human individual is unique. It is not this literal fact which is important here; what counts is that human beings are self-aware, aware of their particularity. Thus it is just as important for the individual to exercise and experience his uniqueness as it is for him to relate to the group. Socialization and individuation are the principal vectors in the development of the mature individual. Participation and privacy alike are necessary conditions for the fulfillment of the human being. This is the operational assumption underlying the discussion below.

There is no question of dealing adequately, in a brief paper, with all aspects of the subject of privacy in the tradition of the Western world. Although awareness of privacy as such is relatively recent, it has a long and complex history, which alone is worthy of a monograph. The subject is further complicated by the diversity of sub-cultures and class structures in the Western world, each with its own special features.

Accordingly, I shall focus here on three issues which diagnose the situation of privacy in the Western world and, further, reveal some of the complexities of the notion of privacy itself: (*a*) the spatial–territorial conception of privacy in the Western tradition; (*b*) contemporary exhibitionism as an apparent voluntary cession of privacy; and (*c*) the technological invasion of privacy—its socio-cultural context and its significance.

THE SPATIAL–TERRITORIAL CONCEPTION OF PRIVACY

Privacy has many meanings and many levels of meaning. Psychologists and social scientists seek to articulate its more general properties, but different peoples exhibit different forms of the exercise of privacy and regard different things as private. In Western culture, privacy is satisfied in a variety of minor forms and in one major form. Let us begin with a look at some of the minor ways in which we achieve privacy.

Non-spatial Limits on Privacy Maintenance

A number of European languages have two ways to say "you." The second person singular (*Du* in German, *tu* in French) is the pronoun of choice between intimates. The plural (*Sie* in German, *vous* in French) is obligatory in all encounters beyond the most intimate. Speakers of English do not have recourse to this distinction, but there are other alternatives. A proper British shopkeeper or servant will use the third person, viz., "Perhaps *the gentleman* might enjoy this fine Havana cigar." Americans, who tend to equate familiarity with friendliness, do not do this. But even Americans will, on rare occasions, hide behind the use of "one" as a substitute for "you" as in "One shouldn't do that sort of thing," or even as a substitute for "I" as in "On hearing the music of Bach, one feels his religious inspiration." The general contrast between European reticence and American familiarity is also expressed in the European reluctance to use first names early in an acquaintance and the American insistence on first names on first encounter. In the patterns of use of "you" and in first-naming, we have a variable socio-linguistic form, a minor form, of privacy maintenance. Differences between Europeans and Americans occur in choice both of forms and of contexts in invoking privacy.

Americans are more reticent than Europeans when it comes to eye contact, the most extreme form of which is staring. Americans are brought up to think that it is rude to stare. In Europe, on the streets, in cafés, in other public places, staring is common and, indeed, represents one of the more intriguing accompaniments of a brief stop for refreshment at an outdoor café.

There are a number of other forms of privacy maintenance, some more general, some more specific, all minor.

The formulaic politeness of many Europeans (the French and Germans have brought this to the level of high art) shrouds its user in a virtually impenetrable cloak of privacy.

Funerals are often more public than the widow, for example, can bear. A typical solution is recourse to the veil. Equally poignant is the use of the veil in formal wedding ceremonies.

While I am on the subject of clothing, it might be useful to note that, among its many practical and aesthetic functions, not the least of these is the protection of privacy, as in the concealment of "the private parts."

Anthropologists long ago identified the "joking relationship" in primitive cultures. It is a form of avoidance of intimacy with key relatives, usually of the opposite sex, with whom one lives in close proximity. Thus, a young man living with the parents of his wife might have a joking relationship with his mother-in-law. This relationship is a kind of intentional mock-intimacy, which is by no means limited to primitive societies. It is widespread in American business and governmental bureaucracies, where this mock intimacy leaves actual privacy intact.

Another, rather specialized, minor form of privacy maintenance is the so-called analytic incognito, an essential tactic in classical Freudian psychotherapy. The analytic incognito allows the patient to ruminate and to vent his feelings, fantasies, and secrets as if he were not being monitored. The analyst, having withheld his own personality from the patient, has thereby allowed the patient to function in an atmosphere of quasi-privacy.

Finally, here is a minor form of privacy maintenance which departs from a definition. I am talking about the widespread application of the concept of the stranger. It occurs in its most extreme form among the Basques, who constitute an ancient isolate on both sides of the Pyrenees in southwest France and northwest Spain. These people, who appear to have kept their linguistic, their biological, and, to some extent, their cultural integrity intact since the last Ice Age, have a narrow and rigid definition of The Stranger which they apply impartially to anyone, Basque or non-Basque, who comes from more than seven kilometers away. The designation *maketo* ("stranger") is pejorative. It is the most extreme form of the "we–they" syndrome, which is probably universal.

These, then, are examples of minor but important forms by which privacy is maintained. They have in common that they do not depend on a physical or territorial void as a precondition of privacy. Thus, I call them non-spatial forms. They are minor not because they are unimportant but because Western tradition has conceived of privacy first and foremost in territorial terms, viz. "A man's home is his castle," or "Good fences make good neighbors." Note also the rich difference in connotation between "house" and "home" in American English, a house being a building while a home is a sanctuary, a context for intimate life.

Spatial–Territorial Basis for Privacy

Despite the number and variety of non-spatial forms of privacy maintenance, our tradition perceives the physical enclave as the *sine qua non* of privacy. The most extreme form of this tradition occurs in Europe. Americans are surprised that a European, otherwise amiable and hospitable to the point of taking their American guests to dinner in an expensive restaurant, will nevertheless rarely invite them home for a dinner *en famille*. When a European family entertains at home, it tends to be a formal, relatively elaborate affair with many guests. The behavior and ambience are extremely mannered and bear little or no resemblance to the everyday, intimate family scene.

The tradition of the European home as an inviolable sanctuary probably goes back to the Bronze Age. An ancient form of this tradition survives today among the Basques. Their culture is one of the most conservative in Europe, and they retain many customs long abandoned by others. Among these is the relationship between house and owner, worth exploring as an example of the territorialization of identity and for its value as a model on which privacy is conceived in spatial terms.

Every Basque house bears a name and, over the front door, a carved stone lintel giving the name of the owner-builder and the date of construction. I have studied two Basque villages in France for a number of years and have a map for one of them going back to the year A.D. 1245. Seventy percent of the house names on the map exist today in the same location. When I was going through the villages on a house-to-house census survey, this was a typical experience: approaching a section where I knew a certain M. Amestoy lived, I stopped a peasant on the road to ask more specific directions. Asking for M. Amestoy's house, I drew a blank. But when I added "the man who lives in the house called 'Hiriartia,' " my informant responded "Ah, M. Hiriartia, yes, it's the third house up the road!"

Calling a man by his house name goes back to a time when the family name and the house name were the same. The present disparity bespeaks ownership changes over the centuries. But the names of the houses have not changed. The immutability of the house names and the persistent use of the house name to identify the owner underline the primacy of the house in conferring identity on its owner rather than the other way around. This is further confirmed by a common family name in Basque and in many European languages which means, literally, "new house": Etcheverry (Basque), Casanova (Italian), Cazenave (Gascon), Maisonneuve (French), Neuhaus (German), Nijhuis (Dutch) and Newhouse (English). Cadets who did not inherit the family property often went forth to establish a new household. The property, locally known as the new house, conferred the name "Newhouse" on the owner. The widespread occurrence of this name today attests the prevalence of this custom at one time. So does the survival, among contemporary European royalty, of the designation "House" of Windsor, Hapsburg, Bourbon, etc.

Extension of Privacy to Include the Concept of Personal Life-Space

This literal link between a man's identity and his property is the model on which Western man has built the conception of a personal life-space. From this it is but a short step to think of privacy in territorial terms as well. And then it becomes almost inevitable that privacy be endowed with the status of a right, and a species of property right at that. This is what happened in American jurisprudence with respect to privacy. The landmark document is the article entitled "The Right to Privacy" of Warren and Brandeis (1890) which was published in the *Harvard Law Review*. It is worth reviewing here, not as jurisprudence, but for its codification of the Western tradition of an "inviolate personality" and the perception of the right to privacy as a kind of property right.

Typical of legal innovators, Warren and Brandeis feel constrained to show that they were not saying anything new but simply spelling out the implications of a legal tradition "as old as the common law." This tradition is the right of the individual to full protection of his person and property from trespass. The authors call attention to the evolution of trespass from physical injury to moral and emotional injury, citing the development of the law of nuisance and remedy for alienation of affections and even a "superficial resemblance" to the trespass involved in libel and slander.

Warren and Brandeis (1890) introduce a diagnostic element which makes the territorial conception of privacy rather more than a vivid metaphor:

> The protection afforded to thoughts, sentiments and emotions, insofar as it consists in preventing publication . . . is merely an instance of the en-

> forcement of the more general right of the individual to be left alone. It is like the right not to be assaulted or beaten, the right not to be imprisoned, the right not to be maliciously prosecuted, the right not to be defamed. In each of these rights, as indeed in all other rights recognized by the law, there inheres the quality of being owned or possessed—and (as that is the distinguishing attribute of property) there may be some propriety in speaking of these rights as property [p. 205].

To the question "What is it which represents the property being protected by the right of privacy?" Warren and Brandeis say in reply "an inviolate personality" (p. 205). American jurisprudence, then, codifies the conception of an individual who has a life-space, a space which is as bounded and inviolate before the law as an owned piece of real estate, bounded by a surveyor. Given the long tradition of the link between identity and physical property, it is not surprising that this relatively recent legal document should shelter the inviolate personality under the rubric of property, thus perceiving the invasion of privacy as an injury comparable to trespass on property and remediable. This, then, is how we conceive of the formal aspect of privacy in the Western tradition.

There is no arguing that privacy is not under attack in the contemporary Western world. The nature of that attack is something else again. Our perception of the menace is not just a simple matter of fact. It is shaped in part by our conception of the nature of privacy itself; and I think we have just seen that this conception is anchored in an equation of privacy with a literal, spatial enclave. There is no question that voluntary physical isolation is disappearing under the pressure of densely packed urban living. We are at the point now at which it can be said that the amount of space available to anyone in the city of New York is in direct proportion to his income. It can be anticipated that, if current trends continue, no amount of money will be able to buy physical isolation in a city such as New York or London or Tokyo. But this is not necessarily the end of privacy, just the phasing out of a particular form of privacy to which our tradition has accustomed us. We will be obliged to advert to different forms of privacy maintenance; and if privacy is the human necessity which it appears to be, we will adapt to such different forms. Again, this does not mean that privacy is not menaced, but the threat does not derive from the increasing anachronism of a particular form.

Beyond the question of the form of privacy maintenance, there are real questions about what, at any one time or place, is regarded as private. I mean the substance of privacy as against the form which I have just been talking about. The substance of privacy is also undergoing change, and this change has been interpreted as a willful surrender of privacy. Is the change in substance a rejection of privacy, or does it originate in an entirely different socio-cultural source?

EXHIBITIONISM AND PRIVACY IN CONTEMPORARY WESTERN CULTURES

Changing Cultural Norms and Lifestyles

What do we mean by the substance of privacy? Simply this: it is any and every answer which people might give to the question "What is private?" The traditional stuff of privacy embraced personal finances; interior family life; sexual predilections, fantasies, and practices; bathroom activities; day-dreaming, artistic creation; and so on. Now, not only are many of these former contents of private life exposed to public view; they are flaunted, proclaimed as if on a public address system, and illuminated as if by klieg lights. Wedlock is scorned by college-age lovers who announce rather than conceal their relationship. Drug use among the affluent has achieved a certain chic. Homosexuality has gone institutional and political. Every kind of sex act may be seen on the movie screen, like a medical textbook come to life in technicolor and Vista Vision. Families in trouble invite television in to document their decay. Artists allow the camera to watch them make paintings and sculptures. Patients talk more freely about their psychoanalysis at cocktail parties than at the analytic sessions themselves.

This is not an "invasion" of privacy. I am not talking here about the salacious reportage of Peeping Toms or disgruntled blackmailers. This is a voluntary, vivacious exhibition of attitudes and activities which not too long ago were kept behind locked doors. But it is not a surrender of privacy any more than it is an invasion of privacy. In short, this exhibitionism represents a radical change in the substance of privacy, but in no way represents a diminution of the will to privacy itself. Three issues, supporting this thesis, require attention. First, very briefly, why do we confuse changes in the stuff of privacy with the end of privacy? Second, if such radical changes in substance do not betoken a desire to do away with privacy, what do they betoken? What is the cause of these changes? Third, if the will to privacy survives, how is it being expressed parallel with this exhibitionism?

As to the first question, we are prone to see in the current exhibitionism the end of privacy because we equate what has always been kept private with privacy itself—like the traditional European, who takes two hours for lunch, looking at an American grabbing a sandwich at a counter and saying "That's no lunch." Neither the form nor the substance of privacy is the same thing as privacy itself. Different cultures, different circumstances, exhibit wide variations in both. To equate particular forms and particular contents of privacy with privacy itself is ethnocentrism pure and simple. It is a perspective on behavioral forms and substance through the peculiar formula of a single set of cultural eyeglasses. Thus, though privacy may indeed be in mortal peril in Western society today, the changes in form and substance do not in and of themselves demonstrate that fact. And to think so is only to conceal the actual origin of these changes in an entirely different socio-cultural context which has nothing to do with privacy.

Sources of the Cultural Shift

With what, then, does the current wave of exhibitionism have to do? This brings us to the second question, which is more important and more complex. For nearly a hundred years, sociologists and social psychologists—Durkheim (1893/1964), Simmel (1950), Freud (1930/1949), Fromm (1955), Riesman (1950), and others—have been telling us about the evolving character of modern urban industrial society and the changing quality of life therein. The upshot of all they have been saying is, grossly, this: our society is progressively vast and dense in population, complex and precariously interdependent in structure. The members of this society, as individuals, are assigned progressively smaller, more specialized, functions vis-à-vis the whole, while at the same time being coerced into a high degree of reliability in the performance of these functions.

The quality of life in such a socio-cultural environment features a progressive reduction of the total individual in all his dimensions to the limited parameters of his age, sex, and role. The social system as such is progressively liberated from the control of the human will, evolving according to its own premisses. Not only is the individual deprived of the experience of being perceived as a whole person (and thus experiencing himself as a whole person); he is deprived of a sense that he can participate creatively and effectively in shaping the social universe in which he works and lives. A cog in a complex structure, the demi-person stands helplessly by while that structure itself changes at an accelerating pace, making even adaptation and accommodation obsolete (Levine, 1971). To begin with, the individual, qua individual, lives in an unsupportable state of isolation. He ends up alienated from the very structure on which he depends and which depends very much on him.

Exhibitionism is a counterattack against isolation and alienation. That this is so becomes clearer when one considers the difference between isolation and privacy. Though there is a superficial resemblance between the two—both share the quality of aloneness—there is at least one factor which makes all the difference in the world to the affected individual. Isolation is enforced aloneness, imposed by the structure and function of the social universe out of its own premisses. But the aloneness of privacy both is willed by the individual and is not only voluntary but positive. For privacy is perceived by the individual as the privileged life-space within which he functions as himself, in which he experiences, exercises, and enjoys his uniqueness. It fulfills a need as profound as his need to be social. So, although isolation is a kind of exile or exclusion or imprisonment, privacy is a voluntary retreat in behalf of self-experience and spiritual regeneration. The isolation of the individual from a system within which he cannot participate as a whole person and which seems impervious to any influence which he can exert translates into the sense of being an outsider in his own milieu. This is the source of exhibitionism.

The accelerating and intensifying isolation/alienation of the individual has produced, as might be expected, an equal and opposite reaction. This reaction has not been of a piece, in either character or intensity. On the level of philosophy and art, it has produced the counter assertion of existentialism. This philosophy, in essence, asks the question "Where is the locus of reality, out there or in me?" and answers, unequivocally, "In Me!" This is not the first occurrence of the same kind of phenomenon under similar circumstances. It was at the height of the domination of Confucian philosophy in China (a role-sociology projected to the status of a religion) that Taoism broke out. It was in rigidly feudal Japan that Zen manifested itself. In each case, a society pre-empted the individual in favor of his social role; in each case a counter assertion in the form of a religious cult emphasizing individual experience arose.

In the West, the existentialism of Kierkegaard came as a religious manifestation, but it lost its religious ties in the later existentialism of the Paris cafés and Expressionist art. These and related movements aggressively asserted concern with and value in individual experience, individual reality. They responded to the leveling, dehumanizing trend in Western civilization by making the inner world of the artist—sometimes fantastic, sometimes absurd, sometimes lyrical, sometimes atrocious—the subject matter of the arts.

This was, if you will, the most exalted reaction to progressive homogenization and robotization. It was exhibitionism on a high level. But if the problem to which it responded was universal in Western society, it was only a matter of culture lag before the reaction was more general and more vulgar. It was not long before the reaction appeared on the level of the middle class in the form of the numerous rejections of the traditional stuff of privacy to which I referred earlier. In a variety of forms, more or less concrete or spiritual, productive and destructive, the middle class joined the philosophers and artists in a collective scream against depersonalization in an intensely secular society. The recent exhibitionism, then, was no abnegation of privacy but an effort to break out of isolation, to bridge the alienation between the individual and other individuals and between all individuals and their society. And thus the exposure, the shocking confrontation, the symbolic, collective streaking.

At the beginning of this paper, I noted man's dual need for sociability and privacy. In the analysis presented immediately above, there was an ironic interplay: isolated Western man, alienated, jettisons the traditional stuff of privacy, desperately exhibits himself in an attempt to move back into contact with others, to break out of the prison of isolation. Does this extreme attempt to reach out to others at the expense of the habitual substance of privacy entail the rejection of privacy itself? This is the question which I want to confront now.

A Countermovement to Avoid Alienation

Recent decades have seen the appearance of many new individual and group activities which promise self-realization. The oldest of these in point of widespread popularity is psychoanalysis. I should note at once that I am concerned here not with the scientific psychological validity of analysis but with the popular recourse to this therapy as one route to restoring the self. The influence of Oriental religions came to the West in the '50s with a special interest in Zen Buddhism. More recently, in the realm of psychology, we have seen the advent of primal therapy. Transcendental meditation and yoga exercises are current. There has also been a florescence of Christian cults, for example, that of the Reverend Sun Myung Moon. And again I want to note that I am concerned not so much with questions of validity as with the nature of the promise. And, finally, there has been a trend to the traditional religions and traditional churches, as well as to the exotic religions and newborn sects of Christianity.

There is a trend in the same exhibitionist middle class to seek out a wide variety of activities and involvements which promise or appear to promise inner, personal, private experience. The fact that some of these activities have a communal aspect does not take away from the individual's personal, indeed private, experience. And others of these activities (TM, yoga, retreats) are indeed literally solitary. What is especially interesting about this trend is that it has religious overtones. It would be a great mistake to interpret this as escapism or otherworldly resignation. What is happening is actually both straightforward and positive: in meditation, in prayer, in confession, in communion, the individual recovers himself and finds, in the totality of Existence, the very realm in which he can fully participate with the whole of himself. Whatever the particular route chosen, the objective is both the exercise of privacy—i.e., the experience of one's own nature—and participation in the total scheme of things with the fullness of one's being.

A contagion of yearning is spreading across Western society, taking, on the one hand, the form of exhibitionism and, on the other, the form of recourse to psychological and religious exercises. The former represents a protest against isolation and a rejection of alienation; the latter, an active attempt to recover the self and once again to belong.

THE SOCIOGENIC AND TECHNOLOGICAL INVASION OF PRIVACY

Whereas contemporary exhibitionism only seems to be an attack on privacy and actually turns out to be something else, privacy is in fact under assault. The attack is sociogenic, originating in the socio-cultural system as such. And it begins with the system's need to know.

The revolution in information technology is no accident in a society such as ours, so vast in population, so complex in organization, so vulnerable to the slightest breakdown in the coordination of individuals and institutions and the delivery of services and the maintenance of security. Such a society has a voracious and expanding need for information. It is always taking its temperature in a broad range of demographic, economic, and even public opinion indicators. It is natural, therefore, that such a society will support the development of a vast arsenal of matériel which gathers, stores, classifies, analyses, retrieves, and puts out this information. Use any metaphor you prefer: if you compare the system to a machine, information is the oil, grease, and fuel on which it runs; if the comparison is with an organism, information is its life's blood. But one feature of the information process should be noted: statistical data originate in data about individuals; the treatment of individual data is not a one-way street from the particular to the group. Data gathered to develop statistics can as well be retrieved and traced back to individuals. And once collected, coded, and stored, information about each and every individual source is accessible in seconds at the push of a button. The folk-wisdom that a secret, once told, is no longer a secret was never more true. For the essence of secrecy is control over who, if anyone, knows the secret. Today, no one knows any longer who has access to what information and for what purposes. And this is the rub. For, although the data-gathering of business and government begins with a rational need to know, the unknown ramifications of data bank exploitation are a real threat to the individual. And so is the constantly expanding definition of what information is relevant.

Other contributors to this volume will be dealing with specific aspects of this problem. Accordingly, I shall limit myself to three issues. First, I want to explore the criminal abuses of privacy in business and government. Secondly, I want to discuss the potential for the invasion of privacy in normal, theoretically justified, gathering of data by business and government. Finally, I want to call attention to the need to distinguish between privacy and secrecy, and to suggest that the latter may have to be elevated to the status of a right.

Criminal Abuses of Privacy in Business and Government

Criminal invasion of privacy immediately calls to mind the activity of snoopers and blackmailers who collect information about the personal lives of people for the purpose of extortion. In a cultural context in which media feed on sensation, there is a ready market for revelations about well-known or powerful figures in government, business, society, or the arts. These people have existed as targets for a long time. Those who prey on them represent a limited group. Blackmail is recognized as a formally criminal act. Consequently, it is by far the least significant of the invasions of privacy characteristic of present-day Western society.

What is new, or recent anyway, is criminal invasion of privacy by business and government. Two outstanding examples are: (1) the pursuit of Ralph Nader by General Motors (GM) when, after the publication of *Unsafe at any speed* (Nader, 1965), he became the nemesis of the automobile industry in general and of GM in particular; and (2) the Watergate–Huston Plan conspiracies of the Nixon administration. The difference between these criminal activities and those of garden-variety blackmailers lies in the respective motives of the two classes of criminals. In the case of the common criminals, the motive is personal profit. In the case of the corporate or governmental criminals, the motivation originates in a sense of responsibility run amuck; it is defensive in nature and, hard as it may be to believe, even righteous in origin.

In the case of GM, we have a vast industrial enterprise whose welfare is, like it or not, linked to the welfare of the country. If one limits oneself to the perspective of the corporation, it is no great act of imagination to turn the relationship around, as did "Engine Charlie" Wilson, onetime president of GM, who made the famous pronouncement before a congressional committee "What's good for General Motors is good for the country." The investment in a single model automobile is enormous. Its failure is a serious menace to the financial well-being of the company. Management is charged with the preservation, protection, and defense of that well-being. From the limited point of view of corporate welfare, management is obliged to defend the company against damaging attack. In a culture brought up in the tradition of adversary legal proceedings, it is not surprising that the corporation did not stop to ask whether fault, indeed, lay with them. Instead, they had recourse to a procedure with which we are quite familiar in courts of law, i.e., the tactic of discrediting the witness. Thus, the impulse to which GM executives gave way was to launch a series of operations designed to uncover facts about Nader's private life which might drive him from the witness stand in shame. The fact that anything one might find about his private life or his character was totally irrelevant in assessing the safety of the Corvair was ignored, just as a defense attorney will try to discredit a witness to a murder because the witness has a prison record.

The Watergate–Huston Plan caper, malevolent as it was, originated in a similar mentality. It is of the utmost importance to understand this, because therein lies the explanation for rumors of similar depredations of former Administrations as well as the real possibility of recurrence. Richard Nixon came to the presidency determined to preside over the affairs of the nation, determined to take the reins of government and its vast, inchoate bureaucracy and make it responsive to his will. From hindsight, one can imagine the contempt with which he regarded those who claimed the apparatus of government was virtually unmanageable. When, on acceding to power, he found this claim to be well-grounded, he took this as a challenge. We must, to understand properly what happened, stipulate that he thought he had a mission to do what he thought was right for the country. He had a responsibility to give effect to what he believed ought to be done.

It was thus that foot-dragging by the bureaucracy, opposition to his policies in the form of bureaucratic watering-down and inaction on his dictates, leaks to the press, and so on, were taken as insupportable obstacles to effective governing. That the Democrats and other opponents were enemies, he took for granted. He had a long history prior to gaining the White House of accusing opponents of being Communists or traitors. He brought this mentality with him to the oval office and extended it to "enemies" within the structure of government. His solution was to mobilize his power as president to "get something" on these enemies, Democrats or bureaucrats, and thus was born the Huston Plan and, later, Watergate. It was the same adversary mentality which led GM to spy on Ralph Nader. It was born of the same limited, asocial sense of responsibility to his own plans and policies which brooked no opposition. Originated in frustration, his plans to "get something" on the Democrats and to institute surveillance and blackmail in order to render the bureaucracy malleable to his purpose were not perceived by him as criminal but as the proper behavior of a fighter who would do what was necessary to make his Administration both durable and efficacious. It may be a measure of his quality of mind and of his moral stature that he still cannot see what he did as criminal. But we would miss the point and betray our future if we should fail to recognize the sincerity of his conviction that what he did was perhaps mistaken (as a tactic) but surely not evil.

Jimmy Carter already finds himself obliged to ask for a united front from members of his Administration. So will every president. They will never get it; and they will always have to deal with leaks (which we ought to welcome since they are the safety valves of democratic administration); but what they do about it will show their political sophistication, moral character, and capacity for democratic leadership. They will always be potentially paranoid in the face of inevitable opposition and obstruction; and they will always, as did Nixon, find paradigms for response in a culture born and bred in the tradition of admiration for fighters, winners, lawyers, and district attorneys who thrive on victory rather than truth.

Infiltration of Privacy as Part of the System

But even criminal invasion of privacy by business and government is limited compared with the infiltration of the life of the individual by business and government, an enterprise linked not to paranoia or evil but to the needs of the system in which we live and work, the system which sustains us and dominates us at the same time.

In the realm of business the institution which moves into our private life-space is credit and the whole apparatus of charge accounts, charge cards, and computerized accounting. This system will reach a new climax with the universal adoption of electronic funds-transfer, which will simply permit deposits and withdrawals and transfers of funds by computer, making checks obsolete and money largely so.

In the realm of government, the decennial census grows in detail as the appreciation of what constitutes relevant information evolves. The other instrument is the annual income tax return. These are good examples of information rightfully obtained and essential to the proper functioning of government, but it is clear that they contain a great deal of information about the private lives and status of individuals. Every citizen, again for purposes normal and essential to the system, now bears a number uniquely assigned to him, which identifies him virtually from the womb to the tomb: the social security number. Ironically, this token of the irreducible uniqueness of the individual, is the token of his vulnerability to the retrieval of all kinds of private data about him by an unknown array of persons and institutions beyond the banks, companies, and government bureaus to which he gave these data for specific purposes.

Contemporary technology has grown by leaps and bounds to accommodate the system's "need to know." Once gathered and coded, the information is stored in great data banks and, most important, is retrievable within seconds on command by anyone with access to the button. That credit supervisors and agents from the Internal Revenue Service (IRS) should have access is understood. The problem lies in the unknown array of others who may have such access for other than the accepted primary purposes. Not only do we not know, we have no control over such access.

Admittedly, data gathered by the census bureau and the IRS, find their way into large-scale statistical abstractions of demographic and economic value. But, by virtue of the social security number, such data are retrievable as well on an individual basis. And, as long as the question "Retrievable by whom?" persists, our privacy (if that is the word we want to use) evaporates.

But there is another level of information gathered about individuals which strikes more directly at the privacy, properly speaking, of the individual. Personnel managers in all institutions, private and public, have become increasingly sophisticated, increasingly aware of the relevance of behavioral science for their assessment of people and their prediction about adequacy and reliability of job performance. This echelon of data deals not with fiscal matters but with personal conditions and habits: state of health, personal habits, strengths and weaknesses of character, elements of lifestyle, and so on. The higher one goes in the ranks of institutions, the more important or the more sensitive the jobs, the more detailed and poignant such data become.

A social system whose very equilibrium rests on a high degree of reliable role fulfillment has found a deep need for information of this kind which allows managers to weed out the unreliable and keep tabs on those on whom they have placed their bets. Again, the need for such information and the gathering of such data originate not in some conspiracy against privacy but in the system's burgeoning and intensifying need to know. On the other hand, we never know who, beyond these managers, may think he too needs to know and for what purposes and with what effects on the life of the individual.

The extent to which individual behavior has become a matter of interest and concern to institutions is reflected in recent disclosures about Central Intelligence Agency (CIA) experiments and research in this field. These studies have ranged, according to a series of recent articles in *The New York Times* (1977a, p. 34; 1977b, p. 27; 1977c, p. 28), from the development of psychological profiles of domestic and foreign notables to assessments of the effects of various drugs on behavior. This gives us a glimpse of the future, suggesting that 1984 is not so far off as we might think (Orwell, 1949). Beyond the gathering, storage, and exploitation of information about individuals—this is the tip of the iceberg—there lies ahead the potential use of psychology and psycho-pharmacology to modify and control the behavior of individuals. As Western society turns to nuclear power, just to cite one example, and the menace of subversion and theft of nuclear materials becomes immediate, it is not difficult to envisage the growing "need" of the system not only to know but to control.

This said, it must also be noted that the problem does not go unrecognized by government. In 1974, Congress passed a Privacy Act establishing a study commission which has recently completed and is about to publish its work (*The New York Times*, 1977c, p. 28). Among other things, the report of the Privacy Protection Study Commission recommends the establishment of a kind of privacy panel within the executive branch which would continuously study the problem and monitor the vicissitudes of privacy. Also recommended are remedies at law for abuses in the dissemination and use of information about individuals. The report defines as sensitive areas those of employment, education, banking, insurance, public assistance and social services, mailing list use, credit and government research, and statistical activities. It proposes that information gathered about individuals be made available to them on request, echoing the Freedom of Information Act passed with respect to Federal Bureau of Investigation (FBI) and other government files.

The one thing we can be sure of is that the system, for good and sufficient reasons, is going to feel the need to know more and more; and the present relatively mild responses to the endangerment of the species privacy will multiply and intensify. As remedy tends to lag behind trespass, it is doubtful whether it will ever overtake and really control what is being called the invasion of privacy. Skinner (1971) has already published the gloomy prediction that individualism and individual freedom are doomed. If he is right, the robotization of man is right around the corner. I do not share his premature despair, but given the human record of awakening to danger too late, I am convinced that it is not too soon to regard the trend as a crisis.

Privacy and Secrecy

The reaction to the crisis must, however, be an informed reaction. And one troublesome aspect of all discussions of the future of privacy is the fuzzy embrace of the term itself. In referring to the various manifestations of the attack on privacy originating in the social system, one must be aware, not only of the variety of the categories of data blanketed under the term, but also of the question of who gets to know what. For example, one goes to a dinner party and engages a neighbor in conversation. Very soon, this stranger refers to something which his psychoanalyst told him. Emboldened by this apparent openness, you say to this person "As long as you have been so frank about your personal life, would you mind telling me something else?" The dinner partner invites you to go ahead. You say "Would you mind telling me how much money you have in the bank?" The question is met with disbelief and a certain outrage at your impertinence, and, of course, he does not tell you.

But consider the exchange, precisely in terms of categories of privileged data and in terms of who gets to know what. Your dinner partner revealed something intimate about his private life: (1) he is undergoing psychoanalysis; (2) he reveals something of the content of that analysis. This is a category of data quite distinct and more centrally personal than how much money he has in the bank. Further, it is information which is known only to him and to his analyst with whom, one would hope, he has a confidential relationship. But he tells you, a stranger, about this at a dinner party, while at the same time he would be very unhappy were such information to become part of his employment dossier. Information about his finances, on the other hand, is perforce beyond his control since it is known not only to his bank but to credit bureaus and to the IRS. Thus, he appears to be more protective of information which is to a limited extent public than about information which he has the power to keep private.

In the previous section on exhibitionism, I dealt at some length about this apparent cession of privacy and need not repeat it here. In the present context, what I ought to consider is the real question of whether that dinner guest's finances have anything to do with privacy at all. And this leads us to a distinction of some importance: namely, the distinction between privacy and secrecy. As I defined it earlier, privacy, in whatever form and regardless of the substance defined as private, is a condition or status. It is the maintenance of a personal life-space within which the individual has a chance to be an individual, to exercise and experience his own uniqueness.

Secrecy, on the other hand, is not so positive a status or condition. Indeed, secrecy is in essence negative. It involves keeping to oneself information which one feels would render one vulnerable to some kind of damage, either practical damage or damage to self-esteem. If the limits of your assets were known to a potential landlord, he might not grant you a lease. If the charming young woman to whom you are attracted, and who appears to reciprocate, were to know how old you are she might think twice about getting involved with you. These are secrets, practically and sometimes hypocritically endowed with the status of private substance to justify not revealing what another person or even an institution has a right to know.

The distinction between privacy and secrecy is not made here to suggest that privacy is a right and secrecy not. On the contrary, the frank recognition of another right, the right to secrecy, is long overdue and would contribute much to a clearer understanding of what needs to be protected, from whom, and under what circumstances. For example, homosexuality used to be a secret. It deserves to attain the status of privacy. Fiscal secrecy used to be sanctimoniously covered by the right to privacy. It needs to be redefined as a secret, and the conditions under which this secrecy might be breached need to be spelled out with safeguards for both the individual and those entities, such as the IRS, which have both the need and the right to know.

The invasion of both privacy and secrecy is here to stay and will grow in scope and intensity. The system's need to know is overwhelming; the stake of every individual in the continuity of the social system is felt, even if that feeling is not consciously articulated or even if, on grounds other than inertia, it is not justified. Consequently, there is no question of blindly running against the tide. Our only hope is to spell out our values, with respect to both privacy and secrecy, and to seek protection against the obliteration of our individuality and the betrayal of our secrets in codes which disregard the needs and rights of both individuals and society. This will surely be a matter of negotiation and trade-offs, not unlike that embodied in the constitutional right not to be forced to testify against oneself. This right may allow criminals to escape justice, but it recognizes the stake of a just society in the protection of the innocent, even at some social cost.

CONCLUSION: IS PRIVACY A VANISHING VALUE?

Privacy is not a vanishing value in the Western world, but it is a value which is becoming increasingly hard to maintain. We cannot hope, in modern urban society, so complex and so populous, to retain privacy in the form of a literal physical enclave as we have enjoyed it in the past. But physical isolation is not the only form of privacy, and we shall have increasingly to adapt to non-territorial forms. As for substance, the stuff of privacy, this is also subject to redefinition. The recent exhibitionism which has flaunted what used to be private originates, not in any attempt to do away with privacy, but in a protest against the isolation enforced by contemporary social life. So, even here, privacy as such is not threatened.

The threat to privacy originates in a complex social system which needs information to survive and which is forever expanding the scope and intimacy of data regarded as relevant. The walls of privacy, and those of secrecy, are crumbling before the battering ram of the need to know. If we let this continue—i.e., if we continue to allow the social system to evolve out of its own premisses instead of responding to human needs and values—then privacy may persist as a value, but it will be a value unfulfilled. The issue is not whether privacy is a vanishing value but whether we will tolerate its disappearance as a reality.

REFERENCES

Durkheim, E. *The division of labor in society* (G. Simpson, trans.). New York: Free Press of Glencoe, 1964. (Originally published, 1893.)

Freud, S. *Civilization and its discontents* (J. Riviere, trans.). London: Hogarth, 1949. (Originally published, 1930.)

Fromm, E. *The sane society*. New York: Rinehart, 1955.

Levine, M. H. Human adaptation to the contemporary urban milieu. In G. Bouloux & J. Ruffie (Eds.), *Adaptation et préadaptation génésique*. Paris: L'Institut National de la Santé et de la Recherche Medicale, 1971.

Nader, R. *Unsafe at any speed: The designed-in dangers of the American automobile.* New York: Grossman, 1965.
The New York Times. March 17, 1977. (a)
The New York Times. April 8, 1977. (b)
The New York Times. May 15, 1977. (c)
Orwell, G. *1984: A literary prediction of a robot society.* New York: Harcourt, Brace, 1949.
Riesman, D. *The lonely crowd: A study of the changing American character.* New Haven: Yale University Press, 1950.
Simmel, G. The metropolis and mental life. In K. H. Wolff (Ed. & trans.), *The sociology of Georg Simmel.* New York: Free Press of Glencoe, 1950.
Skinner, B. F. *Beyond freedom and dignity.* New York: Knopf, 1971.
Warren, S. D., & Brandeis, L. D. The right to privacy. *Harvard Law Review,* 1890, *4,* 193–220.

Various Meanings of Privacy: A Philosophical Analysis

ROBERT C. NEVILLE

Robert Cummings Neville earned all his academic degrees at Yale University: the A.B. in 1960, the M.A. in 1962, and the Ph.D. in 1963. From 1965 to 1973 he was a faculty member in the Philosophy Department at Fordham University; in the interval he was Professor of Philosophy at the State University of New York at Purchase; currently he is a faculty member in the Departments of Religious Studies and Philosophy at the State University of New York at Stony Brook. Dr. Neville is a frequent contributor to professional journals, principally in the fields of philosophy and theology, and is the author of God the Creator: On the transcendence and presence of God *(1968),* The cosmology of freedom *(1974), and* Soldier, sage, saint *(1978). He is a member, among other organizations, of the American Philosophical Association, the Metaphysical Society of America, and the American Theological Society.*

The concept of privacy takes its significance from its contrast with public life. In the archaic, preclassical days of ancient Greece the aristocrats had only public life. Their concepts of self and of legitimate activity had to do with the responsibilities, virtues, and rituals of the public conduct of affairs. Public life for them was not a public role which they played on certain occasions, but life itself. The non-aristocrats, on the other hand, had no public life. Except for the results of their work they were irrelevant to public affairs, and had little or no sense that public responsibility was basic to their identity. Nor did the common people have a sense of privacy, a domain of life *free* from the demands of public responsibility; they were not private, only unpolitical.

TWO CLASSICAL TRADITIONS

The city-states of the subsequent classical period were significant precisely because they required public responsibility of everyone. The aristocrats' prime loyalty to personal virtue was superseded in the values of the city-state by the loyalty of the citizens to the laws and welfare of the polis. Civic loyalty demanded of every citizen a portion of time and energy devoted to public deliberation and welfare, and it thus allowed a distinction to be drawn between that aspect of life and those aspects which had to do with tending one's own affairs rather than the city's. As Werner Jaeger (1965) put it:

> The polis gives each individual his due place in its political cosmos, and thereby gives him, besides his private life, a sort of second life, his *βίος πολιτικός*. Now, every citizen belongs to two orders of existence; and there is a sharp distinction in his life between what is *his own* (*ἴδιον*) and what is *communal* (*κοινόν*). Man is not only "idiotic," he is also "politic." As well as his ability in his own profession or trade, he has his share of the universal ability of the citizen, *πολιτικὴ ἀρετή*, by which he is fitted to co-operate and sympathize with the rest of the citizens in the life of the polis [p. 111].

Greek Tradition of Political Loyalty

Plato and Aristotle, though imbued with the spirit of the polis, ran somewhat against the grain of its ideal in their belief that public life itself requires expertise. For, clearly, if a statesman requires skills as a carpenter requires skills, then not all citizens are equally fit for the exercise of public responsibility. However we might evaluate the fact, Plato and Aristotle were right: politics does demand special skills; or rather, those lacking the skills quickly lose out on the power to exercise public responsibility.

The heritage of Greece regarding the public and private is therefore complex and somewhat contradictory. On the one hand, personal identity, at least for male citizens, consisted in both public life and idiotic or private life. Personal skills in one's work were idiosyncratic and belonged to private or non-public life. Yet the exercise of public responsibility required a special political skill or virtue, and the fact that most citizens lack this meant that it was something of a sham to say that they participated in public life. The reality then as since is closer to what Plato described when he noted that only one class of people rule, those capable of it in one sense of capability or another. For Plato, the rulers were supposed to rule by persuasion, not by the adroit use of political force; yet the effective skills have usually been those associated with force.

Social Contract Theory and Self-Interest

The social contract theorists who were the founders of modern political thought were self-consciously imbued with the classic Greek ideal, and aware of its contradiction: that all citizens are supposed to be political yet only a few have the skill to be. There was an important added dimension to the political thinking of the moderns, Hobbes and Locke. Instead of loyalty to the polis, the spring of political action for them was self-interest. Because of a variety of interests (one of which was their Christianity), they could hardly conceive of basic motivations other than self-interest. Individualism meant the fulfillment of personal interest. Political life, therefore, was explained not as an intrinsic part of personal identity but rather as a means for securing personal interest, a matter of self-serving prudence.

Hobbes (1651/1950, Pt. 1, chaps. 14–16; Pt. 2, chaps. 17–21, 26–28) accordingly argued that the interest of all is best served by ceding to a sovereign the powers to cause violence and to make laws restricting interactions. Through this ceding of authority, the citizens in a delegated sense are the authors of all that the sovereign does; but since they have in fact alienated their authorship to him, the sovereign is the only real author in the state regarding public life. Citizens have public life only to the extent that they act in accord with the dictates of the sovereign; but to act in accord with those dictates is to be ruled by them, not participate in their formation. Personal life therefore has alienated its principal public responsibilities and retains only those of obedience to the sovereign's commands. The rest of personal life is private in something like our contemporary sense of privacy: it is whatever is not regulated by law.

Locke (1689/1956) was even more definite than Hobbes in linking public life to self-interest. For Locke, a person is what he makes and owns, beginning with his own body. The state is an instrument for securing property, and the limits of state authority are set by the self-interest of the governed. Instead of alienating their authority to act, citizens delegate authority to their representatives skilled in political virtue; delegated authority may be recalled, and the underlying conception is that the delegates are the voices of the citizens themselves, disposing of their own property. The American battle cry "No taxation without representation" reflected the Lockean belief that the state has no legitimate authority of its own to dispose of citizens' goods; it has only the delegated authority of the citizens themselves resident in elected, recallable representatives.

In contrast to Hobbes, Locke emphasized a far greater public role for the universal citizen. Instead of merely being public through obedience to the laws of the sovereign, each citizen participates in the making of the laws (particularly concerning taxation) through the exercise of the voting franchise. Because of the vast and complicated scramble for public office, the sphere of politics was greatly expanded so that many more common people could participate in ways more involved than mere voting.

The liberal democracies derivative from Lockean political theory in one sense solve the Greek contradiction by establishing a hierarchy of political responsibility. Only those most skilled in political life make it to the top of a complex, bureaucratic political structure; but those with perfectly common skills can participate on the ward level.

Threat to Privacy in Liberal Position

A special problem arises in the liberal democracies, however. Precisely because the state is seen as the agency of the citizens' own authority, its independent power is feared, and limitations on the power of the state, such as the Bill of Rights, were established in order to protect private life. Privacy then comes to be viewed as that area of personal life in which the state should make no claim, at least not without due process designed to protect privacy. One of the strong connotations of privacy today is the negative sense that it is where others have no right to intrude.

Has liberal privacy any positive value over and above its negative freedom from external infringement? If there is any value, it would be in the ways in which private affairs contribute to one's essential sense of personal identity. I suggest that there are two basic kinds of factors which distinguish what is important in private life from what is trivial, in liberal democracies.

The first is that the important things are those which enhance our economic status and property. This is a function of the fact that we define our personal identities very much in terms of property possessed. Whether our society reinforces economic egoism because it is an important trait of human nature, or whether it is an important part of our nature because society reinforces it, I shall not hazard to debate.

The second factor in making private things important is their relative contribution to political power, or those skills which give one more public power than otherwise. Again, the most important private sphere is the economic, because with wealth usually goes political clout. But education and in some circumstances, though apparently not in others, religion also contribute to political effectiveness. The other aspects of private life, for instance, personal morality, religion in most circumstances, ethnic culture, beliefs about most non-political things, the use of leisure, and a host of other things, are relatively unimportant. Although we engage in them, they are relatively meaningless in terms of what counts in life, and the more power boats and trailers we have to vacation with, the less satisfying they seem.

Marxian critique of political life in a liberal society

Marx pointed out this difficulty well over a hundred years ago. Political life in a liberal civil society involves an alienation of certain abstract and universal characteristics of people as citizens from the more concrete social life of private affairs. But precisely because society recognizes the public political sphere as the more important, the relative concreteness of private life loses its meaning. Human emancipation, said Marx (1844/1964, pp. 1–31), is not the same as political emancipation: the latter serves to alienate people from their concrete life while freeing them from political bondage. The task of human emancipation requires the cultivation of what Marx called "species being," the potential character which people have in association with one another by virtue of belonging to the developing human species. The species being of mankind includes common action and individual perspectives, but within the overall context of a common history regarding emancipation. The aim of the emancipatory process is the absorption of abstract universal human characteristics into the concrete social nature of all people acting together.

Attractive as the ideal of species being is, combining as it does individual freedom with concrete social participation, Marx came to see that the conditions for its realization require serious changes in the liberal social order. These changes in turn require a revolutionary period in which the need for group solidarity far overshadows the historical uniqueness of individual freedom. Indeed the revolutionary government has the Marxian blessing when it restricts individual liberties to the absolute needs of the social revolutionary process. The dictatorship of the proletariat then turns back again to the very situation feared by the liberal democrats: that in which their individual liberties cannot be protected against the public demands of the government. The Marxists argue, of course, that this is a temporary expedient and not at all a matter of preliberal tyranny; but then any pre-liberal tyrant would have said the same thing. At any rate, with the possible exception of China, Marxist countries' attempts to transcend an abstract distinction between public and private life with the ideal of free species being in practice turns out to degrade private life without much compensation.

An alternative view of privacy

Privacy and Personal Creativity

That last remark, however, betrays a sense of what is important in private life which extends beyond those items of importance listed above. For the

Marxist would rightly insist that the private source of economic and political spheres is *de facto* immoral. Indeed, the genuine value in private life, I contend, is that it is the arena of creativity, and creativity is one of the most important values in human life. In order to elaborate this point, let me turn to a philosophical characterization of the distinction between the public and the private which is appropriate for our historical situation (Neville, 1974, chap. 9).

Private affairs are those which have to do with personal creativity. Public affairs are those which have to do with establishing and maintaining an environment which allows for prized kinds of creativity. Several points need to be made in order to explain the logic of this distinction.

Public and Private Dimensions of Creativity

First, most human actions have both public and private dimensions, both affecting the environment regarding the options for creativity, and being creative in their own right. This point acknowledges Marx's valid insight that the public sphere can be separated from the private sphere only at the cost of great abstraction and alienation. Whereas some actions obviously are most important for their public effects, and others for their creative aspects, the concrete quality of action includes both. Public acknowledgment of persons ought therefore to recognize their private characters inextricably involved in their public roles. Private expressions of creativity ought always to be responsible to public environmental effects.

Second, responsibility is a norm uniting both public and private dimensions of action. That is, responsibility involves the sense in which an action should be held accountable not only for the value-qualities of its consequences, but also for the spontaneity and critical freedom involved in its subjective, creative expression. It makes sense, in other words, to judge a person whose actions are most importantly public, such as a public official, by the moral and aesthetic norms of honest creativity as well as by the norms of good public action. Conversely, to be responsible in creative activity is also to be responsible for the public effects on the environment.

Third, the distinction between privacy and publicity is always a relative one. In any situation, a life activity takes place in an environment, the support of which is a public affair; but that environment itself depends on a wider environment, and so on. Furthermore, environments are constantly changing and affecting one another. To take an overly simple example: an individual's creative action at home takes place within the public context of the family. The person can also act in a way creative of the family situation which presupposes the environment of the neighborhood; neighborhood creativity has the town as its public context, and so on.

Fourth, the distinction as here drawn between public and private life is close to the ancient Greek distinction between work and leisure. Work is the activity necessary for sustaining life and providing the environment for normative human living. Leisure (σχολή—from which we derive the word "scholar") is the use of non-work time to cultivate the specifically human virtues. In the conception which I am propounding, following Marx in a sense, any activity should be both a work and an exercise of cultivation of the human good; any action totally devoid of either is humanly deficient and perhaps irresponsible. The distinction is not so much one of time spent in different activities, as of different dimensions of the same activity. This is not to deny, of course, that the work in some activity may be far more important than its leisureliness, and vice versa for other activities. Interestingly, neither work nor leisure is plain rest. Rest is a vital function of human life, but it is not quite right to call it a human activity (though the parts of the body may be acting). Since rest is vital for creativity, the provision of rest is a public responsibility, contrary to the common assumption that rest is a private matter. Most people do not adequately distinguish between rest and leisure, and therefore engage in minimally creative activity, so strenuous as to be useless work, thinking that they are resting.

Creativity's Relevance for the Concept of Privacy

What is the practical upshot of this distinction between public and private for the conception of privacy? In contrast to the liberal tradition, it makes privacy a positive affair, not defined merely negatively as the sphere in which public determinations do not apply. Privacy is the life of creativity. In contrast to the Marxist tradition, privacy stands as the norm for public life, not the other way around. A publicly demanding environment is good to the extent that it supports prized kinds of creativity, whereas creativity is good in itself, though it ought not to be publicly detrimental.

The most important element in this conception of privacy is the notion of creativity in human life. There are many reasons for construing creativity as the metaphysical and moral center of personal living. By creativity I have in mind the fairly strict sense of that term as defined by process philosophers (Hartshorne, 1970; Neville, 1974; Whitehead, 1929). A person is a series of occasions of experience, each one of which is creative. An occasion begins with the appropriation of the occasions of the past, limited in the resources for its own development by what the past presents. But the subjective existence of an occasion is its own immediate happening, in which the past data are sorted, graded, and integrated so that the occasion produces itself as a completed new entity; each occasion is thus self-created in the sense that it makes up elements from the past into a new reality. Once a completed new reality, it is then among the raw material for subsequent occasions. Within a person, each occasion takes in occasions from the past of that person; this provides for personal continuity. Each personal occasion also takes in occasions from the larger environment. The character of personal experience is largely determined by the various structured environments in which it takes place.

Creativity according to this conception is therefore an existential category. Hence the importance of privacy: privacy is the sphere in which people come to terms with and determine their own existence. Each person's existence depends on a larger environment; and when the environment is social, this is a public environment. Because each person's experience is a datum for the larger environment, the effects of that creative existence are public ones, for which each person should be responsible. The special moral importance of privacy is that it is the locus of responsibility. Even where one is responsible for public actions, the exercise of that responsibility takes place within the creative immediacy of self-constitution.

Creativity and Responsibility

Because the exercise of responsibility is a function of creativity, two kinds of concern pertain to privacy. One is the immediate concern of creating responsibly and well. The word "immediate" here is important: it indicates that action in the creative sense is that in which the actor is perfectly "present." Unlike what we sometimes identify as actions, where there is a mediating series of actions or even instruments, immediate action is not only the initiation of a causal process but the direct self-constitution of a person. If we learn to pay attention to what we are doing, a very difficult thing for many to learn, it is possible for this sense of immediacy to become directly available to consciousness.

The second concern is with developing the character which conduces to creativity. On the human level, creativity is not merely a requirement for existence: people can exist in many different ways, and some are more creative than others. It should be noted that values are involved in the very meaning of creativity. Merely to exist is to achieve the values of coherence and definiteness relative to the limitations for integration imposed by the environment. Where the environment allows different ways of achieving coherence and definiteness, creativity is obligated by norms for higher values, relative to what is possible. For human beings, creativity is so complicated as to be obligated by moral norms for its consequences and by spiritual norms for the more inward movements of creativity, including norms for self-knowledge and honesty. An essential private concern of each person, therefore, is the development of character which fosters creativity.

JUSTIFICATION OF THE VIEW PROPOSED

The hypothesis which I have suggested, aligning privacy with creativity and public life with sustaining creativity's environment, is subject to a very important criticism. Does not the hypothesis render the distinction between private and public virtually useless? For the point of that distinction is to demarcate the duties of citizens, on the one hand, and to limit the legitimacy of state intrusions, on the other, and our distinction fails to do this. Should our distinction not throw light on the justification for asserting the rights to be free from unwarranted search and seizure, from having the government quarter troops in our house, or from police spying in our bedrooms to determine whether contraceptives are being used?

Public Affairs vs. *Public Institutions*

In response to this criticism, let me draw a distinction between public affairs and public structures. Public structures are organized institutions which attempt to maintain or control the environment. According to John Dewey (1927), public structures arise from the perception of a group of people that they have a common interest in controlling the indirect consequences of certain private transactions in their society. Each kind of private transaction affecting others indirectly has a potential "public" with an interest to organize so as to control those consequences. Dewey himself did not distinguish systematically between such publics themselves and their organized structures; but he should have, because the organization of a group of people according to a structure relative to certain effects to be controlled is different from those people functioning in the totality of their public ways. This difference is highlighted by my concept that every action has both private and public dimensions.

The importance of the distinction between public affairs and public structures is that it is only with respect to the latter that there can be an interest in determining specific duties and limitations of intrusions. Only with regard to organized institutions such as governments, businesses, schools, or clubs can there be duties prescribed in a legal way. Similarly, it makes sense to determine legal limits to instrusions only when there is an institutional way of identifying the intrusion and its agent. This is not to say that only institutions intrude, but that the mode of intrusion must be legally codifiable as an institution; for instance, there must be an institutional definition of one's property that ought not to be trespassed, or of one's mail that ought not to be read without permission.

Setting of Institutional Boundaries

What is frequently sought in the use of the distinction between the public and the private is a definition of institutional boundaries, where institutions fall wholly within the public realm. For instance, the institution of the family is bounded off from the intrusions of the institutions of education; or the institution of one's personal dwelling is bounded off from the intrusions of the institutions of a military needing quarters; or the institution of home television entertainment perhaps should be bounded off from the intrusions of organized advertising of soap, cigarettes, or pornography.

In all these cases, and others, the definitions of the institutions and of their boundaries is a public matter, definitions which have been forged out of the struggle of civilization to provide a maximal environment for creativity. If we were to accept the institutional distinction as the proper distinction of the public realm from the private realm, in effect, that would be to allow that distinction to be set by the public. Yet I believe the truth of the matter is that, although the struggle to establish institutional boundaries takes place in the public arena, the most important norms for that struggle are those having to do with creativity—that is, private norms.

The modern liberal tradition has tried through its doctrine of natural rights to resist the consequence that the distinction between public and private institutions is set by the public. If it could be argued that there are natural rights in the proto-private domain, the justification of which is prior to the justification of public institutions such as government, those natural rights might provide norms for setting boundaries between public and private. Such was Jefferson's argument, for instance. But I believe that it is impossible to defend the notion of natural rights as normative prior to an organized social life which is both public and private.

Eighteenth-century theorists could appeal to our common sense that people are not reducible in their values to those bestowed upon them by the authority of the government, and that the irreducible core is more important and valuable than—indeed, even incommensurable with—the values of structurally sanctioned social roles. But this is not to make sense of rights in a state of nature. It is only to appeal to the point made earlier, that the values of any actions include those of private creativity as well as those of public worth. Contemporary contract theorists such as Rawls (1971, chaps. 1–3) can interpret natural rights as the values and protections which any intelligent person would want to see attached to any position in society for fear the person might by chance occupy that position himself or herself; but the justification of such "rights" is contingent upon each person's being a rational egoist, and I suspect many people are not egoists at all. As a result of the failure to maintain a justification for natural rights in a domain prior to social distinctions, liberals have frequently been reduced to appeals to convention, for instance to the United States Constitution, to justify the establishment of boundaries for privacy. Yet why, in a moral sense, are the constitutional principles valid?

A Context for Creativity

My claim is that actions are at once public and private. The establishment of public structures, including the setting of boundaries between those structures denominated public and those denominated private, takes place within the public arena as a matter of establishing environments; but it does so under obligations stemming from creativity. I would agree with Dewey that the particular boundaries drawn reflect the efforts of those affected by indirect consequences to control direct transactions. But the reasons for making those efforts, I submit, have to do with protecting the context for creativity, for subjective experience; even where people are unconscious of these reasons, or where the reasoning is confused and ill-formed, it reflects the sense that the center of life is individual activity in a social context of the sort which I have characterized as creative.

Dewey was also right on another important point: namely, that governments themselves are public structures in one sense, private agents in another; when governments engage in transactions with individuals, businesses, or educational institutions, those transactions may have indirect consequences for yet other people who then must form an extra-public structure to cope with them. As a heritage from both the Greek sense of the polis and the modern liberal sense of the government as the embodiment of civil society, we sometimes think that the government is the paradigm institution for public action. Perhaps in a broad sense, governing is another word for public action aimed at establishing and maintaining environments for prized kinds of creativity; but governments are particular structures.

If privacy means protection against government intrusion into the contexts of creativity, it also means protection against the intrusions of business, education, and a variety of other organized environmental factors. But creativity also requires protection from inadvertent effects of elements of the environment which are not socially organized in institutional ways, effects of weather, disease, and various other factors. Everybody needs to act publicly to secure an environment for his own career, which might be unique to himself. Action which sustains an environment for creativity is public even when it does not deal with public institutions. And action which involves personal creativity is private even if it does not take place within an institution commonly denominated private, such as the home.

In answer to the basic criticism, then, I would say that the distinction between public and private based on the conception of creativity properly addresses the real issues concerning action for the good of the social environment and what that environment is good for. Other distinctions should be drawn between institutions subject to further regulation, institutions usually denominated public, and those protected from intrusions; but both kinds of institutions are public in that they provide the contexts or media in which we live our own existential lives.

CONCLUSION

What then is the content of private life, if not just what goes on within certain institutions such as the family which have been labeled private? That content, I believe, is the living of life so as to maximize its excellence, both objectively and subjectively. In other words, private life is creative life, the rewards and norms of which are those of creativity. To be sure, no action or way of life is merely private, since everything affects the environment. But its center is creativity. There is no sense in which creative life needs to be individualistic or isolated: most creativity involves living in concert with nature and other people. Indeed, I believe that Marx's ideal of human life as species being really intended all people to have only private lives harmonized together, with no public effort aimed at impersonal forces required to control the environment. But I do not share Marx's optimism, or historical determinism. We will most likely always have to form our creative lives with an eye to their public obligations and needs. But there is no way by which we may cast our responsibilities onto merely public roles; our responsibilities are exercised in, and normative for, our very private existence.

REFERENCES

Dewey, J. *The public and its problems.* New York: Holt, 1927.
Hartshorne, C. *Creative synthesis and philosophic method.* LaSalle, Ill.: Open Court, 1970.
Hobbes, T. *Leviathan.* New York: Dutton, 1950. (Originally published, 1651.)
Jaeger, W. *Paideia: The ideals of Greek culture* (Vol. 1; G. Highet, trans.). New York: Oxford University Press, 1965.
Locke, J. *Two treatises of government* (T. I. Cook, Ed.). New York: Hafner, 1956. (Originally published, 1689.)
Marx, K. *Early writings* (T. B. Bottomore, Ed. and trans.). New York: McGraw-Hill, 1964. (Originally published, 1844.)
Neville, R. *The cosmology of freedom.* New Haven: Yale University Press, 1974.
Rawls, J. *A theory of justice.* Cambridge: Harvard University Press, 1971.
Whitehead, A. N. *Process and reality.* New York: Macmillan, 1929.

II

THE INDIVIDUAL'S NEED FOR PRIVACY

Privacy and Human Development

CONSTANCE T. FISCHER

Constance T. Fischer received her A.B. degree from the University of Oklahoma in 1960 and her graduate degrees from the University of Kentucky: the M.A. in 1963 and the Ph.D. in 1966. Currently, she is Associate Professor of Psychology at Duquesne University. She is co-editor of the second volume of Duquesne studies in phenomenological psychology *and of* Client participation in human services: The Prometheus principle. *In addition, Dr. Fischer is the author of some 30 chapters and articles dealing primarily with empirical phenomenological research and a human-science approach to psychological assessment. Dr. Fischer is a member of the American Psychological Association and is active in state and local professional organizations.*

This paper will have two main parts. In the first we shall review what is already known in a common sense way about the importance of privacy for the various stages of human development. Here, privacy is defined in the usual way as an environmental condition, that of the absence of surveillance and intrusion. The second part of this paper will look at the experience of being in privacy, where we shall discover that it is not the same as being alone, out of sight, or in secrecy. We shall see this privacy's importance for openness and creative growth. Finally, we shall explore some practical implications of the experience of being in privacy, particularly those for building conditions conducive to nonsecretive privacy. So we shall be going from externally defined conditions to experience, back to conditions now in a modified light.

PRIVACY AS A CONDITION FOR HUMAN DEVELOPMENT

"Human development" refers to growing up through infancy, childhood, adolescence, and adulthood. The stages and tasks of development identified by Erikson (1950, 1959) will serve as an outline for a consideration of the importance of privacy for optimal growth through the stages. Remember that here we are thinking of privacy in the usual way as an absence of surveillance and intrusion.

The infant, we hope, learns that he can count on his environment for security—for ending hunger, wetness, fright. This basic trust is foundational for later development. This trust will be most thorough, however, when it develops even in the intermittent physical absence of the caretakers. Perhaps this also is an occasion for the evolving of a sense of the existence and stability of what later becomes "self."

It is in toddlerhood that the child strives for a certain sense of independence. Here we find him seemingly forever testing limits; stompingly asserting "No!"; following his curiosity into a clattering exploration of kitchen drawers; and so on. The developmental danger at this stage is that overly demanding supervision can truncate the youngster's evolving sense of independence, leaving him with an accompanying sense of shame for his impulses and doubt in his competence. Occasional privacy, albeit with an adult in hearing distance, tells the child that at least to that extent he is independent. He builds his block castle without fear of being told how to do it better or more safely; he gleefully or angrily kicks it down without fear of being shamed. Note, however, that this independence is still accompanied by shame and doubt whenever the child's non-observed activity is experienced as secrecy.

In the preschool years the child's developmental task is to take initiative, to try himself out in play. Here we find him unabashedly (we hope) converting his pillowcase into batman's cape, informing mommy that he is going to marry her when he grows up, and making up his own rules as he plays "fish" or "war" cardgames with other youngsters. The danger in this stage is that vigilant supervision render him guilty of transgressing reality, rules, or parental norms. Privacy, of course, allows the child to try himself out without anticipating condemnation. Two notes here: (1) again, guilt will accompany initiative which occurs in secrecy rather than privacy; (2) the youngster does not have to be physically alone to be in privacy—he can play without fear of guilt-provoking intrusion in the presence of his caretakers if they are not worrying about what the world would think of them because this child is breaking assorted norms.

At this point I should point out several general qualifications about the relation of privacy to Eriksonian stages of development. Erikson himself does not make mention of privacy; I am drawing out its implications for what he and others have noted about developmental tasks and dangers.

In doing this, I am not claiming that privacy is an adequate condition for optimal development; rather, I see privacy as a facet of the complex structure of growing and maturing. I also should make clear for any non-Eriksonians that the person struggles with the tasks of later life in ways which are partially shaped by the outcomes of his earlier stages of development. Of course, the person also continues to live out and develop each of the earlier achievements.

Following the above preschool years, there comes, of course, the school age. Here the youngster finds his own ways of mastering and enjoying work—spelling, book reports, kickball, making his bed, baking brownies, building model planes, playing Startrek. Note that play is also the work of childhood; through play as well as through assignments, the child continues to try out new understandings and skills. The danger of this stage is the possibility of his feeling *inferior* rather than accomplished. Along with opportunities for trying out, with encouragement, appropriate suggestions, and praise, the child also requires chances to try things on his own—to risk mistakes without threat of intrusive correction or ridicule.

This latter requirement is more obvious during adolescence, when the major task is to develop a sense of personal identity, and when the danger is that of being left instead with only a diffuse or fragmented sense of self. Privacy is critical for daydreaming, introspecting, imagining personal futures. Freedom from fear of ridiculing intrusion is similarly important when adolescents get together to check out judgments on teachers, parents, and other adolescents, to exchange information about sex and new fads, and, in general, to develop their own stands, postures, and goals. Speaking of postures brings to mind the importance of literal postures/gestures—of trying out poses, smiles, hairstyles, first with the mirror, then with friends, and finally with people at large. Note that parents who understand the task of this stage, and who are perceived as supportive rather than critical, are invited to witness and assist in the adolescent's development, e.g.: "Hey Mom, does my hair look more sophisticated this way?" As in all the stages, privacy as the absence of surveillance and intrusion can exist in the presence of others. Guardians need not be perceived as guards.

Privacy continues to be important in much the same manner throughout adult development. In young adulthood the developmental task is said to be that of evolving an un–self-conscious intimacy with one's spouse, immediate family, and co-workers. One must find ways of sharing what one cares about, and who one is, even while attuned to the sometimes different concerns of others. The danger of this period is that of developing instead a sense of isolation from others.

The task of middle adulthood is to shape the world for one's self and the next generation in a productive and creative way. By now one is perhaps the parent of adolescents challenging the old ways; the parent and other "authorities" must protect the good of those old ways while also earnestly trying to understand the rightness of the challenge. The danger is that of slipping into stagnation, stunting personal and societal growth.

Finally, in elder adulthood, the task is to integrate one's sense of "who I am" with a sense of mankind—what I would call "the family of man." The danger here is that the person remain non-integrated, experiencing instead despair about his world and his place in it. In each of these adult stages, openness is essential—openness toward the differences among people, openness to personal shortcomings and change, openness to the ambiguity of existence, and openness to the frailties and magnificence of the human journey. This non-defensive stance of openness requires, among other conditions, a general sense of freedom from surveillance and intrusion—privacy.

PRIVACY AS A LIVED EXPERIENCE

The above review of the importance of privacy for psychological development assumed the customary definition of privacy as an environmental condition. Then it looked in a common sense way at what such a condition might mean for Erikson's developmental stages.

Now let us hold those assumptions and that common sense in abeyance for a while, and look instead directly at the experience of the person who is in a state of privacy. We shall find that what was said in the review of privacy as a condition is sustained, but that we understand it more richly. Moreover, looking more directly at what the person was experiencing will lead to very different practical implications.

About ten years ago I began asking for written descriptions of moments in which individuals had been in privacy. After subjecting these descriptions to empirical phenomenological analyses, and then checking them with the original reporters and with additional reports and researchers, I developed compact but concrete revisions of the original (usually much longer) reports. Each compact instance retained the themes which had been present in all the reports but deleted material which did not appear in all the others. In this way I developed a series of compact instances of being in privacy, each of which describes what was essential to the living of privacy in a particular situation. Below are several examples:

> (1) After grousing around the house, arranging coffee, pens, etc. on the dining room table, I had finally squared off against the journal manuscript. Even with the two-day deadline somehow there had to be a way to revise it to the editor's specifications and yet retain my message. Why in the world couldn't he see the point?! Through an ambience of labor I eventually lose myself in a field of outlines, notebooks, marginal pencilings. My pen is not yet poised, but somehow I am sensing the whole which my editor and I had seen from different perspectives. Vigilance

has turned into attentiveness to new possibilities. The telephone suddenly demands to be answered. As I run to shut it up, I try desperately to hold on to where I had been. I realize fleetingly that I don't know how I had gotten into my new relation with my project; that damned phone had torn me away, leaving no strands to hang on to, I am barely civil to the graduate student wanting to know if I couldn't read his late paper in one day. Back at the table I bitterly (helplessly) condemn the student's opacity, the futility of trying to fill all my roles responsibly, my manuscript's absurdity, and my own multifarious limitations. It is many hours before I rediscover a place similar to where I was when the phone rang [Fischer, 1975, pp. 29–30].

(2) Toward the end of the semester my graduate assessment class is meeting in its discussion groups of 10–12 persons. On this day in effect we are colleagues as we struggle together to reformulate the differences between my "collaborative approach" and mainstream practices. By now we share a common ground of a semester's creative laboring over actual assessments. As we talk, new phrases come into being throwing our work into different light. We both delineate the limits of our past efforts and strongly affirm their preferability to traditional procedures. There is an aura of discovery / humility / hopefulness. A bearded stranger slips into the room, brusquely explaining "Dr. Murry sent me." In my perturbance over losing the mood and train of our "thought," I am leery of asking who he is lest my voice be too harsh. Having lost the appropriate moment to inquire, I now steal glances at him, wondering if he is an applicant, a busybody, an administrator, an opponent of collaborative assessment. After self-conscious efforts to pick up where we left off, I discover that I have pulled my chair somewhat out of the informal circle; the rest of the session degenerates into my lecturing rather curtly about what I already had worked out [Fischer, 1975, pp. 30–31].

(3) I'm lying in bed reading *Newsweek*. Or I was; now I'm gliding among reveries about a Utopia in which all people participate in basic forms of work and thus share broader perspectives and possibilities for peace. I haven't formulated the details; they are to come later, after I prereflectively soak up unverbalized wanderings. It's a rich landscape, inviting my attention in all sorts of promising directions. My husband remarks that he thinks the shower floor leaks. "Uh huh," I say, easily flowing along my landscape. But now he's discussing what should be done about it. I mumble some more, trying to stay within my territory, but I must also listen to what he's saying. Finally I hear the irritation in my mumblings, and toss aside *Newsweek* and my lost, unretrievable world. Now we discuss plumbing costs, remaining vacation time, etc. I wonder abstractly what I had been so caught up with before [Fischer, 1971, pp. 152–153].

As my co-researchers and I developed condensed descriptions such as these, we discovered that they were distinctly different from some others which we eventually recognized as ones involving either guarding something private or as secrecy. In contrast to those states, privacy involved a forgetfulness of external judgment, an un–self-conscious receptivity to changing perception. There was a sense of oneness, of flow—out of which respect for ambiguity and revised understandings might grow. This lived privacy occurred among people as well as when one person was alone. It occurred when one was merely musing as well as when one was working at something. And lived privacy was present during physical activity and mental tasks as well as during quiescent musing.

In a more formal way, in consultation with co-researchers, I examined the condensed instances and derived a summary description of what they all had in common, stated in a way which preserved the experiential whole. The resulting structural summary has held up well since then, when it was worded in the following way:

> In Summary, Privacy Is When: the watching self and the world fade away, along with geometric space, clock time, and other contingencies leaving an intensified relationship with the intentional object. The relationship is toned by a sense of at-homeness or familiarity, and its style is one of relative openness to or wonder at the object's variable nature [Fischer, 1971, p. 154].

Because people cannot report their experiences of privacy until they are looking back at them, we also discovered that the reports included an implicit structure of how being in privacy came to an end. Sometimes the person finished musing and was ready to turn attention elsewhere. But very often privacy was disrupted by intrusion. The structural summary which we abstracted from descriptions of the disruption turned out to be relevant to psychological development in a way quite different from the mere absence of privacy.

> In Summary, Disrupted Privacy Is When: attention is jerked from its prior object, and shifts repeatedly among the intruder, self as caught by the other, and the peripheral world, as well as the lost object. There is a jarring aura of control being still out of grasp, with return to privacy being in the hands of the intruder. Intentional relations are now in the styles of task, manipulation, or withdrawal. Time is lived in that future to be somehow achieved, or in helpless, fixed present or past. Both time and space thrust forth as inescapable contingencies, limitations to be suffered or reckoned with. As attention flits among its three focal objects, affect varies with felt ability and desire to do something about each of them. Specifically, the intersection of ought–must (do something) with uncertain–can't is the location of such affects as irritation, anger, and impotent, frightened rage where the focus is on the intruder. Where oneself is the object (at the same intersection), the affect is unease, embarrassment, or shame as one finds himself fixed. Finally, where the prior

object is sought, the affect includes agitated despair, inadequacy, or anxiety [Fischer, 1971, pp. 157–158].

Before discussing the implications of lived and disrupted privacy for psychological development, we should first point out that although both structural summaries have been affirmed by additional reports and analyses over the years, they certainly could be written in somewhat different language and yet evoke the same themes and phenomena. The structural summaries are of course general, and perhaps therefore do not convey the special meanings of being in privacy, such as spirituality, personal integration, respite from demands, creativity, aloneness, etc.

RELEVANCE OF PRIVACY FOR INTEGRATED PSYCHOLOGICAL GROWTH

Back to being in privacy. Having clarified what we knew only implicitly before about the living of privacy, we can now speculate about its importance for psychological development (for adults, since only adults served as subjects in the study). One aspect of what privacy provides is an opportunity to get in touch with one's self while not worrying centrally about other people's judgments; we might call this "being at home with one's self." Privacy is also a condition for imagining different possibilities —of freeing one's self from perceived contingencies. Growth toward optimal fulfillment requires both at-homeness and visions of what else might be. We are speaking here of creative productions (art, cuisine, writing, etc.) as well as of personhood. A related opportunity provided by privacy is that of getting in touch with other people, of "where they're coming from"; a prerequisite for this process is the un–self-conscious, non-defensive openness to changes in one's own perceptions. Finally, in privacy one can experience a sense of unity, not only with other people, but with events and the world at large. Emerging from such dwelling, one can be much more patient and understanding of others' projects and differences. Note how very different the above process has been from secrecy or other defensive stances.

Having thought now of privacy explicitly as a mode of consciousness, I think we can look back at what was said about Erikson's stages of development and see them with richer understanding. As an exercise, with the structural summary of lived privacy in mind, think back to the following tasks/achievements and to how they are involved for the adult: trust, independence, trying out personal accomplishments, personal identity, un–self-conscious intimacy, creative productivity, integration.

Privacy does not always lead to growth. One's openness, unity, and flow may be with, or even restricted to, negative, limited, or evil profiles. In addition, one may enter privacy as an escape and thus avoid coping constructively with problems. Even where within privacy the person has been awed by the newly discovered facets of something and his own connectedness with it, there is no guarantee that this experience will later "go" anywhere. Being-in-privacy is not sufficient for positive growth. But it does seem necessary.

Now, back to disrupted privacy. Reflecting upon the structural summary, we see that disruption of intense privacy is not only a disruption of opportunities for growth, but (depending upon one's relation to the object of one's musing and to the intruder) also a negative experience in itself. By "negative experience" I mean more than just that it feels bad. There may be negative developments in the person's relations with the intruder, from whom he finds himself withdrawing, objectifying, attempting to manipulate, and perhaps wishing to annihilate. Even perceived threats to future privacy may lead to such negative involvement. Think, for example, of how in relation to our own lives we vilify the dormitory supervisor, the neighborhood gossip, the Central Intelligence Agency. Besides threatened external judgment, there are simple threats to the flow of consciousness: jangling telephones, door-to-door salespersons, breakdowns of appliances, the roar of motors and of television sets.

True, sometimes psychological development is best served by intrusion into privacy, for example when the person's dwelling is one of pervasive depression, or condemnation of others, or simply when it is time to transform the growth of consciousness into action. But where one is not "at home" with his musings and with the disrupter, threats or actual disruptions of privacy can build into restricted/restricting interpersonal relations.

PRACTICAL IMPLICATIONS

By way of closing this exploration of privacy and psychological development, let us look at some practical implications. Traditionally, most efforts to safeguard privacy have been just that—defensive maneuvers to keep others out. These maneuvers are not in the interest of positive psychological development since they enhance secrecy—a defensive, closed, restricted position in which one views outsiders as potential enemies. So a general practical implication is that to promote human development, we should think beyond the environmental condition (that absence of surveillance and intrusion) to encourage privacy as the opportunity to dwell intensely and openly in the richness of things, events, people—their multiple and changing aspects, and their inherent relation to us.

Thus, housing planners would do well to build not high-walled fortifications, but low walls and shared space where residents can see, and hence feel more a part of, their community. Here they can be in privacy nondefensively. Here they can meet and explore their differences and commonalities rather than guard their private worlds against residents as intruders. Such a process probably accounts in part for lessened crime rates in this kind of architecture.

In classrooms we could think beyond separate toilet facilities for faculty and students, for boys and girls, and even beyond inviolable lockers and desks. We could promote classroom opportunities for un–self-conscious musings about new facets and about one's connectedness with just about everything.

Closed meetings can be seen as necessary for a subgroup to explore explicitly but non–self-consciously its feelings and options. But private meetings must occasionally open themselves to reflection through outsiders' eyes if the subgroup is to maintain a healthy connectedness with, and sense of, its larger context. Lived privacy is a state of openness to difference in unity.

Medical staffs could provide not only the privacy of dressing rooms, examination gowns, divider curtains, etc., but also concern for the examination's relation to the patient's life in general. Even behind sheets the patient too often still experiences himself as reduced to a body, and he has difficulty integrating its possible deficiencies/defects/diseases with his ongoing life. The doctor or nurse who is more than technician helps the patient to be himself, to remain open to possibilities, to stay in touch with his ability to cope. This is lived privacy, wherein the person retains his sense of connectedness, wonderment, non-defensiveness.

Other areas to consider might be closed files, journalism's reporting of facts, club meetings, family living arrangements, integrated schools. In each case, privacy as the condition of protection from surveillance or intrusion runs the danger of becoming defense and isolation rather than the lived privacy of un–self-conscious dwelling.

REFERENCES

Erikson, E. H. *Childhood and society*. New York: Norton, 1950.

Erikson, E. H. Identity and the life cycle. *Psychological Issues*, 1959, *1*, No. 1 (Monograph 1).

Fischer, C. T. Toward the structure of privacy: Implications for psychological assessment. In A. Giorgi, W. F. Fischer, & R. von Eckhartsberg (Eds.), *Duquesne studies in phenomenological psychology* (Vol. 1). Pittsburgh: Duquesne University Press, 1971.

Fischer, C. T. Privacy as a profile of authentic consciousness. *Humanitas*, 1975, *11*, 27–43.

Justice, Privacy, and the Civil Order

WILLIAM P. BAUMGARTH

William P. Baumgarth received his A.B. degree from Fordham University in 1968, and his graduate degrees from Harvard University: the M.A. in 1971 and the Ph.D. in 1976. He spent the year of 1972 in England as a travelling Fellow, and from 1973 to 1975 he taught at Wake Forest University. He joined the faculty of Fordham University in 1975, where he is currently Assistant Professor of Political Science. Dr. Baumgarth is a member of the Political Science Association, and is the author of a growing number of panel presentations and articles in the field of political science.

The issue of privacy rarely arises explicitly in the history of political thought. Yet the substance of what we mean by privacy is indeed treated at some length by political philosophers when they investigate the nature and limits of the family and of private property: those institutions which sustain private ways of life and which compete with explicit political duty for the citizen's attention. I intend in this paper to set forth the outline of a classical argument critical of the notion of privacy, and then I shall turn to another classical source for a criticism of that first argument. Next, I shall proceed to *The Federalist Papers* for the reactions of the founders of our nation to the problem of the private citizen's desires conflicting with the public order's needs. Finally I should like to relate the question of privacy to the meaning of politics itself and briefly examine some modern views concerning the necessity of privacy for the enhancement of, indeed the survival of, political life.

THE GREEK POLIS AND SOCRATES' DILEMMA

Origin of Political Philosophy in the REPUBLIC

What sort of light does the history of political philosophy shed upon "privacy"? To begin with, political philosophy is younger than philosophy proper (Strauss, 1959). Although many searchers for wisdom pursued their philosophical investigations before Socrates, it is with Socrates (or, perhaps, with his death) that political philosophy commences. We moderns have a hard time understanding the precarious position of a Socrates because we think so readily in seemingly philosophical terms. Yet philosophy is not merely a mode of analysis: in its beginnings at least, it was a way of life.

The philosophical lifestyle, if we take Socrates as its examplar, was a most radical way of life, and since it consisted so visibly in the asking of embarrassing questions, it could not but come into conflict with the demands of particular public orders. It would appear to the ordinary Greek citizen that the philosopher was placing his own private lifestyle above the duties which politics enjoined. It also appeared that the philosopher was elevating his private "wisdom" above the wisdom embodied in the laws and, more ominously, above the wisdom contained in the tales about the gods. Worse still, the philosopher insisted upon making a public show of his sagacity by openly questioning popular opinions about morals and religion, and teaching the young to do the same (Neumann, 1972, pp. 546–548). The tension between philosophy and politics culminated in the condemnation of Socrates by an Athenian jury. In this respect the political action of Athens cannot be faulted as inferior to that of any other ancient regime. Some political orders, like Sparta, would never have permitted even the notion of philosophy; Athens at least tolerated the prodding of Socratic questioning until Socrates' old age. The Athenians, after all, always seemed attracted to novel ideas which more conservative regimes readily eschewed.

The *Republic* may be interpreted as Socrates' most comprehensive political defense. The philosophical attitude may be viewed as one of questioning; the political attitude, on the other hand, demands answers. Philosophical man is inclined toward a leisurely, disinterested approach to perennial issues; political man, on the other hand, operates within a partisan, temporally restricted, realm. After all, philosophy must weigh the merits of a just war; politics, however, must come to grips with who the friend and who the foe are this minute. It is with this tension between theory and practice, between theoretical disinterest and partisan commitment, that the *Republic* is concerned.

Tension between Philosophy (Wisdom) and Politics (Justice)

After having successfully silenced the sophist Thrasymachus, who had reduced justice to a mere question of self-interest, of might makes right, Socrates is confronted by the two brothers Glaucon and Adeimantus. These aristocrats demand some answer as to what justice is, and whether it is choiceworthy in itself or merely as a means to some other end. It would seem as if this question was aimed directly against Socrates: the philosopher, after all, seems more interested in the quest for wisdom than in the pursuit of justice. Socrates is forced by his questioners to found political philosophy. That is to say, he must provide a defense of philosophy in terms which the better elements of the political community, at least, can comprehend (Plato, Bk. 2, 357A–367E; Strauss, 1964, pp. 50–138). Philosophy, that is, must be shown to be in conformity with justice. Justice, however, seems concerned primarily with here-and-now decisions. Philosophy, as long as it is the quest for wisdom, is occupied with a search for eternal answers. Must the two not always be in a state of tension?

In answer to the brothers' query, Socrates refers to the myth of Gyges, the possessor of a ring of invisibility. With the assistance of this device, Gyges is enabled to kill the king, sleep with his queen, and perpetrate various other atrocities (Plato, Bk. 2, 359C–360D; Machiavelli, 1515/1976, chap. 15). Injustice is thus assisted by "invisibility"; or, less allegorically, crimes against the community are facilitated by the protection which institutions such as the family or private property afford. The lesson is clear: to have the perfectly just regime, it is necessary to abolish those institutions which stand between the individual and the scrutiny of the community. That is to say, it is necessary to abolish privacy.

Socratic Solution: Rule of Philosopher–King

Justice, in one of its senses, means a full commitment to the demands of the community. The *Republic* reveals what that demand entails: the abolition of every such possibility of invisibility. This is a radical demand, yet one which the philosophical Socrates does not shy away from. Socrates does not spare his philosophers from the type of duties which the political order imposes upon its citizens. All philosophical individuals are compelled to partake of the duties of citizenship, even when those duties conflict with the type of love of wisdom which philosophy engenders. The guardian class, which includes all potential philosophers, is, by its education, fully devoted to the common concerns of the political association.

As such, it is completely communistic: all ownership of goods, all marriages, all raising of children are left entirely in the control of the community (Plato, Bk. 7, 540B; Bk. 3, 416D; Bk. 5, 462A).

The various private interests of the several classes of the political community are reduced to a single common good ascertained by a single ruling class singularly divorced from the pursuit of self-interest. All this is effected by the wisdom of the philosopher–kings who alone can provide a social order in which each man is given what is his due, which is another way of expressing the notion of justice. The city described by the *Republic* would seem to correct the injustices arising from private conventional institutions, such as property and family, by reference to a standard derived from nature: the natural superiority of wisdom over foolishness. In this regime resources are taken from the haves and given to the have-nots on the basis of appropriate need and proper talent. No potential pianist goes without music lessons; nor do unused antique pianos pile up in the homes of the rich.

Consequent Dethronement of Privacy

All this does not occur without considerable paradox. In the name of nature, children are taken from their natural parents and given to those better equipped to educate them. From this perspective, the most natural of all relationships, that of husband and wife and of parents and children, appears really as radically conventional and utterly unjust (Plato, Bk. 5, 456C). These corrections of convention (the equality of sexes, the communism of property, of marriage, and of children) are possible only if privacy itself is abolished, if no individual, including the philosophers themselves, is permitted to escape from public view (Cropsey, 1973). The wisdom of the philosophers is displayed no longer in private dialogues, but in public duties. Socratic questioning generates, out of the exigencies of community need, politically relevant answers, and philosophy itself becomes defensible only in the light of its usefulness. This would seem to be a distortion of its very nature, since the quest for wisdom, like good conversation or love-making or other private activities, appears as something delightful in itself, even without reference to public utility. In the *Republic* theory and practice are made to appear inseparable, and this coincidence of philosophy and politics is achieved only at the expense of the philosopher's private lifestyle.

Here, in short, is a society dedicated to procuring services from each person according to individual talents, and bestowing goods upon each inhabitant according to need. The demands of Marxist socialism with respect to the good society seem not quite as radical as the conditions of life which the *Republic* envisions: if the *Republic* seems less universalistic than the Marxist world community, the Platonic dialogue is at least less ambiguous about the tension between the needs of the community, on one hand, and the individual's freedom to hunt, fish, and philosophize, on the other.

CRITICAL REACTION TO THE *Republic*

The assault launched by Socratic philosophy on the vaunted wisdom of the polis did not go unanswered. Aristophanes in *The Clouds* shows how Socrates' natural right of the wise to rule over the foolish implies a wise child's right to beat his foolish old father. The conventional family arrangement, to which all decent men seem to assent, and the law itself, which rests upon accounts of the gods challenged as mythical by the Socratic philosopher, would be endangered if philosophy were to have a free critical hand. The most impressive attack on the Socratic critique of the polis arises, however, not from the poetic critics of philosophy, but from a philosopher himself: Aristotle's account of the *Republic* in Book II of the *Politics*.

Aristotle Rejects Notion of Analogy to Family

The *Republic*, according to Aristotle, is defective on two grounds: the end which it envisions is not in conformity with the nature of politics, and the means which are set forth would not accomplish that mistaken end. The political association is an aggregation of sorts: if the citizens had nothing in common, there could not be such an association. Yet the unity achieved in the political association must not be mistaken for the coordination of the activities achieved in a household. There the father rules over his children in a regal fashion and over his slaves in a despotic way. The political association is a more perfect mode of aggregation than the family: for one thing, the political association places justice ahead of love, which surely eclipses the former in many familial circumstances. Plato's scheme would reduce the political association to a household and then, farther, to a single individual. The classes of the *Republic* are like parts of a single soul (Aristotle, *Politics*, Bk. 2, 1261A).

Not only does the political association consist of a number of men, more importantly it contains different kinds of men: more exactly, men belonging to different classes reflecting different interests. The political art consists of the ability to reconcile these interests, to give each such class its due. Thus the political association with its diversity of interests and of classes is like some piece of music consisting, of course, of various musical notes. The statesman's art is the harmonization of these notes, and the unity achieved is a unity in harmony, in which the politician has "saved the phenomena"—that is, not obliterated the various notes.

> It is true that unity is to some extent necessary, alike in a household and a *polis*; but total unity is not. There is a point at which a *polis*, by advancing in unity, will cease to be a *polis*: there is another point, short of that at which it may still remain a *polis*, but will none the less come near to losing its essence, and will thus be a worse *polis*. It is as if you were to turn harmony into mere unison, or to reduce a theme to a single beat [Aristotle, *Politics*, Bk. 2, 1263B].

The end envisioned in the *Republic* proves questionable, and the means, communism, is equally defective. It appears as if each one of the citizens will view the others as kin: as sibling or parent. But for Aristotle there is a natural limit to man's knowledge and his emotional capacities. Surely the polis ought to be like a family, but the close association between familial members can only be approximated politically. Even this political comradery is but a watered-down form of friendship.

> What is common to the greatest number gets the least amount of care. Men pay most attention to what is their own: they care less for what is common; or, at any rate, they care for it only to the extent to which each is individually concerned. . . . The scheme of Plato means that each citizen will have a thousand sons: they will not be the sons of each citizen individually: any and every son will be equally the son of any and every father; and the result will be that every son will be equally neglected by every father [Aristotle, *Politics*, Bk. 2, 1261B].

This is as true for the family as it is for property. Given men as they are, there is every chance for an improvement of laws respecting what is one's own. But all such reform must take into account the passion for one's own which cannot be obliterated by any such reform. Even Plato's *Republic* makes a concession to this constitutional limitation: the Platonic polis is not a world-state (Neumann, 1972, p. 561). It is small enough so that political knowledge and political spiritedness, patriotism, will not have to cope with human numbers and geographical immensities of such a magnitude that only the lowest common denominators will dominate political conversation. The citizens in such a polis will be familiar with each other in a way which approximates true familial intimacy. Aristotle's concept of the nature of politics also elevates to a central position this politics of "smallness."

Plato's Republic Ignores Diversity of Interests Among Classes

The political association is concerned with what is due to each: what should be justly considered as one's own. The peculiar political problem is that each of the various classes in the political association views this question of justice from a biased point of view, since each such group is a bad judge of the issues when adjudicating cases involving its own interest. Thus, the free-born, yet poor, members of a polis, who constitute the vast majority of the citizenry in most circumstances, will agree that justice consists of treating equals equally. The rich members of the community readily assent to the proposition that justice consists in treating unequals unequally. Yet the former believe that being born free entails an equality in every respect with all other citizens, while the latter group believes that inequality in one respect—wealth—entails inequality in all decisive respects. To complicate the situation still further, the aristocrats, the gentlemen of leisure means, assume that, by justice, they alone should rule. After all, politics should be concerned, not with mere survival, but with the good life—the life of virtuous gentlemen. Those who embody the life of virtue are rightfully those entitled to reign (Aristotle, *Politics*, Bk. 3, 1281A).

Aristotle notes that the claims put forward by each of these classes of citizens contain some important truth, but a truth which is distorted because it is partisan. Every political society is characterized by a notion of justice and by a class which exemplifies that notion and rules by virtue of it. Those societies are in Aristotle's term democratic if they are devoted to a certain type of equality; oligarchic, if dedicated to a type of inequality of wealth as a claim to rule; and aristocratic, if it is virtue in the sense of gentlemanly civility which constitutes the political society's civic ideals. Yet most such associations are not political at all, but rather examples of domination, of exploitation of one class by another. In a democracy the rich are servants of the many; in an oligarchy the rich exploit the poor. Most existing regimes have no "common good," no sense of justice which goes beyond the self-interest advocated by Thrasymachus in the *Republic*.

But the apparent Platonic remedy to this injustice, the suppression of self-interest, of one's own, of privacy, is not the course chosen by Aristotle. Each class in the community, it will be recalled, expresses some justice in its demands. The poor do, indeed, contribute substantially to the survival of the community in terms, say, of its military defense. The rich do, of course, also provide for the community's subsistence and even magnificence in the commerce which they undertake. The aristocratic sorts do embody the type of wholehearted commitment to civic life which a leisurely, yet virtuous, life affords. Yet political life is more than mere military alliance, more than commercial treaties, however necessary these things might be to the physical survival of the community. Since both these classes provide for the necessary conditions of political life, it would be unjust to withhold from them their right to participate in it. The aristocratic class may embody in its nature the end for which politics exists, the good life, but virtue cannot rule alone: it has neither the numbers requisite for self-defense nor the wealth necessary for commerce (Aristotle, *Politics*, Bk. 3, 1283A).

Art of Statesman Concerned with Pursuit of Common Good

The genuine body politic is constituted by a statesmanlike art which harmonizes, in accordance with justice, the various class interests. The rich and the gentlemen are made to see that the poor are not defective in terms of political intelligence when their collective judgment operates. The classes of the few are also persuaded by the statesman that the claims to rule based upon inequality are capable of being employed by the richest or strongest members of the community as an invitation to tyranny. The poor, on the other hand, learn to view their right to participate in politics not merely on the basis of numbers (another claim which could be employed by a potential tyrant), but on the basis of virtue: the type of political wisdom reflected in deliberative assemblies or juries (Aristotle, *Politics*, Bk. 3, 1282B).

Thus, the poor, by just claim, should participate in political bodies where the excellence generated in numbers will be apparent. The rich and the gentlemen, whose political skills are more apparent on an individual level, will justly participate in the executive offices, where energy and prudence, rather than lengthy deliberation, are required. Out of self-interest each class expands its own notion of the content of that self-interest until, by political midwifery, a common good is perceived. In oligarchies and democracies, the most common regimes, political devices are introduced by the statesman which will moderate the dominant inclinations of these regimes. In particular, the political actor will strive to create a "middle class" by encouraging a voting alliance between the poorer members of the wealthy class and the wealthier members of the poorer class. This class would constitute the politically ideal class of the type of political order which Aristotle would judge as best in most circumstances: the polity. The middle class so formed would be moderate indeed, neither possessing great wealth nor suffering poverty. If it could come to enjoy its moderation, then we should have the best political order without qualification: the rule of virtue (Aristotle, *Politics*, Bk. 1, 1259B).

Like a skilled doctor, the wise statesman understands that an aristocratic constitution can no more be forced upon a people enjoying a democratic or oligarchic constitution than an olympic athlete's exercise routine can be taken up overnight by a middle-aged, slightly overweight university professor (Aristotle, *Politics*, Bk. 3, 1288B). There are limits placed upon the statesman as there are limits placed upon the artist who works only with driftwood. Yet within the limits of the driftwood, there are so many possibilities. In the breeding and training of animals the creative possibilities are so much greater than those available to inorganic matter. How much more imagination must contribute to the work of the statesman, who plants constitutional seeds now which may bear issue in centuries, can be easily inferred. But of course "centuries" does indeed pose the greatest limitation in both the Aristotelian and Platonic political philosophies: the factor of chance.

Reconciliation of Justice and Self-Interest of Classes

Suppose, however, that an aristocracy does come into being. It is the rule of the virtuous, yet the virtuous must, it may be rightly supposed, possess a sense of justice. Therefore, the true aristocracy (like that constituted under a philosopher–king) would be, at least on the surface, indistinguishable from a polity or mixed regime. Yet the polity, it might be further imagined, might appear, at least to some unskilled outsider, as but a very virtuous type of democracy. In short, might not the best Aristotelian regime be exemplified in modern times by British democracy under Churchill?

The Aristotelian regime is one based upon a notion of justice which is fully appreciative of the claims made by self-interested political classes. The political association grows out of and enhances the types of social institutions, such as the family, which are apparently dismissed by the *Republic* as mere conventional devices. The most exalted political class, the gentlemen, enjoy both public discussion and the private pleasures which come from property and family. Friendship, the most agreeable of all interpersonal relations not completely familial, is never, in Aristotle's thinking, equated with political comradery, but maintains its habitation in the realm of privacy. "But these institutions [marriage connections, kin-groups, religious gatherings, and social pastimes] are the business of friendship. It is friendship which consists in the pursuit of a common social life" (Aristotle, *Politics*, Bk. 3, 1280B). Even though Aristotle elevates the good life above social life, he does not demand the abolition of the former, since it appears as a necessary means to the achievement of the political end.

THE *Federalist* DEBATE

Although he places great emphasis upon the diversity of interests present in political society, Aristotle, as noted above, does not depart from the model of the compact polis when discussing the nature of the just regime. Neither the Aristotelian good regime nor its Platonic counterpart is achievable until a certain coincidence of politics and philosophy comes about. It is with respect to both these characteristics, the element of smallness and the role of chance, that the writers of *The Federalist Papers* take exception. For the *Federalist* authors, the Aristotelian notion of self-interest, of class, and of privacy would appear to be still too Platonic for a practical science of politics involved in changing decisively the political world.

Republican Position of Opponents to Federal Constitution

The opponents of the proposed federal Constitution were, for the most part, convinced republicans. For the anti-federalist theorists the source book on the nature of republicanism was Montesquieu (1748/1949), who, in classical fashion, had restricted the possibilities of republicanism to rather limited geographical areas, quite similar to the size of the Platonic and Aristotelian polis. Large geographical areas, if governable at all, were consigned by Montesquieu and the anti-federalists to the rule of a despot. Such large areas, it was argued, could be managed only by indirect popular rule, by representatives of the people. But what would keep these delegates committed to their constituents' interests, they being so far removed in their capital city from day-to-day popular political pressure?

Only the small republic permitted this constant review of the government's actions by the governed. Furthermore, large political associations with sufficient commercial ingenuity become wealthy and hence an object of envy to their neighbors. Thus such states must develop considerable military expertise and foster the martial virtues. The spirit of the soldier and the self-governing virtue of the free republican citizen did not seem harmonizable. If such a professional military is not to be established, then it would be necessary to rely upon a citizen army. A citizenry jealous of its independence, vigilant over its representatives, and willing to fight if necessary for its self-preservation could only be the product of a small community wherein, as we have seen, the fellow-citizens are united with each other by an almost familial bond of affection. Love of one's own and the distrust of things foreign would be fostered in the political culture of the small popular republic.

The FEDERALIST *Rejoinder*

The Federalist Papers argue that not only is the small-republic theory defective with respect to the most fundamental political goal, self-preservation, but even its most attractive feature, its view of political community, is flawed. The small-republic theorists had believed that confederal alliances between sovereign republics would provide for an adequate defense of their independence. Yet such confederal schemes as the colonies had adopted in the Articles of Confederation fell short of the type of military and commercial coordination of policy which only a central government with real sovereign power could effect. For them, faced with strong European foes and confronting the possibility of defection of states to these enemies, political survival entailed a strong, centralized large nation state. The imagined isolation of a utopian small republic simply did not describe the actual conditions of the newly liberated colonies.

Just as important, however, is the critique which *The Federalist Papers* formulate with respect to the very idea of the small republic. Surely Publius would agree with Aristotle about the necessity of a diversity of interests, of classes within a political community. The suppression of separate interests, of "factions," could not be accomplished without at the same time abolishing freedom (Madison, 1788/1966). But such a goal could not, of course, be accepted by republicans. But the history of small republics does not prove to be a history of liberty, of the harmonization of classes politically. Rather, it is a history of domination: of the rich exploiting the poor or, more often, of the poor expropriating the rich. Differences between degrees of wealth are all too visible in the small republic, and such differences will remain in spite of attempts to constitute a moderate middle-class regime. Life in the small republic is life in a goldfish bowl. Everybody knows everybody else's affairs immediately. What real differences of interests or tolerance of views could ever arise in such a setting?

Improbability of Privacy in Small Republic

When the tyrant is a local majority, whether defined by religious or political views or by economic status, it is difficult or impossible to achieve any degree of "invisibility." Privacy in the small republic appears improbable, and with an absence of privacy comes a deadening uniformity of action and opinion. The eternal vigilance of the small republic respects no borders of private property, private opinion, or even matters relating to marriage and the family. The most successful examples of the small republic in America are the best models of majoritarian tyranny: the Puritan communities and their town meetings. In short, the classical polity only appears to be political. The absence of any real diversity of interests therein reveals this community to be one more species of political domination: no common good appears except the interest of the dominant class.

Publius spends some time discussing the type of constitutional devices which, by tapping the ambition of the representative and his professional pride, will prevent the national government from escaping from the control of the electors. But all such systems of checks and balances are but paper obstacles to a patient tyrannic majority if that majority coalesces within a small political community. Expand the size of the republic and you make it difficult for such a majority faction to arise in the first place. After all, most such factions require, for their success, some degree of secrecy impossible to maintain for a national oppressive majority. And if such a faction did materialize, the effort needed to keep it together within the federal scheme of checks and balances and time lags would make it all but impossible to keep such a faction together to see through to the end its pernicious schemes (Madison, 1788/1966).

Thus, measures injurious to a minority undertaken in some state or states may be contained in that region and not become national in scope, given the extensiveness of the envisioned republic. But Publius is not only recommending an extended republic: the type of polity which he advocates has a distinctly commercial nature. The destruction of tariff barriers between the states and the mobility which national citizenship offers (being itself an escape device from oppressive state majorities) would induce commerce to flourish and the division of labor to intensify as never before possible in a small republic. Thus various kinds of jobs and varieties of property, all supported by a dynamic economy, would blur the distinction between the extremities of wealth so visible in small republics. The citizen of the commercial republic is given every reason to view his ties with his fellow-citizens as increasingly economic. Differences in religious belief or political persuasion become less important when day-to-day commercial activity dominates the heart of the self-interested citizen's concerns. As religious and provincial interests are forgotten, professional affiliations would provide a focal point for the citizen's desire for community. Thus the family, so exposed to community pressure in the homogeneous small republic, becomes the primary basis of both self-interested concern and of privacy in the extended republic. The expanding middle class, together with its professional organizations and leisure-time institutions, views its local community as, by and large, merely a place of dwelling. The concerns of this class become national in scope, and with its perspectives broadened beyond the provincial community, a freedom from parochial pressures, a new possibility for privacy, is effected.

Advantages in an expanded polity. Publius would seem to agree with Aristotle on the need for such a middle class as a bulwark for the political community's coherence. Though Publius' middle class enjoys avocational activities, some of which are political in nature, it is not quite the type of leisurely middle class which Aristotle described. The identification of self-interest and the common good in Aristotle is accomplished only by wise statesmanship. The self-interest which Publius recommends is, of course, geared toward economic advancement, and the self includes the individual and his family and close friends. The means by which this self-interest leads to a community good is best explained by the cunning plan of political and market institutions which function to lead the individual to such ends, in Adam Smith's terms, by "an invisible hand" (Diamond, 1963, pp. 590–592). In order to enhance his private sphere, the citizen must contribute economically to his fellows' improvement. The rather organic community of the small republic gives way to more of an emphasis on immediate family, on friends, and on professional associates. The commercial life, it would seem, makes fewer demands upon a person with respect to those activities undertaken after working hours. Private leisure-time enjoyments are both the object which spurs on the life of the commercial republic as well as being themselves enhanced by the economic success of that society. In short, the public realm appears to be, at least on the surface, merely a means to procure that which is enjoyed in privacy.

A form of Lockean liberalism. The political philosophy entailed in *The Federalist Papers*' view of the relation of state and society is recognizable as a form of classical liberalism. The classical liberal championed the cause of the individual against the claims of the centralized, paternal state. Classical liberalism formulated a notion of freedom which viewed liberty as beneficial not only in the sphere of ideas but also in the economic and political realms: free men, free speech, and free markets. Although its proponents varied greatly with respect to the theoretical foundations of their enterprise, most classical liberals were agreed upon their political prescriptions: a polity favorable to life, liberty, and property. Of course, this formulation of the liberal credo goes back to perhaps the first explicit individualist libertarian, John Locke. It is largely due to the impact which Lockean liberalism has had upon social thought that our modern concern with privacy arose, particularly with respect to liberal natural law teachings. Contemporary liberal opinion tends, however, to view the matter of privacy from a point of view seemingly distant from Locke's emphasis upon natural rights. We shall turn now to two such genuinely liberal yet philosophically diverse proponents of this libertarianism: Friedrich von Hayek and Michael Oakeshott.

TWO MODERN PROPONENTS OF POLITICAL LIBERALISM

Hayek's "Rule of Law" and Privacy

Hayek believes that classical liberalism's greatest achievement was the formulation of the notion of the "rule of law." The rule of law is not identifiable with mere constitutionalism. Rather, it is a statement about what constitutes genuine law as opposed to the mere dictates of whatever the powers that be desire (it is an opinion of the school of legal positivism that any decree capable of sovereign enforcement is *ipso facto* law). The following characteristics are distilled by Hayek from the history of liberal legal theorizing regarding genuine laws: such laws must be general (containing no proper names), they must bind both the governors and the governed, and they must be certain (Hayek, 1960a, p. 208). These attributes create a legal space around the individual within which he will be free to act. In short, their main effect is to provide a realm of privacy for the citizen.

According to Hayek, laws are essentially different from commands insofar as commands generally tell an actor what specifically to do, and laws provide parameters within which the citizen can utilize his own personal knowledge of circumstances to achieve desired ends. If we wish to create a crystal, observes Hayek, we do not arrange every molecule individually in a certain fashion. Rather, we set up a certain solution within which crystalline patterns will emerge (Hayek, 1955, p. 30). In a complicated industrial society, the individual actors are like the separate molecules which, given a proper legal "solution," will form "as if by an invisible hand" certain social patterns. The social arena abounds with various examples of ordered patterns arising from the interacting of individuals with one another—such as language, customs, the prices on the market, all of which display such rule-governed laws that they appear to be the result of purposeful creation, though they are planned by no one actor purposefully (Hayek, 1967, p. 243).

Certain legal frameworks (those described by the "rule of law" notion) assist the aforementioned spontaneous orders; others, like a political system based upon command, interfere with these workings. Substituting political commands for the rule of law entails attempting to replace the individual actor's knowledge of specific circumstances of time and place with the perhaps mistaken knowledge of the autocrat. At any rate, to attempt this substitution on a large scale is to permit a single intellect or a small group of minds to restrict the social division of knowledge manifest in spontaneous order to the rather limited information of the planners (Hayek, 1960b, p. 10).

The citizen is permitted by the rule of law to plan his own activities as he sees fit, the incentives of the market serving to alert him as to where such services are profitably to be proffered. It is not that the classical liberal believes that every person is the best judge of his own interest; it is merely that nobody can be sure of who would know that interest better (Hayek, 1948, p. 15). This is to say, the philosopher–king may be a wise man or a maniac. Given this possibility, Hayek opts for a political system in which bad men can do the least amount of harm, rather than one which seeks some positive notion of the nature of the good. Just as Aristotle finds Plato's notion of "the Good" not particularly helpful in defining what is good for this political community here and now (Aristotle, *Ethics*, Bk. 1, 1096A–1097A), so Hayek finds problematic the claim that any ruler could so discern talent and social need as to distribute ability to projects more accurately than the way in which the market does.

In short, privacy, guaranteed by that sphere circumscribed by the rule of law, is necessary both because of our epistemological limitations in knowing what is good for others and because of the positive benefits which arise when men, acting out of self-interest "rightly understood," create the various goods and services demanded by the consuming population of a commercial republic. To the extent to which a right to privacy is an effective right, it seems inexorably linked to the question of property. Or, put a lot differently, when I enjoy any privacy legally, the law at the same time creates a property right: some place which I can call my own where I enjoy the benefits of Gyges' ring (at least from the point of view of the political community). Hayek's notion of privacy, entailed in the concept of the rule of law, is also a statement about the meaning and necessity of private property.

Oakeshott's Critique of Rationalist View

Michael Oakeshott's conservatism seems at first glance less politically motivated than Hayek's brand of liberalism. More precisely, Oakeshott judges that the major assault upon sound political practice arises from a theoretical disposition which he terms "rationalism." Rationalism is the theoretical belief that all knowledge truly so termed is knowledge of the kind embodied in a manual directive of some technique, say a cookbook. What can be known can be fully expressed in the form of rules or formulas governing given activities. Rationalism demands that knowledge begin at some indubitable starting point (where it breaks in upon sheer ignorance) and proceed, by rigorous deductive logic, to its determined end (Oakeshott, 1962, pp. 5–6, 8). When I learn to play bridge, for example, I can clearly determine the before and after of bridge knowledge (the period preceding and following my reading of the bridge guide).

The rationalist position. The rationalist mind requires in political life the identical detached objectivity and skills relevant to puzzle-solving which it so admires when coming upon well-organized engineering techniques. The rationalist does not have much use for the untidiness of political practice, particularly when the objects and methods of political actors seem so blurred by reliance upon tradition. If the objective mind needs to start, Cartesian-like, from some indubitable departure point, then the practice of politics had better begin with a clean sweep of all the biased, muddled premisses hitherto guiding political action (Oakeshott, 1962, p. 86).

The rationalist does not view politics as a problem. A problem, after all, may not admit of *a* solution. Rather, the rationalist tends to see political life as a series of technical puzzles amenable to impartial solutions. Rationalism, unfortunately, seems to be a genus with many species. Some rationalists view political life, as currently constituted, as an obstacle to improving mental health; others see it as impeding the elimination of pollution and other environmental hazards. In short, because he is antipolitical in a most pronounced fashion, the rationalist fails to see that the selection of ends to be grappled with communally is by no means something impartial or purely scientific. The rationalist, by pushing one or more projects as being more important than political give-and-take, abandons entirely the only means by which deliberation, as opposed to force, can achieve those goals: politics.

The rationalist belongs to an intellectual tradition which includes such diverse theorists as Bacon, Comte, and Marx. The common feature of this intellectual disposition is a view of the political community as an enterprise: an association of actors bound together for the sake of pursuing some common substantive end (Oakeshott, 1975, p. 292). The Platonic Republic, it will be remembered, was made possible only by a collapse of practical knowledge into theoretical knowledge, concretized in the rule of the philosopher-kings. Aristotle had criticized that scheme by drawing attention to the difference between the common good politically conceived and the good of an individual or of a class, such as the philosophers. The Republic has no common good because it is not a community but an individual: no truly political art arises in the Republic.

The rationalist tradition in like fashion views the political good as a single project or set of projects to be achieved by substituting theoretical expertise for current traditional practices. Its notion of the political good confuses the substantive goods pursued by individual actors with the political reconciliation of perhaps variant class demands. When the nature of political life becomes effectively like that of an enterprise, then the private substantive goals of the citizens are subordinated to whatever project the political enterprise emphasizes. In short, there must be a tension between privacy and political life when the rationalist theoretician's visions of political community are put into effect (Oakeshott, 1975, pp. 315–317). If these projects constitute the very nature of a "political" community, then non-subscription to them is no more tolerable than opposition to philosophical rule would be in the Republic.

Defect in rationalist view. According to Oakeshott, both the rationalist conception of knowledge and the rationalist vision of politics are defective. Techniques in any art can be applied only if, in addition to technical knowledge expressed in rules, we also possess practical knowledge, knowhow. In all human activities, from cooking to theoretical mathematics, the human actor is guided not only by the knowledge which can be aphoristically stated and learned, but also by skills which can be acquired only by example, by apprenticeship (Oakeshott, 1962, p. 8). Knowing how to solve a mathematical problem means more than knowing a technique, like addition or calculus. It means recognizing a problem as being amenable to some technique. Knowing how to cook entails more than a cookbook can state: it means recognizing when the food is done, the water is boiling, and the hollandaise sauce is smooth. The rules of some art never dictate what to do on a given occasion. Grammatical norms, although enabling me to avoid being grossly misunderstood, do not tell me what to say here and now.

Furthermore, such practical knowledge tells me *how to do* something, technical knowledge informs me as to *what to do*. In an art such as medicine, diagnosis is largely a function of such know-how. After all, it is precisely when the medical book indicates two diseases may be present under one type of symptom that the competent physician is of the greatest value. As long as the circumstances surrounding human action are open to change, it will be necessary to have both a knowledge of the logic of some art and the type of practical skill requisite for working out that logic in a concrete setting. As far as the rationalist insistence that "true" knowledge must be characterized by its relationship to some indubitable starting point, Oakeshott notes that we never seem to find ourselves in a position where pure knowing breaks in upon pure ignorance. All acts of knowing appear to be reformations, amendments, of things already known. I could not learn to play bridge, for example, unless I already knew what it is like to play a game (Oakeshott, 1962, p. 12).

The Critique as Applied to Politics

Rules, techniques, methods, and systems of rules, such as the cookbook, would seem to be abridgments of some ongoing activity where practical knowing predominates. This is true not only of cooking or of medicine or of speaking a language, but also of morality. In this sphere the injunction to do good and to avoid evil is too general to be of much use without the type of knowledge of circumstance which would make that advice operative. And the same relation between the logic of a practice and its concrete exemplification exists in politics. Just as I do not deduce from the rules of language what I shall say at this time, but rather I illustrate my understanding of language through my substantive linguistic performance, so the political actor attempts, in confronting a political problem, to discover the intimations which a political tradition entails for the solution, tentative though it may be, of that situation (Oakeshott, 1962, p. 124). The living tradition of a political community may be abridged in the form of ideology, including the rationalist vision of scientific public administration. Yet, like the relation between a medical text and actual surgery, such abridgment does not supply all that is necessary to the political art. Indeed, in pretending to do so and attempting to usurp practical political skill, ideology will interfere with the attainment of even the restricted goods which politics may provide.

The notion of political association as enterprise is not the only concept of politics discoverable in Western political thought. Alongside it stands the idea that the political community may be thought of as akin to moral phenomena. That is to say, the logic of morality sets certain parameters around all actions which may be considered ethical. Surely all particular ethical acts reflect the moral actor's concrete perception about what is right here and now: they fulfill his substantive needs, providing him with a means for moral self-disclosure. The political association which Oakeshott terms *civitas* enables its citizens to fulfill diverse needs and to undertake varied projects because the *civitas* itself is not a project. It is based upon law (Oakeshott's term is *lex*) which, like the norms of morality or the rules of grammar, dictates, not what an actor is to do, but rather how he is to follow through any of his chosen projects (Oakeshott, 1975, pp. 90, 122).

This law, like most such activity-governing techniques, is largely negative, informing the actor of what not to do, as the rules of logic inform us as to how *not* to express ourselves if we wish to be understood. Just as there is no one positive moral action which everyone at all times must perform, yet all actors can refrain from some actions (such as murder), so what forms the political community is not a substantive project but a commitment to certain ways of doing things, or rather an agreement to refrain from given types of actions. Public life is thus inseparable from some condition of privacy for:

> In the civil condition, "private" and "public" refer to relationships, not to persons, to performances, or to places. And they meet in every substantive engagement: the private "interest" in its success and the public concern that it shall not be pursued without taking account of considerations (specified in *lex*) which are indifferent to its success or failure [Oakeshott, 1975, p. 146].

Thus the common good of the political association is not to be found in the pursuit of some extrinsic good to which politics is merely a means. Rather, like morality, a life of lawful activity is self-justified, self-complete. Political association, like friendship, is entered into for its own sake, because it is intrinsically satisfying. Just as friendship is not comradery, in the sense of association for a single given purpose, so also the commitment to *lex* may be viewed as a formal subscription exemplified or illustrated in many concrete, substantiated projects (Oakeshott, 1975, p. 118). Such public life, as Oakeshott construes it here, necessitates a rich private existence, for the *civitas* is

> an association, not of pilgrims traveling to a common destination, but of adventurers each responding as best he can to the ordeal of consciousness in a world composed of others of his kind, each the inheritor of the imaginative achievements (moral and intellectual) of those who have gone before and joined in a variety of prudential practices, but here partners in a practice of civility the rules of which are not devices for satisfying sub-

> stantive wants and whose obligations create no symbiotic relationship [Oakeshott, 1975, p. 243].

The public order is necessarily formal; it gets its substantive meaning from the way in which concrete, private actors choose to illustrate its logic as they disclose themselves in substantive enterprises.

Politics, as characterized by Aristotle, is the art of attending to the affairs of a community consisting of diverse classes and interests. As such, it involves, as Oakeshott clearly indicates, continuous activity, because the extrinsic problems facing such a community and its internal life, consisting of the reconciliation by political persuasion of its various classes, offer no final solution. The political art consists of those tentative settlements which satisfy, at least for a while, the competing interests within the community with respect to the demands of justice regarding adequate representation of those interests in the formation of public policy. It is not as if politics is merely an instrumental means to the solution of given problems: the political art is not a passive one. Rather, politics itself creates political constituencies, political problems, and those precarious agreements. The politician, like the entrepreneur, may be the first to perceive a problem, and hence act to create some new interest, to give the word "people" a substantive meaning within a context where the people, as a numerical mass, neither knows about some difficulty nor cares. As *The Federalist* sees it, there is all the difference in the world between the "people" drunk and the "people" sober, and that difference is, to a major extent, the effect of political life, rather than its cause.

CONCLUSION

Politics is a precarious activity. After all, persuasion may occasionally have to give way to force: sovereignty, rather than reconciliation, might be the order of the day (Crick, 1972, p. 28). The decision to use sovereign force is itself a political act, although the successful putting aside of such coercion is a much better illustration of what politics is all about. Politics is also a precarious activity because it seems so slow and so meandering in its effects to those enamored of quick or precisely engineered solutions. Yet politics is not merely a means toward some other end; like sex or good conversation, it is intrinsically rewarding (Crick, 1972, pp. 25–26).

As Hayek shows, privacy and politics are necessarily related terms. Or, put differently, the good political order is a self-limiting one. "Politics are the public actions of free men. Freedom is the privacy of men from public actions" (Crick, 1972, p. 18). The vitality which privacy generates is the only real source for that energetic expression of interests which forms the matter upon which the political art operates. This also reflects the precarious nature of the activity we term "politics."

> True politics cannot treat *everything* in political terms. The Marxist attempt to politicize all social relations is, in fact, the attempt to eliminate politics. For politics is concerned with limited purposes. Art, for example, cannot be politicized while remaining art. Love cannot be politicized while remaining love [Crick, 1972, p. 41].

The Platonic Republic, seemingly true to the dedication to the community which justice demands, proves mistaken about the sort of justice which preserves genuine community. When once we understand the crucial role which prudence plays in political life, and abandon the attempt to replace practical understanding with theoretical precision, we can see that the proper understanding of "giving each man his due" justifies privacy and its corollaries: private property and the family. For a rich public life, there must be assets and talents brought by the citizens to that public arena, and these are, within the boundaries of the rule of law, cultivated in the domain characterized by privacy. Is privacy, then, helpful in sustaining civil order? It is not only helpful but necessary, for there can be no community when a diversity of citizens is lacking, and no such diversity unless the realm of private affairs is adequately secured. The "common good" created and sustained in political activities would be, in reality, only the good of some individual or class if it did not arise out of the give-and-take encouraged by the multiplicity of interests begotten in the private sphere. And the private sphere lacking a proper political context would, it appears, merely generate communities characterized by domination. Privacy and political order are but different aspects of the same phenomena: the human civil condition.

REFERENCES

Aristotle. *The Nicomachean ethics* (E. Rhys, Ed.; D. P. Chase, trans.). New York: Dutton (Everyman's Library, No. 547), 1911.

Aristotle. *The politics* (E. Barker, trans.). Oxford: Clarendon, 1946.

Crick, B. *In defense of politics* (2nd ed.). Chicago: The University of Chicago Press, 1972.

Cropsey, J. *Toward reflection on property and the family*. Paper presented at symposium on the origins and development of property rights, University of San Francisco, January 19, 1973.

Diamond, M. *History of political philosophy*. Chicago: The University of Chicago Press, 1963.

Hayek, F. A. von. *Individualism and economic order*. Chicago: The University of Chicago Press, 1948.

Hayek, F. A. von. *The political ideal of the rule of law*. Cairo: National Bank of Egypt, 1955.

Hayek, F. A. von. *The constitution of liberty*. Chicago: The University of Chicago Press, 1960. (a)

Hayek, F. A. von. Kinds of order in society. *New Individualist Review*, 1960, *3* (2), 3–12. (b)

Hayek, F. A. von. *Studies in philosophy, politics, and economics*. Chicago: The University of Chicago Press, 1967.

Machiavelli, N. *The prince* (J. B. Atkinson, trans.). Indianapolis: Bobbs-Merrill, 1976. (Originally published, 1515.)

Madison, J. The union a check on faction. Essay no. 10 in R. P. Fairfield (Ed.), *The Federalist papers: A collection of essays written in support of the Constitution of the United States* (2nd ed.). Garden City, N.Y.: Doubleday, 1966. (Originally published, 1788.)

Montesquieu, C. L. *The spirit of the laws* (T. Nugent, trans.). New York: Hafner, 1949. (Originally published, 1748.)

Neumann, H. Is philosophy still possible? *The Thomist*, 1972, *36*, 545–565.

Oakeshott, M. *Rationalism in politics and other essays*. New York: Basic Books, 1962.

Oakeshott, M. *On human conduct*. Oxford: Clarendon, 1975.

Plato. *The republic* (B. Jowett, trans.). New York: Modern Library, 1941.

Strauss, L. *What is political philosophy? and other studies*. Glencoe, Ill.: Free Press, 1959.

Strauss, L. *The city and man*. Chicago: Rand McNally, 1964.

Privacy and Spiritual Growth

JOSEPH G. KEEGAN, S.J.

Joseph G. Keegan, S.J., received his A.B. degree from Woodstock College in 1929 and his M.A. (1943) and Ph.D. (1949) degrees from Yale University. He has been a member of the Fordham University faculty since 1942, and is currently Associate Professor Emeritus of Psychology. Father Keegan was Chairman of the Psychology Department from 1949 to 1958, and Director of the Counseling Center from 1961 to 1966. He is a member of the British Psychological Society and the American Psychological Association. Father Keegan has been intimately associated with the entire series of Pastoral Psychology Institutes, having been a member of the Organizing Committee for each Institute.

Having from nature bodily as well as spiritual needs demanding fulfillment, the human person necessarily encounters difficulty in maintaining a just balance in striving for acceptable goals. It should be admitted at the outset that any personal need for privacy may have to be attenuated or accommodated to other demands for harmonious fulfillment within the human condition.

The theme being advanced in this complex set of demands requiring reconciliation is that, by and large, various analyses of human nature, as well as historical accounts of man's search for a balanced solution, suggest a basic and recurrent role for the individual's religious orientation and the setting of a high value on religious ideals. Such a theme must be carefully examined, for it is not immediately evident that all individuals actually achieve their personal fulfillment or self-actualization in a manner which can properly be called religious or a quest for intimacy and union with the Absolute One.

It is to be hoped that these brief remarks may indicate that the core of the present inquiry may reside in the analysis of related concepts, as well as in considerations about the relationship of the individual's need of privacy for personal spiritual growth. However central to our theme this latter relationship must be, there are other concepts—religious values, spirituality, spiritual growth toward union with God—which will need clarification. Following a hurried exposition of these relevant notions, spiritual growth will be discussed, first in the light of an abbreviated historical overview, and, secondly, in terms of principles which are intended to assist the individual in his or her spiritual pilgrimage.

CLARIFICATION OF RELEVANT CONCEPTS

Because religion can, and often does, differentially permeate the individual's personal life, consciousness, and behavior, it should not be surprising that it has been variously defined. Apart from the diverse forms of its manifestations through formalized creeds and rituals, religion is notably multifaceted among individuals who are said to be religious.

Religious Values

The scope of the present discussion would seem to require that we emphasize that facet which concerns the individual's encounter with God, be it the realization of a corresponding need, or at least the urgent desirability of recognizing and reverencing a suprapersonal and supramundane Being of highest value. With this emphasis in mind, it might give some definitional clarity to note:

> A man's religion is the audacious bid he makes to bind himself to creation and to the Creator. It is his ultimate attempt to enlarge and to complete his own personality by finding the supreme context in which he rightly belongs [Allport, 1950, p. 142].

The taboos associated with the various primitive modes of expressing such attitudes to a supreme being suggest the secrecy surrounding the thought of, and more frequently the naming of, the deity. By some extension of this reverential secrecy, or respect for the sacred, one tacitly accepts that going apart, seeking the isolation of a shrine or place of seclusion, or opting for solitude as the appropriate occasion for prayer and meditation, mark the individual's effort to give assent to communion with his or her supreme religious value. Perhaps it would be too exclusive a characterization to accept the statement that "religion is what the individual does with his own solitude" (Whitehead, 1926, p. 16). Though the need to withdraw into solitude or to practice abstention from uttering the name of the deity hardly captures what true religion really *is*, much less the way most people speak about it, there remains an aura of mystery about an individual's converse with God.

Such emphasis on personal solitude, however, will not deny a social component in a person's worship of God or in the development of his or her "godliness." For it is not only contemporary thought which has drawn attention to the "interpersonal field" as the appropriate milieu in which, through dynamic confrontation with others, one's own personality *becomes* what it actually *is*. In recent psychological and philosophical inquiry this view is practically axiomatic. In the context of religious development and the achievement of a mature religion, the reciprocity of the individual and the community has long been acknowledged by theologians. Doubtless the individual's need of community for a total expression of the religious urge is hardly accidental. Buber's (1923/1970) *I–Thou* is as relevant in this context as Angyal's (1941) biosphere or Lewin's (1959) Life-Space in personality description. The problem will be to discern in such polarities proper balance and mutuality rather than the antagonism of opposites. The apparently contrasting poles must be seen as synergic. With T. S. Eliot some can find a "resolution of forces" between life in solitude and life in community:

> Even the anchorite who meditates alone,
> For whom the days and nights repeat the praise of God,
> Prays for the Church, the Body of Christ incarnate
> [Eliot, 1971, p. 101].*

Spirit and Spirituality

In the history of spirituality esteem of privacy, as an explicit referent—though not necessarily in the form of a near-equivalent concept—is largely a term of recent coinage. The occurrence of the word itself would scarcely ever, if at all, be found in the indexes of the classics among spiritual writings. Even Vatican Countil II in its praiseworthy Declaration on Religious Freedom omits mention of the word "privacy." However, it rests its case for religious freedom on the twin foundations of human reason and the revealed Word of God, each bearing witness to the sense of dignity of the human person.

> It is in accordance with their dignity as persons—that is, beings endowed with reason and free will and therefore privileged to bear personal responsibility—that all men should be at once impelled by nature and also bound by a moral obligation to seek the truth, especially religious truth. They are also bound to adhere to the truth, once it is known, and to order their whole lives in accord with the demands of truth [Vatican Council II, 1966, p. 679].

* Quoted by permission from the poem "Choruses from 'The Rock' " in the *Collected Poems, 1909–1962*.

The thrust of the Council's Declaration was to decry all coercion or interference with the individual's right to believe and worship, and the basis of the individual's right rests upon his or her dignity as a person. If this is so in our own times, it may not be so strange to find in Christian tradition a certain *implicit* regard for privacy as one of the options suitable to the cultivation of the interior life of the spirit.

It is also pertinent to note that a rigid dichotomy of flesh and spirit or of body and mind would run counter to biblical history. Even though the early Christian and patristic efforts to wed biblical tradition and Hellenistic metaphysics generated some departures, the central trend was toward an essential unification of body and soul constitutive of the holistic, autonomous person.

The term "spirit" conjures up the concept of spirituality, especially in its meaning which looks to human *moral* perfection. Precisely because they are free does the possibility exist for God's people of actualizing their highest values. In other terms, it is in the free, responsible direction of personal actions in the light of values consciously known and accepted that we can in any reasonable sense speak of human spiritual growth. This mention of human freedom implies some prior consideration of the spirituality of the soul, which we cannot here elaborate to the degree which it certainly deserves. Suffice it to say that some modern philosophers (Heidegger, 1927/1963, to cite one example), as well as more traditional metaphysics, stress the analysis that the intellect, in knowing its own act, which is being, arrives at some knowledge of its own being, or of its own nature as well as of its existence. The spirituality of the soul in this sense is attested first in judgment and consequently in volition or willing.

Since the human will reveals an openness to being in all its universality comparable to that of the intellect, the individual can love all that partakes of the goodness flowing from being as such. As things are known in their intimacy and interiority, the will can tend to others and treat another human being *as another*, that is, as a person in his or her intimacy and interiority, and can love God in and for Himself. That these capacities will always be realized or universally executed is not the contention in subsequent discussion. The point is that the theme under inquiry—that the individual should have autonomy in the direction and control of his or her spiritual growth—would be a vain exercise in rhetoric apart from its basis in human freedom and a life of the spirit.

Spirit and Growth

Growth or development may be taken as synonymous in designating a quantitative and qualitative sequence of continuous change in a system. The process may be considered as occurring over a time span, usually through phases which are predictably ordered. Often there is implied a sequence of irreversible change, as in a tree or animal organism. As applied to age-related changes in human psychological functioning (Developmental Psychology), the concept is in wide usage, although not all psychologists are in agreement as to the criteria by which the stages of psychological growth can be plotted. One notes, however, some general comparability among the several "systems" of Freud (1916/1966, pp. 303–338), Erikson (1964), and Havighurst (1972), for instance. They have in prospect a goal called maturity; their stages involve sequential, age-correlated progress; and the maturational process is a patterned one.

The citing of examples of organic development should not come as a surprise to one familiar with New Testament literature, especially the gospel parables of Jesus. In the thirteenth chapter of St. Matthew's Gospel are to be found three parables in which there is a clear implication of the patterned, sequential development toward maturity which is to be found in plant life. They are: the parable of the sower and the seed, the parable of the weeds (darnel) sown among the grains of wheat, and the parable of the mustard seed. In each of the first two of these parables the explicit "lesson" cautions us about the need to avoid damaging environmental factors which might impede an otherwise predictable maturation. In all three, one senses the clear implication that some ordered developmental sequence has its application to growth of the spirit. For promising beginnings to come to proper maturity, care must be exercised throughout the course of spiritual growth.

In a context in which empirical studies are admittedly sparse, it has, nevertheless, been noted that in questionnaire studies (Braden, 1947) early training was high on the list of reasons influencing religious orientation in later life. As another writer has noted, "The self is the accrued results of its faith response to the decisive grace of God revealed in opportune moments of life" (Oates, 1973, p. 87). In a broad sense, "opportune moments" may correlate with Erikson's (1964) critical stages or Havighurst's (1972) developmental tasks (of which we shall have more to say later). Such opportune moments are obviously not to be taken as fleeting instants of time which must be seized by the forelock; one is rather inclined to accept them as the more indeterminate periods of spiritual development in which the individual consolidates successive gains.

PRIVACY IN HISTORICAL PERSPECTIVE

Although some threats of invasion of privacy are, admittedly, of recent or even of contemporary origin, one should not lose sight of the timeless element in the human need to preserve personal autonomy in the matter of self-disclosure with regard to the inner life of the spirit. Despite the admittedly disastrous invasion of privacy associated with the inquisitorial pursuit of heretics and alleged witches engaged in by religious bodies in medieval and Renaissance times, it is not correct to infer that respect for individual liberty and the need for privacy were the product of modern "enlightenment." Judaeo-Christian experience has created a tradition which contains elements which are timeless and which constitute the base source for recognizing the human person's inherent need to exercise freedom in his or her choice of modes of interiority. Yet it is of relevance to explore within this tradition some historical manifestations or "movements," which carry the flavor of their own particular era. History provides a plethora of such movements. We shall have to content ourselves with a small sampling in which the effort will be made to note the accent which was placed upon privacy as a desideratum. The selected manifestations within which the quest for spiritual growth and advancement appears to have been significant are: the practice of confession; the flight to the desert in early Christian times; monasticism, especially Benedictinism in the West; and the rise of the more "modern" religious orders, particularly the mendicant friars in the High Middle Ages. Of course, mysticism has also been a notably individualistic phenomenon, but in view of its scant and dubious relationship to purely personal effort, it will not be explicitly presented as illustrative of human spiritual growth.

Practice of Confession

As is obvious, sacramental confession enjoins self-disclosure. But in this sacrament, traditionally known as the Sacrament of Penance or Confession (now the Sacrament of Reconciliation), the penitent's privacy is and has been protected by the inviolability of the "seal of confession," as declared in canon 889 of the Code of Canon Law. It is therefore a matter of positive law, but it can reasonably be argued that it is also a provision which flows directly from the penitent's need to have his or her intimate revelations of conscience protected against unapproved or unlicensed disclosure. That the inviolability of the seal does not seem to have been an explicit point of ecclesiastical law for some centuries is no argument that the privacy involved was a need guaranteed only by positive law. From earliest times it was recognized that the divine command to confess implied a corresponding obligation of strict secrecy on the part of the confessor—otherwise the approach to the sacramental tribunal would be repugnant to a degree of being impossible of fulfillment.

Evidently for the first four centuries or so, the practice of public confession was not a matter of church legislation but a manifestation of the openness and sense of community on the part of the faithful and of their eagerness to make reparation and to accept public penance freely. However, gradually, but certainly by the ninth century, there was explicit recognition of the principle that sins confessed by a penitent should be revealed to no one save God. In this historical setting, necessarily abbreviated as here presented, one can infer as prior to any legislation the individual's exclusive ownership of his or her "internal forum" and its secrets. In the context of our topic, this is the core of the life of the spirit.

In an analogous setting, Westin (1967, pp. 32ff.) writes of an inner "core zone" of hopes, fears, and prayers beyond all ordinary sharing. To secure emotional relief and additional means of maintaining this "core zone," the individual may under stress seek to reveal in a confessional manner some of his or her ultimate personal secrets. But in so doing, one does not thereby declare that the inner sanctuary becomes public property. This partial and privileged sharing is always by way of exception and subject to the will of the autonomous person.

In this connection, one is reminded of the words of Pope Pius XII, who in speaking, not of sacramental confession, but of psychotherapeutic intervention, addressed as follows the International Association of Applied Psychology: "The best psychologists are quite aware that the most skillful use of the existing methods will not succeed in penetrating the zone of the mental life which constitutes, so to speak, the center of the personality which ever remains a mystery" (1958, p. 13).

Incidentally, that public appraisal may distort or even misinterpret what one says or does is one reason for valuing privacy, but it is not the essential basis of the need for privacy. For the latter, we must go to the fundamental dignity of the individual as an autonomous person. Every person has intimations of unrealized or of incompletely formulated goals, of gaps between the realizable and the currently realized self, of discontinuities in his or her philosophy of life, of potentialities yet to be explored, or of skills yet to be exercised. To have their defenses torn away is tantamount to a shaming exposure to unwanted scrutiny. Certainly, the contents of the inner zone of ultimate secrets, and of the surrounding zone of intimate, but not necessarily ultimate, secrets, are requisite for the person's continued "becoming" and growing toward a fuller realization of "who I am." "The free man is the private man, the man who still keeps some of his thoughts and judgments entirely to himself, who feels no overriding compulsion to share anything of value with others, not even those he loves and trusts" (Rossiter, 1958, p. 17).

Fathers of the Desert

Evangelical ideal. There is a certain danger of creating misunderstanding when one attempts to express spiritual values in an idiom more consonant with ancient usage than with our own. Such terms as "self-abnegation," "emptying of self," or "the folly of the saints" tend to create an entirely negative impression in falling upon the modern ear. Yet for the thoroughgoing ascetic and the mystics of history the evangelical ideal has consistently been seen as something close of realization, provided one could seriously accept the means thereto; and such means clearly envisioned obstacles along the route to that freedom which was reckoned to be "the freedom of the children of God" (Rm 8:21). For the early martyrs the obstacle may have been encountered in a tribune's command to offer incense before the image of the emperor. External obstacles can be either avoided or surmounted. But those which were internal, including the issue of self-will, were seen, according to evangelical principles, as needing to be eradicated. Hence, the notion of purgation (in this life or in the next) was consistently seen as a most appropriate metaphor.

It may help if one considers the life-experience of Origen (ca. 185–253) a point of transition from martyrdom to purification of self as the readiest path to spiritual perfection. The shift was from regarding actual martyrdom as the seal of one's salvation toward the ideal of a spiritual "martyrdom" in the active overcoming of self. One might be tempted to say that, deprived of the opportunity of a martyr's crown, the serious Christian must undertake the more gradual method: a dying to self and "the world."

Whether or not the so-called "desert fathers" were inspired by Origen's spirituality is debatable. It could just as well be inferred that the "flight to the desert" was something in accord with the temper of the times. At any rate, there were many hermits and cenobites, particularly in Egypt (ca. 250–500), and three regions of Egypt made the desert famous: the Thebaid; the Nitrian desert and valley (Scete); and Middle Egypt between the Nile and the Red Sea.

Flight to the desert. To the hermits and monks of the desert (such men as Anthony, Athanasius, and a host of others) the cities were as dungeons; the sands of the desert by comparison were bedecked with the glorious flowers of the Christ-life. Not all, of course, who called themselves Christians, but many, women as well as men, were attracted by the inviting vision. Such were the people for whom self-surrender went beyond the avoidance of sin and for whom total commitment signified devoting the whole person to an ideal. In another age it will be called the Imitation of Christ. The Apostle Paul (Rm 7:21–25) can be cited as authority for the view that the acquisition of self-mastery may require stern measures. The means to the achievement of the "vision" (likeness to Christ) involves spiritual combat. That the means must always be the contending with cold nights and torrid days in sultry, arid deserts is another matter. Evidently, in their view, the need for solitude and hardship was part of the package for one who wished to see God.

Though they were the last persons capable of giving it philosophical definition, nevertheless it was the genius of these early "athletes of Christ" to discover privacy's relevance as a proper setting for spiritual contemplation and prayer. One might conjecture as to their motivations, such as a firm conviction about the proximity of the second coming, parousia, of the Son of Man. However, whether parousia was envisioned as near or remote, it constituted a call for preparedness, and to these early Christians privacy became a key element for the purchase of that "treasure lying buried in a field" (Mt 13:44). Choosing as their "field" the barren reaches of Egypt and Syria, they sought in prayerful solitude to be worthy of that eternity which Boethius and others would later define.

Needless to say, we cannot altogether neglect the cultural and social factors involved in this flight to the desert. It is plausible that it was in part a protest against or rebuke of the established order of Roman law and custom. In another age a new religious movement might have had recourse to other methods—perhaps passive resistance, or some form of political activism. The Christian response, on the contrary, has almost universally been one of accepting the legitimacy of established authority and the seeking of a *modus vivendi* through patient accommodation. Nor can we overlook the extent to which the flight into the desert was also a rejection of the "worldly" values centered in the ease and comforting security which followed in the wake of the cessation of persecution under previous Roman emperors. In much of its thrust early Christian asceticism was a lay protest against the notion that formal ritual is the only route leading to salvation. Speaking of monasticism in the East, Dom Cuthbert Butler (1898/1967) could write: "The dominating principle that pervaded Egyptian monasticism in all its manifestation was a spirit of strongly marked individualism" (Vol. 1, p. 237).

It is a reasonable inference that men and women of that era—even as they gradually came to change their anchoritic lifestyles for community living in monasteries and convents—placed priority on personal sanctification somewhat over cultic worship. The movement accented such matters as the awareness of sinfulness and the need for purification and penitential practices, as well as learning to systematize the steps to holiness. The term "athletes of God" was not an unfamiliar one among them or among admirers who came from Caesarea and Rome, and even from Spain, as pilgrims or "tourists."

In any case, whether it promoted more than its share of fanaticism as well as fervor, the movement was definitely one in pursuit of privacy and solitude. The ideals associated with the lifestyle of these ascetics were surrender of self, cultivation of solitude, contemplation, and ascetical penance. It was a wholehearted acceptance of Christ's invitation as expressed in the Gospel according to St. Luke (9:23): "If anyone wishes to be a follower of mine, he must leave self behind; day after day he must take up his cross and come with me."

Monasticism in the West

The quest for solitude seen as conducive to prayer and the cultivation of the presence of God was doubtless the keynote of the anchorites, whether we look to Christianity of the East or to its "migration" to western Europe and the foundations made by John Cassian and his disciples. In addition to solitude, high on the list of characteristics of this earlier movement were marked individualism, an almost competitive emphasis on asceticism, and a contemplative orientation which might be regarded as "angelic" in its direction. But monasticism in Europe gradually took on the coloration of Benedictinism. St. Benedict (ca. 480–547), notably at Monte Cassino in 528, replaced the earlier, more individualistic practices with a rule within which the emphasis was on community, obedience to a superior, moderation in penances, and a greater orientation toward prayer as vocal prayer and recitation of the divine office.

It is clear that the descriptive phrase *ora et labora* ("pray and work") is aptly employed to designate such a life; but it is hardly a life in which privacy is left unprotected. As given by Benedict, the rule places no emphasis on apostolic endeavor; it does, however, stress the individual, more by way of giving the self for God through love than by a combative conquest of self. The uppermost question facing a prospective novice entering a monastery of St. Benedict would have to be: Do I truly seek God? If so, all the rest—liturgy, penance, scholarship, and contemplation—will follow.

In some respects it may be true that feudal monasticism was too much geared to its times. Was the relationship among abbot, choir monks, lay brothers, and *conversi* a model or a replica of lord, knight, and peasant? However many their contributions to the cultivation of the spiritual life during the turbulent feudal times, the educational and devotional efforts of the monasteries hardly touched the lives of the multitude. Yet it was this very multitude which was to take on a new significance in the eleventh and twelfth centuries with the waning of feudalism and the advent of a new age.

Religious Orders

The monks of St. Benedict as well as those of Cluny and of Cîteaux were, of course, religious. Except for the surmise that it was probably weak, if not moribund, it is difficult to know how much piety prevailed outside the monasteries in the feudal era. But it is known that the collapse of feudalism led to entirely revolutionary economic and social change. Trade and commerce on a scale previously unknown and the consequent gathering of tradesmen, artisans, and consumers led to enormously increased city-dwelling. And no less revolutionary was the emergence of an altogether new kind of religious movement in the medieval era. This movement was largely the result of the influence of two great leaders: St. Francis of Assisi (ca. 1182–1226) and St. Dominic (1170–1221).

Mendicant friars. In creating two new religious orders (Franciscan and Dominican), these dynamic saints, together with the followers whom they inspired, revolutionized regard for poverty and esteem for preaching, respectively. Both orders contributed greatly to the spread of theological learning as doctors and masters at famous medieval universities. But it is their influence upon Europe's piety which chiefly interests us. Given the confusing aftermath of the early crusades, the unheralded rise of trade and travel, the thronging of people from the land into cities unprepared for the influx, and the political weakness of the Church, piety at the beginning of the thirteenth century must have been at a low ebb. Francis' love of God and of prayer and penance diverted him from a confining solitude or monastic cell to find Christ in his brethren, among the poor and the most miserable beggars of the streets. Going beyond "selling all to gain all," he literally renounced all and established for himself and his followers a way of life which embraced absolute poverty with dependence upon alms alone.

For Francis, life in Christ was to be found in the living of it. The "desert fathers" had cultivated the love of God in solitude; monks sought it in the prayerful quiet of a cell or during the hours poring over a text to be transcribed; Francis found the crowded city a more fitting arena in which to exemplify that emptying of self which he had contemplated at the foot of the cross. Doubtless his credo was that the freedom provided by poverty enables love to burn more brightly. Not every last feature of medieval life was celestial, but it may safely be claimed that whatever spiritual light there was burned more brightly because of Francis' evangelical love of simplicity and his realization of the meaning of the Incarnation.

It is possible to deal more briefly with the contribution of St. Dominic and his Order of Preachers. It was Honorius III who first sanctioned this order in 1216, according it the status of a mendicant religious order with a strict vow of poverty for its members. As was the case with the Franciscan friars, the Dominicans were to have no commitment to a single house or foundation. Furthermore, the sons of St. Dominic received papal permission to be excused from canonical prayer (performance of the "hours" in choir) in order to devote themselves to the study of Scripture and the sciences. Doubtless it was this flexibility or permissiveness which largely contributed to the fact that members of these two orders were almost the exclusive luminaries among the thirteenth-century schoolmen of Europe—Aquinas, Albertus Magnus, Roger Bacon, Bonaventure, and Theodoric of Freiberg, to cite just a few. In the development of theology they pursued the cause of learning both of Scripture and of the sciences, and thus transmitted for the profitable use of the clergy and others the fruits of study and contemplation.

Much as we honor the contribution of these two orders to learning and the search for truth, it is important not to underestimate what they did for, and the appreciative response they earned from, the downtrodden and the forgotten poor. What the mendicant orders did was to convince the lowly and the near-forgotten that they too could partake of the enlivening springs of religious truth. For them also the life of the spirit became reality.

Active apostolate. Every individual has a need to integrate experience, insights, and conclusions so as to arrive at a meaningful manner of influencing events via his or her own individuality. As Westin (1967) states it, this involves much self-evaluation, for which privacy is a *sine qua non.* The necessary intellectual reflection requires some removal from events in order that the processing of information, the weighing of alternatives, and the planning of strategy for personal action be conducted prudentially. In the realm of the spirit at least two comparable processes are of tremendous importance: examination of conscience and the discernment of spirits. The examination of conscience, as the forerunner of any reasoned sorrow for sin, is, of course, an integral part of the Sacrament of Reconciliation. But the examination of conscience in prospect here is that time-honored religious practice whereby the person striving to be pleasing to God seeks to *maintain* the purity of his or her conscience. Employed twice daily, it is a spiritual exercise calculated to increase the innocence of one's conscience through the weakening of habits and tendencies which may well be suspected of leading to disorder unless held in check. Such is its general function. The name of St. Ignatius (ca. 1491–1556) is usually associated with the particular examination method, although the examination of conscience had its roots in earlier Christian asceticism.

Special rules for the discernment of spirits are also associated with the name of Ignatius of Loyola and his *Spiritual Exercises* (Puhl, 1951, p. 141). A word is in order concerning Ignatian spirituality, since its orientation toward action might superficially suggest a disregard for privacy needs. But his influence in history is being introduced here precisely because he carried forward psychologically what was latent in the practices introduced by Francis of Assisi and Dominic. The innovative aspect of Ignatius' doctrine was this: contemplative prayer is somewhat subordinate to the active, apostolic life. But one must recognize in the Ignatian way the totality of union with God, lest one arrive at the faulty inference that prayer is being reduced to a lower level of significance. It is to be admitted that in his Constitutions for his order he departs from tradition with respect to the time allotted to his followers for formal prayer. Ignatius, more explicitly than Francis or Dominic, was attempting to solve a question which had variously vexed many a theologian: to what extent may a monk become involved in missions beyond the walls of the monastery without ceasing to be a monk?

For Ignatius, priority was accorded the union of the human will with the will of God, even though activity oriented toward the love of God might reduce somewhat the time of formal prayer. This was an orientation which grew out of his personal experience and about which he spoke firmly toward the close of his life (Gannon & Traub, 1969, pp. 160–169). And it was from experience too that he derived his insights about the rules for discernment. The complex mental operations referred to in these rules may be thought of as the constituent elements of the cardinal virtue of prudence in traditional Christian literature. Hence, as in the case of the examination of conscience, so also with respect to discernment and its decision-making, privacy is much in demand. The proper discharge of discerning between good and evil urging of the spirit necessarily implies personal reflection and often wise consultation. Recalling that prudence is a virtue of the intellect, one can conclude that intelligent reflection and the consideration of alternatives and their consequences require the umbrella, so to speak, which only privacy can supply. Proper discernment is a task which scarcely yields to contemplation in its demands upon the individual's experience in solitude.

CONTEXT OF INDIVIDUAL SPIRITUAL GROWTH

Life of the Spirit

At the same time as it is a quest for authentic encounter with God, the life of the spirit is a search for the meaning of all life, especially one's own. Although other approaches may be available, religion should rank high among the paths open to individual inquiry about life's meaning. In a study previously noted, it was reported from an empirical investigation, in which more than 2,000 persons were asked why they were religious, that the most frequently occurring response was "religion gives meaning to life" (Braden, 1947). Since the acquisition of such meaning is initiated most generally within the confines of the family, in person-to-person interchange between mother and child, father and child, and among siblings, when the latter are present in the home, it cannot be emphasized too strongly how important it is that these interactions be valued for their intimacy and privacy.

Apropos in a context of meaning and values, Clark (1958) attempts to relate religious development to the operation of the so-called four wishes, the motivational forces which Thomas proposed: *security*, *response*, *recognition*, and *experience* (Thomas & Znaniecki, 1927).

Motivational Aspects

Security. In a religious setting Thomas' security would best relate to the religious person's estimate of personal dependence on God, not merely for material sustenance, but more particularly for assistance and support in the more abundant supernatural way of life. Familiar is the prayer refrain "for the temporal and spiritual welfare of all those in peril or exposed to danger." Most of us possess a sense of decorum or propriety and apply some measure of reasonable restraint in stating the dangers from which we desire our fellow-creatures to be protected by the divine favor; but it still holds true that an authentic religion will show concern for the basic yearnings of mankind.

Response. This is best seen as a religious need in the Christian acts of generosity and supererogation in requiting God's love for His creatures. In any consideration or reflection upon one's personal meaningfulness, gratitude to God must have a high priority, and the religious person will be conscious that such an appreciative response is but a repayment, however inadequate in expression, of undeserved divine beneficence. Though it is true that religion is not the only vehicle for the expression of love and friendship, it is par excellence the embodiment of the human person's most sublime recognition of the I–Thou relationship of intimacy and mutual love. In fact, it is the relationship which gives all meaning not only to one's attitude toward God as Supreme Being but also to one's fellow-creatures. Perhaps Murray's (1938) affiliation need is conceptually preferable to response need in our effort to capture the fuller content of the I–Thou relationship as the religious person sharpens his or her stance before God. Again, if Otto's (1917/1958) notion of God as *tremendum* is to be taken as even nearly literal, and our mode of comprehending Him a kind of "sixth sense" operation, response does seem to be a term of considerable dilution.

Recognition. In a truly religious context this must be seen as an implicit fulfillment of a spiritual way of life rather than as an explicit, primary quest. After all, in its naked form as primary motivation, how can it escape the charge of a tendency toward self-display or the assumption of a "holier than thou" attitude? Rather must it be seen in the light of an accompanying humility which realistically takes into account the disparity between the *tremendum* and the creaturely recipient of divine love. It is well represented in such Old Testament characters as Joseph, who had been sold into bondage by his brothers and came unexpectedly to a position of prominence, or in the New Testament parable of the prodigal son. On the other hand, the theme of recognition may prove to be detrimental to the cause of religion as in the instances of those who exploit ecclesiastical position or church membership for personal display or rise to fame.

New experience. As a motivating force in the spiritual life, this is perhaps more subtle and more diversified in its manifestations than any of the other Thomas' "wishes." At its highest levels, it is to be seen in the favors granted to the great authentic mystics, to a Catherine of Siena or Teresa of Avila. Its genuine worth has been poetically elaborated in Francis Thompson's *Hound of Heaven* and by John of the Cross in his *Ascent of Mount Carmel.* Less remarkable manifestations of novelty, or of variety at least, apparently find a place in Christian liturgy and worship. The recent charismatic and Pentecostal movements in several churches traditionally known as institutional would attest to some basic attraction for variety and new experience. And it might be noted that Spranger accepted a definition of religion as "the highest and absolutely satisfying value experience" (1916/1928, p. 213).

Developmental Stages

In every culture the learning basic to the acquisition of norms, values, and ideals occurs in the context of interaction with adults. What takes place in spiritual development can hardly be the exception. Hence, it should scarcely surprise us that religious ideals of the young are dependent upon parents who are willing to accept responsibility for the early training of their children. It is a most serious responsibility and hardly by mere happenstance is it that religious groups entrust its initiation and early phases to parents within the sacred and protected precincts of the family setting. It is within this milieu of the intimate family setting that the child's need for privacy can be recognized and most judiciously satisfied. Essentially this is so because within the family, better by far than elsewhere, can society and religion have confidence that the ambient "atmosphere" will be one of love and patient, understanding acceptance.

From the beginning of his or her spiritual growth the child is certainly no less fragile than in other areas of need, such as those for physical, intellectual, and emotional development. His or her first steps in the manifestation of all such needs, including those of the spirit, will necessarily be tentative and inchoate, vulnerable to harsh or inconsiderate criticism, and easily thwarted to the point of total or partial extinction. It is hardly necessary to elaborate the analogy of the care required for the proper maturation of seedling and plant. More in perspective is the importance to be placed on the protective function of privacy.

One may ask: What are the advantages to be gained through the sedulous provision of such privacy? Several such advantages may emerge from a consideration of a scheme of patterned development. We shall cite the one proposed by Erikson (1964). As has already been mentioned in passing, others—Freud (1916/1966) and Havighurst (1972), for instance—have proposed somewhat diverging schemata of growth in personality. Though we recognize that there is no great unanimity among psychological theorists in specifying stages of human development, Erikson's eight-stage scheme recommends itself because it attempts to cover the entire lifespan and because the respective critical stages or "crises" (problem areas), which he associates with each of the eight stages respectively, appear to be relevant in a consideration of spiritual and religious growth. There is the added advantage that Erikson's work and his formulations are sufficiently well known to excuse the brevity of the following discussion.

First stage. By limiting consideration to the tasks which he assigns to the earlier stages of growth, it is intended to illustrate in which light the successful accomplishment of Erikson's serial "tasks" may relate to the proper, unimpeded development of religious values. In the crisis of the psychosocial "problem" faced by the infant in the first year of life, successful solution should be the acquisition of basic trust in the parents, vested particularly in the mother in the general case; by extension, to other people seen as "caretakers"; and more remotely in God. This last, of course, is by considerable extension and will hardly be operative at any conscious level until some later date. Most observers who accept this analysis in a religious light would probably interpret the acquisition of trust as an affective preparation for the later acceptance of God in the guise of a father-image or of a powerful person who is warm and supportive. On the other hand, a negative outcome—i.e., failure to solve the task proposed—would be mistrust, or the emotional disposition for seeing God as cold, indifferent, or rejecting.

Second stage. In the second of Erikson's stages (that of the child in the second, third, and perhaps into the fourth year of life), the psychosocial task to be mastered is that of autonomy, or the emerging with a sense of selfhood involving at least personal separateness, if not relative independence. Perhaps the negative outcome or failure in this stage, which Erikson designates as shame and doubt and which connotes self-worthlessness, serves to increase our appreciation of the importance of the conflictual nature of this developmental phase. It is, to be sure, an emotional, not a reasoned, conclusion reached by the child; yet to entertain the deep-seated conviction that one is worthless or non-productive must certainly be an obstacle to openness in any future encounter with God. Again, it should be clear that the emotional conflict attending the child's struggle can be visualized as promising a better resolution if its dénouement is allowed to occur within the family setting, where love and forbearance can we hope be assumed to prevail. Have most of us not noted the public annoyance on the part of strangers, when they behold the antics of a resistive, stubborn child? We assume a greater tolerance on the part of family members.

Third stage. In this stage (fourth, fifth, and sixth years of life), the issue has to do with the child's success in learning that it is permissible to express initiative and that such expression is not something about which to experience guilt. Again, it is a lesson which is to be learned mostly at an affective level, but it might be said that the religious dimension has relevance for the very important matter of being branded as either sinful and damned or feeling capable of being redeemed. Since the area touched upon in this stage (Freud's Oedipal stage) is the twin *bête noire* of sexual and aggressive impulse, it should be even more obvious that the setting for the resolution of these problems should be one of comforting privacy and tolerant understanding. As will be pointed out subsequently, the individual's need for privacy in the growth of the spirit is tempered by a comparable need: namely, a need for self-disclosure.

The need for self-disclosure may be occasional or periodic, freely indulged, and characterized by one's imposition of secrecy upon the person to whom the disclosure is made. Hence, the desideratum is a fine balancing between these two needs. Since it is not to be assumed that such balance will be achieved automatically, our thinking is that it is within the protected enclosure of the family that excessive privacy will best be prevented from taking the path of lonely isolation and shame-ridden guilt. In like manner, self-disclosure will be so regulated as not to become needless exposure or vulgar exhibitionism. A prime example may be found in the near universality of some form of training in modesty. Such training is most frequently accompanied by religious overtones, as instanced by subtle and explicit reference to the all-seeing eye of God or to the close presence of angelic beings. But it is undoubtedly the manner in which it is taught more than the image employed which contributes to the acquisition of modesty as a trait or attitude.

Fourth stage. With the advent of Erikson's fourth stage, which generally occurs in what was once simply called the latency period and which presupposes as its task the mastery of societal skills (industry as opposed to inferiority), the individual is less within the protective shadow of the home and more dependent on his or her own endeavors. As far as privacy is concerned in this and subsequent stages, its safeguarding will be ever more related to the individual's esteem for values previously learned. It will be a time of testing and of evaluating such values in interaction with schoolmates, other peer-group members, and adult models encountered outside the family. It will provide the opportunity to make comparisons and even to compete on a wider scale for successful accomplishment. Such success will undoubtedly be enhanced by retention of the fruits of prior trust, autonomy, and initiative. Generally speaking, there is in this period a diminishing of emotional urgency and more input from developing rationality, unless, of course, the task is not mastered, and inferiority prevails.

Without entering into any intricate analysis of theological positions regarding "works" or the so-called "work-ethic," but assuming a generalized stance, one might look for the spiritual significance of the work–rest cycle in regard to the composing of secular–religious activities and their respective satisfactions. The alternation of fast days and feast days, of sacrifice and celebration, may not be fully comprehended at this age level, but certainly some intimation of their relevance should be appreciated. Apart from some insights along these lines, it is not likely that in later life there will occur a positive responsiveness to such movements as Christian Awakening, prayer renewals, and closed retreats.

Final stages. Recognizing as we must that growth of the spirit is also a lifelong enterprise, for the sake of brevity it behooves us to collapse somewhat the last four phases of Erikson's scheme: the struggle for personal identity in adolescence to the recognition of life's meaningfulness in one's final years. It is for these stages that the first four have been a preparation, and one would like to think that they will constitute the most consciously rewarding for the mature religious "pilgrim." Among recent writers, perhaps Allport (1950) best presented the differential characteristics separating a mature from an immature religion, and it is a mature religion which should be the goal of one's spiritual growth, the end-product of a fulfilling pilgrimage.

A Place for Self-Disclosure

In our previous discussion of the individual's general need to protect privacy, it was conceded that such need was not to be regarded as inexorable. There are some persons in every population—and times, perhaps, in the lives of most—for whom it is not regarded as essential to personal integrity that their inner aspirations for personal holiness, or even their more intimate conversation with God, be maintained in strictest secrecy. They would, however, appear to be the exceptions among persons religiously oriented. An exception might be found within groups wherein openness and community spirit are to be fostered through mutual sharing. Another exception to the need for privacy can be found in the extent to which religious persons seek selective disclosure for guidance and direction in the conduct of their spiritual lives. Such guidance and direction is sought voluntarily, implies trust to be invested in the director or confidant, and leaves to the individual determination of the scope and extent of such self-revelation. Even when such self-disclosure (traditionally called manifestation of conscience) is highly recommended or explicitly required, as in monastic and religious orders, its extent is left to the discretion of the individual.

As a matter of fact, especially in recent times the exercise of the manifestation of conscience can hardly be regarded as a dictate of obedience. Rather, in view of its purpose in seeking to help the individual to establish spiritual ideals and appropriate methods in their pursuit, this exercise is explicitly recommended as related to the virtues of docility and prudence. Within this framework what the individual seeks and what the director is supposed to provide is a prudential exposition of options based on the person's level of spiritual progress and the presumed greater experience of the director in spiritual matters.

From the standpoints of theological doctrine and moral guidance, there is a vast literature concerning this type of self-disclosure and any perusal of it will reveal such primary considerations as:

(*a*) the retention by the individual of freedom with respect to the amount and depth of such self-revelation;
(*b*) the assurance that the director is acting as a spiritual "father" and that he possesses sufficient objectivity, as well as knowledge and experience to detect what otherwise might be latent illusion or other obstacles to further progress in spirit;
(*c*) the guarantee of absolute confidentiality with regard to all that is disclosed; and
(*d*) the realization that freedom of choice remains with respect to the acceptance in whole or in part, or as accommodated to one's own personal needs, of any suggestions which are offered.

It need hardly be emphasized that these and related safeguards associated with the literature of personal spiritual direction point up the esteem and respect accorded the individual's need for privacy in relation to spiritual formation and growth. It should be pointed out, however, that although the spiritual director, whether appointed by authority (as in novitiates and seminaries) or freely chosen, is usually a priest, his discharge of this particular role is merely analogous to, and not a part of, his office in the hearing of sacramental confessions. In the confessional the priest may, and usually does, dispense spiritual advice or brief, general direction, but hardly with the same individualized and personally-oriented consistency which comes with the knowledge of the personal needs which he can acquire over time as one's director of conscience.

SUMMARY

It has been pointed out that any in-depth consideration of the topic proposed would require a careful sorting out of several highly relevant concepts, and the effort was made to clarify the pertinence of some of these. Beyond this initial search for definitional clarity, a two-pronged approach to an analysis of the role of privacy in relation to spiritual growth was undertaken. The first was a highly selective choice among religious movements of the past, which seemed to offer promise of furnishing illustrative features of humanity's need for a large measure of privacy and non-interference in the individual's pursuit of spiritual goals. Though the examples selected were specifically related to the history of Christianity, it was felt that they were sufficiently diverse and spread over differing cultural epochs to offer a reasonable background against which to look for the presence of a common theme. The movements examined were the practice of confession, the spirituality of the "desert fathers," and the growth of religious orders, especially Benedictinism, in the West. In varying amounts a cult of privacy as a safeguard and protection for growth in spirit seemed to emerge.

A second approach attempted to search for a similar theme through an analysis of what might be considered a reasonably acceptable stage-like program of personality development. Admittedly, the pattern of growth or the program selected, that of Erikson, though not embraced by all psychologists who treat of human development, is one which is representative and frequently cited. Its several stages in the growth of the individual were examined for developmental features which could be regarded with some confidence as applicable to spiritual growth. Finally, notice was taken of the role of limited or selective self-disclosure, especially in situations in which absolute cultivation of privacy might in itself obstruct the individual's spiritual progress.

REFERENCES

Allport, G. W. *The individual and his religion.* New York: Macmillan, 1950.

Angyal, A. *Foundations for a science of personality.* New York: Commonwealth Fund, 1941.

Braden, C. S. Why people are religious—A study in religious motivation. *Journal of Bible and Religion*, 1947, *15*, 38–45.

Buber, M. *I and Thou* (W. Kaufmann, trans.). New York: Scribner's, 1970. (Original German edition, 1923.)

Butler, Dom Cuthbert (O.S.B.) *The Lausiac history of Palladius: A critical discussion together with notes on early Egyptian monachism* (2 vols. in one). Hildesheim: Olms, 1967. (Originally published, 1898.)

Clark, W. H. *The psychology of religion: An introduction to religious experience and behavior.* New York: Macmillan, 1958.

Eliot, T. S. *Collected poems, 1909–1962.* New York: Harcourt Brace Jovanovich, 1963.

Erikson, E. H. *Childhood and society* (2nd ed.). New York: Norton, 1964.

Freud, S. *The complete introductory lectures on psychoanalysis* (J. Strachey, trans.). New York: Norton, 1966. (Original German edition, 1916.)

Gannon, T. (S.J.) & Traub, G. (S.J.). *The desert and the city: An interpretation of the history of Christian spirituality.* New York: Macmillan, 1969.

Havighurst, R. J. *Development tasks and education* (3rd ed.). New York: McKay, 1972.

Heidegger, M. *Being and time* (J. Macquarrie & E. Robinson, trans.). New York: Harper & Row, 1963. (Original German edition, 1927.)

Lewin, K. *A dynamic theory of personality: Selected papers* (D. K. Adams & K. E. Zener, trans.). New York: McGraw-Hill, 1959.

Murray, H. A. *Explorations in personality.* New York: Oxford University Press, 1938.

Oates, W. *The psychology of religion.* Waco, Texas: Word Books, 1973.

Otto, R. *The idea of the holy* (J. W. Harvey, trans.). New York: Oxford University Press, 1958. (Original German edition, 1917.)

Pius XII. Allocution to the International Association of Applied Psychology, April 10, 1958. *Acta Apostolicae Sedis*, 1958, *50*, 268–282. English translation: *The Pope Speaks*, 1958, *5*, 7–20.

Puhl, L. (S.J.). *The spiritual exercises of St. Ignatius.* Westminster, Md.: Newman, 1951.

Rossiter, C. The pattern of liberty. In M. R. Konvits & C. Rossiter (Eds.), *Aspects of liberty.* Ithaca, N.Y.: Cornell University Press, 1958.

Spranger, E. *Types of men, the psychology and ethics of personality* (P. J. W. Pigors, trans.) Halle: Niemeyer, 1928. (Original German edition, 1916.)

Thomas, W. I. & Znaniecki, P. *The Polish peasant in Europe and America.* New York: Knopf, 1927.

Vatican Council II. W. M. Abbott (S.J.) (Ed.). *The documents of Vatican II.* New York: Herder & Herder, 1966.

Westin, A. *Privacy and freedom.* New York: Atheneum, 1967.

Whitehead, A. N. *Religion in the making.* New York: Macmillan, 1926.

III

THE INDIVIDUAL'S RIGHT TO PRIVACY

The Citizen's Right to Privacy: Basis in Common Law

PETER A. LANCE

Peter A. Lance received his A.B. from Northwestern University (1971), his M.S. from Columbia University, where he was Consumer Reports Fellow (1972), and his J.D. from Fordham University School of Law (1978). A former journalist and documentary filmmaker, he has been the recipient of three Emmys, two San Francisco State Broadcast Awards, the Roy W. Howard Award of the Scripps Howard Foundation, the Ohio State Award, and the Gabriel Award. In 1974 he won the Robert F. Kennedy Journalism Award for his production of The Willowbrook case: The people v. the State of New York. *He is co-author of* The Nader report: The workers *(1971), and a novel,* The short, thick man *(1979). Currently, Mr. Lance is a producer for ABC News.*

On the afternoon of September 22, 1975, Sara Jane Moore pointed a .38 caliber revolver at President Gerald R. Ford as he was leaving the St. Francis Hotel in San Francisco. As she pulled the trigger, a man standing nearby knocked her arm downward. The gun discharged, but the bullet missed its mark. President Ford was unharmed. Sara Jane Moore was taken into custody, and Oliver W. Sipple, the 32-year-old ex-Marine who had spoiled her shot, found himself, all at once, a national hero (Note 1).

As the media spotlight focused on Sipple, reporters learned that he was an active member of San Francisco's gay community. Word of his homosexual ties flashed across the country (Note 2). The private life of the man who saved the President became public, and Oliver W. Sipple filed a $15,000,000 damage suit for invasion of privacy (Note 3).

In essence, the Sipple case represents another face-off in the constant tug-of-war between two important interests in American society: the right of the press to inform vs. the right of the individual to be left alone. Both interests are protected by law; but while the right to publish is grounded firmly in the First Amendment, the right of privacy is somewhat more abstract (Bloustein, 1974). The word "privacy" does not appear in the Constitution, and not until 1965, in the landmark *Griswold* decision, did the Supreme Court elevate the "right to privacy" to constitutional status (Note 4). Since then, the Court has limited the constitutional privacy "right" to "matters relating to marriage, procreation, contraception, family relationships, . . . child-rearing and education" (Note 5). Moreover, since the Constitution protects citizens only from the power of government, not from each other, the constitutional "right of privacy" is relevant only to incursions by the state (Richards, 1977, 1980).

The privacy case of Oliver W. Sipple falls outside the constitutional sphere, yet his cause of action has survived a motion for summary judgment and continues through the California courts. For Mr. Sipple is seeking redress under a privacy theory grounded not so much in the Constitution as in common law (Dionisopoulos & Ducat, 1976; Parker, 1974).

THE RIGHT OF PRIVACY

Legal History

Prior to 1890 there was no legal theory upon which an American citizen whose privacy was breached could recover damages in a court of law. The common law of torts provided a host of remedies for civil wrongs but, like the Constitution, was devoid of any cause of action for invasion of privacy. At the same time, not a single state or federal statute recognized personal privacy as an interest worthy of protection.

Then, sometime in the late 1890s, a prominent Boston matron named Mrs. Samuel D. Warren held a series of elaborate social entertainments at her home. The daughter of Senator Bayard of Delaware, Mrs. Warren was the wife of a paper magnate who had recently given up the practice of law. Her social affairs were immensely popular among the Brahmin elite of Marlborough Street and Beacon Hill, and the object of intense coverage by the Boston press. The *Saturday Evening Gazette* which specialized in "blue blood" items reported on Mrs. Warren's parties in highly personal and embarrassing detail. After the particularly lurid coverage of her daughter's wedding, Mrs. Warren became annoyed and turned to her husband for help. Mr. Warren proceeded to consult his former partner, Louis D. Brandeis, a man who would not be forgotten by history (Prosser, 1960).

Tort Theory in Common Law

Since there was no recognized legal theory upon which Mrs. Warren might counter the excesses of the "yellow journalist" press, Mr. Warren and Mr. Brandeis set about to devise one. The result was an article published in the *Harvard Law Review* of December 15, 1890 (Warren & Brandeis, 1890). No other single law review piece has had a comparable impact on American law. Almost three-quarters of a century after its publication, William L. Prosser, the dean of contemporary tort law, wrote an article in the *California Law Review* (Prosser, 1960). After painstaking research he identified more than 300 cases traceable to the privacy principles set forth by Warren and Brandeis. Eleven years later, in the fourth edition of his encyclopedic *Handbook of the Law of Torts*, Prosser (1971) noted that privacy-case law had grown by another 100 decisions. Today, largely as a result of the legal scholarship of Warren, Brandeis, and Prosser, the "right of privacy" has become central to the law of torts. It has been recognized by statute or common law in 40 states and the District of Columbia, and it is viewed by a number of First Amendment scholars as the single greatest counterweight to the power of the press (Abrams, 1977).

The *tort* privacy theory therefore runs parallel to the *constitutional* privacy principles set forth in *Griswold* and its progeny. While the constitutional "right of privacy" offers some protection against incursions by the state, the tort theory provides a broader remedy for breaches of privacy by persons or entities outside government. It is upon this latter theory of civil redress that Oliver W. Sipple has mounted his case; or, more accurately, he has mounted it upon *one* of the privacy-tort theories (Prosser, 1971; Prosser & Wade, 1971). As Prosser discovered, the case law which followed the Warren and Brandeis article developed along four separate lines. Today the all-embracing tort known as "invasion of privacy" actually comprises four distinct kinds of invasion of four distinct privacy interests. Roughly defined, the four torts have generally been set forth as follows:

(1) *public disclosure* of embarrassing private facts about the plaintiff;
(2) *intrusion* upon the plaintiff's seclusion or solitude, or into his private affairs;
(3) publicity which places the plaintiff in a *false light* in the public eye; and
(4) *appropriation* for the defendant's advantage of the plaintiff's name, image, or likeness [Prosser, 1960, p. 389].

As we consider the categories one by one, the reader should bear in mind the countervailing interests at work. It may be fairly stated that whatever is added to the field of privacy is taken from the field of free discussion and business enterprise. Thus, in this area of the law there has been continuing conflict between the press and the private person, a conflict which has produced partial victories for both sides.

PUBLIC DISCLOSURE OF PRIVATE FACTS

Setting in Warren–Brandeis Article

Warren and Brandeis forged their privacy theory by extracting principles from existing common law remedies. Piecing together prior decision where relief had been granted for defamation, invasion of property rights, and breach of confidence, they concluded that the law had always supported "the general right of the individual to be let alone" (1890, p. 195). Later, their reasoning would be used to mount lawsuits against a host of defendants, both corporate and individual. But Warren and Brandeis made no secret of the fact that their privacy remedy was being offered primarily as a shield against the press:

> The press is overstepping in every direction the obvious bounds of propriety and of decency. Gossip is no longer the resource of the idle and of the vicious, but has become a trade, which is pursued with industry as well as effrontery. To satisfy a prurient taste the details of sexual relations are spread broadcast in the columns of the daily papers. To occupy the indolent, column after column is filled with idle gossip which can only be procured by intrusion upon the domestic circle [p. 196].

Prior to the Warren–Brandeis treatise, the traditional remedy for injury to reputation was an action for defamation, which included the torts of slander (by spoken word) and libel (by printed, and later broadcast, matter). A defendant could invariably defeat a libel or slander claim, however, by showing that the defamatory matter uttered or printed was *true* (Prosser, 1971, p. 796). Under the privacy theory advanced by Warren and Brandeis truth was no longer a defense. As they saw it, privacy "implies the right not merely to prevent inaccurate portrayal of private life, but to prevent its being depicted at all" (1890, p. 218).

Thus, in the first case known to rely on the public disclosure theory, a newspaper was enjoined from publishing a picture of an actress clad in tights (Note 6). There was no dispute as to whether the young lady's legs were accurately reproduced. The issue was whether a newspaper could reproduce them without her consent. The court thought not, and the first of four privacy categories was born. Over the years the public disclosure tort grew in several directions.

Growth of Public Disclosure Tort

In 1927 a man named Brents put up a sign in the window of his garage which read:

> Dr. W. R. Morgan owes an account here of $49.67. And if promises would pay an account this account would have been settled long ago. This account will be advertised as long as it remains unpaid [Note 7].

Shocked at the public airing of his indebtedness and lacking a remedy in libel because of the truthfulness of the notice, Dr. Morgan sued Mr. Brents and collected $1,000 for invasion of privacy.

In 1931 the tort was expanded to provide protection for the embarrassing disclosure of facts pertaining to plaintiff's early life. In the 1920s a young prostitute named Gabrielle Darley had been the defendant in a sensational murder trial (Note 8). Once acquitted, she repented, abandoned her life of shame, and married a respectable man named Melvin. For the next seven years she lived a quiet life in polite society among friends who knew nothing of her past. Then a motion picture company released a film called *The Red Kimono*, depicting the true story of Gabrielle Darley and disclosing Mrs. Melvin's current identity. Her new life was shattered, and she went to court. The Fourth District Court of Appeals in California held that the unnecessary use of Mrs. Melvin's name and the revelation of her past to new friends constituted an actionable invasion of her right of privacy.

Eight years later recovery was permitted where a plaintiff's name was used in the radio dramatization of a robbery in which he was the victim (Note 9). At the same time various state courts broadened the public disclosure theory to protect against revelations of embarrassing physical traits. Relief was granted where x-rays of a woman's pelvic region were used in a newspaper (Note 10); where the photograph of a plaintiff's deformed nose was published in a medical journal (Note 11); and where a doctor attempted to use pictures of a patient's facial disfigurement taken while the patient-plaintiff was unconscious (Note 12).

Limits to its Application

The public disclosure tort came to protect a wide range of personal interests, but it was not without limits. First, as Prosser (1960) noted, the disclosure of private facts had to be "a public disclosure and not a private one" (p. 393). In short, for a plaintiff to recover he had to show that he had been the victim of *publicity* in some form (Bloustein, 1964, 1968).

The debtor–creditor cases provide good examples of what the courts meant by "publicity." As mentioned above, the posting of a public notice that a plaintiff did not pay his bills was held to be an invasion of privacy

(Note 7). The same result was found where a plaintiff's debts were published in a newspaper (Note 13) or shouted aloud in the public streets (Note 14). But the mere communication of a plaintiff's indebtedness to his employer or even to a small group of people proved insufficient grounds for recovery (Note 15).

Furthermore, the cases almost uniformly held that the facts disclosed to the public must be *private* facts and not public ones. Thus, matters such as a plaintiff's date of birth or marriage (Note 16), his occupation, and his military service record (Note 17) were held to be outside the scope of the public disclosure tort. Even Warren and Brandeis acknowledged that information contained in public records (1890, pp. 216–217) should be exempt, and in 1975 the United States Supreme Court agreed. In *Cox Broadcasting Corporation v. Cohn* (Note 18), the father of a rape victim sued the parent company of a television station which had disclosed the young girl's name on its evening news program. In rejecting the father's public disclosure claim, the Court per Mr. Justice White held that ". . . the prevailing law of privacy generally recognizes that the interests in privacy fade when the information already appears on the public record" (Note 18, p. 1046).

By the same reasoning courts over the years have denied recovery where plaintiffs were photographed in public places such as streets (Note 19), markets (Note 20), courtrooms (Note 21), and sporting events (Note 22). Again, the thinking has been that there is no harm in "giving publicity to what is already public and what anyone present would be free to see" (Prosser, 1960, p. 395). Of course, where plaintiffs were filmed in private places such as a hospital bed (Note 23) or operating room (Note 12), relief was granted. So also, a cause of action was upheld when hospital orderlies, in a breach of faith, made public the picture of a deformed child, and a newspaper published it (Note 24).

A third limitation on the public disclosure tort was a long-standing requirement that the matter made public be such that it would offend "a reasonable man of ordinary sensibilities" (Prosser, 1960, p. 396; Note 25). Here the pre-eminent case is *Sidis v. F–R Publishing Corporation* (Note 26). William James Sidis was an infant prodigy who had graduated from Harvard at the age of 16, having lectured to noted mathematicians on the fourth dimension as early as at the age of 11. In his late teens Sidis underwent an unusual psychological change. He experienced a revulsion toward mathematics and the publicity which his early accomplishments had brought him. Dropping from public view, he led an obscure life as a bookkeeper, spending his off-hours collecting streetcar transfers and studying the folklore of the Okamakammessett Indians. In 1937 his desire to remain aloof was ruined when *The New Yorker* published an article describing his present whereabouts and activities as part of a regular feature entitled "Where Are They Now?" The account was not unflattering but the effect on Sidis was devastating, and he brought suit for invasion of privacy.

The Second Circuit Court of Appeals held that Sidis had no cause of action since there was nothing in the magazine story which would have been objectionable to a normal person. A lower federal court had already distinguished the *Sidis* case from *Melvin v. Reid* (Note 8), where the onetime prostitute was allowed recovery. In *Melvin*, the court noted, the plaintiff sustained "an unwarranted attack upon her reputation," whereas Sidis was depicted in "a fair statement of facts relating to him" (Note 26, p. 21). Prosser saw the difference between the two cases in terms of a "mores" test, under which courts were more prone to condemn publicity surrounding "those things which the customs and ordinary views of the community will not tolerate" (1960, p. 397).

INTRUSION ON PRIVATE AREAS

Application of This Tort

The very term "invasion of privacy" suggests some sort of physical violation of the privacy interest. Yet Warren and Brandeis, in focusing their logic on the press, appeared concerned less with the *act* of intrusion and more with its publication and embarrassing effect. In fact, by Prosser's count, the tort of intrusion predated the famous *Harvard Law Review* piece by nine years. The seminal case involved a young Michigan woman named Roberts who lay in the pangs of childbirth one dark and stormy night (Note 27). Her husband summoned the country physician, a Dr. Demay, who was forced to travel a great distance by horseback to reach her. Feeling sick and tired from overwork, Dr. Demay requested the company of a man called Scattergood to carry his lantern, umbrella, and medical instruments. At the Roberts house the two men were admitted, and soon with Scattergood's help the child was delivered. Later, upon learning that Scattergood was a layman, and an *unmarried* layman at that, the shocked Mrs. Roberts brought suit. Observing that "the plaintiff had a legal right to the privacy of her apartment at such a time" (Note 27, p. 162), the court awarded Mrs. Roberts substantial damages without specifying the grounds.

Over the years the tort of intrusion took on a broader legal profile. It came to serve as a remedy for all violations of a plaintiff's rightful physical solitude or seclusion (Ezer, 1961). The protected areas were held to include a plaintiff's home (Note 28), his temporary quarters (Note 29), and even the parcels which he carried into a public store (Note 30). Three separate jurisdictions allowed recovery to the victims of Peeping Toms (Prewett, 1951), and the tort was also used to stop harassing phone calls by creditors (Note 31). Eventually the principle was extended to forbid non-physical intrusions by means of telephoto lens, wiretap, or microphone (Note 32). It was on this theory that consumer watchdog Ralph Nader was able to collect a $425,000 settlement from General Motors Corporation (GM) after a federal court recognized a prima facie case against the big automaker for intrusion by "unauthorized wiretapping and eavesdropping" (McGarry, 1972, p. 28; Note 33).

Some Limitations Imposed

As the courts acknowledged a wider zone of privacy, they also limited the intrusion tort on three fronts. First, to invoke the remedy, a plaintiff had to demonstrate something in the nature of "prying or intrusion" (Prosser, 1960, p. 391). Hence, noises which disrupted a religious service (Note 34), name-calling, and obscene gestures in public (Note 35) were insufficient to merit relief. The courts also demanded that the privacy intrusion be of the sort which would offend a reasonable man. As a result, a Kentucky judge dismissed the claim of an irate tenant who became incensed when his landlord stopped by to collect the rent on a Sunday morning (Note 36).

The paramount limit on the intrusion tort was the requirement that the area or interest invaded be one which was entitled to privacy. Thus, where the police, acting within their power, subjected a plaintiff to post-arrest fingerprinting, photographing, and search, he had no cause of action (Note 37). Similarly, on the street or in a public place a plaintiff had no right to be left alone. He had no remedy if his picture was taken or even if he was followed about (Note 38). In response to Mr. Nader's claim that GM had him "shadowed," the federal court noted that "mere observation of a plaintiff in a public place does not amount to an invasion of his privacy." Still, the court observed, "under certain circumstances, surveillance may be so 'overzealous' as to render it actionable" (Note 33, p. 563).

Such was the case in 1972 when Jacqueline Onassis, the widow of President John Kennedy, filed a $1,500,000 damage suit against photographer Ron Galella for invasion of privacy, assault, harassment, and intentional infliction of mental distress (Note 39). Galella, self-styled *papparazzo*, made his living by snapping pictures of the rich and famous. His particular approach involved the close shadowing of subjects, capturing them on film at times when they were offguard. One such encounter with actor Marlon Brando resulted in fisticuffs, and Galella sustained a broken jaw.

For some time in the early 1970s Galella concentrated on Mrs. Onassis and her two children. The court record established that the photographer resorted to physical assaults, offensive language, and "incessant surveillance" in order to film the former First Family:

> Outside of movieland, reporters do not normally hide behind restaurant coat racks, sneak into beauty parlors, don "disguises," hide in bushes and theater boxes, intrude into school buildings, and, when ejected, enlist the aid of school children, bribe doormen and romance maids [Note 39, p. 198].

Finding that Galella had "insinuated himself into the very fabric of Mrs. Onassis' life," the court enjoined the photographer to remain a specified distance from the plaintiff and her children. Galella had claimed immunity in the action. He argued that the First Amendment shielded newsmen from any liability for their conduct while gathering the news. The court was not convinced: "Crimes and torts committed in newsgathering are not protected. . . . There is no threat to a free press in requiring its agents to act within the law" (Note 39, p. 987).

As we shall discuss later, the right of privacy has always been balanced by the courts against the right of the press to cover "public figures" and "matters of public interest" (Prosser, 1971, p. 823). At the same time, the intrusion tort, by its very nature, is often accompanied by charges that a defendant trespassed or subjected a plaintiff to mental distress. Thus, while the First Amendment might protect the right of a defendant to *publish* the results of his intrusion, it has generally been held to offer little protection against the act of intrusion itself. The primary case in point is that of *Dietemann v. Time, Inc.* (Note 40).

In November of 1963 *Life* magazine published an exposé entitled "Crackdown on Quackery." The article focused on one A. A. Dietemann, a journeyman plumber who claimed to be a scientist-healer. As noted by the court, Dietemann, "a disabled veteran with little education, was engaged in the practice of healing with clay, minerals, and herbs—as practiced, simple quackery."

Through an arrangement with the Los Angeles County District Attorney's office, two *Life* reporters entered Dietemann's home on September 20, 1963. One of the reporters, a Mrs. Jackie Metcalf, told Dietemann that she had a lump on her breast. Dietemann then placed his hand on her chest and proceeded to wave a wand of some kind over a series of gadgets. He concluded that Mrs. Metcalf had eaten rancid butter eleven years, nine months, and seven days prior to that time. The two reporters surreptitiously recorded the encounter by using a radio transmitter, and photographs were taken with a hidden camera. On October 15, 1963, Dietemann was arrested and charged with practicing medicine without a license. Following the publication of the *Life* story, he filed a suit for invasion of privacy.

A trial court ruled in favor of Dietemann and granted him $1,000 in general damages for "injury to [his] feelings and peace of mind." On appeal, defendant *Time Inc.* raised the First Amendment as a defense, arguing that the hidden camera and recorder were "indispensable tools of investigative reporting." Writing for the Ninth Circuit Court of Appeals, Judge Shirley Hufstedler disagreed:

> The First Amendment has never been construed to accord newsmen immunity from torts or crimes committed during the course of newsgathering. The First Amendment is not a license to trespass, to steal, or to intrude by electronic means into the precincts of another's home or office [Note 40, p. 247].

In conclusion, Judge Hufstedler clearly distinguished between the intrusion (which she held merited no protection) and the subsequent publication of the story and photographs (privileged under the First Amendment).

PLACING PERSON IN FALSE LIGHT IN THE PUBLIC EYE

Roots of this Tort

Publicity which places the plaintiff in "a false light in the public eye" is the third type of illegal invasion of privacy (Prosser, 1960, p. 398; Wade, 1962). The roots of this tort extend as far back as 1816 when Lord Byron was successful in enjoining the distribution of an inferior poem falsely attributed to his pen (Note 41). Since then the tort of false light has been invoked in several classes of cases where misrepresentation was the common element.

Following the thrust of Lord Byron's action, a number of cases involved the spurious use of plaintiffs' names. For example, in 1905 a Georgia policyholder sued his insurance company for the unsanctioned use of his picture and name along with a fictitious testimonial in a company advertisement (Note 42). In 1941 a public servant in Oregon brought suit when his name was signed to a telegram urging political action and addressed to the governor (Note 43). There has likewise been a host of suits involving books and articles falsely attributed to various plaintiffs (Note 44).

Another line of cases involved the use of plaintiffs' pictures to illustrate writings with which they had no connection. As we shall see, the "newsworthiness privilege" (Note 45) permitted such use in some instances. But recovery was granted in extreme cases where, for example, the images of innocent plaintiffs were used to set off stories on "dishonest cab drivers" (Note 46), "man-hungry women" (Note 47), "juvenile delinquents" (Note 48), and narcotics dealing (Note 49). In these cases there was also somewhat of an overlap with the appropriation tort which we shall examine later.

A third, more limited, category of false light actions involved the fictionalization of events involving actual identifiable persons. Here, as in *Dietemann*, the key case revolved around an article in *Life*.

Landmark Case

In 1952 three escaped convicts entered the Pennsylvania home of Mr. and Mrs. James J. Hill. For the next 19 hours the Hills and their five children were held prisoner (Note 50). Significantly, they were not molested or treated violently at any time during the siege. A few days after the incident two of the three escapees were killed in a shoot-out with police.

The following year Joseph Hayes (1954) wrote a best-selling novel based on the seizure of the Hills. It was entitled *The Desperate Hours.* The Hills were not mentioned by name in the book, but the author peppered the story of their ordeal with a number of incidents which never occurred. For example, the family in the novel was made to suffer violently at the hands of the convicts. The father and son were beaten and the daughter subjected to verbal sexual insult. Later the novel was adapted as a Broadway play.

In 1955 *Life* published an article about the play, illustrated with pictures shot at the Hill home where the actual drama had taken place. The actors from the play were portrayed under a headline which read: "True Crime Inspires Tense Play." One picture was captioned "Brutish Convict." Another showed an actress in the role of the daughter biting the hand of one of the convicts in an attempt to force him to drop his gun. The caption read "Daring Daughter." This time the Hill family was named, and they filed suit for invasion of privacy. The case of *Time, Inc. v. Hill* went all the way to the United States Supreme Court, and the holding was something of a landmark. While the Court noted the validity of the false light tort, it held that liability could be established only upon the showing of "malice" or "reckless disregard for the truth" (Note 50, p. 382).Thus, the Court recognized a major limitation on the false light tort where media defendants were involved.

In 1974 the Supreme Court held to its rigid standard of proof in *Cantrell v. Forest City Publishing Co.* (Note 51). That case involved a *Cleveland Plain Dealer* story on the family of a bridge-collapse victim. The reporter who wrote the piece interviewed and photographed the children of the victim while their widowed mother was not at home. In the subsequent article he stressed the family's "abject poverty, the children's old, ill-fitting clothes and the deteriorating conditions of their home." The story contained a number of inaccuracies and falsehoods, not the least of which was the distinct implication that Mrs. Cantrell had been present during the reporter's visit. The Cantrells brought suit against the publishing company, arguing that the story placed them in a "false light" and made them the object of pity and ridicule. On appeal the Supreme Court underscored the "actual malice" standard of *Time, Inc. v. Hill* (Note 50), but ruled in the Cantrells' favor. Thus, while false light cases have become more difficult to win, damages are not beyond reach if a plaintiff can show that the offending publisher acted with "actual malice" or "reckless disregard for the truth."

COMMERCIAL APPROPRIATION AND EXPLOITATION

Protection of Person's Image

Warren and Brandeis centered their privacy thesis in the right of a plaintiff to be free from damaging disclosures. Yet the bulk of early privacy-case law focused on another interest: the right of a plaintiff to protect his name, image, or likeness from commercial exploitation.

The first recorded case in this sphere concerned one Abigail Roberson, a woman of considerable pulchritude, who found her likeness on thousands of boxes of flour (Note 52). Not having consented to the use of her picture, Abigail Roberson brought suit against the Rochester Folding Box Company. In a 4–3 decision, the New York Court of Appeals held against her. The court could find no legal precedent for granting relief. Outraged at the ruling, the New York legislature enacted what became the first privacy statute in the country, making it both a crime and a tort to appropriate the name or likeness of any person for "trade purposes" without his or her consent (Note 53).

The first judicial acceptance of appropriation as a tort came in *Pavesich v. New England Life Insurance Co.* (Note 42). The 1905 Georgia case concerned a newspaper advertisement featuring an unauthorized picture of Pavesich proclaiming that he had bought life insurance and was the better man for it. Ruling counter to the New York Court of Appeals, the Georgia Supreme Court found a common law right of privacy and reversed a trial court's order dismissing Pavesich's complaint. Prosser came to recognize this precedent-setting case as a basis for the false light tort category as well as the seminal ruling against appropriation.

Whether based on statute or the common law, the holdings in favor of plaintiffs in appropriation actions have been legion. A Los Angeles woman named Marion Kerby recovered when a movie studio promoting the motion picture *Topper Returns* sent out letters signed, "Your ectoplasmic playmate, Marion Kerby" (Note 54). A young Illinois girl collected after her photograph was used to promote the sale of dog food (Note 55), and a North Carolina woman obtained relief when a snapshot of her in a bathing suit found its way into a newspaper ad for a slimming product (Note 56).

As we shall discuss, the courts have traditionally ruled in favor of the media when the privacy interests of "public figures" were in question. Nonetheless, the courts have recognized the right of all persons (even celebrities) to protect their names and images from "commercial use." For example, Warren Spahn, the famous Milwaukee Braves pitcher, was awarded $10,000 following the publication of his unauthorized and fictionalized biography (Note 57). This book dramatized such matters as Spahn's relationship with his father, his war record, the courtship of his wife, and even his private thoughts while on the pitcher's mound. Although the recovery was granted under New York's Appropriation Statute, the court recognized elements of all four tort categories including public disclosure, false light, and intrusion.

Still, in the interests of the First Amendment, the courts have strictly construed the term "commercial use" where "public figures" have been the subject of coverage in bona fide reports (Prosser, 1971, p. 806; Note 58). In such instances relief under the appropriations tort has generally been denied, even though the media outlets which published the reports clearly were profit-making entities.

Contrasting Decisions

The United States Supreme Court radically altered that view in 1976 in the case of *Zacchini v. Scripps Howard Broadcasting Co.* (Note 59). Billed as a "human cannonball," Zacchini was an entertainer who performed the feat of being shot from a cannon into a net some 200 feet away. His entire performance lasted approximately 15 seconds. In August and September of 1972 Zacchini was hired to present his act at the Geauga County Fair in Burton, Ohio. He regularly performed in a fenced-in area for members of the public who paid an admission fee to enter the fairgrounds. When a local television station videotaped his performance and aired it in its entirety on a newscast, Zacchini brought suit. After a trial court dismissed his complaint, the Ohio Court of Appeals held that the plaintiff had stated a proper cause of action for infringement of common law copyright. One concurring justice found that Zacchini had a healthy appropriation cause of action, based on his "right of publicity." The entire court agreed that the First Amendment did not privilege the television station where the plaintiff's entire act was telecast.

On appeal, the highest court in Ohio agreed with the concurring justice and rested Zacchini's claim on the "right to publicity," but ultimately the court ruled in favor of the media defendant, relying on *Time, Inc. v. Hill* (Note 50). The Supreme Court reversed. In a 5–4 decision Mr. Justice White noted the distinction between *Time, Inc. v. Hill* and the case at bar. *Time, Inc. v. Hill,* he observed, was a false light action in which the First Amendment interest won out over the interest of "reputation." By contrast, he noted, the "right of publicity" in *Zacchini* was a "proprietary interest . . . closely analogous to the goals of patent and copyright law."

In conclusion, Justice White declared that "the First and Fourteenth Amendments do not immunize the media when they broadcast a performer's entire act without his consent" (Note 59, pp. 4956–4957).

The common thinking among First Amendment scholars is that *Zacchini* will have limited application because there are very few "entire acts" which can be accommodated within a news broadcast. Still, it is a noteworthy decision, for it reveals something of the Burger Court's priorities when the privacy interest is measured against the media's right to publish.

NEWSWORTHINESS DEFENSE: A LIMIT TO PRIVACY

Warren and Brandeis acknowledged that "the right to privacy does not prohibit any publication of matter which is of public or general interest." Moreover, they insisted that "to whatever degree . . . a man's life has ceased to be private . . . to that extent the protection [of privacy] is to be withdrawn" (1890, pp. 214–215). Thus, without ever expressly mentioning the First Amendment, the fathers of the privacy tort planted the seed for what became the greatest limit on "the right to be let alone"—the "newsworthiness" defense. Over the years that defense served to defeat privacy claims in two of the tort spheres where the press was most often the defendant: public disclosure and false light. Accordingly, most state and federal courts refused to grant relief where actions involved "public figures" or "matters of public interest" (Prosser, 1960, p. 411).

Assessing the case law, Prosser described a "public figure" as "a celebrity—one who by his own voluntary efforts has succeeded in placing himself in the public eye," or "anyone who has arrived at a position where public attention is focused upon him as a person" (1960, pp. 410–411). This category was held to include actors (Note 60), athletes (Note 61), public officers (Note 62), inventors (Note 63), explorers (Note 64), and war heroes (Note 65).

The term "public interest" came to have more to do with the public "curiosity" then the public "good." "News" was defined as "that indefinable quality of information which arouses public attention" (Note 66), and banking on the First Amendment, the courts generally acknowledged the press as the final arbiter in such contexts. Thus, a number of people "caught up and entangled in the web of news and public interest" were held to be beyond the protection of the privacy tort, and those who found themselves "public figures for a season," whether they had sought out the limelight or not, could not recover damages against the media (Prosser, 1960, p. 413). This list of plaintiffs included the innocent victims of crime and tragedy as well as eccentrics. William James Sidis, the math–*Wunderkind*-turned-recluse, was among this group (Note 26). In throwing out Sidis' privacy suit, Judge Charles E. Clark concluded that "at some point the public interest in obtaining information becomes dominant over the individual's desire for privacy" (Note 26, p. 811). As to when that "point is reached," the courts have yet to agree on a uniform test.

THE CONSTITUTIONAL PRIVILEGE

Extension of Press Protection

In the mid 1960s the "newsworthiness" defense was raised to the level of "constitutional privilege" through a series of decisions by the Supreme Court. First acknowledged in the landmark libel involving *New York Times Co. v. Sullivan* (Note 67), the privilege was later extended to the privacy sphere in *Time, Inc. v. Hill* (Note 50).

Prior to the *New York Times* decision, the truth of a matter published was sufficient to defeat any defamation claim, but there was some concern that even the defense of truth would be an inadequate shield for the press as it began to report on the civil rights movement in the South (Abrams, 1977). The fear among some First Amendment scholars was that libel actions brought by southern officials might inhibit coverage of the struggle for equality. It was in this climate that the Supreme Court used the *New York Times* case to expand the umbrella of press protection.

Montgomery, Alabama, Police Commissioner L. B. Sullivan had sued the *Times* for publishing an advertisement containing minor factual errors about police handling of the Freedom Riders Movement. Although he was neither named nor indirectly referred to in the advertisement, Commissioner Sullivan alleged that he had been personally defamed. Since Alabama did not recognize a limited press privilege for good faith misstatements of fact, Sullivan was awarded $500,000 by a trial jury for injury to reputation. The Alabama Supreme Court affirmed the holding.

Reversal by the United States Supreme Court was unanimous:

> The constitutional guarantees require, we think, a federal rule that prohibits a public official from recovering damages for a defamatory falsehood relating to his official conduct, unless he proves that the statement was made with "actual malice"—that is, with knowledge that it was false or with reckless disregard of whether it was false or not [Note 67, pp. 279–280].

The theory of the holding was that the Constitution is best served by the free discussion of public interest matters.

In 1967 the Supreme Court extended the "constitutional privilege" to include coverage of "public figures" as well as "public officials" (Note 68). Four years later in *Rosenbloom v. Metromedia* (Note 69), a plurality opinion, Mr. Justice Brennan suggested that the "privilege" hinged, not on the status of the party defamed, but on a consideration of whether the defamatory publication concerned a matter of "public or general interest." Sixteen states followed this rationale. In those jurisdictions, whenever a story in question was deemed to affect "the public interest," liability was limited to a showing by the plaintiff that the media defendant was guilty of "malice" or "reckless disregard." In a sense, this approach harked back to the common law "newsworthiness" defense in the privacy sector.

Its Subsequent Restriction

Then in 1974, a decade after the *New York Times* ruling, the Supreme Court put the brakes on the media's expanding "constitutional privilege" to defame. In *Gertz v. Robert Welch* (Note 70) the Court overruled *Rosenbloom*, limiting the "constitutional privilege" once again to coverage of "public officials" and "public figures."

In recent years the Supreme Court has further narrowed the scope of the media "privilege" by limiting the "public figure" category (Note 71). Still, the impact of the "privilege" upon the law of privacy has been profound. In *Time, Inc. v. Hill* (Note 50), the *Desperate Hours* case, the Court extended the *New York Times* rule to false light privacy actions, and, at the same time, expanded the rule to protect even "matters of public interest." Here the Court did not limit the "privilege" to the coverage of "public officials" or "public figures," as it did in the defamation sphere.

After *Time, Inc. v. Hill*, a plaintiff "linked to . . . a matter of public interest" had to prove "malice" or "reckless disregard" in order to collect against a media outlet which cast him in a false light. Since the public disclosure tort involves the publication of true facts, the *New York Times* "actual malice" rule does not apply. Still, there is a growing controversy among First Amendment scholars as to whether or not the press should have some special protection against the public disclosure cause of action. In *Cox Broadcasting Corporation v. Cohn* (Note 72), the Court recognized the television station's "privilege" to publish the name of a rape victim, but limited its holding to the facts of the case. Thus far, in the balancing test between the privacy interest and the right to publish, the Supreme Court has refused to tip the scales in either direction for public disclosure of private facts.

CONCLUSION

The privacy claim of Oliver W. Sipple hangs on such a balancing test. Sipple, whose heroic act literally thrust him into the public eye, was clearly a "public figure" at the time he saved the President's life. But did his public figure status render his entire life subject to public scrutiny? Did the "public interest" in Sipple extend to his sexual preference? Lawyers for the *Los Angeles Times* have argued that its coverage of Sipple's background was "responsive to the consistent urging of the homosexual community that news respecting its activities be published," and that "such news would have the effect of dispelling stereotypes . . . respecting those involved in the gay community as being weak or ineffectual" (Note 73, p. 3).

Sipple's attorney has countered by questioning whether his client would have acted "if he had known that saving the life of the . . . President would subject his sex life to the speculation and scrutiny of the national news media" (Note 74, p. 6). In a recent California decision the Ninth Circuit Court of Appeals fashioned a test for public disclosure actions which may control the Sipple case.

> The line is to be drawn when publicity ceases to be the giving of information to which the public is entitled, and becomes a morbid and sensational prying into private lives for its own sake, with which a reasonable member of the public with decent standards would say that he had no concern [Note 45, p. 1129].

The final outcome in the Sipple case may not be known for years. Just what effect, if any, that decision will have on the public disclosure tort is unclear. But one point is certain. If the media defendants are victorious, the credit (or blame) must be shared in part with the men who framed the First Amendment. At the same time, if Oliver W. Sipple prevails, he need look to only three individuals to pay his respects: Samuel D. Warren, Louis D. Brandeis, and William L. Prosser. For the birth and development of the American tort of privacy must surely be laid to them.

REFERENCE NOTES

1. *Los Angeles Times,* September 23, 1975, I, 1, 2, 3.
2. *Los Angeles Times*, September 25, 1975, I, 1, 34; September 26, 1975, I, 3, 23; September 27, 1975, I, 23.
3. *Oliver W. Sipple v. The Chronicle Publishing Company.* Superior Court of the State of California for the City and County of San Francisco, Docket No. 695–989.
4. *Griswold v. Connecticut.* U.S., 1965, 381, 479.
5. *Paul v. Davis.* 96 S. Ct. 1155, 1166 (1976).
6. *Manola v. Stevens.* N.Y. Sup. Ct., 1890; *The New York Times,* June 15, 18, 21, 1890.
7. *Brents v. Morgan.* 221 Ky. 765; 299 S. W. 967 (1927).
8. *Melvin v. Reid.* 297 Pac. 91 (1931).
9. *Mau v. Rio Grande Oil, Inc.* 28 F. Supp. 845 (N.D. Cal. 1939).
10. *Banks v. King Features Syndicate.* 30 F. Supp. 352 (S.D.N.Y. 1939).
11. *Griffin v. Medical Society.* 11 N.Y.S. 2d. 109 (Sup. Ct. 1939).
12. *Clayman v. Bernstein.* 38 Pa. D & C 543 (C.P. 1940).
13. *Trammell v. Citizens News Co.* 148 S.W. 2d. 708 (1941).
14. *Biederman's of Springfield, Inc. v. Wright.* 322 S.W. 2d. 892 (1959); *Tollefson v. Price.* 430 P. 2d. 990 (1967).

15. *Timperley v. Chase Collection Service.* 77 Cal. Rptr. 782 (1969); *Harrison v. Humble Oil & Ref. Co.* 264 F. Supp. 89 (D.C.S.C. 1967); *French v. Safeway Stores, Inc.* 430 P. 2d. 1021 (1967).

16. *Meetze v. Associated Press.* 95 S.E. 2d. 606 (1956).

17. *Stryker v. Republic Pictures Corp.* 238 P. 2d. 670 (1951); *Continental Optical Co. v. Reed.* 86 N.E. 2d. 306 (1949).

18. *Cox Broadcasting Corporation v. Cohn.* 95 S. Ct. 1029 (1975).

19. *Humiston v. Universal Film Mfg. Co.* 178 N.Y.S. 752 (1919).

20. *Gill v. Hearst Pub. Co.* 253 P. 2d. 441 (1953).

21. *Berg v. Minneapolis Star & Tribune Co.* 79 F. Supp. 957 (1948).

22. *Gautier v. Pro-Football, Inc.* 304 N.Y. 354 (1952).

23. *Barber v. Time, Inc.* 159 S.W. 2d. 291 (1942).

24. *Bazemore v. Savannah Hospital.* 155 S.E. 194 (1930).

25. *Reed v. Real Detective Pub. Co.* 162 P. 2d. 133 (1945). *Davis v. General Finance & Thrift Corp.* 57 S. E. 2d. 225 (1950). *Samuel v. Curtis Pub. Co.* 122 F. Supp. 327 (N.D. Cal. 1954).

26. *Sidis v. F-R Publishing Corporation.* 113 F. 2d. 806 (2d. Cir. 1940), affirming 34 F. Supp. 19 (S.D.N.Y. 1938).

27. *DeMay v. Roberts.* 46 Mich. 160, 9 N.W. 146 (1881).

28. *Young v. Western & A. R. Co.* 148 S.E. 414 (1929).

29. *Newcomb Hotel Co. v. Corbett.* 108 S.E. 309 (1921); *Byfield v. Candler.* 125 S.E. 905 (1924).

30. *Sutherland v. Kroger Co.* 110 S.E. 2d. 716 (1959).

31. *Carey v. Statewide Finance Co.* 233 A. 2d. 405 (1966).

32. *Rhodes v. Graham.* 37 S.W. 2d. 46 (1931) (wiretap); *McDaniel v. Atlanta Coca-Cola Bottling Co.* 2 S.E. 2d. (1939); *Roach v. Harper.* 105 S.E. 2d. 564 (W. Va. 1958) (microphone).

33. *Nader v. General Motors Corporation.* 25 N.Y. 2d. 560 (1970).

34. *Owen v. Herman.* 11 W. & S. Pa. 548 (1841).

35. *Lisowski v. Jaskiewicz.* 76 Pa. D & C 79 (C.P. 1950); *Christie v. Greenleaf.* 78 Pa. D & C 191 (C.P. 1951).

36. *Horstman v. Newman.* 291 S.W. 2d. 567 (1956).

37. *Voelker v. Tyndall.* 75 N.E. 2d. 548 (1947); *McGovern v. Van Riper.* 54 A. 2d. 469; *Norman v. City of Las Vegas.* 177 P. 2d. 442 (1947); *Walker v. Lamb.* 254 A. 2d. 265 (1969).

38. *Chappell v. Stewart.* 33 A. 542 (1896); contra: *Pinkerton Detective Agency v. Stevens.* 132 S.E. 2d. 119 (1963).

39. *Galella v. Onassis.* 353 F. Supp. 196 (S.D.N.Y. 1972); affirmed in part: 487 F. 2d. 986 (1973). Originally, Galella brought suit in federal district court asking $1.3 million in damages from Mrs. Onassis, her two children, and three Secret Service agents assigned to protect them. Galella alleged false arrest and malicious prosecution and sought to enjoin their interference with the practice of his trade. The district court dismissed Galella's complaint and denied his motion to dismiss Mrs. Onassis' countersuit.

40. *Dietemann v. Time, Inc.* 449 F. 2d. 245.

41. *Lord Byron v. Johnston.* 2 Mer. 29, 35 Eng. Rep. 851 (1816).

42. *Pavesich v. New England Life Insurance Co.* 50 S.E. 68 (1905).

43. *Hinish v. Meier & Frank Co.* 113 P. 2d. 438 (1941).

44. *D'Altomonte v. New York Herald Co.* 154 App. Div. 453 (1913); *Hogan v. A. S. Barnes & Co.* 114 U.S.P.Q. 314 (Pa. C.P. 1957).

45. *Virgil v. Time, Inc.* 527 F. 2d. 1122 (1975), cert. den. 44 U.S.L.W. 3670 (May 24, 1976).

46. *Peay v. Curtis Pub. Co.* 78 F. Supp. 305 (D.D.C. 1948).

47. *Martin v. Johnson Pub. Co.* 257 N.Y.S. 2d. 409 (Sup. Ct. 1956).
48. *Metzger v. Dell Pub. Co.* 207 Misc. 182, 136 N.Y.S. 2d. 888 (Sup. Ct. 1955).
49. *Thompson v. Close-Up, Inc.* 277 App. Div. 848, 98 N.Y.S. 2d. 300 (1950).
50. *Time, Inc. v. Hill.* U.S. 1967, *385*, 374.
51. *Cantrell v. Forest City Publishing Co.* U.S., 1974, *419*, 245.
52. *Roberson v. Rochester Folding Box Co.* 171 N.Y. 538 (1902).
53. New York Sess. Laws, 1903, ch. 132, sec. 1–2. Now as amended in 1921, N.Y. Civil Rights Law, sec. 50–51. Held constitutional in *Rhodes v. Sperry & Hutchinson Co.*, 193 N.Y. 223 (1908), affirmed, U.S. 1911, *220*, 502.
54. *Kerby v. Hal Roach Studios.* 127 P. 2d. 577 (1942).
55. *Eick v. Perk Dog Food Co.* 106 N.E. 2d. 742 (1952).
56. *Flake v. Greensboro News Co.* 195 S.E. 55 (1938).
57. *Spahn v. Julian Messner, Inc.* 18 N.Y. 2d. 324; 274 N.Y.S. 2d. 877 (1966).
58. *Colyer v. Richard K. Fox Pub. Co.* 162 App. Div. 297 (1914); *Booth v. Curtis Pub. Co.* 223 N.Y.S. 2d. 737, affirmed 11 N.Y. 2d. 907 (1962).
59. *Zacchini v. Scripps Howard Broadcasting Co.* 45 U.S.L.W. 4954–4959 (1977).
60. *Paramount Pictures v. Leader Press.* 24 F. Supp. 1004 (1938); *Chaplain v. National Broadcasting Co.* 15 F.R.D. (S.D.N.Y. 1953).
61. *Ruth v. Educational Films.* 184 N.Y.S. 948 (1920).
62. *Martin v. Dorton,* 50 So. 2d. 391 (1951) (sheriff); *Hull v. Curtis Pub. Co.* 125 A. 2d. 644 (1956) (policeman).
63. *Corliss v. E. W. Walker Co.* 64 Fed. 280 (Mass. 1894).
64. *Smith v. Suratt.* 7 Alaska 416 (1912).
65. *Stryker v. Republic Pictures Corp.* 238 P. 2d. 670 (1951).
66. *Sweenek v. Pathe News.* 16 F. Supp. 746, 747 (E.D.N.Y. 1936).
67. *New York Times Co. v. Sullivan.* U.S., 1964, *376*, 254.
68. *Curtis Publishing Co. v. Butts.* U.S., 1967, *388*, 130. *Associated Press v. Walker.* U.S., 1967, *388*, 130.
69. *Rosenbloom v. Metromedia.* U.S., 1971, *403*, 29.
70. *Gertz v. Robert Welch.* U.S., 1974, *418*, 323.
71. *Time, Inc. v. Firestone.* U.S., 1976, *424*, 448.
72. *Cox Broadcasting Corporation v. Cohn.* U.S. 1975, *420*, 469.
73. *Oliver W. Sipple v. The Chronicle Publishing Co.* Docket No. 695–989; Notice of Motion by Times, Mirror and Chandler for Summary Judgment and Memorandum of Points and Authorities in Support Thereof; January 2, 1976.
74. *Oliver W. Sipple v. The Chronicle Publishing Co.* Docket No. 695–989; Opposition of Motion for Summary Judgment per John Eshleman Wahl.

REFERENCES

Abrams, F. The press, privacy, and the constitution. *The New York Times Magazine*, August 21, 1977.

Bloustein, E. J. Privacy as an aspect of human dignity: An answer to Dean Prosser. *New York University Law Review*, 1964, *39*, 962–1007.

Bloustein, E. J. Privacy, tort law, and the constitution: Is Warren and Brandeis' tort petty and unconstitutional as well? *Texas Law Review*, 1968, *46*, 611–629.

Bloustein, E. J. The first amendment and privacy: The Supreme Court justice and the philosopher. *Rutgers Law Review*, 1974, *28*, 41–96.

Dionisopoulos, P. A., & Ducat, C. R. *The right to privacy.* St. Paul: West, 1976.

Ezer, M. J. Intrusion on solitude. *Law in Transition*, 1961, *21*, 63–76.

Hayes, J. *The desperate hours.* New York: Random House, 1954.

McGarry, C. *Citizen Nader.* New York: Saturday Review Press, 1972.

Parker, R. B. A definition of privacy. *Rutgers Law Review*, 1974, *27*, 275–296.
Prewett, B. Crimination of Peeping Toms and other men of vision. *Arkansas Law Review*, 1951, *5*, 388–389.
Prosser, W. L. Privacy. *California Law Review*, 1960, *48*, 383–423.
Prosser, W. L. *Handbook of the law of torts* (4th ed.). St. Paul: West, 1971.
Prosser, W. L., & Wade, J. W. *Cases and materials on torts.* Mineola, N.Y.: Foundation Press, 1971.
Richards, D. A. J. Unnatural acts and the constitutional right to privacy: A moral theory. *Fordham Law Review*, 1977, *45*, 1281–1348.
Richards, D. A. J. The jurisprudence of privacy as a constitutional right. In W. C. Bier (S.J.) (Ed.), *Privacy: A vanishing value?* New York: Fordham University Press, 1980.
Wade, J. W. Defamation and the right of privacy. *Vanderbilt Law Review*, 1962, *15*, 1093–1125.
Warren, S. D., & Brandeis, L. D. The right to privacy. *Harvard Law Review*, 1890, *4*, 193–220.

The Client's Right to Privacy

JAMES J. HENNESSY

James J. Hennessy received his A.B. (in 1963) and M.A. (in 1966) degrees from St. John's University, Jamaica, New York, and his Ph.D. (in 1974) from New York University. From 1966 to 1970 he was Assistant Director of the Counseling Center at St. John's University. Subsequently, he was a Counselor, College Community Center, Queensborough Community College, and later still Assistant Coordinator, Project in Individualized Instruction, Patchogue, New York. In 1974 Dr. Hennessy joined the faculty of Fordham University, where he currently is Associate Professor in the Division of Psychological and Educational Services of the School of Education. Dr. Hennessy is a member of a number of professional organizations, among them the American Psychological Association and the American Personnel and Guidance Association, and is the author of an increasing number of articles in professional journals.

A careful review of the recent literature examining the effectiveness of counseling and psychotherapy suggests that success or failure of treatment is determined to a large extent by the quality of the relationship established between the therapist and client. This is the case in the dynamic psychotherapies (Malan, 1976), and in the behavioral therapies (Kazdin & Wilcoxon, 1976), and is also true when the dynamic and behavioral therapies are compared (Staples, Sloane, Whipple, Cristol, & Yorkston, 1976). The willingness of a client to enter into the therapeutic relationship is based, to an extent, on the trust which the client has that the therapist is capable of providing assistance with some of the most private and personal concerns of the individual.

This trust can exist only when there is some reason to believe that one is safe when revealing personal information and feelings. Thus, rapport, willingness in self-disclosure, and openness to the therapeutic process are affected by the client's belief that what is said will be held in confidence and that there are valid therapeutic reasons for divulging highly personal information. These beliefs deal with client rights to confidentiality and to privacy, two overlapping but different areas, and with the ethical and legal responsibilities which the therapist assumes when entering the therapeutic relationship.

The issues which this paper will address bear on the ethical and legal limits of confidentiality and privacy in therapy. Before dealing with specific rights and issues, however, it is important to clarify the distinctions between confidentiality and privacy, and between ethics and law.

CLARIFICATION OF RELEVANT CONCEPTS

Privacy

The term "privacy" was defined by Supreme Court Justice William O. Douglas to mean that "the individual should have the freedom to select for himself the time and circumstances when he will share his secrets with others and decide the extent of that sharing" (Nygaard, 1973, p. 42). From the point of view of a client's rights, this definition not only reserves to the client the right to enter into a therapeutic relationship, but also leaves to the client the freedom to determine how much to share with the therapist.

Nygaard (1973) also gave a more inclusive definition of the right to privacy as contained in *Black's Law Dictionary*:

> The legally protected right of an individual to be free from unwarranted publicity and to be protected from any wrongful intrusion into his private life which would outrage or cause mental suffering, shame, or humiliation to a person of ordinary sensibilities [p. 42].

Black's definition includes elements of both confidentiality (unwarranted publicity) and privacy (wrongful intrusion) as used in this paper.

Confidentiality

Confidentiality refers specifically to the retention or the sharing with others of information received by a therapist in face-to-face interaction with a client. Though the legal conditions of it will be given in greater detail below, confidentiality can be defined as the right of the client to have communications or exchanges of information given in a professional–client relationship kept secret. It is a concept which is concerned specifically with the protection from outside intrusion into the therapeutic relationship; privacy is a right concerned both with outside interference or intrusion, and, perhaps more importantly, with what occurs *within* the therapeutic relationship. Client rights to privacy come into play when a therapist is called upon to share information with third parties, and when the therapist manipulates a client to gain access to the "secrets" of the client. The issues of confidentiality and privacy will be explored separately since different threats to client rights are involved.

Ethics

As defined in this paper, ethics refers to a highly developed personal values system which guides the therapist as he makes moral decisions. Ethical principles are the guides for what ought to govern human conduct, and, as such, they spring from the individual's beliefs in the value and nature of man. Each person has a unique style of ethics, although there may be many common elements consistent with societal expectations, religious convictions, and standards of professional, social, or cultural groups.

The ethical values of the counselor or therapist will determine the therapeutic strategies and goals which he strives to reach. The importance of these values, from the client's point of view, is evident in the contrast between the utilitarian system of ethics of Freud (1954) with the humanistic system of Maslow (1962) or Rogers (1961). The Freudian emphasis on the instinctively driven pursuit of pleasure and avoidance of pain as the prime determinants of behavior will lead to very different strategies and goals of therapy from those to which the humanistic principles of Maslow, which view man as being basically good and moving toward self-actualization, will lead.

Aware of it or not, every counselor and every therapist functions from a personal ethical system. This system may be poorly developed, and the counselor or therapist may not consistently adhere to it, but as Van Hoose and Kottler (1977) state:

> One could even say that the regulation of all therapist behavior is based entirely on a belief system for what is right for a particular client. . . . the core of a therapist's system of what is right, wrong, good, bad, effective, ineffective, appropriate, and inappropriate is based on a philosophical ethical system [p. 39].

Because of the central value of ethics to the therapeutic process, it is important for the therapist to develop this system to highest levels so that moral decisions affecting the client can be made systematically in a logical, rational, and critical manner.

Law

Law, as used in this paper, refers to the statutes enacted by legislatures or established by courts which apply to all people of a specified group or area. The law defines the legal constraints which govern conduct, and spells out sanctions for those who violate them. Laws are binding on all, even though a person may challenge them. The ethical standards of a therapist may differ from the legal standards of society, thus placing the client in a position where some basic rights to privacy may be threatened. The remainder of the paper will speak to some of those threats, and offer some recommendations for lessening them. The client's right to confidential or privileged communication will be discussed first, followed by a discussion of the right to privacy within the therapeutic relationship.

CLIENT'S RIGHT TO CONFIDENTIAL COMMUNICATION

A Landmark Case

Any casual reading of the current professional journals and newsletters will bring to the reader's awareness the concerns and issues which psychologists, counselors, and other mental health providers face when they attempt to keep client communications confidential. The most widely known example of this issue is the *Tarasoff v. Regents of the University of California* case in which the Supreme Court of California found a therapist and his employers guilty of negligence for failure to warn a third party of threats which a client in therapy made against her life. Although the therapist reported the threats to local police, the client was released after a short period of detention, and subsequently followed through on his threats and killed his former fiancée. The defendants were found guilty of negligence for not advising the girl and her parents of the threats. Van Hoose and Kottler (1977), in their summary and analysis of the case, quote the court's ruling, which confronted directly the issue of confidentiality or privileged communication:

> Public policy favoring protection of the confidential character of patient–psychotherapist relationship must yield in instances in which disclosure is essential to avert danger to others; the protective privilege ends where the public peril begins [p. 88].

As Van Hoose and Kottler indicate, this case highlights the conflict between ethical and legal aspects of confidentiality, a conflict which has not as yet been successfully resolved by either the law or the professional associations of psychologists, counselors, and other mental health providers.

Ethical Principles Involved

Ethical principles were defined as moral or philosophical guidelines which therapists and counselors establish to aid in deciding what should be done when conflict arises. Yet because many practitioners have not clearly and fully developed a personal code of ethical practice, both the American Psychological Association and the American Personnel and Guidance Association have formulated standards of ethical conduct for their members. Though these standards are not intended as a substitute for a personal code, they could be viewed as minimal standards of ethical behavior, and counselors and psychologists are expected to act in accordance with the principles of confidentiality established by their respective professional associations.

The need for a firmly established code of ethics was amply demonstrated recently by the American Psychological Association (APA), but at this time, principles of confidentiality have not been satisfactorily developed. In the most recent revision of its ethical standards, the principles pertaining to confidentiality were left unchanged, but this restatement, rather than reflecting professional agreement on the principles, underscores the inability of the profession to resolve the complex problems in the area. The principle now in effect states:

> Safeguarding information about an individual that has been obtained by the psychologist in the course of his teaching, practice, or investigation is a primary obligation of the psychologist. Such information is not communicated to others unless certain important conditions are met [American Psychological Association, 1977, p. 22].

These conditions are not clearly specified, although information can be released without the client's consent when there is clear and imminent danger to the individual or to society.

A more detailed statement of a client's right to confidentiality is given by the Association in its Standards for Providers of Psychological Services (American Psychological Association, 1975), which directs psychologists to explain to the client any limits which exist for maintaining confidentiality, such as institutional policies, legal requirements, and accessibility of records. It then states (p. 21):

> Unless otherwise directed by statute or regulations with the force of law or court order, the psychologist shall not release confidential information, except with the written consent of the consumer directly involved or his legal representative.

The confusion which many practitioners feel is exemplified by the obvious contradiction between the ethical standards and the standards for providers of services, in that the former directs the practitioners to break confidence if threats to life are involved, while the latter states such breaches can occur only with client consent or when the psychologist is legally required to do so. This confusion is further exacerbated by the ambiguities of laws relating to confidentiality.

The ethical standards of the American Personnel and Guidance Association (APGA) are somewhat more detailed, and specify certain conditions which would override the confidential nature of the counseling relationship. The APGA standards also set guidelines for establishing the primacy of client's rights and the obligations which the counselor has to the institution or agency in which the counselor works. Members of the association are expected to perform in accordance with institutional regulations, but when there is an unresolvable conflict between institutional policies and the welfare and rights of the client, the counselor is advised to consider seriously terminating affiliation with the institution. Thus, if a school official demands access to information obtained in a counseling relationship, the counselor is ethically bound to refuse to respond, *unless legally compelled to do so.*

The ethical standards of both the APA and the APGA stress that the clients' rights to confidentiality are to be protected; at the same time both standards recognize that these rights are not absolute, and can be waived under certain serious conditions. Thus the codes demonstrate an awareness of society's need for protection from possibly dangerous individuals. Ethically, then, the client's right to confidential communication is a qualified right, which can be waived only under compelling circumstances.

Legal Protection of Confidentiality

The legal basis for confidentiality stems from the concepts of privileged communication which originated in early English common law to protect the communications between a client and an attorney. Because its purpose was to prevent a lawyer from divulging information given by a client, the concept of privileged communication was established as a right of the client's, which only the client could waive.

Confidentiality, as a legal right of therapy clients, exists only where it has been expressly recognized by statute or court precedent, and then only if the particular communications meet four criteria:

(1) the communications must originate in the confidence that they will not be disclosed;
(2) the elements of confidentiality must be essential to full and satisfactory maintenance of the relationship between the parties;
(3) the relationship must be one which, in the opinion of the community, should be sedulously fostered;
(4) the injury inflicted on the relationship by disclosure of the communi-

> cations must be greater than the benefit gained for proper disposal of litigations [Burgum & Anderson, 1975, pp. 15–16].

According to Burgum and Anderson, statutory protection exists in at least 17 states for the clients of psychologists and in nine states for clients of school counselors. They were pessimistic about the likelihood that additional states would grant this privilege, and concluded that courts would not extend legal recognition to the confidential nature of the therapeutic relationship where it does not already exist. While ethical standards prohibit the revealing of client communications except in certain instances, these standards do not have the support of law in most states. Counselors and psychologists may be required to give testimony, or be held liable for failure to do so if they do not divulge these communications.

Specific Areas of Potential Violation

There are other, less obvious, but potentially more serious, threats to confidentiality than the unlikely instances that a counselor or psychologist would be subpoenaed to testify in court. Four concerns will be mentioned here, but no doubt the reader can envision other possible breaches of confidentiality.

Group therapy. Over the past decade, the popularity of group counseling and psychotherapy has increased tremendously. As this popularity has increased, so have the instances of questionable professional practices. For the most part, these practices involve ethical questions which go beyond confidentiality and touch on other aspects of the right to privacy which will be discussed later. The threat to confidentiality which groups pose has both legal and ethical implications.

Many authorities have suggested that, from a legal viewpoint, the principle of privileged communication, even for licensed persons protected by statute, does not apply when more than two people participate in the communication. Confidentiality, in effect, can exist only in one-to-one communication. Thus communications given to several others are not given in confidence, and those who receive the communications (other group members) may be compelled to share that information. Though the professional may or may not be protected by a client's right to privileged communication, this protection does not extend to any other group members. It is unlikely that most group leaders advise group members of their lack of protection from disclosure and merely request that members hold everything said in confidence. By so doing leaders may give members a false sense of assurance about the confidentiality of the sessions. Ethically, group leaders should advise members as to the limits on confidentiality, even though to do so may inhibit some members or prevent discussions of certain topics.

Reimbursement by government or agency. A second possible threat to confidentiality is of concern primarily to psychologists and counselors who are eligible for third-party reimbursements through private or public medical insurance plans. In order to receive payment, the practitioner must complete forms which often call for very specific information about the "condition" of the client. State and federal regulations for reimbursement also require that fairly specific records of each session be kept and be available for audit by the reimbursing agency. The threat to confidentiality is posed when the insurer records these reports in its filing system and then gives other people access to the files. The federal government is currently attempting to develop safeguards against these intrusions into the private concerns of its citizens and is awaiting the report of a commission appointed to suggest modifications of the federal privacy laws and regulations (Fields, 1977). Until stringent safeguards are enacted, professionals who submit reports to insurance carriers do so without the sure knowledge that the reports will not be used in some way to harm the client.

Tape recording. The widespread use of video and audio tape recording of counseling and therapy sessions presents a third threat to confidential communications. Recording without the consent of the client is specifically prohibited by the ethical standards of both the APA and the APGA, and by state and federal laws and regulations on electronic eavesdropping. The threat to privacy comes, not from clandestine recording, but from the improper disposal of tapes obtained with the permission of the client. The client has the right to expect that such tapes will not be shared with others without consent, or kept as permanent additions to case records. Certain limiting conditions must be acknowledged. In training facilities, tapes are often reviewed by supervisors or other traineees, and tape transcripts may be made as part of research or case study analysis. In these instances the obligation to obtain consent is still present, and if a client refuses permission, those sessions cannot be taped.

Possibility of role confusion. A fourth issue is especially germane to the Institute. Pastoral counseling is now a major area of activity of specially trained priests and ministers. A question of role confusion, by either the counselor or client, may lead to problems in maintaining confidentiality. Most states and courts grant the right of privileged communication to priests and penitents. Clients may assume that because the counselor is a priest all communications must legally and ethically be held in confidence. This assumption is erroneous, at least from a legal and possibly from an ethical point of view. When acting in the role of a counselor or therapist, the pastoral counselor enjoys the same legal protection as do his professional colleagues. The pastoral counselor may refuse on ethical and moral grounds to break confidence, but if compelled to do so legally, he must be prepared to accept the consequences of violating a lawful request. The priest–penitent relationship is not the same as the pastoral counselor–client relationship, and the privileges and prerogatives of one do not transfer to the other, even though one person is functioning in both roles.

The resolution of the ethical and legal issues dealing with confidentiality will not occur until the professional associations and, to a lesser extent, state legislatures and courts, define more specifically the limits and conditions under which the therapeutic relationship exists. It is the professional associations which should take the lead in this activity.

> Some legal methods for controlling the professional activities of therapists, particularly if these methods weed out the incompetents, are probably legitimate. Professionals, however, should not rely solely upon legislatures and courts to solve their problems unless they are prepared to give up some freedom and professional activity [Van Hoose & Kottler, 1977, p. 126].

The development of workable ethical standards by APA and APGA which reflect the ethical positions of their members ought to be given high priority. Until this is done the client is placed in a tenuous position, for he is not sure of the extent to which his privacy will be protected from outside interference.

RIGHT TO FREEDOM FROM UNJUST INTRUSION

The above discussion was concerned with that aspect of privacy which dealt with the right to be free from unwarranted publicity. But the right to privacy also includes protection from any wrongful intrusion into one's private life. This aspect of privacy has received considerably less attention in the literature, although opponents of behavior modification have cited it as one argument against those techniques. The client's right to privacy, or freedom from wrongful intrusion, is acknowledged in the *Revised Ethical Standards* of the APA (1977).

> Psychologists respect the integrity and protect the welfare of the people and groups with whom they work. . . . Psychologists *fully inform consumers* as to the purpose and nature of an evaluative, treatment, educational or training procedure, and they freely acknowledge that clients . . . *have freedom of choice with regard to participation* [p. 23; emphasis added].

Although the principle is quite explicit, its implementation in everyday practice is beset with difficulties which pose threats to a client's right to privacy. We shall focus on only a few of these threats as they might occur in individual and group treatment.

Application in Behavior Modification

Psychotherapy is now recognized as a positive social force which can be used to effect socially desired changes in individuals whose behaviors, thoughts, or feelings are considered to be deviant. The recognition of the prominence of psychotherapy in bringing about these changes can be seen in the widely-held belief that the rehabilitation of criminals is brought about not by the deprivation of certain freedoms and punishment through confinement, but through a therapeutic process aimed at changing behavior or underlying personality structures.

Szasz has suggested (1974) that we are moving toward a "therapeutic state" in which individuals who are "different" are labeled such and forced into a psychotherapeutic relationship so that socially desired changes can be effected. The powerful techniques of behavior modification, aversion therapy, and systematic desensitization have been utilized with inmates in hospitals and prisons, usually without their consent. Civil libertarians raised such strong objections to these practices that the federal correctional system has severely limited the use of these techniques on "captive clients."

The possibility of the abuse of clients' rights in the use of behavioral techniques with both "captive" clients and clients freely seeking professional help has long been recognized by experts in the field. Mahoney (1974), for example, wondered if, "When we systematically assess and modify thought patterns, are we pursuing a 'benevolent brainwashing,' which is unwittingly subversive and pervasively immoral?" (pp. 283–284). Although Mahoney was specifically concerned with behavior therapy, his question is equally valid for other therapeutic techniques, as virtually all therapies attempt to influence or change behavior, thoughts, or feelings in therapist-valued directions. Because the techniques of even the client-centered and psychodynamic therapies are subtly applied to elicit certain client responses and bring about specific changes, the therapist has an obligation to make clear his or her role and values in the process. Though it may not be possible or desirable to avoid influencing a client, the therapist must openly and honestly express his or her values so that the client can freely decide whether or not to participate in the process. For "The therapist who unwittingly shapes the values of the client is more deserving of professional concerns than one who acknowledges that element as an important consideration in the clinical enterprise" (Mahoney, 1974, p. 286).

As long as a client is capable of competent decision-making, the right to decide to enter therapy and to change behaviors, thoughts, or feelings resides with the client. The question of whether an individual has the necessary competence to make such a decision may be difficult to answer in some hospital settings, but in other instances the therapist cannot violate the client's right to choose, and must not covertly or overtly attempt to bring about changes valued by either the therapist or society. To do so is wrongfully to intrude into a client's private life and to deprive the client of a basic right to privacy.

Freedom in Self-Disclosure

There is a pervasive sentiment at many levels of American society that openness and complete honesty with one another will somehow cure the ills of individuals and society. Sunshine laws now require that all deliberations of government at all levels be open to public inspection, and "truth-in-" advertising, packaging, communications, etc. regulations are binding on many private, non-public institutions, businesses, and agencies. These laws and regulations are designed to protect the public by giving people sufficient data to enable them to make informed decisions.

In the mental health field, openness and complete honesty have been viewed as positive therapeutic forces since Freud first enunciated the principles of free association. Many therapists long ago decided that the initial concerns and problems which a person brings to therapy are merely surface manifestations of deeper issues which can be gotten to only after patient resistance has been overcome. An analysis of the development of therapeutic techniques from Freud (1954), to Rogers (1961), to Perls (1969), to the technicians of therapy now offering packaged counseling procedures reveals that each of them was seeking methods which would allow a client to express highly personal attitudes and feelings, on the assumption that open confrontation with these secrets would lead to growth, self-actualization, or non-neurotic functioning. Clients are encouraged (reinforced) to be totally honest and immediate, to deal with feelings by sharing them with others, even though the feelings shared may have little bearing on the problems which brought the client to the therapist. Progress in therapy is often measured by the willingness of the client to disclose highly personal material, and the therapeutic failure is the person who cannot or will not disclose his or her full self to the therapist.

The threat to the client's right to privacy, or wrongful intrusion, arises when the therapist's probing is guided more by his or her allegiance to a therapeutic theory or technique than by the specific needs of the individual client. For example, the therapist who denies the validity of a client's initial statement about vocational indecision and begins to explore sexual attitudes or attitudes toward parents, under the guise that these are the more important issues, is intruding into the client's private life and thus violating a right to privacy.

The rise of group counseling and therapy techniques during the past two decades provides other examples of invasions of privacy to satisfy a theory or method rather than help a client. The "hot seat" technique of the followers of Perls and the marathon sessions of many encounter-group specialists are designed to get individuals to "open up" and to divulge their secrets. The group exerts tremendous pressure on members to "self-disclose," and the group values only those willing to do so. The person who values silence, who chooses when and what will be shared, or who merely does not want to respond, can have his defenses mercilessly attacked by a group which prizes only sharing, not privacy. Rather than encouraging such behavior, the group leader must be willing to intervene when those rights are threatened. The uncritical acceptance of the notion that full self-disclosure is always therapeutic and therefore should be a goal both of individual and group counseling and of psychotherapy must be tempered with a respect for the individual's right to privacy. There must also be an understanding that client-sought changes in behavior, thoughts, or feelings can occur without the client's laying bare of all aspects and dimensions of the self.

CONCLUSION

As the foregoing suggests, the issue which this Institute sought to address —"Is privacy a vanishing value?"—is quite appropriately asked of the practitioners and theoreticians of therapy and counseling. As we become more skilled in interview techniques, we are better able to elicit deeper, more closely held, information from our clients. Concurrently, as the techniques of behavior therapy become better understood and more sophisticated, it becomes possible to bring about behavior changes, even with reluctant clients.

These developments place a burden on the professional to become more sensitive to the types of activities which might infringe on the client's right to privacy. This sensitivity must be rooted in an ethical code which views each person as a valuable, free individual who has a right to determine his own course of action. The development of this ethical code is the responsibility of the profession, the universities which train professionals, and, ultimately, the individual.

REFERENCES

American Personnel and Guidance Association. *Ethical standards.* Washington, D.C.: Author, 1974.

American Psychological Association. Standards for providers of psychological services. *APA Monitor,* March 1975, pp. 19–22.

American Psychological Association. Revised ethical standards of psychologists. *APA Monitor,* March 1977, pp. 22–23.

Burgum, T., & Anderson, S. *The counselor and the law.* Washington, D.C.: American Personnel and Guidance Association, 1975.

Fields, C. A growing problem for researchers: Protecting privacy. *Chronicle of Higher Education,* May 2, 1977, pp. 1, 15.

Freud, S. *The origins of psychoanalysis* (M. Bonaparte, A. Freud, & E. Kris, Eds.). New York: Basic Books, 1954.

Kazdin, A., & Wilcoxon, L. Systematic desensitization and non-specific treatment effects: A methodological evaluation. *Psychological Bulletin*, 1976, *83*, 729–758.

Mahoney, M. *Cognition and behavior modification*. Cambridge, Mass.: Ballinger, 1974.

Malan, D. H. *Toward the validation of dynamic psychotherapy*. New York: Plenum, 1976.

Maslow, A. *Toward a psychology of being*. New York: Van Nostrand, 1962.

Nygaard, J. *The counselor and students' legal rights*. Boston: Houghton Mifflin, 1973.

Perls, F. *Gestalt therapy verbatim*. Lafayette, Cal.: Real People Press, 1969.

Rogers, C. *On becoming a person*. Boston: Houghton Mifflin, 1961.

Staples, F., Sloane, R., Whipple, K., Cristol, A., & Yorkton, N. Process and outcome in psychotherapy and behavior therapy. *Journal of Consulting and Clinical Psychology*, 1976, *44*, 340–350.

Szasz, T. S. *The myth of mental illness* (Rev. ed.). New York: Harper & Row, 1974.

Van Hoose, W., & Kottler, J. *Ethical and legal issues in counseling and psychotherapy*. San Francisco: Jossey-Bass, 1977.

The Believer's Right to Privacy

RICHARD P. MCBRIEN

Richard P. McBrien is a priest of the Archdiocese of Hartford, Connecticut. He obtained his Doctorate in Theology from the Gregorian University in Rome, and is currently Professor of Theology at Boston College and Director of its Institute for the Study of Religious Education and Service. Father McBrien is past president of the Catholic Theological Society of America, and former chairman of the joint Graduate Program of Boston College and Andover Newton Theological School. He is the author of nine books, among them: Church: The continuing quest*;* The remaking of the Church: An agenda for reform*; and* What do we really believe? *In addition to contributing to professional and popular journals, Father McBrien is the author of a syndicated weekly theology column for the Catholic press, which won an award in 1974 and again in 1975 from the Catholic Press Association as the best column in its field.*

The category of "privacy" appears in no theological dictionary or encyclopedia. Annual bibliographical compilations provided by the *Ephemerides Theologicae Lovanienses* contain few references to the subject. And one will look in vain in the standard textbooks of moral theology for extensive, or even glancing, treatments of the question. Surprisingly, there is no explicit mention of the right to privacy in an otherwise forthright Christian Bill of Rights proposed by an interdisciplinary symposium of the Canon Law Society of America (Coriden, 1969).

NARROWER FOCUS OF TRADITIONAL VIEW

When the topic *is* discussed, the exploration is often narrowly focused. The right to privacy is understood as the right to the protection of one's secrets, of one's confidences, of one's psychic self. Thus, my privacy is violated if someone reads my mail without permission, or photographs my medical records surreptitiously, or tape records my conversations without my knowledge, or tells other persons something communicated in the strictest confidence, or wiretaps my telephone without legal warrant, or probes into my credit records without my consent.

Sacramental and Non-sacramental Confidentiality

Given this more restricted notion, the *believer's* right to privacy is almost inevitably construed as a question having to do with the seal of confession or, on a slightly less solemn level, the non-sacramental exchange between a Catholic and his or her spiritual director or between a member of a religious community and his or her religious superior. A confessor cannot divulge material given him in the context of the Sacrament of Penance, not simply because it is against the law of the Church (*Codex juris canonici*, 1917/1957, canons 889–890), but also because such material is given him *in persona Christi* and not as a private individual. Confessional matter is not his to share; it is Christ's alone. The priest is His consecrated instrument.

Extension to Other Areas

This regard for sacramental confidentiality has occasionally been extended into other areas. More than 15 years ago, when psychological testing was first being proposed and introduced into the admissions and evaluation processes of Catholic seminaries and religious houses, much resistance was mounted against it. One of the most influential American Catholic moral theologians of this century, John C. Ford, S.J., expressed his own reservations in a lengthy and carefully argued paper for the Catholic Theological Society of America in 1962. "A man's interior psychic life is of its nature secret," he wrote. "It is a secret that belongs to him alone" (p. 85). The content of this psychic life is manifold: the data of the moral conscience, the consciousness of one's own thoughts good and bad, of one's own graces and temptations, of one's own passions good and bad, one's own emotional tendencies, instincts, and dispositions good and bad, conscious and unconscious, and the memory of one's own secret deeds good and bad.

Father Ford called upon Pope Pius XII (1958) for support:

> In itself, the content of the psyche is the exclusive property of the person himself . . . and is known only to him. . . . And in the same way as it is illicit to take what belongs to others or to make an attempt against a person's corporal integrity without his consent, neither is one allowed to enter his interior domain without his permission, whatever be the techniques or methods used [p. 362].

Proper Limits of this Right

There are limits, of course, to such a right, and Father Ford readily acknowledged them. First, a Catholic is obliged to reveal in confession the matter necessary for absolution. His or her revelations are, in that case, strictly protected by the seal of confession. Secondly, a Catholic may be obliged outside of confession to "manifest his conscience" to a spiritual director or a religious superior in order to receive appropriate spiritual direction or to facilitate the larger corporate purposes of the religious congregation. But, again, such revelations are protected by the strictest secrecy, short of the seal itself. By "protected" is meant that "the material manifested cannot be used externally in any way without the consent of the subject" (Ford, 1962, p. 86). Accordingly, if a superior, through the "manifestation of conscience," properly or improperly should come into the possession of knowledge damaging to the person involved—even if, for example, such knowledge could disqualify the person from vows or sacred orders—the superior's hands would be tied. Only the subject could loose them. Thirdly, there are other circumstances where a believer might be required by charity, prudence, or even justice to reveal portions of his or her psychic life. The person may need psychiatric help. He may be a candidate for a religious order, and some measure of self-revelation may be obligatory. But such revelation is always done with the subject's consent.

So cherished has this right to privacy been in traditional Catholic thought that some writers have begun recently to complain about its exaggeration. A religion editor at *Time* magazine, Richard N. Ostling, noted in his book *Secrecy in the Church*, that "the right is easily abused if it is applied thoughtlessly to shield institutions, or to shield the conduct of individual officials within institutions. In these cases the moral principle of the 'common good' . . . takes hold" (1974, p. 98).

Although some Catholic moral theologians and canon lawyers continue to frame the question of privacy in this narrower context—i.e., as an invasion of one's personal and secret domain—they do argue that the believer's right to privacy must increasingly be conditioned by the Church's right to know. This principle would be pertinent especially in the processing of candidates for sacred orders or in the examination of candidates for sensitive ecclesiastical offices. It is also pertinent to the new situation of faculty supervisors (as distinguished from "spiritual directors") in Catholic seminaries. What can be revealed about a student who may have indiscreetly and/or unintentionally disclosed to his academic supervisor some serious deficiency of character, of behavior, or of attitude? Is the faculty adviser bound by the same laws of confidentiality as bind the spiritual director? If so—i.e., if the seminarian is to be "protected" from damaging disclosures of this kind—who is to "protect" the Church from unsuitable candidates for the priestly ministry?

There are, of course, occasional inconsistencies in the formulation of this narrower, more traditional notion of privacy. In reaffirming the prevailing discipline regarding the reception of First Confession and First Communion, Cardinal James Knox, of the Congregation for the Sacraments and Divine Worship, and Cardinal John Wright, of the Congregation for the Clergy, issued a joint letter in which they argue that First Confession must come before First Communion in order to safeguard and protect "worthy participation in the Eucharist" (1977, p. 2). But how would this particular sacramental sequence insure "worthy participation" in the Eucharist? Suppose a confessor were convinced that a Catholic, about to receive Holy Communion for the first time, had made a sacrilegious confession. Does the confessor have the right to expunge the penitent's name from the list of prospective communicants? "Of course not," their Eminences would insist, "because that would be a direct violation of the seal of confession." How, then, is "worthy participation" in one's first Eucharistic meal "safeguarded" and "protected" by prior reception of the Sacrament of Penance?

BROADENING THE BELIEVER'S RIGHT

Argument for Equating Privacy and Self-Determination

But there is a broader and more positive understanding of privacy. The right to privacy can also mean the right to self-determination. This argument has been advanced most persuasively by Richard McCormick, S.J., a Roman Catholic moral theologian whose scholarly authority needs no buttressing from this quarter. Father McCormick develops that argument in the context of the Karen Quinlan decision reached by the New Jersey Supreme Court. The key issue in that decision was precisely the right to privacy: not understood as the right of Karen Quinlan to have her medical records kept secret, but the right of Karen Quinlan (and of those closest to her) to decide whether she wanted to prolong an essentially inhuman life by artificial means alone. The New Jersey court held in its March 31, 1976, decision that the right to privacy is broad enough to encompass a patient's decision to decline medical treatment under certain circumstances. Karen Quinlan, the court declared, was not to be deprived of her right to privacy simply because she was incompetent. Her guardian and family should be permitted to render their own best judgment as to whether she would exercise her right.

Critique of the Argument

There were, as expected, many negative reactions to the New Jersey Supreme Court decision, and many opposed it precisely on the grounds that the "right to privacy" had no relevance at all to the case: Dr. Mildred Jefferson, Chairperson of the National Right to Life Committee; Msgr. James T. McHugh, of the United States Catholic Conference; Eugene Schulte, Director of Government and Legal Services for the Catholic Hospital Association; and editorial writers for such Catholic publications as *America*, *The Voice* (Archdiocese of Miami), *The Catholic Standard and Times* (Archdiocese of Philadelphia), and the *Idaho Register* (Diocese of Boise). The *America* editorial faced the issue directly: "In recent years courts have shown a disturbing tendency to confuse 'privacy' with 'self-determination' " (1976, p. 327).

But Father McCormick does indeed equate the right of privacy with the right to self-determination, and he bases his argument on his understanding of the Catholic moral tradition itself. He summarizes that tradition as follows:

> there is first a *duty* to preserve one's life, and following on that a *right* not to be interfered with in making moral decisions with regard to this duty. The right of privacy or self-determination is a necessary means because, given the personal or individual character of the considerations that limit this duty and given the personal character of the situations that activate this duty, it is the person himself or herself who is best situated to implement decisions. . . .
>
> This self-determination (or privacy) is a conditional or instrumental good. That is, it is a good precisely insofar as it is the instrument whereby the best interests of the patient are served by it. If, for example, the best overall good of patients would be better achieved without self-determination, it would be senseless to speak of self-determination as a right [1976, p. 41].

RIGHT TO SELF-DETERMINATION DELIMITED

In Traditional Catholic Theology

The right to self-determination is not unlimited (and Father Ford [1962] made the same kind of qualification regarding his own more restricted treatment of the subject):

> First, when the exercise of this right is de facto and in the circumstances no longer to the overall good of the person involved, then the very reason for self-determination or privacy has disappeared. . . .
>
> Second, self-determination as a means to the overall good of the person or patient says nothing about the exercise of this right to the detriment of others. That is another judgment altogether. That is, how the overall good of the patient is related to and perhaps limited by the good of other patients is simply not to be derived from the notion of privacy or self-determination itself [McCormick, 1976, p. 41].

Thus, in the first case, a person could not justify suicide on the basis of his right to self-determination or privacy. And, in the second case, he could not refuse to give food to a starving person on the grounds that the food is his own private property. These two limitations flow from traditional Catholic moral theology's understanding of rights. There is a limitation, first, on the right itself, and, secondly, on its exercise. The right to privacy, in summary, is "an instrumental right in service of and subordinate to a good—*the best interests of the person*" (McCormick, 1976, p. 42).

In the Documents of Vatican Council II

If one were to accept Father McCormick's broader definition of the right of privacy as the right to self-determination, then it is clear that there is more material in support of this right in the official teachings of the Catholic Church than might at first appear. Otherwise, the only explicit conciliar mention of the right of privacy would have been in the twenty-sixth article of the Pastoral Constitution on the Church in the Modern World:

> there must be made available to all men everything necessary for leading a life truly human, such as food, clothing, and shelter; the right to choose a state of life freely and to found a family, the right to education, to employment, to a good reputation, to respect, to appropriate information, to activity in accord with the upright norm of one's own conscience, to protection of privacy and to rightful freedom in matters religious too [Vatican Council II, 1966, p. 225].

However, taking privacy to mean also self-determination, one finds that the same Pastoral Constitution is concerned elsewhere with the right to privacy in religious life:

> Only in freedom can man direct himself toward goodness. . . . For its part, authentic freedom is an exceptional sign of the divine image within man. For God has willed that man be left "in the hand of his own counsel" so that he can seek his Creator spontaneously, and come freely to utter and blissful perfection through loyalty to Him [p. 214].

The subject of privacy as self-determination is treated even more directly and more extensively in the council's Declaration on Religious Freedom. According to the Declaration, religious freedom means that

> all men are to be immune from coercion on the part of individuals or of social groups and of any human power, in such wise that in matters religious no one is to be forced to act in a manner contrary to his own beliefs. Nor is anyone to be restrained from acting in accordance with his own beliefs, whether privately or publicly, whether alone or in association with others, within due limits [pp. 678–679].

This doctrine of freedom (privacy, self-determination) has roots in divine revelation, the council's Declaration argues. Revelation discloses "the dignity of the human person in its full dimensions" (p. 688). There is evidence as well in the attitude and teachings of Christ, particularly in the way in which He formed his own disciples. Furthermore, religious freedom is also consonant with the freedom of the act of faith itself. "It is one of the major tenets of Catholic doctrine that man's response to God in faith must be free. Therefore no one is to be forced to embrace the Christian faith against his own will" (Vatican Council II, 1966, p. 689). Compelling a person to become a Christian believer, in other words, is an invasion of privacy, a right which is grounded at once in human dignity and divine revelation.

IMPLICATIONS FOR BELIEVER'S RIGHTS

The believer's right to privacy, therefore, goes far beyond his or her right to protection from the unwarranted exposure of secret knowledge and information. The issue of privacy within the Christian community goes far beyond the question of the seal of confession, or the spiritual relationship between subject and spiritual director, or the filial relationship between subject and religious superior. It also goes beyond the many questions arising from the new situation of Catholic seminaries, particularly with regard to the wider availability of information about seminarians through academic advisement within the seminary or through pastoral supervision of field education projects outside the seminary.

The believer's right to be a believer at all is itself a matter of privacy. The believer's right to follow a spiritual program best suited to himself or herself for the sake of Christian growth and ultimately for the sake of personal salvation is a right of privacy. The believer's right to decide how much physical and psychic energy he or she can realistically expend on behalf of the gospel is covered by the right of privacy. The believer's right to decide how to regulate his or her leisure activities, friendships, modes of recreation, and so forth, is similarly a matter of privacy.

To ridicule or harass a so-called dissident believer is to attack that believer's right of privacy. To demand that a candidate for the priesthood or for religious profession adopt specific cultural values or customs is to challenge that person's right of privacy. To impose a particular kind of devotional life or to judge another harshly because he or she does not assume a particular devotional style is to deny that believer's right of privacy.

Many who have been close to the internal operations of religious congregations, seminaries, and dioceses can testify to the fact that authentic religious activity has at times suffered from the seemingly unbridled desire of ecclesiastical functionaries to control the lives of their fellow-believers. Lay persons, priests, sisters, brothers, seminarians, novices, postulants, and others have been told how to think, how to pray, how to recreate, how to dress, how to manage one's personal resources (if at all), how to work, whether or not to marry, whether or not to have children—and how many to have.

The right of privacy is not unlimited. That has already been made clear. But it *is* a right, and it is a right which has far more to do with the shaping and directing of one's whole personal life than with protection from Nixonian excesses. Privacy is a matter of self-determination, of freedom in the pursuit of one's own humanity, and, finally, of one's own salvation by the grace of God. In this process of self-determination, computerization is not the principal enemy. It is, rather, the residual inclination—at times naïvely innocent and at other times perverse and sinister—of religious people to try to control the lives of other religious people.

That is why the ongoing institutional reform of the Church is more relevant to the protection of the believer's right of privacy than is a new lock on the door, a prison sentence for an errant attorney general, or a decision against enrolling in a seminary or religious community.

REFERENCES

America. Karen Quinlan and the right to die. April 17, 1976.

Codex juris canonici. Westminster, Md.: Newman, 1957. (Originally published, 1917.)

Coriden, J. (Ed.). *Human rights in the Church.* Washington, D.C.: Corpus Books, 1969.

Ford, J. C. (S.J.) Religious superiors, subjects and psychiatrists. *Catholic Theological Society of America Proceedings*, 1962, *17*, 63–129.

Knox, J., & Wright, J. Text explains ruling on confession and communion. *The Witness* (Diocese of Dubuque), May 26, 1977.

McCormick, R. A. (S.J.) The moral right to privacy. *Hospital Progress*, 1976, *57*, 38–42.

Ostling, R. N. *Secrecy in the church.* New York: Harper & Row, 1974.

Pius XII. Morality and Applied Psychology. Address to the International Congress of Applied Psychology, April 10, 1958. *Acta Apostolicae Sedis*, 1958, *50*, 268–282. English translation: *Catholic Mind*, 1958, *56*, 353–368.

Vatican Council II. W. M. Abbott (S.J.) (Ed.). *The documents of Vatican II.* New York: Herder & Herder, 1966.

IV
LEGITIMATE LIMITATIONS: SOCIETY'S RIGHT TO KNOW

The Jurisprudence of Privacy as a Constitutional Right

DAVID A. J. RICHARDS

David A. J. Richards received his A.B. and J.D. degrees from Harvard University, and the degree of D.Phil. from Oxford University. At the time of the scheduled Institute in 1977 he was Associate Professor of Law at the Fordham University School of Law; currently he holds the same position at the School of Law of New York University. Dr. Richards is the author of A Theory of Reasons for Action *(1971) and of a growing number of articles in law reviews and journals throughout the country. He is a frequent symposium speaker on legal–philosophical topics. He is a past member of the Board of Directors of the Society for Philosophy and Public Affairs, New York Chapter, and is currently President of the Austinian Society, a research foundation in law and philosophy.*

The proper philosophical elucidation of the constitutional right to privacy is a major challenge to constitutional jurisprudence. Elsewhere, I have made some suggestions regarding the scope of this constitutional right in the area of sexual autonomy (Richards, 1977a, 1977b). Here, I should like to develop those suggestions into a more general theory of the constitutional right to privacy, i.e., the application of this right not only to sexual contexts but, as commentators and some courts have suggested, to styles of dress, the use of marijuana, the right to die, and the like. Is it possible, in a philosophically cogent way, to develop a form of philosophical explication which casts light on how and why the constitutional right to privacy has been applied in certain ways and ought to be applied to a number of seemingly disparate and diverse situations? I should like here, in rather brief and summary compass, tentatively to propose a kind of sketch to a prolegomenon of such a theory. I begin with a description of the present forms of the right to privacy in the law, which naturally invites reflection on the jurisprudential foundations of the constitutional right to privacy which is our concern here.

THE HISTORICAL EVOLUTION OF THE RIGHT TO PRIVACY

The value of privacy, as an independently protected legal right, was first formulated in a famous law review article by Warren and Brandeis (1890). It was there suggested that the mere intrusion upon certain personal matters—in itself not compensable under then-existing law—should be regarded as an independent tort. Since then, the "right of privacy" has been successfully invoked in a wide range of tort cases. Dean Prosser in 1960 examined 300 such cases in an attempt to discover exactly what interest was being protected. He concluded that no single thing was common to every loss of privacy. But he did note four characteristics, at least one of which was present in each case: namely,

(1) Public disclosure of embarrassing private facts about the plaintiff;
(2) Intrusion upon the plaintiff's seclusion or solitude, or into his private affairs;
(3) Publicity which places the plaintiff in a false light in the public eye; and
(4) Appropriation for the defendant's advantage of the plaintiff's name, image, or likeness [Prosser, 1960, p. 389].

Subsequent commentary has sought to reduce Prosser's disparate list to one unifying theme: privacy as the capacity to control information about oneself or one's experiences (Fried, 1970; Gross, 1971; Miller, 1971; Parker, 1974; Westin, 1967). For broader definitions, others (Bloustein, 1964; Van Den Haag, 1971; Weinstein, 1971) may be cited.

Relevant Court Decisions

In constitutional law, privacy is a notion of more recent vintage. At least prior to 1965, privacy in constitutional law was not regarded as an independent constitutional right. The word "privacy" nowhere appears in the Constitution. At most, privacy was viewed as an interest protected in certain limited respects by various specific constitutional provisions—for example, the Third Amendment prohibition of quartering soldiers in the home, the Fourth Amendment guarantee against unreasonable searches and seizures, and the Fifth Amendment protection against self-incrimination.

The idea of an independent constitutional right to privacy was introduced in 1965 in *Griswold v. Connecticut* (Note 1, p. 479). There the Supreme Court invalidated a Connecticut statute forbidding the use of contraceptives as applied to a married couple on the ground that it violated a constitutional right to privacy protecting the marital relationship. Justice Douglas, writing for himself and for Justice Clark, found that an independent right to privacy could be inferred from a number of constitutional provisions (Note 1, pp. 484–486). Justice Goldberg, joined by Chief Justice Warren and Justice Brennan, also found a fundamental right to marital privacy, inferrable chiefly from the Ninth Amendment (Note 1, pp. 486–499). Only Justices Harlan and White, who concurred in the judgment, would find the statute to be violative of the Fourteenth Amendment's substantive due process guarantees in that it had no rational relation to any proper state purpose (Note 2).

In 1969 in *Stanley v. Georgia* (Note 3, p. 557) the Court held unconstitutional a state statute criminally punishing the merely private possession of obscene materials. After mentioning the defendant's First Amendment right to receive information, the Court, citing *Griswold*, invoked the constitutional right to privacy: "For also fundamental is the right to be free, except in very limited circumstances, from unwanted governmental intrusions into one's privacy" (Note 3, p. 564). The Court agreed that individuals have the right to satisfy their "intellectual and emotional needs in the privacy of [their] own home[s]" (Note 3, p. 565).

In 1972 the Court in *Eisenstadt v. Baird* (Note 4, p. 438) invalidated the conviction of a campus lecturer for giving a contraceptive device to a young woman of undisclosed marital status (Note 5). Four justices were prepared to hold on equal protection grounds that unmarried persons must be allowed the same access to contraceptive devices as the relevant statute accorded married persons alone (Note 6). The following expansive dictum of the plurality opinion appears to give broad support to the idea that the *Griswold* right to privacy is not strictly limited to marital relationships:

> It is true that in *Griswold* the right to privacy in question inhered in the marital relationship. Yet the married couple is not an independent entity with a mind and heart of its own, but an association of two individuals each with a separate intellectual and emotional makeup. If the right of privacy means anything, it is the right of the *individual*, married or single, to be free from unwarranted governmental intrusion into matters so fundamentally affecting a person as the decision to bear or beget a child [Note 4, p. 453].

The scope of the right to privacy was further expanded in 1973 in *Roe v. Wade* (Note 7, p. 113). The Court there held that a Texas statute forbidding abortion except to save the life of the mother violated the mother's fundamental right to privacy, "founded in the Fourteenth Amendment's concept of personal liberty and restrictions upon state action . . ." (Note 7, p. 153). In adopting this rationale, the Court made clear what all but two justices in *Griswold* had avoided saying: that the constitutional right to privacy is among the liberties guaranteed by due process of law (Note 8).

Finally, in *Paris Adult Theatre I v. Slaton* (Note 9, p. 49) the Court rejected a privacy-based challenge made by owners of an adult movie house to a Georgia civil provision allowing injunctive relief against the presentation of obscene materials (Note 10). The Court held that no general privacy right—such as that protecting a woman's right to an abortion—protects the use of obscene materials (Note 9, pp. 65–66), and that a commercial theater is not sufficiently analogous to a private home to merit limited, place-oriented privacy protection such as was extended in *Stanley* (Note 3).

The implications of these precedents for other areas have been a matter of considerable dispute. For example, in the sexual area, Justice Harlan's dissent in *Poe v. Ullman* (Note 11), which first discussed marital privacy as a fundamental right, explicitly excluded homosexual practices (Note 12). Justice Goldberg's opinion in *Griswold*, in which Chief Justice Warren and Justice Brennan joined, also excluded deviant sexual conduct from the right and cited Harlan's language in *Poe* with approval (Note 13). Thus, at least four of the *Griswold* justices appear to have been unwilling to expand privacy to include homosexual conduct. The Supreme Court's recent summary affirmance in *Doe v. Commonwealth's Attorney for City of Richmond* (Note 14), though of doubtful lasting precedential value (Richards, 1977a, p. 1320, n. 206), suggests that a majority of the present Court concurs. On the other hand, a number of lower courts have either held (Richards, 1977a, p. 1302, n. 116) or stated in dictum (Richards, 1977a, p. 1302, n. 117) that statutes forbidding homosexual relations between consenting adults are unconstitutional on privacy grounds. Outside the sexual area, comparable controversy prevails. One state supreme court invoked the right to privacy in invalidating the state's prohibition on the use of marijuana (Note 15). Other courts have invoked the idea of privacy in justification of the right to die (Note 16).

Need for Clarification of Underlying Theory

The difficulty in predicting the implications of the right to privacy cases is symptomatic of the unprincipled, amorphous form which the constitutional right to privacy has had from its inception. Its history has been suggestive more of legislative fiat than of judicial reasoning (Note 17). This sense of intellectual legerdemain is suggested even by the name of the right—"the right to privacy." As we have seen, the right of privacy, as conventionally understood both in the law of torts and in constitutional law, with relation to illegal searches and seizures and the like, turns on an individual's right to withhold personal information or experience from others (Fried, 1970; Gross, 1971; Miller, 1971; Parker, 1974; Westin, 1967). However, the constitutional right to privacy, as developed since *Griswold*, cannot be characterized as merely a right protecting information control (Note 18). It involves affirmative personal rights. This feature of right-to-privacy cases, which commentators have observed even about *Griswold* (Gross, 1971), was made quite clear by *Roe v. Wade* (Note 7). In *Roe*, the challenged law subjected the person performing the abortion to criminal sanctions and was unconstitutional because it made it difficult for women to obtain the desired service. There is not the remotest suggestion in *Roe* that the state could cure the constitutional infirmity by removing any criminal sanction from the woman while continuing effectively to restrict abortion by attacking suppliers of the service (Note 19). Indeed, since *Roe* the Court has insisted that the *Roe*-defined right extends to "the doctor's office, the hospital, the hotel room, or as otherwise required to safeguard the right to intimacy involved" (Note 9). In short, there is no evidence that the constitutional right to privacy depends on outrageous government surveillance violative of conventional right-to-privacy interests.

Undoubtedly, there are significant relationships between the conventional right of privacy and the value which it protects, and the kind of personal liberty involved in *Griswold* and its progeny. First, the enforcement of laws limiting sexual liberty (e.g., anti-contraception laws) would often involve particularly egregious forms of interference with the conventional right of privacy (e.g., searching the bedroom) (Note 20). Second, one of the primary underlying values, made possible by the conventional right of privacy, is the capacity, by informational control, to create different kinds of intimacy with some but not others, a capacity fundamental to the growth of friendship and love (Fried, 1970, pp. 137–152). *Griswold* and *Roe* were apparently intended to enhance the growth of intimate relationships by granting forms of intimacy freedom from governmental control. Third, privacy in the conventional sense (being left alone without anyone observing) is a generally accepted prerequisite to human sexual intercourse (Ford & Beach, 1951, pp. 68–72), and the protection of sexual activity seems to be one aspect of certain of the constitutional right-to-privacy cases (Richards, 1977a, nn. 180–204.

These similarities between the conventional right of privacy and the kind of liberty established in *Griswold* and its progeny are persuasive analogies. Reasoning by analogy is, of course, one traditional mode of legal reasoning by which courts gradually extend or develop precedents in a principled way. The Court cannot be faulted for using such a mode of reasoning in developing the implications of constitutional values. The challenge of the right-to-privacy cases is to articulate in a principled way the constitutional considerations which motivate the courts in this area (Wechsler, 1959).

The constitutional right to privacy, as we have observed, clearly does not rest on some kind of right of information control. Rather, it turns on some form of substantive liberty or autonomy (Gross, 1971) to act in certain ways without threat of governmental sanction, interference, or penalty. The Court's remarks about the nature of this substantive right are suggestive. Activities protected by the right implicate individuals' "beliefs, their thoughts, their emotions and their sensations," central values of the "right to be left alone" (Note 21). These experiences are at the core of "protected intimate relationships" (Note 9) and require some kind of sanctuary in order to be cultivated properly and perfected (Note 22). These remarks cry out for more fundamental examination of the right to privacy in the light of jurisprudential theory.

JURISPRUDENTIAL FOUNDATIONS OF PRIVACY AS A CONSTITUTIONAL RIGHT

Privacy, understood as a substantive constitutional liberty independent of issues of information control, rests, I submit, on the concurrence of several variables: (1) that there is, in the light of contemporary evidence, no good moral reason to believe that certain conduct, traditionally conceived as morally wrong, is wrong at all; (2) that the conduct in question relates to basic issues of the definition and integration of the self in which the liberty of the agent to decide whether or not or how to engage in such conduct crucially determines the coherent rationality of a person's life plan; and (3), consequent on (2), that there is no compelling paternalistic reason which may justify the limitation of liberty. Let me amplify the description and force of these variables *seriatim*. Then, in conclusion, we can assess how they clarify the proper scope of the application of the constitutional right to privacy.

Perceptions Relevant to Morality

The constitutional right-of-privacy cases typically arise in areas (for example, sex, death, the use of drugs) in which there is a strong conventional wisdom to the effect that certain conduct is morally wrong and in which the justice of that wisdom is under fundamental attack. It is, I believe, no accident that privacy here is conceived by its proponents, not as an advisable or charitable or benevolent or even wise thing to concede, but as a *right*. Proponents, here and in general, conceive matters involving *rights*, not as human weaknesses or defects which others should benevolently overlook, but as positive moral goods which one may demand and enforce as one's due. Accordingly, the constitutional right of privacy is, in part, to be understood in terms of a transvaluation of values: certain areas of conduct, traditionally conceived as morally wrong, are now perceived as either affirmative moral goods or as not raising serious moral questions at all. How, philosophically, are we to interpret such claims?

The idea, I believe, is this. Philosophically, we must distinguish the concept of morality and the associated class of moral principles from the lower-order moral rules and conventions which have traditionally been justified by the notion of morality and its principles. In the light of contemporary evidence and conditions, certain lower-order conventions are no longer justified by ultimate moral considerations. For example, one influential model of sexual function perceived the only proper use of sex to be procreation. However, contemporary evidence indicates that the distinctive force of human, as opposed to animal, sexuality is that it is not rigidly procreational (Richards, 1977a, 1977b). To the extent that the traditional model of sexuality is discarded in favor of a more plastic, non-procreational model of the role of sexuality in human life, rigid moral rules prohibiting forms of non-procreational sex are no longer perceived as justified by ultimate moral considerations. One important ingredient of the constitutional right to privacy is, I believe, this underlying shift in moral perception.

Opponents of the constitutional right to privacy correctly formulate their opposition in terms of moral argument which questions the transvaluation of values which right-to-privacy arguments presuppose. Unfortunately, these moral arguments typically assume that the relevant concept of morality and moral principles is to be identified with existing social convention, determined, as Devlin (1965) suggests, by taking a man at random from the Clapham omnibus. Just as we prove the standards of negligence for purposes of civil or criminal liability by appealing to the judgment of ordinary men acting as jurors, so the applicable standards of morality can be proved in the same way. Ordinary men morally loathe homosexuality; accordingly, homosexuality is immoral and must be legally forbidden. But there is no good reason to make this identification of morality and social convention, since it is based on an indefensible and naïve moral philosophy as well as on an unexamined and unsound sociology (Hart, 1967).

Recent moral philosophy has been increasingly occupied with the clarification of the conceptual structure of ordinary moral reasoning (Baier, 1958, pp. 187–213; Gauthier, 1963; Grice, 1967, pp. 1–35; Hare, 1952, 1963, pp. 86–185; Rawls, 1971; Richards, 1971). The concept of morality or ethics is not an openly flexible one; there are certain determinate constraints on the kind of beliefs which can be counted as moral in nature (Foot, 1958, 1958–1959; Foot & Harrison, 1954; Warnock, 1967, pp. 55–61, 1971, pp. 35–70). Some examples are the principles of mutual respect—treating others as you would like to be treated in comparable circumstances (Baier, 1958, pp. 187–213; Gauthier, 1963, pp. 81–94; Grice, 1967, pp. 1–35; Rawls, 1971, pp. 130–132; Richards, 1971, pp. 75–91); universalization—judging the morality of principles by the consequences of their universal application (Hare, 1963, pp. 91–94; Richards, 1971, pp. 83–85, 216); and minimization of fortuitous human differences (like clan, caste, ethnicity, and color) as a basis for differential treatment (Kant, 1785/1959, pp. 65–71). It follows from this conception that a view is not a moral one merely because it is passionately and sincerely held, or because it has a certain emotional depth (Devlin, 1965, p. 114), or because it is the view of one's father or mother or clan, or because it is conventional. On the contrary, the moral point of view affords an impartial way of assessing whether any of these beliefs, which may often press one to action, is in fact worthy of ethical commitment (Baier, 1958, pp. 187–213; Gauthier, 1963; Grice, 1967, pp. 1–35; Hare, 1952, 1963; Rawls, 1971; Richards, 1971).

Thus, moral views of the kind which the law enforces do not rest on mere social convention. Rather, moral questions are marked by a special, universalizing form or kind of reasoning. For example, the view that non-remedial preferential quotas are immoral rests on a principle which a morally aware person would defend whether he was helped or hurt by it. Hare (1963, pp. 86–185) gives examples of the force of this kind of reasoning. A minimal condition for a serious moral theory is that it give expression to such features of moral reasoning. Devlin's (1965) theory, if it can be so called, does not; it is based on quite non-moral instincts, social tastes, and accepted conventions. No serious moral philosopher of stature, including those who defended Devlin's substantive conclusion, has defended such a theory.

The attraction of Devlin's theory for judges is its seeming objectivity; it affords a definite criterion for the morality which the law enforces without appeal to subjective considerations. The classic statement of this view by an American judge is Cardozo's (1949, pp. 108–112). But the empirical objectivity of existing custom has nothing to do with the notions of moral impartiality and objectivity which are, or should be, of judicial concern in determining the public morality on which the law rests. The idea that the pursuit of the latter must collapse into the former is a confusion of inquiries, arising from an untenable and indefensible distinction between subjective moral belief and the public morality of the law. There is no such distinction. Views, to be moral, require a certain kind of justification. Judges, interpreting legally enforceable moral ideas, must appeal to the kind of reasoning which is moral. They do not as judges abdicate their capacity as persons for moral reasoning. On the contrary, competence and articulateness in such reasoning comprise the virtue which we denominate judicial.

Surely, moral arguments regarding the constitutional right to privacy are eminently proper. Undoubtedly, opponents of certain applications of the right to privacy can develop serious moral arguments, at least in some cases with at least some degree of force which must receive the dignity of an answer. In general, however, such opponents have not taken seriously or responsibly the task of moral argument incumbent on them or on any serious moral thinker. Rather, like Devlin (1965), they appeal for justification precisely to the social conventions which proponents of the enlarged application of the right to privacy attack.

One non-social conventional form of such a moral argument, certainly implicit in Devlin and others, is, frankly, that of theological ethics, i.e., that moral principles at bottom are moral because they are the will of the Judaeo-Christian God. Whatever the constitutional plausibility of such a proposal in Devlin's England where church and state are not constitutionally separate, in the United States the establishment-of-religion prohibition of the First Amendment presumably stands as an absolute bar to the frank and candid enforcement of theological ethics of the form implicit in Devlin's argument (Henkin, 1963, p. 393). However, even assuming *arguendo* that there is no constitutional impediment of the kind which there undoubtedly is, there are powerful philosophical objections to theological ethics in the simplistic form here under discussion. For example, a powerful tradition of Christian theology rejects the idea that the force of moral ideas derives from God's will, insisting, rather, that moral concepts have a natural authority antecedent to divine will. Accordingly, moral concepts must be explicable without a circular appeal to divine will (Note 23). Aside from theology, there are convincing philosophical arguments which render implausible a theological account of ethical principles (Brandt, 1959, ch. 4).

These moral arguments cannot be further pursued here. It suffices, for present purposes, that one see the kind of shift in moral judgment underlying the constitutional right to privacy and that one perceive the form of moral argument appropriate to the assessment of this shift. I have discussed elsewhere why I believe this shift to be appropriate in the area of sexual autonomy (Richards, 1977a), and I submit that a comparable kind of moral assessment must be applied to the other controverted applications of the constitutional right to privacy.

The Self and Rational Choice

I take it to be elementary that moral principles define the constraints or boundary conditions within which a person may rationally pursue his or her ends, whatever those ends are (Richards, 1971, chs. 6, 12). Within moral limits, people are at liberty to design their lives and purposes in rationally coherent fashion; moral principles importantly define those limits. For example, human beings clearly possess much larger capacities for aggressiveness than, in the present state of social living, it is morally appropriate for them to develop and cultivate, in themselves as adults and in the young, through family training and later education. Accordingly, since moral principles forbid the full development and display of these capacities, we do not regard it as appropriate that individuals regard themselves as being at liberty to design their lives to give such capacities full and untrammeled expression, however rational this might be in the individual case. I take it to be an uncontroversial truth of human psychology that man is, compared to lower animals, extraordinarily plastic and adaptable. Sacrifices of personal happiness, regarded as unthinkably onerous and burdensome in a later historical period, were undertaken with natural facility in an earlier period. To the extent that moral principles demand it, human nature can sustain quite onerous demands, or, at least, demands eventually perceived to be onerous.

An additional crucial variable, in the constitutional right-to-privacy cases, follows naturally from the shift in moral judgment just discussed: namely, that certain ranges of conduct, previously conceived as being tightly regulated by moral principles, are now perceived, in the light of new facts, perspectives, and circumstances, as no longer being morally determined in the same way. For example, forms of non-procreational sexual intimacy, marital and non-marital, are no longer justifiably judged to be immoral per se. Moral principles still importantly regulate sexual matters but not as gross prohibitions on kinds of intercourse per se; rather, moral issues now cluster around consent, fraud, candor, sensitivity, fidelity, and the like (Wilson, 1965). To the extent that moral principles no longer rigidly prohibit certain forms of conduct, the scope of permissible liberty in rationally designing one's life enlarges accordingly. Forms of conduct previously forbidden per se are now among the permissible forms of life which mature people are free rationally to undertake; human capacities, previously narrowly and rigidly confined, are now permissibly cultivated and developed, often with creative and exploratory imagination and even artistry.

Among those ranges of conduct now morally at liberty, the constitutional right to privacy identifies those issues the rational decision on which crucially determines the coherent rationality of a person's life plan. At points throughout human life, people have the capacity and opportunity to make choices which bear fundamentally on the design of their life plan, which is, I believe, not unnaturally described as the choice of self. Ordinary people, uncontaminated by philosophical discussions of personal identity (Note 24), typically identify other people (in response to the query: Who is X?) in certain characteristic ways, for example, by occupation, education, marital status, children, family connection. Certain choices in life are taken to bear fundamentally on the entire design of one's life, for these choices determine the basic decisions of work and love, which in turn order many of the subsidiary choices of human life. Obvious examples of such choices are the matters of whether and where to be educated, the choice of occupation and avocation, the choice of whether and whom to love and befriend and on what terms (marriage), the decision whether and to what extent children will be a life's concern, and the like.

A central aspect of modernity is, I believe, that moral judgments on many of these matters have changed in ways and for reasons previously discussed. Traditional moral judgments on many of these matters are under fundamental attack. For example, the traditional judgment that it is immoral for women to undertake "masculine" occupations has now been largely discredited, so that choice of such occupations, at least in terms of formal institutions, is among women's liberties. In other areas, traditional moral judgments yield less easily, for example, in sexual matters. In such cases, where reasonable moral judgment no longer can sustain absolute prohibitions and the issue in question is one among the fundamental life choices, the constitutional right to privacy, understood as a right of personal autonomy, finds its natural home. Here, the language and thought of rights is naturally adopted in order to sustain the claims of individuals against a traditional wisdom which has lost its moral foundation.

Inappropriate Paternalism

Even if no moral judgment may appropriately be made about the probity of certain conduct, we may still believe that undertaking such conduct is sufficiently irrational that we have moral title to interfere on paternalistic grounds (Note 25). The final crucial variable, in the application of the constitutional right to privacy, is the radical inappropriateness of such forms of argument in a case properly invoking the constitutional right to privacy. This inappropriateness is a consequence of the nature of the rational choice involving basic life choices, and can be understood by considering such choices.

The idea of rationality, employed in the context of life choices, importantly takes as the fundamental datum the agent's ends, as determined by the agent's appetites, desires, capacities, and the like. The process of rational choice in such contexts importantly regulates its decision by principles of rational choice which call for the most coherent plan of satisfying these ends over time (Note 26), understanding that the choices in question determine a number of subchoices which will have effects throughout the agent's life and indeed probably determine the duration of that life (Fried, 1970, pp. 155–182). If the agent in question has the requisite developed capacities of choice and deliberation (is not an infant, mentally defective, or insane) and understands the nature and consequences of the choice before him or her (Dworkin, 1971; Richards, 1971, pp. 192–195), paternalistic interference in this process substitutes the interferer's own quite personal ends for the ends of the agent, and fails to take seriously the fundamental datum of rational choice in these matters: that the agent's ends are given and that rationality makes adjustments among them. The temptation to such paternalistic distortions is especially grave in a transitional period of transvaluation of values in matters of basic life choices.

Paternalistic judgments often are masks for the now discredited traditional moral wisdom in which people have invested deep significance, making their own quite personal and idiosyncratic past life-choice decisions of metaphysical import invoking the ordinary person's deepest ideology and philosophy—"the meaning of one's life." But past choices in these matters, often premissed on now inappropriate moral judgments, are no proper guide in circumstances in which the underlying moral judgments are invalid. For, since rigid moral prescriptions in many of these areas are no longer appropriate, people must make these choices in as imaginative, creative, exploratory, and inventive a way as human wit can devise, consulting one's personal desires, wants, needs, competences, and how one most harmoniously wishes them concurrently to develop and be satisfied over a lifetime. Freedom from paternalistic interference in these choices is crucially necessary if people are to be able to identify those choices as *their own*, if they are to be afforded the inestimable moral and human good of having chosen their own lives, to the greatest extent feasible for human creatures, as free and rational beings. The right of privacy, in this context, protects a person's moral title to his or her self—to his or her body, emotions, sentiments, fantasies, aspirations, and how they will unfold in the integrated life plan which is a human life (Reiman, 1976).

APPLICATION OF THE CONSTITUTIONAL RIGHT TO PRIVACY

I have quite pointedly characterized this account of the constitutional right to privacy as a sketch of a prolegomenon to the theory of the right to privacy, for the account is in many obvious ways undeveloped. For example, my account turns on a view of the central role of moral theory in clarifying the proper application of moral principles over time, but I have not here fully defended such a theory; and I appeal to the limited role of paternalistic considerations, but I have not explained in satisfactory detail what those limits are. I believe that these tasks can be accomplished (Richards, 1971, 1977b), and thus that this account can be given plausible theoretical support. It suffices, for present purposes, that the theory proposed here elucidate the *form* of considerations which must be assessed in evaluating issues involving the constitutional right to privacy: namely, (1) whether, in the light of contemporary evidence, there is any good moral reason to believe that certain conduct, traditionally conceived as morally wrong, is wrong at all; (2) whether the conduct relates to basic life-plan choices; and (3), consequent on (2), whether paternalistic considerations are radically inappropriate. I do not propose here to engage in detailed casuistry of how these considerations should decide particular cases. But certain general clarifying remarks may be briefly and usefully made.

I have noted that the constitutional right to privacy has been applied, *inter alia,* to sexual issues (contraception, abortion, use of pornography in the home, homosexuality), drug use (marijuana), and the right to die. Certain of these cases fall, I believe, quite uncontroversially within the criteria for the proper application of the right to privacy here discussed. Many of the sexual issues (for example, contraception and homosexuality) can, I believe, convincingly be shown properly to call for application of the constitutional right to privacy. In these cases, traditional moral judgments can be decisively rebutted; the issues of life choice are profound, involving the basic integration of work and love in a life plan; and paternalistic arguments are radically inappropriate, since they clearly here are colored by distorting perceptions not rationally connected to the issue at hand (Richards, 1977a, 1977b).

Non-sexual applications of the right to privacy may be similarly analyzed with greater and lesser degrees of cogency. The right-to-die cases, for example, involve issues in which moral judgments regarding permissible killing are decidedly in flux; the question of choice of one's death seems clearly among basic life choices; and paternalistic judgments may, at least in certain of these cases, be radically inappropriate. At any rate, in some such cases the fear of one's own death will unwarrantably distort one's perception of another person's right to die. However, to the extent to which the paternalistic issue is here somewhat less clear, the application of the right to privacy is accordingly more moot (Foot, 1977). Drug control (marijuana use) probably satisfies the first and third criteria for application of the right to privacy, but may be somewhat more controversial as regards the issue of basic life choice. The controverted point would be whether or to what extent soft drug use implicates a strategic life decision.

CONCLUSION

In conclusion, I have argued that the constitutional right to privacy is a sensible development in constitutional law, which rests on a convergence of three criteria, which in turn are based not on the conventional privacy interest in information control, but on a broader personal right or liberty relating to certain kinds of basic life choices. Undoubtedly, there is some latitude for reasonable controversy about the proper application of the constitutional right to privacy. But it is important to see that this range of controversy must be disciplined by appeal to the kinds of considerations specified by the three criteria discussed here. Inevitably, the resolution of such issues must rest on interdisciplinary cooperation among philosophy, law, and the social sciences. This should be wholly unsurprising. No serious issue in the law is without its roots in philosophical presuppositions and empirical assumptions. Accordingly, philosophical analysis, companioned with the social sciences, affords a powerful and beneficent tool to shape so practical an activity as the law in the light of humane moral intelligence.

REFERENCE NOTES

1. *Griswold v. Connecticut.* U.S., 1965, *381.*
2. *Griswold v. Connecticut.* U.S., 1965, *381*, 499–502 (Harlan, concurring); 502–507 (White, concurring).
3. *Stanley v. Georgia.* U.S., 1969, *394.*
4. *Eisenstadt v. Baird.* U.S., 1972, *405.*
5. *Eisenstadt v. Baird.* U.S., 1972, *405*, 440, No. 1. The Court noted that while the lower court had described the woman as unmarried, the record contained no evidence as to her marital status.
6. *Eisenstadt v. Baird.* U.S., 1972, *405*, 446–455. Justice Brennan wrote the opinion of the Court, in which he was joined by Justices Douglas, Stewart, and Marshall. Justice White, joined by Justice Blackmun, concurred in the result, but reached neither the equal protection nor the right-to-privacy issues. Justices Powell and Rehnquist took no part in the decision.
7. *Roe v. Wade.* U.S., 1973, *410.*
8. *Board of Education v. LaFleur.* U.S., 1974, *414*, 632. The Court invoked the idea of a woman's right to decide whether to bear a child, recognized in *Roe*, as part of its reasoning holding unconstitutional a mandatory pregnancy leave after only four months of pregnancy. See also pp. 639–640.
9. *Paris Adult Theatre I v. Slaton.* U.S., 1973, *413.*
10. Addressing the question of the applicability of the First Amendment, the Court reiterated its holding in *Miller v. California*, U.S., 1973, *413*, 15, that obscenity is not constitutionally protected expression, and vacated and remanded the trial court's finding of obscenity for reconsideration in the light of the new standards enunciated in Miller. See also pp. 54–55. For a criticism of the *Miller* and *Paris* opinions, see Richards (1974).
11. *Poe v. Ullman.* U.S., 1961, *367*, 497.
12. *Poe v. Ullman.* U.S., 1961, *367*, 553 (Harlan, dissenting).
13. *Griswold v. Connecticut.* U.S. 1965, *381*, 498–499 (Goldberg, concurring).
14. *Doe v. Commonwealth's Attorney for City of Richmond.* U.S. 1976, *425*, 901, affirming without opinion E.D. Va., 1975, *403*, F. Supplement 1199 (three-judge court).
15. *Ravin v. State.* Alaska S. Ct., 1975, *537*, P. 2d, 494. For commentary, see Note (unsigned): On privacy: Constitutional protection for personal liberty. *New York University Law Review*, 1973, *48*, 670–673; and Baker (1974).

16. Several courts have cited the constitutional right to privacy as encompassing the right to die. See, e.g., *In re Quinlan*. N.J. 1976, *70*, 10,355 A. 2d 647; and *In re Yetter*. Docket No. 1973–533 (Pa. Ct. of Common Pleas, Northampton Co., Orphans Ct., 1973), citing U.S. Supreme Court decision in *Roe v. Wade*. For commentary see Davis (1967) and Malone (1974).

17. See generally Ely (1973), and for a comment Gelinas (1973), and the note (Unsigned): *Roe v. Wade*—The abortion decision: An analysis and its implication. *San Diego Law Review*, 1973, *10*, 844–856.

18. For an example of such a strained interpretation, consider Justice Douglas' view of *Roe v. Wade* as involving information disclosure issues in the context of the doctor–patient relationship. *Doe v. Bolton*. U.S., 1973, *410*, 179, 219.

19. Note Justice Rehnquist's dissent which indicates that the problems implicit in enforcing abortion laws are completely different from those involved in *Griswold*. *Doe v. Bolton*. U.S., 1973, *410*, 172 (Rehnquist dissenting).

20. These issues were obviously central in Justice Douglas' mind in the majority opinion in *Griswold*, in which he contrasted the Connecticut criminal statute with other measures, such as the regulation of the sale and manufacture of contraceptives, which would have achieved the state's goal of discouraging use. *Griswold v. Connecticut*. U.S., 1965, *321*, 485.

21. *Stanley v. Georgia*. U.S., 1969, *394*, 557, 564, quoting *Olmstead v. United States*. U.S., 1928, *277*, 438, 478 (Brandeis, dissenting).

22. In *Paris*, both the Court's rejection of the principle—well articulated by John Stuart Mill—that liberty should be limited only to prevent harm to others (Mill, 1859/1961, p. 197), and its citation of the adage "a man's home is his castle" (*Paris Adult Theatre I v. Slaton*. U.S., 1973, *413*, 66) suggests that the source of the value placed on the "privacy of the home" in *Stanley*, which *Paris* reaffirms, arises from the significance in one's life of a private sanctuary for personal relationships.

23. St. Thomas, for example, postulates a "special natural habit, which we call synderesis" which contains the first principles of morality (*Summa theologica*, 1a, 2ae, q. 79, a. 12–13). These first principles of natural law, prior to any divine revelation, are known as true by "one standard of truth or rightness of everybody" (Aquinas, 1959, pp. 123–125). The statement is also made that "natural law corresponds to the order of our natural inclinations" (Aquinas, 1959, p. 123). For a more detailed account of the development of Aquinas' thought on moral freedom, see D'Arcy (1961). Similarly, Francisco Suarez (1612/1974, pp. 205–206) argues that the essence of morality is independent of divine will. The separation of the concepts of ethics and divine will is explicit in Grotius, who observed: "And what we have said would still have great weight, even if we were to grant what we cannot grant without wickedness, that there is no God" (1853, Prolegomenon, p. xlvi). Furthermore, "Natural law is so immutable that it cannot be changed by God himself" (Grotius, 1853, Bk. 1, p. 12). Indeed, the view that natural law depends on divine law seems to have been theologically revolutionary and heretical (Oakley, 1961).

24. For important recent philosophical discussions, see Williams (1973), Parfit (1973, pp. 137–169), and Rorty (1976).

25. The distinction here made between moral and paternalistic grounds is one of convenience, as paternalistic grounds certainly are naturally viewed as one among the moral grounds of reasons for action. See Richards (1971, chap. 10). I make and use the distinction here for purposes of articulating with sharpness the different kinds of considerations relevant to the reasonable discussion of the constitutional right to privacy.

26. For the notion of a rational life plan, see Rawls (1971, pp. 407–416); Fried (1970, pp. 105–115); and Richards (1971, pp. 27–48, 63–74).

REFERENCES

Aquinas, T. *Summa theologica of Thomas Aquinas* (Fathers of the English Dominican Province, trans.). London: Barker, 1912.

Aquinas, T. *Aquinas: Selected political writings* (A. P. D'Entreves, Ed.). Oxford: Blackwell, 1959.

Baier, K. *The moral point of view: A rational basis of ethics.* Ithaca, N.Y.: Cornell University Press, 1958.

Baker, T. *Roe* and *Paris*: Does privacy have a principle? *Stanford Law Review*, 1974, *26*, 1161–1189.

Bloustein, E. J. Privacy as an aspect of human dignity: An answer to Dean Prosser. *New York University Law Review*, 1964, *39*, 962–1007.

Brandt, R. B. *Ethical theory*. Englewood Cliffs, N.J.: Prentice-Hall, 1959.

Cardozo, B. N. *The nature of the judicial process.* New Haven: Yale University Press, 1949.

D'Arcy, E. *Conscience and its right to freedom.* New York: Sheed & Ward, 1961.

Davis, D. J. The dying patient: A qualified right to refuse medical treatment. *Journal of Family Law*, 1967, *7*, 644–659.

Devlin, P. *The enforcement of morals.* New York: Oxford University Press, 1965.

Dworkin, G. Paternalism. In R. Wasserstrom (Ed.), *Morality and the law*. Belmont, Cal.: Wadsworth, 1971.

Ely, J. H. The wages of crying wolf: A comment on *Roe v. Wade*. *Yale Law Journal*, 1973, *82*, 920–949.

Foot, P. R. Moral arguments. *Mind*, 1958, *67*, 502–513.

Foot, P. R. Moral beliefs. *Proceedings of The Aristotelian Society*, 1958–1959, *59*, 83–104.

Foot, P. R. Euthanasia. *Philosophy and Public Affairs*, 1977, *6*, 85–112.

Foot, P. R., & Harrison, J. When is a principle a moral principle? *Proceedings of The Aristotelian Society* (Suppl. vol.), 1954, *28*, 95–134.

Ford, C. S., & Beach, F. A. *Patterns of sexual behavior*. New York: Hoeber, 1951.

Fried, C. *An anatomy of values: Problems of personal and social ethics.* Cambridge: Harvard University Press, 1970.

Gauthier, D. P. *Practical Reasoning: The structure and foundations of prudential and moral arguments and their exemplification in discourses.* Oxford: Clarendon, 1963.

Gelinas, A. J. A. *Roe v. Wade* and *Doe v. Bolton*: The compelling state interest test in substantive due process. *Washington and Lee Law Review*, 1973, *30*, 628–646.

Grice, G. *The grounds of moral judgment.* Cambridge: Cambridge University Press, 1967.

Gross, H. Privacy and autonomy. In J. R. Pennock & J. W. Chapman (Eds.), *Privacy* (Nomos XIII: Yearbook of the American Society for Political and Legal Philosophy). New York: Atherton, 1971.

Grotius, H. *Hugonis Grotii De jure belli ac pacis libri tres* (W. Whewell, trans.). London: Parker, 1853.

Hare, R. M. *The language of morals.* Oxford: Clarendon, 1952.

Hare, R. M. *Freedom and reason.* Oxford: Clarendon, 1963.

Hart, H. L. A. Social solidarity and the enforcement of morality. *University of Chicago Law Review*, 1967, *35*, 1–13.

Henkin, L. Morals and the Constitution: The sin of obscenity. *Columbia Law Review*, 1963, *63*, 391–414.

Kant, I. *Foundations of the metaphysics of morals, and What is enlightenment?*

(L. W. Beck, trans.). Indianapolis: Bobbs-Merrill, 1959. (Originally published, 1785.)

Malone, R. J. Is there a right to a natural death? *New England Law Review*, 1974, *9*, 293–310.

Mill, J. S. On liberty. In M. Cohen (Ed.), *The philosophy of John Stuart Mill: Ethical, political and religious.* New York: Modern Library, 1961. (Originally published, 1859.)

Miller, A. R. *The assault on privacy.* Ann Arbor: The University of Michigan Press, 1971.

Oakley, F. Medieval theories of natural law: William of Ockham and the significance of the voluntarist tradition. *Natural Law Forum*, 1961, *6*, 65–83.

Parfit, D. Later selves and moral principles. In A. Montefiore (Ed.), *Philosophy and personal relations.* Montreal: McGill-Queen's University Press, 1973.

Parker, R. B. A definition of privacy. *Rutgers Law Review*, 1974, *27*, 275–296.

Prosser, W. L. Privacy. *California Law Review*, 1960, *48*, 383–423.

Rawls, J. *A theory of justice.* Cambridge: Harvard University Press, 1971.

Reiman, J. H. Privacy, intimacy, and personhood. *Philosophy and Public Affairs*, 1976, *6*, 26–44.

Richards, D. A. J. *A theory of reasons for action.* Oxford: Clarendon, 1971.

Richards, D. A. J. Free speech and obscenity law: Towards a moral theory of the First Amendment. *University of Pennsylvania Law Review*, 1974, *123*, 45–91.

Richards, D. A. J. Unnatural acts and the constitutional right to privacy. *Fordham Law Review*, 1977, *45*, 1281–1348. (a)

Richards, D. A. J. *The moral criticism of law.* Encino, Cal.: Dickenson, 1977. (b)

Rorty, A. O. (Ed.) *The identities of persons.* Berkeley: University of California Press, 1976.

Suarez, F. On laws and God the lawgiver. In *Selections from three works* (G. L. Williams, A. Brown, J. Waldron, & H. Davis, trans.). Oxford: Clarendon, 1974. (Originally published, 1612.)

Van Den Haag, E. On privacy. In J. R. Pennock & J. W. Chapman (Eds.), *Privacy* (Nomos XIII: Yearbook of the American Society for Political and Legal Philosophy). New York: Atherton, 1971.

Warnock, G. J. *Contemporary moral philosophy.* New York: Macmillan, 1967.

Warnock, G. J. *The object of morality.* London: Methuen, 1971.

Warren, S. D., & Brandeis, L. D. The right to privacy. *Harvard Law Review*, 1890, *4*, 193–220.

Wechsler, H. Toward neutral principles of constitutional law. *Harvard Law Review*, 1959, *73*, 1–35.

Weinstein, M. A. The uses of privacy in the good life. In J. A. Pennock & J. W. Chapman (Eds.), *Privacy* (Nomos XIII: Yearbook of the American Society for Political and Legal Philosophy). New York: Atherton, 1971.

Westin, A. F. *Privacy and freedom.* New York: Atheneum, 1967.

Williams, B. *Problems of the self: Philosophical papers, 1956–1972.* Cambridge: Cambridge University Press, 1973.

Wilson, J. *Logic and sexual morality.* Baltimore: Penguin, 1965.

Privacy and the Protection of National Security

BRUCE ANDREWS

Bruce Andrews received his B.A. and M.A. degrees from Johns Hopkins University and his Ph.D. from Harvard University. He has been on the faculty of Fordham University since 1975 where he currently is Associate Professor of Political Science. Within political science the special interest area of Dr. Andrews is World Politics and International Relations. While still a student, he was Research Assistant to the President's Commission on International Trade and Investment Policy, and subsequently served as Rapporteur to the Council on Foreign Relations (1980s project). His book Public constraint and American policy in Vietnam *(1976) is part of the Sage Professional Papers in International Studies. Dr. Andrews is a member of the Political Science Association and the International Studies Association.*

> Perhaps it is a universal truth that the loss of liberty at home is to be charged to provisions against danger, real or pretended, from abroad.
>
> James Madison to Thomas Jefferson
> May 13, 1798

The relationship between privacy and national security is more tangled than most. In recent years, it has taken on a new complexity, as the claims of security have expanded to fill most crevices of national life and as new and more efficient means for infringing upon people's private lives have been developed. In the postwar American social order, privacy has been under vigorous attack, fueled by the alleged imperatives of foreign policy. Those imperatives, occasioned by the nature of the international environment and the character of America's enemies, have been thought to prescribe continuous vigilance. Abroad, they have suggested the need for an interventionist and hegemonic foreign policy; at home; they have accompanied the intrusions of the government into the private lives of its citizens.

These intrusions have been made possible by, and have helped to sustain, a widespread popular indifference or caution. In subtle and in not so subtle ways, a foreign policy has been able to generate one of its own domestic preconditions. The infringements on civil liberties, on the constitutional framework, and on established political institutions have therefore seemed all the more insidious. At times, of course, official policymakers acknowledge the trade-off between national defense and the protection of democratic liberties. Their rhetoric still induces the public to sacrifice some of the latter in order that the former might be better protected. But the general public has been less conscious of what or how much it is sacrificing. The corrosive impact which prevailing definitions of the national interest have upon a sensitivity to civil rights and civil liberties has not been fully acknowledged. Until recently, the public has accepted many of these trade-offs and many of these official definitions without a great deal of thought. Such a political somnambulism has been helped along by an atmosphere of confusion, secrecy, consumerist fulfillment, and Cold War hysteria. In the process, limits on state power and bulwarks against tyranny have been removed. The political changes engineered in the name of security have led to widespread personal insecurity. Political defenselessness and the cancellation of constitutional rights became the price of foreign policy achievement.

THE PROBLEM

Each aspect of this relationship between security and privacy bears examining. Because the record of secret state activity has finally been disclosed in recent years—if only by fits and starts—we can now begin to deal with it more openly and more analytically. The problem is not whether electronic surveillance and other attacks on privacy are legal or constitutional, but whether they are socially intelligible—whether they make sense in view of the society which spawned them. Also, the problem is not whether honorable men can strike a balance between national defense and constitutional restraints, but whether the requirements of a social system like that of the United States—in regard to a foreign policy aimed at advancing its interests, for example—will tend to sweep those restraints aside. A brief look at the empirical record of state activity in this sphere will therefore be helpful. Besides serving as a "negative role model" with a capacity for inducing shock and reform, it can set the stage for a discussion of the larger issues which need to be explored. These include: the use of security as a "totem" to justify police-like activity on the part of state actors; the connection between success in the foreign policy realm and the anesthetizing of the domestic public; the definition of national security and its relationship to a war in Indochina which was the occasion, in the Nixon years, for a dramatic increase in official invasions of privacy and attempts to stifle dissent. At the end, the connection between an interventionist foreign policy and the inhibition of democratic control will be considered.

EMPIRICAL RECORD OF STATE ACTIVITY

> It may well be that the national security of this country could be aided by acts which violate our Constitution.*

CIA Techniques Adopted by FBI

As the status quo at home and in the empire abroad met with increased domestic resistance in the 1960s, the role of America's intelligence agencies assumed greater prominence. They took their cue from the growing centralization of power in the executive branch and from an implicit theory of virtually limitless executive prerogative in the realm of foreign affairs. The Federal Bureau of Investigation (FBI), in particular, acted as the domestic counterpart of the Central Intelligence Agency (CIA), mimicking that agency's cloak-and-dagger operations with a campaign of surveillance, "counterintelligence," and covert activity all its own. No longer were operations limited to suspected foreign agents or violent criminals, although this was their statutory and programmatic rationale. Now they were directed against an entire spectrum of organizations and individuals opposed to official government policy, encompassing such civil rights groups as the Southern Christian Leadership Conference, free universities, the feminist movement, Students for a Democratic Society, the Jewish Defense League, the American Friends Service Committee, and a host of anti-war groups opposed to America's interventions in Southeast Asia.

Access to confidential sources of information was central to these operations and was acquired through contacts with college registrars and deans, telephone company employees, banks, landlords, and the Internal Revenue Service (IRS). The FBI undertook *hundreds of thousands* of separate investigations of groups and persons who were placed in the "subversive" category. Although this should apparently imply a strong potential on the part of these subversives for planning or advocating ac-

* Department of Defense memorandum, supporting a motion for summary judgment in *Bennett v. Dept. of Defense*, 75 Civ. 5005 (LFM) (S.D.N.Y.)

tions to overthrow the government, no one has been prosecuted under the laws covering such crimes in the last 20 years. Nevertheless, the spying, the "trespassory microphone surveillance," and the warrantless wiretaps continued. The attorney general could even claim, in retrospect in October 1974, that "the public record is sufficiently clear that there has been no serious abuse of discretion over the years of national security wiretaps installed for foreign intelligence purposes" (U. S. Senate Judiciary Committee, 1974b, p. 236). In a typical case revealed by the disclosure, through the communications media, of Pennsylvania FBI documents, a meeting of the pacifist Conference of War Resisters was watched to see if "it will generate any anti-U. S. propaganda." These were the sorts of activities justified under the rubric of foreign intelligence purposes. No stone could safely be left unturned. A "preventive detention" list was maintained in FBI field offices specifying the people who might jeopardize the nation's safety in a crisis situation. More than 200,000 names appeared. In all, 500,000 domestic intelligence files were gathered on more than 1,000,000 Americans (U. S. Senate Select Committee, 1976).

Domestic Expansion of CIA Activity

The CIA followed suit, spying on radical and civil rights groups and anti-war newspapers, installing wiretaps and engaging in break-ins without warrants, building close ties with state and local police, and infiltrating activist organizations of all kinds to solicit intelligence (Halperin, Berman, Borosage, & Marwick, 1976). Such domestic snooping and covert activity have always been excluded from the CIA's legitimate functioning. Nevertheless, in the so-called "crisis atmosphere" of the late-1960s and early-1970s, such operations snowballed. The Domestic Contact Service expanded its coverage. Links with college communities continued to threaten the sanctity of academic freedom. Operation CHAOS, as it was called, managed to generate 13,000 files covering 1,000 domestic organizations, after its creation in August 1967. A computerized index of 300,000 names resulted. Along with the 100,000 entries in the army's intelligence dossiers, this information was used to discredit and complicate the work of student dissenters, as well as the draft resistance and anti-war movements.

Other violations of statutes and federal regulations continued apace. The CIA, in its secret HTLINGUAL operation spanning a 20-year period, became heavily involved in tampering with the mail. As many as 28 million pieces of mail sent by or addressed to Americans were screened; 2 million were photographed; almost a quarter of a million were opened and photographed. Another computerized index resulted—this time, involving nearly one and one-half million names. Howard Osborn, the CIA's director of security, agreed with the Rockefeller Commission report: "This thing is illegal as hell" (U. S. Senate Select Committee, 1976, Bk. 3, p. 605). Heavily shrouded in secrecy, the rather mysterious National Security Agency (NSA) added its own contribution. As part of its Project SHAMROCK, it intercepted all the private cables leaving the country, analyzing 150,000 messages a month, and distributing the information to other government agencies. Through the course of the post–World War II period, the NSA characteristically shifted its focus from suspected foreign agents to groups and individuals engaged in anti-war activities which supposedly were under the protection of the law. In Project MINARET, using a "watch list" of such names, it systematically scanned all their international wire, cable, and radio communications. Files on 75,000 Americans were maintained. The Fourth Amendment restrictions on illegal searches and seizures, which certainly applied in these cases, were expediently ignored.

Counterintelligence: Growth Toward Police State

But domestic surveillance alone did not satisfy the officials responsible for protecting the nation's defense and reproducing the social system. The actions of radical dissenters and anti-war activists were to be counteracted, inconvenienced, and disrupted. More and more sections of the federal apparatus devoted themselves to this task. "Counterintelligence" shifted into a manipulation of the domestic political process on an unprecedented scale. Much of the manipulation took its direction from the highest reaches of the executive branch; other actions were sanctioned by zealous officials at the middle levels. It is without any unwarranted melodrama to say that these actions reveal the basic contours of an authentic "American police state" (Wise, 1976)—one which was kept from its full flowering only by vigorous detection, unexpected disclosures, and administrative failure.

The illegal treatment of confidential tax returns provides another revealing example of this domestic thrust. In the Nixon years, groups and individuals involved in "leftist" dissent and "alleged peaceful demonstrations" were singled out for special treatment. As John Dean noted, the President specifically pressed for "the use of the Internal Revenue Service to attack our enemies"; for, according to a White House memo, "What we cannot do in a courtroom via criminal prosecutions to curtail the activities of some of these groups, IRS could do by administrative action" (cited in Lukas, 1976, pp. 29–30). Political criteria of an improper nature began to guide the IRS's auditing of tax returns. Tax law enforcement became both selective and politicized—a weapon of harassment in the hands of the state, to be used against a secret list of adversaries. More than 8,000 individuals and almost 3,000 organizations found themselves in this category. Information gained through these improper investigations and field audits was then improperly distributed throughout the intelligence apparatus—to serve as a spur for additional political counterthrusts.

Grand juries provided another tool in this arsenal, and another officially sanctioned invasion of privacy. They offered an umbrella for the gathering of confidential information which could be more easily obtained under threat of subpoena or coerced from subpoenaed witnesses reluctant to be jailed for contempt. Nearly 2,000 people were subpoenaed in the Nixon years alone. Constitutional safeguards in these instances were held in abeyance, as the privileges of the prosecution were abused; an "accusatorial" system was subtly transformed into an "inquisitorial" one (Copelon, 1977; Mead, 1976). The constructive work of dissenters was derailed or undermined; whole categories of lawful political behavior and even interpersonal association were stigmatized. As with their functional predecessors—the congressional committees investigating "un-American" activities—an atmosphere of suspicion resulted.

Moreover, not all the contributions to this repressive climate originated at the federal level. As recent lawsuits reveal, state and local police formed home-grown "Red Squads" in order to spy on and harass local citizens engaged in political actions to alter the status quo, either at home or abroad ("Lawsuits against Federal, State and Local Red Squads," 1977). Assisted in many cases by federal authorities, these squads provided the local counterparts of the disruption and surveillance undertaken by the CIA, FBI, NSA, IRS, and the Pentagon—in many cases "targeting on" the same individuals. The Mississippi State Sovereignty Commission, as one example, accumulated the names of 10,000 Mississippi individuals and 270 organizations in its "intelligence files"; Chicago police claim to have indexed over 200,000 names from the fruits of their local spying. What cannot be quantified, however, and what is devilishly difficult to gauge, is the contribution which these governmental programs made to inhibiting the movements for peace and for radical social change—for this, after all, was their purpose. The invasion of privacy served as a mere instrument.

COINTELPRO Tactics

Still the most infamous of all these invasions were those which made up the FBI's systematic Counterintelligence Program (named COINTELPRO, and pronounced in four syllables). Desirous of continuing and expanding the same "preventive actions" which had worked so well to hamper the Communist party, the FBI found that the mid- and late-1950s provided a less hospitable climate of opinion than the more virulent heyday of Senator McCarthy, the Smith Act, and the omnipresent Loyalty Boards. When COINTELPRO began, 20 years ago, it "transformed Mc-

Carthyism into an underground operation" (Halperin et al., 1976, p. 113; Atkins, 1976; Blackstock, 1976; U. S. Senate Select Committee, 1976). In doing so, it sustained its coverage—against other Communist organizations, against groups advocating Puerto Rican independence, against the Socialist Workers Party—and then widened it to include the civil rights, student protest, anti-war, and radical movements of the 1960s and early-1970s. "The purpose of this new counter-intelligence endeavor," as the Final Report of the U. S. Senate Select Committee noted (1976, Bk. 3, p. 5) was "to expose, disrupt, misdirect, discredit, or otherwise neutralize" these political activist organizations and individuals. To this task, the tactical virtuosity of the FBI was applied. Although the full record of evidence is only now trickling out in court cases and by means of the Freedom of Information Act, what is already revealed is enough to make the much more publicized crimes of "Watergate" seem rather pale by comparison.

Intensive surveillance of these domestic groups shaded over into harassment, burglaries, and theft ("second-storey jobs" and "black-bag jobs," as they were called). More than 2,000 separate FBI COINTELPRO actions have been acknowledged. Besides the extensive burglaries and break-ins, these included the supplying of derogatory material (often of questionable accuracy) to fuel attacks by a compliant "free press" on specific groups and individuals. To show such things as the "depravity of the New Left," "articles showing advocation of the use of narcotics and free sex are ideal" (cited in Halperin et al., 1976, p. 128). They also worked to discredit political activists by means of anonymous letter campaigns to parents, employers, school officials, etc., and more direct pressure on employers to get their targets fired. At times, activists were "roughed up" in order to disturb and deter them. At other times, more direct intervention was utilized. Agents relied on forged documents and letters to discredit influential individuals *within* their own organizations—to mark them as informants, to destroy their effectiveness, to generate confusion. As one FBI official put it, "you can seed distrust, sow misinformation." The family lives of certain activists became a governmental target. Some radical groups were turned against each other, occasionally by using them as quasi-official spies, occasionally as a way of provoking violence.

Use of Informers and Agents Provocateurs

Through the use of informers, the government infringed upon the sanctity of political association and even of judicial proceedings. Harassment became an *inside job*, a highly valued way of distorting the internal politics and interpersonal relations of groups in order to destroy them or orient them toward the sorts of public violence which might undermine their legitimacy in the eyes of the community. These contacts were officially designed, as the agency's "New Left Notes—Phila." memo of September 16, 1970 put it, to "enhance the paranoia endemic in these circles and further serve to get the point across that there is an FBI agent behind every mailbox."

As one official with the FBI's internal security section in San Francisco put it: "It's very nice to know that the people you're chasing are afraid to use telephones" (cited in Navasky & Lewin, 1973, p. 307). In the same context, reference might be made to the cynical remark of a top-ranking general:*

> If any citizen of this country is so concerned about his mail being read or is concerned about his presence in a meeting being noted, I'd say we ought to read his mail and we ought to know what the hell he has done.

In another example, it was recently revealed that in a six-year operation against the Institute for Policy Studies, a prominent radical research organization in Washington, D.C., more than 60 paid informers were put in place. The Socialist Workers Party injunction against the more than decade-long FBI compaign of burglary, wiretapping, mail tampering, harassment, and the use of informers is also revealing (*Socialist Workers Party v. Attorney General.* 73 Civ. 3160 [S.D.N.Y.]). The party's offices were burglarized at least 94 times during the 1960s, and up to 1,000 informers were used at various times to collect the 8,000,000 pages of files which the FBI admitted accumulating. In such cases, the protection of the Fourth Amendment (for example, the prohibition against general warrants which do not particularize the items to be seized) went by the boards.

Still more darkly, these paid informers took on the clandestine role of *agents provocateurs*. They supplied weapons and explosives, took part in violent crimes, and encouraged the internal *policies* of crime and violence which were supposedly what the government had wanted to quell. Entrapment and negative "public relations" resulted, or at the very least a diverting of these organizations into unproductive or self-destructive channels.

Informers were used in an attempt to destroy the Black Panther Party, even to the point of provoking violent confrontations and setting up key members for political assassination (Cantor, 1976). They were also involved in funding and arming the ultra-rightist paramilitary Secret Army Organization, which was active in threats, break-ins, beatings, bombings, and shootings intended to disrupt anti-war protest activities in southern California. Other recent lawsuits portray a similar range of activity: illegal surveillance and disruption of the Women's Liberation Movement,

* General George Brown, Chairman of the Joint Chiefs of Staff, cited in *The Washington Post,* March 27, 1977.

the Vietnam Veterans Against the War, the use of undercover police agents as "students" in campus unrest, the attempted inducement of campus bombings at Kent State University, etc. One recent study persuasively concludes that "the hand of the secret agent was responsible for a great deal of the political conflict [and campus violence] of the last decade and a half" (Marwick, 1977). The salience of the targets which provided the rationale for these actions could be created by the actions themselves.

Violations at Executive Level

An expansion of the efforts involved in eavesdropping, wiretapping and bugging, illegal mail opening, the use of college campus informants, burglary: all these received the executive imprimatur with Richard Nixon's approval of the "Huston Plan"—which "amounted to nothing less than a blueprint for a police state in America" (Wise, 1976, p. 154). In July 1970, presidential assistant Huston proposed that: "Present procedures should be changed to permit intensification of coverage of individuals and groups in the United States who pose a major threat to internal security" (Weissman, 1974, p. 321). On "surreptitious entry," his famous memorandum stated, "present restrictions should be modified to permit selective use of this technique against other urgent security targets. . . . Use of this technique is clearly illegal: it amounts to burglary."

In spite of this admission of criminality, H. R. Haldeman soon informed Huston that the President had approved the proposal in its entirety. Only J. Edgar Hoover's hesitation over the formal decision memorandum of July 23, 1970, led to the merely "piecemeal" implementation of the plan (Lukas, 1976, p. 49), using the techniques described above. Even so—or perhaps as a result—five years later, FBI Director Kelley could still say of the illegal break-ins: "I do not note in these activities any gross abuse of authority." The Bureau, he felt, had "acted in good faith with the belief that national security interests were paramount."

SOME SALIENT BROAD ISSUES

Use of Security as a Cover

Dean:	You might put it on a national security grounds basis.
Haldeman:	It absolutely was.
Nixon:	National Security. We had to get information for national security grounds. . . . With the bombing thing coming out, the whole thing was national security.
Dean:	I think we could get by on that.*

* Discussion in the Oval Room of the White House relative to the burglary of the office of the therapist Daniel Ellsberg, March 21, 1973.

Does this argument about the claims of national security let the government off the hook so easily? In their most familiar form, encountered with increasing frequency in the postwar period, the requirements of national security are said to be: (1) clear, objective, unproblematical; and (2) overriding many competing claims of personal freedom or civil liberties. Such an argument has been *embodied* in the state practices cited above. Moreover, it attained prominence because it was used whenever the occasion arose for justifying those activities—whether in public or within the confines of the bureaucracy. The frequency of those occasions was not unrelated to the fact that the legal warrant for these practices was a house of cards. The secrecy which customarily enshrouded these matters of security also had an impact, as did the compliance of the media. It made these public accountings much less common. President Kennedy's displeasure with the press over the handling of the Bay of Pigs invasion suggested one mechanism by which these public defenses might be avoided. As he argued on April 27, 1961 (cited in Aronson, 1970, pp. 161–162):

> In times of clear and present danger, the courts have held that even the privileged rights of the First Amendment must yield to the public's need for national security. Today no war has been declared . . . [nevertheless] Our way of life is under attack. . . . If the press is awaiting a declaration of war before it imposes the self-discipline of combat conditions, then I can only say that no war has ever imposed a greater threat to our security.

As foreign policy issues became increasingly "domesticated" in the late-1960s and early-1970s, the recourse *in public* to the claims of national defense did, of course, become more common. At the same time, it proved no less revealing. President Nixon even went so far as to use those claims to justify the Watergate cover-up: "since persons originally recruited for covert national security activities had participated in Watergate, an unrestricted investigation of Watergate might lead to an exposé of those covert national security operations" (Lukas, 1976, p. 462). Without having those operations specified, one simply had to take on faith the idea that such an exposé would be disastrous.

This account has a long lineage. Franklin Roosevelt's original rationale for wiretapping, presented to the attorney general on May 21, 1940, limited it to "grave matters involving the defense of the nation" and "persons suspected of subversive activities against the Government of the United States." In addition, he noted his agreement with section 605 of the Federal Communications Act of 1934 which had said, "Under ordinary and normal circumstances wiretapping by government agents should not be carried on for the excellent reason that it is almost bound to lead to abuse of civil rights" (cited in McClellan, 1976, p. 223). Yet times and foreign policies change, and, with them, domestic policies of this kind. As the Cold War unfolded, Attorney General Tom C. Clark requested on July 17, 1946, that the wiretapping procedure be extended to "cases vitally affecting the *domestic* security" (cited in Theoharis, 1974; emphasis supplied), thereby authorizing the surveillance of political dissidents. President Truman concurred. Even so, FBI Director Hoover had already informed an uncomplaining Congress as early as 1939 that the Bureau was compiling indices of people engaged in "any activities that are possibly detrimental to the internal security of the United States" (Halperin et al., 1976, p. 97). As time went on, Americans discovered just how broad and elastic this characterization could be.

Popular activities threatening the internal security: in this, we find the same category for which the Huston Plan sought "intensified coverage" over 30 years later. COINTELPRO, in addition, would disrupt those "subversive elements seeking to undermine our nation," as Assistant FBI Director Sullivan put it in 1966. In the late-1960s, the Special Service of the IRS was also thought to be carrying on this "overall battle against persons bent on destruction of this government" (U. S. Senate Select Committee, 1976, Bk. 3, pp. 881–882). Surveillance of the Women's Liberation Movement was accounted for in a similar vein, as were the campaigns against Martin Luther King, Jr., the Black Panthers, the Socialist Workers Party, and dozens of other domestic groups pressing for social change—and sometimes for dramatic, though nonviolent, transformations of America's foreign policy and domestic status quo. The intelligence agencies characterized these groups as a "subversion force," whose activities justified the officially sanctioned espionage and trampling of civil liberties. Legitimate political dissent seems to have become indistinguishable from the kind of subversive activity which truly jeopardized the nation's military defense. That a distinction is in order may be recognized in the following statement of Chief Justice Earl Warren:

> This concept of "national defense" cannot be deemed an end in itself, justifying any . . . power designed to promote such a goal. Implicit in the term "national defense" is the notion of defending those values and ideas which set this Nation apart. . . . It would indeed be ironic if, in the name of national defense, we would sanction the subversion of . . . those liberties . . . which [make] the defense of the Nation worthwhile [In *United States v. Robel,* 389 U.S. *258,* 264].

Can Foreign Policy Silence All Public Dissent?

When a conception of the domestic social order or the status quo had achieved something approximating a consensus among the ruling groups, a map of "the nation to be defended" could then be derived.* "The nation," at that point, could be seen as a bundle of distinguishable characteristics. The idea of national security had acquired a specific social content. As I have remarked elsewhere:

> In most cases, even considerations of national security are not intelligible apart from a specific conception of the domestic order which is to be protected or advanced. The international aims of a government, in other words, are very rarely either self-explanatory or ends in themselves. . . . For a complete account, they must eventually be redefined as *means* toward a more inclusive set of *social purposes* [Andrews, 1975, p. 523].

National security thus takes on an instrumental form; it can be *derived* from the reigning conception of the domestic society which is to be protected or advanced. If the particular "moves" of policy can be seen and acknowledged as means toward the end of security, the idea of security itself can be located in a deeper or "second order" relationship of ends to means. But what is interesting for our present purposes is the fact that this "second order" derivation tends to go unrecognized. In postwar American policy, except in periods of crisis or dramatic transition, it has largely been taken for granted. With rare exceptions, the "official" conceptions of the valued status quo have not been an occasion for sharp political division. Nor have the broad conceptions of national security derived from them, at least insofar as we find them inscribed in America's postwar international policy. Instead, domestic debate and political struggle have centered largely in the tactics to be used to protect those shared conceptions.

Because these deeper matters were not heavily politicized, they afforded the policymakers a great deal of leeway in particularizing their conception of the nation, in defining the potential threats to its defense, and in specifying the best means to meet or pre-empt them. Eventually policymakers came to mistake this leeway for the nation's security itself; the maximization of state power, both at home and abroad, was identified with the minimal requirements of security. This was a logical extension of the prevailing official "mind set," since domestic as well as foreign tactics could be derived from a taken-for-granted idea of security, as long as it was well elaborated. And in the American case, because it was a fundamentally conservative and expansionist social system which was being protected, the exertions of state power would have to be both vigorous and successful. This carried with it rather exacting preconditions of both an international and a domestic variety.

For example, acceptable limits of political opposition and dissent were

* For several treatments of the historical evolution of such a mapping in the American case, see Dowd, 1974; Johnson, 1968; Kolko, 1976; and Williams, 1961.

entailed. Groups or individuals who crossed these limits—whether from a disagreement over the nature of the desired society or over the policies recommended to protect it—found themselves in a virtual no man's land. They became a threat to "internal stability," a source of unrest or, increasingly, a target for political redirection through the use of paid agents and counterintelligence disruption. As the consensus over the need for an interventionary foreign policy began to break apart in the 1960s (Andrews, 1976, 1977; Russett, 1975; Tucker, 1972, 1973), these threats loomed larger in the eyes of the arbiters of orthodoxy. As the army's general counsel candidly put it in 1974, "the people on the other side were essentially the enemy" (U. S. Senate Judiciary Committee, 1974a, p. 16).

Resultant Inhibition of the Public Voice

Counteracting the threat required that the state apparatus be mobilized in quite a far-reaching manner, as we have seen. In particular, it began to involve the inhibition of citizens' willingness to exercise the political rights which were guaranteed to them. Not only did such things as surveillance and infiltration violate people's Fourth Amendment right "to be secure in their persons, houses, papers, and effects, against unreasonable searches and seizures," but the chance of these same things occurring helped to create a climate of fear and paranoia which, in turn, undercut the guarantees of the First Amendment. The use of grand jury proceedings against the Vietnam Veterans Against the War may serve as a case in point, for certainly this was "part of an overall governmental tactic directed against disfavored persons and groups . . . to chill their expressions and associations"—as noted in a Fifth Circuit Court decision of 1975 (*U.S. v. Briggs.* 514 F 2nd 794, 805–806). The chilling effect also occurred as the by-product of a politically conservative climate, one which did not evolve accidentally but was a conscious creation of the federal government and the ruling elites. From their point of view, such a creation could be regarded as another entailment of the claims of security.

Like the international policies which overarched it, the domestic task was grounded on a notion of *deterrence.* The social sources of discontent would not be relieved; instead, a more coercive strategy would be followed. Enemies at home and abroad could be inhibited or would engage in avoidance behavior when they found themselves facing the concerted efforts of the state. "Aversive conditioning" and "stigmatization" would be the predictable results (Askin, 1973). Boundaries of acceptable political behavior were to be redrawn, both by means of the intrusions of the government and also as citizens came to internalize the new rules of the game. As Justice William O. Douglas phrased it in the so-called *Keith* decision in 1972 (*U. S. v. U. S. District Court*): "More than our privacy is implicated. Also at stake is the reach of the Government's power to intimidate its critics." Eventually, as the entailments of security expanded, this intimidation came to expand as well. In the end, the government targeted groups outside the established institutional nexus, but also seized upon the task of confronting the media, the Congress, and partisan opponents through officially sanctioned channels. This extension eventually brought down the wrath of the "establishment," as Nixon used to call it, just as it had undermined earlier political figures whose attacks had crossed a similar line: Joseph McCarthy and Henry Wallace, for examples from both sides. In the most recent case, the norms of electoral competition were transgressed by means of large-scale political espionage and disruption; harangues and planned threats of IRS investigation and anti-trust actions were to be effective in changing the views of the media; dissenters and foes in the Congress and the federal bureaucracy were assailed. John Dean's well-known memorandum of August 16, 1971, written at the request of the President's assistants, caught the spirit of this approach by discussing:

> How we can maximize the fact of our incumbency in dealing with the persons known to be active in their opposition to our administration. Stated a bit more bluntly—how we can use the available federal machinery to screw our political enemies.

The isolated "commanding heights" had virtually declared war on all the lower levels of the political system, as if playing out the familiar script for a self-defined "crisis" situation. To combat a dangerous ideological adversary, in the eyes of state actors, appeared to mean that many of the covert tactics and repressive characteristics of that adversary would have to be adopted, at least in the short run. First incorporated into America's Cold War foreign policy, this lesson came to insinuate itself even more deeply into the fabric of domestic life. To combat the equally dangerous currents of social change and partisan opposition at home, these same lessons seemed appealing. When the response to domestic dangers would be wrapped in the flag, or tied to prevailing claims of national defense, the need for a determined counter thrust appeared all the more suggestive.

National Security Needs More Precise Definition

The maximization of executive power was ceasing to be merely a possibility, and certain statements of government officials were no longer naïve slogans. Thus,

> There have been—and will be in the future—circumstances in which Presidents may lawfully authorize actions in the interests of the security of this country, which undertaken by other persons or by the President under different circumstances would be illegal [Richard M. Nixon].

Everything is valid, everything is possible [White House Aide Tom Charles Huston, June 9, 1970].

Experience in Indochina. America's escalation of the war in Vietnam provided these enabling circumstances. By so doing, it brought many of these issues to prominence once again, as the needs of foreign policy seemed to warrant decisive domestic action—of a prophylactic sort. In the late-1960s, Lyndon Johnson had urged that the anti-war movement be investigated to determine whether the turmoil at home was being fomented from abroad—an interesting parallel to the Administration's "external" view of the conflict in Vietnam itself. Although no solid evidence turned up, the surveillance continued to grow. When Richard Nixon occupied the White House in 1969, the same domestic forces beset him and threatened to undercut his authority. The White House saw itself faced with a profound social crisis, one which might paralyze the government and endanger the security of "the nation" as it was officially conceived. Imagery of impotence abounded. But this time the threat would not be "appeased." Instead, it would be "managed," even if by techniques which did not respect constitutional limits and the niceties of the law. The gloves were off. As Egil Krogh, Jr. said at the time: "Anyone who opposes us, we'll destroy. As a matter of fact, anyone who doesn't support us, we'll destroy" (Lukas, 1976, p. 93).

Yet *what* was in crisis? The abuses of surveillance and counter-intelligence cannot be put in a larger social context if we regard them simply as the deficient product of standard bureaucratic process (Halperin, 1975–1976, pp. 149–150) or of personal psychopathology at the top. They were not ends in themselves; nor did they unfold as a mere by-product of bureaucratic autonomy and self-aggrandizement. Certainly the overall directions of domestic and international policy were intersecting and bringing with them the increasingly alarmist visions of American leaders. Speaking of the student rebellion and its opposition to the war on March 22, 1969, President Nixon claimed that: "It is not too strong a statement to declare that this is the way civilizations begin to die" (cited in Schell, 1976, p. 36). And we can regard this as a presidential way of speaking about America's postwar empire or world leadership role and its exacting preconditions, as Nixon applauded Yeats' insight: " 'Things fall apart; the center cannot hold.' " For the domestic turmoil faced by official Washington had come, in large measure, as a response to the continuing American war in Asia. And so it was the identification of national security with that continuing Asian involvement which helped to fuel the patterns of action under analysis: the expansion of state power into previously private spheres, the adoption of paramilitary tactics in the domestic arena, and the infringement of civil liberties. Those who opposed the established social order were undercutting the credibility of American foreign policy; those who struggled against that policy were doing the work of the enemy, whether they recognized it or not; those who were advancing the enemy's cause deserved to be treated accordingly. If the war protected American security—and this was, of course, what the war's critics refused to accept—then anything done to sap the opposition to that war would likewise help protect the nation's security.

Or so the logic went, officially. In May 1969, America's secret bombing of the supposedly neutral territory of Cambodia was revealed by *The New York Times*. The "violation of national security," as Henry Kissinger would later characterize the publishing of such sensitive information, was not merely a diplomatic issue. Government officials also hoped to keep the anti-war movement at home from reawakening. This "extraordinarily damaging" disclosure (to use Kissinger's modifiers) therefore precipitated a well-known series of warrantless wiretaps of 13 government officials and four journalists in an attempt to plug news leaks and quell the opposition. In several cases, the wiretaps were accompanied by what the attorney general called "the other business" (surveillance, etc.). As J. Edgar Hoover's memo of a May 9 call from Kissinger records it, he "hoped I would follow it up as far as we can take it and they will destroy whoever did this if we can find him, no matter where he is" (Wise, 1976, p. 36).

By the time the Pentagon Papers were revealed and published in mid-1971, the anxiety of foreign policy officials simply added to an atmosphere of besiegement. Wiretapping had already been defended as a legitimate security action, designed to stop the public disclosure of information and to allow policymakers to play their cards close to the chest. A legal right would even be claimed for the wiretapping of groups whose activities jeopardized the smooth flow of diplomatic initiative, such as the Jewish Defense League's harassment of Soviet embassy officials. COINTELPRO and the suppression of domestic dissent had been defended in a similar way, with a view toward the protection of "internal security." Kissinger urged that the disclosure of the Pentagon Papers be kept from serving as a precedent, "at all costs."

Sterner and more encompassing measures were to be tested out. In the summer of 1971, the White House set up the Special Investigations Unit or "Plumbers Unit," taking its name from those other domestic professionals whose job it is to "plug leaks." This allowed the men surrounding the President to skirt the hesitations of the intelligence agencies and move directly into political espionage. Among their other responsibilities, John Ehrlichman approved a "covert operation" to examine the medical files of Daniel Ellsberg's therapist, "If done under your assurance that it is not traceable." It was undertaken in September 1971; much later it proved to be traceable and its instigators found themselves open to criminal prosecution. Another, even more bizarre plan which was contemplated involved the theft of documents pertaining to the Indochina conflict from the Brookings Institution, a well-known liberal think-tank in Washington,

D.C.—to be achieved by the planting of a fire bomb in the building and the retrieval of the documents "during the commotion that would ensue" (Wise, 1976, p. 157). And still the full record of the Plumbers' activities has not yet been revealed.

Constitutional limits infringed. Apparently these operations were regarded in much the same terms as the war in Indochina itself—exceptional, even distasteful actions which, however, were needed at the time to preserve America's interests. This at least helps to account for the positive ethical gloss which the nation's leaders were so intent on giving them. If need be, actions would be carried out *in the face of* established constitutional limits, rather than under their protective umbrella, for neither the public nor the guardians of legality could be counted on to understand the kinds of threats which officials saw all around them. As Donald Santarelli from the Justice Department observed in 1973, "Today, the whole Constitution is up for grabs" (cited in Schell, 1976, p. 314). It was as if the perspective of Dirty Harry, the Clint Eastwood character in Don Siegel's 1971 film, had become national policy—a violent individual at the center, butting himself up against legal restraints and attempting to protect an established social system from its own violent symptoms and contradictions.

Because of the endemic uncertainty of international affairs—and this has been a *leitmotif* in diplomatic thinking since the time of Thucydides—someone could usually build a case for aggressive action. When interventions into Third World countries were arranged (in Cuba, Cambodia, Chile, Angola, Zaire, etc.), and when their success depended on the American public's being either supportive or kept in the dark, special problems arose. In some ways, the issues remained constant throughout the postwar era, but the proposed solutions changed from time to time. By the late-1960s, the public depredations of McCarthyism and the more virulent strains of anti-Communism did not seem publicly acceptable. But if the enforced mobilization of the early Cold War period was no longer needed or even desirable in an age of limited wars and the "destabilization" of foreign regimes, an enforced silence or a lack of public scrutiny might yet prove exceedingly valuable. This was especially true as the priorities of the American public began to loosen up and show movement in the 1960s, and as a reluctance in the face of foreign interventions began to display itself (Andrews, 1976). At times, from the official vantage point, ignorance might still look like bliss. If information leaked out, on the other hand—to foreign audiences or to domestic enemies—U. S. leaders could claim that the high ground of diplomatic leeway had been encroached upon.

Not only did the uncertainty of foreign affairs have its counterpart in the uncertainty of domestic politics and civil liberties, the two were wrapped together. An inability to control the information process or to eliminate dissent would foreshadow an increase in a level of uncertainty which was already uncomfortably high. National insecurity would result. In these instances, someone could usually build a case for aggressive action—only this time on the home front as well. For, after all, without surveillance and occasionally some disruption of the "hostile forces" at home, how could one maintain the domestic preconditions for a foreign policy success with any certainty? How could one ever really know what breaches of security were occurring?

In 1974, thinking along similar lines, the Justice Department therefore argued that the warrantless wiretaps of journalists and former government officials had a counterintelligence dimension. Disclosures of "national security information" in the press enabled America's enemies to obtain it without resort to spying—since foreign agents could simply read the newspapers! The way an unfettered free press operated might then be "tantamount to 'foreign intelligence activity' " (Wise, 1976, p. 101). Similar motives lay behind the wiretapping of respected journalists in the foreign policy field such as Joseph Kraft, in 1969. Later on, Attorney General Levi noted that the burglary and "surveillance did not indicate that Mr. Kraft's activities posed any risk to the national security." Yet this was hardly the point; *for only the results of the surveillance* could indicate this in any definitive way.

Attorney General Saxbe testified in October 1974: "But as Voltaire said, 'Has the hawk ever ceased to prey upon the pigeon?' And I do not want to be the pigeon" (U. S. Senate Judiciary Committee, 1974b, p. 247). In these same hearings, Senator McClellan spoke of "disarming" the nation by outlawing electronic surveillance in domestic cases; FBI Director Kelley warned of "burning the house down to roast the pig," and Saxbe claimed that it would be like "pulling the firemen off the ladder." As I have said, in cases of uncertainty someone could always argue that the security risk outweighed the illegality. Moreover, the security risk could be determined only after the intrusion into citizens' private lives had occurred. The same was true of COINTELPRO, but here the dangers to domestic stability could always be contrived with the help of *agents provocateurs* to justify the counterintelligence operations.

CONCLUSION

Just as many had feared, the loss of liberty at home was charged, in the American case, to the efforts made against dangers from abroad. The civil liberties protected by the Constitution, the freedoms embedded in a democratic political process, the privacy of citizens: these would often prove to be luxuries in the face of national security claims. And these national security claims, in turn, would be said to hinge upon the imperatives of world politics, the nature of nuclear deterrence, the need for credibility, and the exacting price of freedom in a hostile world (see, for example, Schell, 1976, chap. 6).

These connections bear examining. For, as I have argued, these security claims—and the infringements of liberty to which they are tied—are not simply features of the international environment which can be taken for granted. Rather, they spring from the requirements of a particular social system or domestic "social paradigm" (Andrews, 1975, p. 524) as government leaders interpret them. The idea of national defense, like the equally opaque or "mythic" ideas of national security and the national interest, will still retain this reliance on a particular domestic *context* and a specific domestic *content*. By retaining these features, or by locating a foreign policy in this "second order" relationship, we can help to make intelligible the expansive foreign policies which go well beyond the needs of direct territorial defense or the protection of sovereignty. In the American case, this will prove especially useful, for it also helps to make intelligible the domestic patterns of surveillance and infringement of liberties which have been uncovered. The expansive international policies and the "restraining" of domestic dissent go hand in hand.

The idea of protecting "freedom" from external threat, for example, may be another way of talking about the international preconditions for reproducing a particular domestic status quo—and its most highly valued aspects of a political, economic, or cultural variety. As in the case of postwar America, those external preconditions may suggest the need for a hegemonic foreign policy, which entails a leadership role over a far-flung "Free World" alliance, the containment of ideological and military competitors, and periodic interventions throughout the system in order to safeguard a hegemonic control and access. In recent decades, this led first to an "imperial America" and then to official anxieties about the *domestic* preconditions of maintaining that hegemonic structure and that capacity for intervention. These foreign policy tasks have consistently been identified with the needs of national defense; the security claims which accompanied them helped to fuel the attacks on civil liberties. This was also true no matter how extravagant or wrongheaded those claims might be. In fact, the curbs on their extravagance—supplied by an active and critical public—were precisely what those security claims had helped to undermine in the postwar years. The depoliticization of the public and the depoliticization of "national security" were joined.

To get beyond the surface presented by the legal or constitutional issues involved in surveillance or wiretapping, we will have to recognize the links which connect foreign policy ambitions to their domestic requirements. In the American case at hand, this seems especially clear. Usually without their approval or even acknowledgment, a reluctant and often neo-isolationist American public has been encouraged to make dramatic sacrifices for such ambitions. The nation has sacrificed democratic freedoms at the altar of "credibility" and "defense," without its being made clear just what is being advanced or defended, and without discovering if the public were willing to play its appropriate political role in sanctioning such an effort. Instead, we have witnessed the U. S. government behaving like the fabled Oroborus: the head devouring the body. Policies would be maintained "at all costs." In the process, to protect a particular "paradigm" or concept of "the nation," the body politic might be consumed. In this fashion, we can see that it would not be citizens' privacy but instead *the privacy of state action* which would be secured.

REFERENCES

Andrews, B. Social rules and the state as a social actor. *World Politics*, 1975, *27*, 521–540.

Andrews, B. *Public constraint and American policy in Vietnam*. Beverly Hills, Cal.: Sage, 1976.

Andrews, B. Representation and irresponsibility in foreign policy. Paper presented at the 18th Annual Convention of the International Studies Association, St. Louis, Mo., March 1977.

Aronson, J. *The press and the cold war*. Boston: Beacon, 1970.

Askin, F. Surveillance: The social science perspective. In Columbia Human Rights Law Review (Eds.), *Surveillance, dataveillance, and personal freedom*. Fairlawn, N.J.: Burdick, 1973.

Atkins, D. The Socialist Workers Party and the FBI. *First Principles*, 1976, *2* (1), 9–13.

Blackstock, N. *COINTELPRO: The FBI's secret war on political freedom*. New York: Vintage, 1976.

Cantor, S. Fred Hampton: A case of political assassination. *First Principles*, 1976, *2* (3), 1–11.

Copelon, R. Reconstitutionalizing the grand jury. *First Principles*, 1977, *2* (8), 1–8.

Dowd, D. *The twisted dream: Capitalist development in the United States since 1776*. Cambridge, Mass.: Winthrop, 1974.

Halperin, M. H. National security and civil liberties. *Foreign Policy*, 1975–1976, *21*, 125–160.

Halperin, M. H., Berman, J., Borosage, R., & Marwick, C. *The lawless state: The crimes of the U.S. intelligence agencies*. New York: Penguin, 1976.

Johnson, B. The democratic mirage: Notes toward a theory of American politics. *Berkeley Journal of Sociology*, 1968, *13*, 104–143.

Kolko, G. *Main currents in modern American history*. New York: Harper & Row, 1976.

Lawsuits against federal, state, and local red squads: A docket of cases. *First Principles*, 1977, *2* (5), 1–4.

Lukas, J. A. *Nightmare: The underside of the Nixon years*. New York: Viking, 1976.

Marwick, C. M. The government informer: A threat to political freedom. *First Principles*, 1977, *2* (7), 1–10.

McCellan, G. S. (Ed.). *The right to privacy*. New York: Wilson, 1976.

Mead, J. Grand juries: An American inquisition. *First Principles*, 1976, *2* (1), 3–8.

Navasky, V., & Lewin, N. Electronic surveillance. In P. Watters & S. Gillers (Eds.), *Investigating the FBI*. Garden City, N.Y.: Doubleday, 1973.

Rockefeller Commission. *Report to the President on CIA activities within the United States.* Washington, D.C.: Government Printing Office, 1975.

Russett, B. The Americans' retreat from world power. *Political Science Quarterly,* 1975, *90,* 1–21.

Schell, J. *The time of illusion.* New York: Vintage, 1976.

Theoharis, A. G. Statement. In U. S. Senate, Committee on the Judiciary, Hearings before the Subcommittee on Criminal Laws and Procedures. Electronic surveillance for national security purposes. October 1–3, 1974.

Tucker, R. W. *A new isolationism: Threat or promise?* New York: Universe, 1972.

Tucker, R. W. The American outlook: Change and continuity. In R. E. Osgood et al. (Eds.), *Retreat from empire?—The first Nixon administration.* Baltimore: Johns Hopkins University Press, 1973.

U. S. Senate, Committee on the Judiciary, Hearings before the Subcommittee on Constitutional Rights. *Military surveillance.* April 9–10, 1974. (a)

U. S. Senate, Committee on the Judiciary, Hearings before the Subcommittee on Criminal Laws and Procedures. *Electronic surveillance for national security purposes.* October 1–3, 1974. (b)

U. S. Senate, Select Committee to Study Governmental Operations with Respect to Intelligence Activities. Final report, *Supplementary detailed staff reports on intelligence activities and the rights of Americans,* 94th Congress, 2nd session, 1976.

Weissman, S. (Ed.). *Big brother and the holding company.* Palo Alto, Calif.: Ramparts Press, 1974.

Williams, W. A. *The contours of American history.* Chicago: Quadrangle, 1961.

Wise, D. *The American police state: The government against the people.* New York: Random House, 1976

Promotion of Openness in a Democracy

MARTIN C. FERGUS

Martin C. Fergus earned his A.B. degree from Miami University (Ohio) in 1965, and his M.A. (1971) and Ph.D. (1972) from Harvard University. He has been on the faculty of Fordham University since 1971 and currently is an Associate Professor in the Department of Political Science. Dr. Fergus is a member of the American Political Science Association and the American Society of Public Administration. He is a specialist in American National Government (the Presidency, Congress, and Politics of Public Administration) and his research, publications, and scholarly addresses are devoted principally to these areas.

The right to privacy is a well-established part of Anglo-American political thought and legal tradition. Nevertheless, the right to privacy is not an absolute one, for there are conflicting rights which also make up a part of this tradition. Foremost among these conflicting rights is the public's "right to know," a right which is the necessary underpinning of a democratic system of government (Bathory & McWilliams, 1977). This paper will concern itself with the conflict between the right to privacy and the right of the people to know, in order to determine more clearly the areas in which the value of promoting openness in a democracy can legitimately limit the right to privacy.

What criteria are to be used in making such a judgment? In the final analysis, they must be normative and subjective and must encompass broad assumptions about the nature of the polity itself (Bathory & McWilliams, 1977, p. 5). A useful starting point for such a discussion is an empirical examination of the existing balance between the right to privacy and the people's right to know. In particular, this paper will focus on several aspects of this problem as it applies to the United States. First, it will look (*a*) at recent legislation which has been designed to ensure that people have the knowledge which they need in order to hold governing authorities accountable, and (*b*) at the limits which the right to privacy has placed on such legislative efforts. An analysis of the role of information in democratic politics will follow. For the conflict between privacy and the public's right to know cannot be understood apart from an understanding of the "information marketplace" (Galnoor, 1977b, p. 302), where control over information leads to economic profit and to influence on government policy. Next, a number of examples will be presented to illustrate the openness–privacy conflict. Finally, in the concluding section, we will be in a position to explicate normative criteria for judging the debate between openness and privacy and to apply these criteria to existing legislation and to the information marketplace in the United States.

RECENT LEGISLATION AND THE OPENNESS–PRIVACY ISSUE

Since the mid-1960s, several pieces of legislation have been passed in an effort to promote a more open government. Two major laws in this category are the Freedom of Information Act, which was passed in 1966 and amended in 1974, and the Government in the Sunshine Act, which was passed in 1976. Both laws specifically address the conflict between the public's right to know and the right to privacy.

Freedom of Information Act

The Freedom of Information Act (1966, 1973, amended 1974), Public Law 89–487, was an amendment to the Administrative Procedure Act (1946) which established a public information policy for government agencies. Although the 1946 Act set procedures for releasing government information, it left a great deal of discretion in the hands of the agencies themselves. Information could be withheld from the public if it were "required for good cause to be held confidential" (Administrative Procedure Act, 1946, p. 238), and there was only minimal judicial remedy to such rendering by an agency. In contrast, the Freedom of Information Act broadened the kinds of information which had to be made available, required public agencies to provide requested records expeditiously, "permitted exemption only of matter which met one of nine specific requirements," and provided for court review of negative decisions on the part of administrators when such a review was requested by the person seeking the information ("Freedom of Information Bill Enacted," 1967, p. 556). Of the nine exemptions from the law, two relate most directly to the question of privacy: the fourth—"trade secrets and commercial or financial information obtained from any person and privileged or confidential"—and the sixth—"personnel and medical files and similar files the disclosure of which would constitute a clearly unwarranted invasion of personal privacy" (Freedom of Information Act, 1966, p. 251).

Since the implementation of the Freedom of Information Law, few exemptions have been contested as often as the privacy exemptions (Saloschin, 1975, p. 11). Some of the specific complaints under exemptions four and six were expressed by John Shattuck of the American Civil Liberties Union during hearings held in 1973. In relation to exemption four Shattuck noted:

> The problem with the existing exemption is that it has been claimed by agencies and sometimes interpreted by the courts to apply to non-commercial and financial information which the *agency* rather than the person who provided the information claims is confidential [Freedom of Information Act, 1973, p. 264].

Shattuck noted further (p. 264) that "agencies have also refused under this exemption to disclose commercial information even though it was not 'obtained from a person' but was developed by the agency." In relation to the sixth exemption, Shattuck indicated (p. 265) that agencies were taking the word "files" too literally, refusing to release records from a file if this information happened to be included with other information which did not qualify under exemption six. When the Act was amended in 1974, although a number of changes which strengthened the Act were made ("Freedom of Information veto overriden," 1975, pp. 648–654), the only change affecting exemptions four and six was a requirement that exempted portions from requested records be deleted and the remainder of the records be released (Amendments to the Freedom of Information Act, 1974, pp. 1561–1564). Exemption four, which is of particular importance for the analysis which follows, remained unaltered.

Government in Sunshine Act

The second major open-government law to be passed in recent years is the Government in the Sunshine Act (Public Law 94–409). While the Freedom of Information Act is designed to make government records available to the public, the Sunshine Act opens agency meetings to public view. Agencies are required to give advance notice of the date, place, and subject of each meeting and, except for exempted agencies where secrecy is a regular part of their operations, meetings can be closed to the public only by a majority record vote of the participants or, under clearly specified conditions, at the request of a person affected by the deliberations. The public can be excluded only for reasons indicated in the ten specified exemptions listed under the law. If a meeting is held behind closed doors, the specific exemption(s) under which this action is taken must be cited by the agency's chief legal officer and a verbal transcript (or, under certain conditions, minutes) has to be kept and, once exempt portions are deleted, released to the public. Appeal to the courts is provided for, and the burden of proof is placed on the agency involved, rather than on the complainant ("Government in the Sunshine Act cleared," 1976, p. 473).

Seven of the ten exemptions under the Sunshine Act are virtually identical to those under the Freedom of Information Act, even down to the numbering of the exemptions. Thus, the two main exemptions which apply to questions of privacy are again number four, which deals with "trade secrets or financial or commercial information obtained under a pledge of confidentiality," and number six, which relates to "information whose disclosure would constitute an unwarranted invasion of personal privacy" ("Government in the Sunshine Act cleared," 1976, p. 473).

The Sunshine Law also strengthens the Freedom of Information Act itself, for several provisions of the earlier Act had actually been used to *restrict* public access to information. Of particular importance were successful efforts to keep meetings of regulatory commissions and government advisory committees secret in spite of a 1972 law—the Federal Advisory Committee Act (Public Law 92–463)—designed to open them to the public. The 1972 law made such meetings public unless the subject matter to be discussed was covered under the exemptions listed in the Freedom of Information Law. But, in practice, all an agency had to do was to indicate in the Federal Register that the subject matter of the meeting qualified under the exemption section of the Freedom of Information Law, and the meeting was closed. Often specific exemptions were not even cited (Relyea, 1975, pp. 5–6). In order to plug this loophole, the Sunshine Act specifically included regulatory commissions and advisory committees under its jurisdiction and "specified that the provisions of this act would take precedence over the Freedom of Information Act . . . in cases of information requests" ("Government in the Sunshine Act cleared," 1976, pp. 473–474).

Although this examination of open-government laws and some of the difficulties of implementing them has revealed aspects of the openness–privacy conflict, this conflict is not just a question of law. It is also a question of politics, of power, and of political influence. Unless the implications of this fact are made clear, the full ramifications of the openness–privacy debate cannot be understood.

THE INFORMATION MARKETPLACE

Privileged Status of Special Groups

If one looking at the Freedom of Information Act and the Sunshine Act should conclude that the basic conflict over openness in a democracy is between the government, on the one hand, and the public, on the other, this would be an erroneous conclusion. The information marketplace is more complicated. A good deal of information, even highly classified information, may be shared by the government with select groups in the public, while other groups are excluded. Similarly, private groups which possess information may choose to share it with the government, yet decide not to make it available to the general public. Thus the conflict between privacy and openness is most often a contest between government and selected interest groups, on the one hand, and the bulk of the public, on the other.

A critical question to be examined, therefore, is why one group gains the privileged status which entitles it to government information while another does not. Part of the answer is relatively simple: those who already have information are in a position to exchange it for new information from the government; those who have little (or no) information are unlikely to get more. Thus the flow of information in society can be thought of as a marketplace, where "transactions are reciprocal and access to information is gained on an exchange basis" (Galnoor, 1975, p. 35). But not every group which possesses information is made privy to what the government knows. "Some groups are not 'established' simply because they have not been recognized as responsible or respectable enough to share government confidence" (Galnoor, 1975, p. 38). Thus groups can be excluded from the exchange process either because they lack information or because their views are not regarded as legitimate by the government and by already established interest groups.

A group which is part of the information marketplace is in an advantaged position, both economically and politically. When information is restricted to a few hands, its value increases, and it translates not only into financial gain (Lowi, 1977, p. 43), but also into political power (Saloschin, 1974, p. 190; Rourke, 1975, p. 2). In fact, the possession of information often results in direct access to governmental decision-making itself; for, in many areas, the making and implementing of government policy are dependent upon both private sources of information and the cooperation of powerful private-interest groups (Galnoor, 1975, p. 34; Lowi, 1977, p. 55; Beer, 1969, pp. 320–330). Such access in the United States has been institutionalized in the form of "government advisory committees," which consist both of representatives from groups in the private sector and of government officials.

Extension of Secrecy in Government

These committees are the very ones described in the last section in terms of their success in maintaining the secrecy of their meetings even in the face of the Freedom of Information Act and the Federal Advisory Committee Act. The mechanism of the government advisory committee has been resorted to so often that one recent inventory counted "over 1,400 advisory committees attached to various agencies in the federal government" (Nadel, 1975, p. 16).

The kinds of relationships established by the government advisory committees also develop in areas where the government is supposed to regulate the interests of private groups for the public good. Thus government regulatory bodies often engage in the same kind of cooperative secrecy as advisory committees and agencies do. The Food and Drug Administration, for example, has withheld brand names of defective products from the public because of the damage which revealing them might cause the offending firms. As one author observes, this represents "a policy that shows far greater concern for the agency's business interests than for its wider public constituency" (Nadel, 1975, pp. 17–18).

One of the impacts of these relationships is on the nature of government secrecy itself. In contrast to the conclusion of some authors that secrecy is largely the product of the standard operating procedures of government bureaucracies (Wellford, 1974, p. 206), the evidence indicates that secrecy results most often from the needs of private interest groups (Galnoor, 1977b, p. 304). Thus the right to privacy, particularly as it is expressed in exemption four of both the Freedom of Information Act and the Sunshine Act, becomes the means whereby certain powerful interests in society influence government agencies while denying such access and influence to other groups and to the general public (Curzon, 1977, pp. 103, 105; Nadel, 1975, p. 21). Any lessening of government secrecy, therefore, has the potential of altering the existing authority structures of society (Lowi, 1977, p. 57; Nadel, 1975, p. 22).

Obviously, the openness–privacy issue is a complex one, and a thorough examination of it will lead into questions concerning the very nature of the polity itself. But before we examine these questions, let us look at some examples of the operation of the information marketplace.

EXAMPLES ILLUSTRATING THE OPENNESS–PRIVACY CONFLICT

This section will examine four areas of the information marketplace which vividly reveal important aspects of the openness–privacy conflict. These include the operation of government advisory committees, cooperation between the government and private groups to withhold records from the public, information sharing between government officials and certain private groups, and, finally, the exception which proves the rule—what happens when a government official publicly reveals information which was meant to be shared only by the government and privileged-interest groups.

Government Advisory Committees

The operation of government advisory committees will be examined by looking at the establishment of U. S. trade policies in three areas: steel quotas, oil imports, and textiles. In the case of steel, pressures for a quota system began to be exerted in 1967 when stiff foreign competition was capturing a larger and larger share of the American market. The State Department determined that the solution to the "problem" was the negotiation of voluntary import quotas with those nations which were the major suppliers of foreign steel. During these negotiations, the State Department consulted with domestic steel producers (but not domestic steel consumers), informing them of the foreign proposals and soliciting their "views, reactions, and concerns" (Frank, 1974, p. 276). The result of these negotiations was a series of agreements which set voluntary quotas, running from 1968 to 1971, for the import of foreign steel.

By 1971, when a new round of negotiations was to begin, the impact of the earlier agreements was clearly being felt by consumers. Concerned with rising steel prices, Consumers Union approached the State Department to express its views. The department willingly listened to the arguments of the group, but was "unwilling to provide, either informally or in formal proceedings, the statistics or analyses behind their decision that limitations were necessary, or to be specific about the status or objectives of the negotiations" (Frank, 1974, p. 277). Clearly, the rules of the information marketplace were in operation, and the interests of some groups were being protected by the government at the expense of other groups and, ultimately, of the public at large. (Subsequent court action on the part of Consumers Union had not reached a final resolution at the time of Frank's study.)

The case of the oil-import program is very similar to the example of steel quotas. Again, domestic companies were suffering from foreign competition, and industry representatives were interested in reducing imports of foreign oil. One legal mechanism for accomplishing this was the Mandatory Oil Import Program, which permitted the establishment of oil-import quotas if this should prove necessary for reasons of national security. On the theory that foreign competition would lead to a decline in the development of U. S. reserves, thus rendering the country vulnerable to foreign boycotts, President Eisenhower invoked the statute in 1959. This was done on the determination of the Director of the Office of Emergency Preparedness that national security was involved and on "the recommendation of a government–business advisory committee . . ." (Frank, 1974, p. 282). Over the years, changes in this program were discussed with oil industry representatives but, in violation of provisions of the Trade Expansion Act of 1962 and the Administrative Procedure Act of 1946, consumer groups were completely excluded from this process. Finally during 1973, while a court challenge by consumer groups was pending, the President eliminated oil-import quotas. Though it accomplished one of the plaintiffs' major objectives, this decision was made in typical fashion, "without the public investigation" required by law and in "intimate collaboration with industry but virtually no contact with the plaintiffs or other consumers" (Frank, 1974, p. 284). Thus, in spite of the fact that in one year alone (1969) the oil-import program had cost consumers $5.26 billion (Frank, 1974, p. 282), consumer groups were not considered legitimate participants in the oil-quota decision-making process.

Our final example of government advisory committees involves the textile industry. In 1962, the Management–Labor Textile Advisory Committee was established to "provide advice and information" to the government "on conditions in the textile industry, and on trade in textiles and apparel" (Frank, 1974, p. 286). This committee, as the name implies, included representatives from both producers and labor, but none from consumer groups. Although by mid-1972 the committee was required under executive order 11671 to open its meetings to the public, a secret meeting was held in August 1972 in violation of this requirement. When the committee was scheduled to meet in September, the meeting was again closed to the public, this time on the basis of the foreign policy exemption, claimed because, in the words of the Secretary of Commerce,

> The Government receives from members of the Committee sensitive information which they receive from various sources on the attitude of foreign governments in the negotiations which the Government is undertaking. The Government discusses with the members of the Committee possible negotiating positions as to specific levels of restraint in order to receive their evaluation of the effect of such proposed levels on the domestic industry. . . . If the meeting were open to the public, the foreign policy interest of the United States Government would be substantially compromised. It would not be possible to have the kind of candid discussion that has existed at meetings of this Committee over the last decade. Public participation at the meeting would reduce its effectiveness to the point where it would be meaningless to hold the meeting [cited in Frank, 1974, pp. 286–287].

Neither the foreign policy exemption, nor the exemption for "privileged or confidential commercial or financial information," was applicable to the kind of subject matter discussed at this meeting. Furthermore, the whole issue of the sensitive nature of the information is thrown into question for, although "its revelation to representatives of concerned consumer groups or public groups" is precluded, "at the same time, it is being revealed to forty-odd representatives of labor and management with presumably diverse interests" (Frank, 1974, p. 287). Clearly, the information marketplace is again in operation, with advantages to some groups at the expense of others.

Withholding Government Records

One can detect a government–interest group collaboration not only in meetings of government advisory committees, but also in the government's reluctance to release certain records to the general public. We have already noted one such case in the refusal of the Food and Drug Administration to release brand names of defective products. Two additional examples involve information on natural gas supplies in the United States and records revealing which American firms were participating in the Arab economic boycott of Israel.

The natural gas controversy developed in 1973, the year in which President Nixon proposed deregulation of natural gas from new wells. The effect of this proposal would have been to remove this particular gas from the authority of the Federal Power Commission (FPC) to regulate the price of natural gas moving in interstate commerce. The theory behind the proposal was that the low price of natural gas was discouraging new exploration and thereby reducing the known supply of natural gas reserves. In support of the President's position, there was a study which had been released by the FPC in February 1973 which indicated that "natural gas reserves had declined 26 per cent between the end of 1969 and mid-1972 and were at a level about 9 per cent below that estimated by the gas industry" ("Natural Gas Deregulation," 1974, p. 641).

A number of Senate opponents of the President's policy were suspicious of both the industry figures and the figures from the FPC. Then in June 1973 James T. Halverson, an FPC investigator, stated that "records of natural gas producers showed gas reserves were up to 1,000 per cent greater than the firms had reported to the American Gas Association ("Natural Gas Deregulation," 1974, p. 641). Documents were then turned over to the Senate Judiciary Antitrust and Monopoly Subcommittee which showed that the 79 questionnaires from producers which had been used to compile data for the FPC study had been destroyed on orders of Lawrence R. Mangen of the FPC's Bureau of Natural Gas. According to Mangen, this was done because "it was his understanding that these confidential reports were to be destroyed or returned" to the firms which had supplied them ("Natural Gas Deregulation," 1974, p. 641). Was there a gas shortage? Though there is no certain answer to this question, it is certain that information which might have helped to provide an answer was deliberately withheld from both the Congress and the public through the cooperative actions of the Bureau of Natural Gas and the natural gas producers.

A second case of keeping information from the public involves the attempt by Arab nations to force American firms to join their boycott of Israel. This was accomplished, for example, by requiring companies which signed contracts with Arab nations to agree to boycott goods made in Israel or goods made by firms which did business in Israel. Under U. S. law and Department of Commerce regulations, U. S. firms were required to inform the Department whenever they received such boycott requests and, furthermore, whether or not they had complied. One irony of the situation was that, although it was the President's stated policy that "Such discrimination is totally contrary to the American tradition and repugnant to American principles," at the same time the Department of Commerce "circulated to U. S. firms business offers or tenders from Arab countries that contain boycott restrictions" ("Arab Boycott Records," 1976, p. 344).

It was under these circumstances that, in July 1975, the House Interstate and Foreign Commerce Subcommittee subpoenaed Commerce Department records in order "to gain information from Commerce Secretary Rogers C. B. Morton on the U. S. participation in the boycott" ("U. S. Policy Probed: Congress Studies Impact of Arab Boycott," 1975, p. 2243). Morton refused to turn over the information to the subcommittee and, in response to a lawsuit instituted by the American Jewish Congress, argued that releasing the names of the firms would only serve to make them subject to "obvious counter measures and pressures by various individuals and groups" ("U. S. Policy Probed: Congress Studies Impact of Arab Boycott," 1975, p. 2244). Throughout the late summer and early fall Morton maintained his position vis-à-vis the subcommittee. Finally, in mid-November, the subcommittee voted, along party lines, to cite Morton for contempt of Congress. Had the full committee also voted to cite him, as it was expected to do, the resolution would have gone to the floor of the House for final action ("Panel Cites Morton: Contempt Recommendation," 1975, p. 2490).

But late in November Morton agreed to turn over the requested information to the subcommittee, on the condition that its chairman, John E. Moss, pledge to keep the material confidential. Morton argued that confidentiality was necessary because the Export Administration Act of 1969 forbade making such information public, but Moss refused to agree to it before seeing the information. Finally, on December 8, Morton promised to provide the subpoenaed records to the subcommittee with the understanding that the information would be released to the public only if a majority of the subcommittee voted to do so. In order to allow Morton to save face,

> both sides agreed to disagree, in effect, over the meaning of the agreement. . . . The department maintained publicly that its understanding from Moss was that the committee would not vote to make the material public. But the subcommittee insisted that it could treat the information as members saw fit ["Moss Subcommittee: Arab Boycott Records," 1975, p. 2708].

Eventually, although the Ford Administration backed off from an earlier pledge, made under the pressure of the re-election campaign, to make public a list of those firms which had been a part of the boycott, the President did agree to release the names of all firms which joined the boycott after October 7, 1976 ("Export Bill Killed Over Anti-Boycott Issue," 1976, p. 259). Attempts legally to require the collection and publication of the names of all firms participating in the boycott failed, however, when legislation containing these provisions died at the end of 1976 with the expiration of the 94th Congress ("Export Bill Killed Over the Anti-Boycott Issue," 1976, pp. 257, 259).

Information Sharing Between Government and Private Groups

This section will examine in some detail one case of information sharing, and then briefly indicate the existence of two related examples. Our central case concerns the relationship between the Central Intelligence Agency (CIA) and the International Telephone and Telegraph Company (ITT) on the matter of policy toward Chile in the early-1970s. The cooperation between the CIA and ITT on this matter was so close that at times their roles seemed almost to merge, the result, in part, of the membership in 1970 of John McCone, a former director of the CIA, on the board of directors of ITT.

The cooperation between the CIA and ITT existed at several different levels, including the sharing of intelligence data, the discussing of policy options and the ways in which both ITT and the CIA could aid in implementing them, and the exploration of the possibility of financing CIA projects with ITT money. In the area of intelligence gathering, McCone described his contacts with CIA director Helms in the following terms: "The purpose of my discussion with Mr. Helms was to reflect to him and through him . . . the views of informed people in ITT on the possible outcome of the election," and to alert him to the implications of an Allende victory ("Multinational Probe Hits ITT Involvement in Chile," 1974, p. 846). After the Helms–McCone meeting, William Merriam, a vice president of ITT, and William Broe, chief of the CIA's clandestine services for the Western Hemisphere, also met and "exchanged information on the situation in Chile" ("Multinational Probe Hits ITT Involvement in Chile," 1974, p. 847). Thus, while the public remained in the dark, the government shared highly secret information with a privileged corporation, and the corporation provided its own intelligence in return.

But CIA–ITT cooperation involved more than an exchange of information. Merriam provided Broe with a list of policy recommendations, and Broe, who agreed with the recommendations, suggested that ITT put pressure on the White House to have the recommendations adopted. Merriam subsequently explored a number of policy options with White House staffers John Erlichman and Peter Peterson, who was an adviser on international economic policy. For his part, Broe met with Edward Gerrity, another ITT vice president, to examine "the feasibility of possible actions to apply some economic pressure on Chile" ("Multinational Probe Hits ITT Involvement in Chile," 1974, p. 847). Options discussed at this meeting included possible actions both on the part of the government and on the part of U. S. business interests. Among the options were "the delay or cessation of bank credits, withdrawal of technical assistance," and "a slow-down by companies in spending money, making deliveries and shipping spare parts" ("Multinational Probe Hits ITT Involvement in Chile," 1974, p. 848). Broe also passed on to Gerrity a list of companies with interests in Chile which might be called upon to cooperate if these plans were implemented ("Multinational Probe Hits ITT Involvement in Chile," 1974, p. 848). Such "joint projects" seemed simply a matter of routine to CIA and ITT officials.

Finally, on two occasions, ITT offered to finance several CIA operations in Chile. In the first instance, before the election was held, ITT offered to supply funds to help finance Allende's opponents. The second offer, made between the time Allende received a plurality at the polls and the time when the Chilean congress would meet to select a president because no candidate had received a majority, ITT offered the U. S. government $1 million for use in influencing the vote and for possible efforts to destabilize the Chilean economy. The suggestion made by McCone and ITT board chairman Harold Geneen during congressional hearings that this $1 million was actually to be used for "constructive" projects such as "housing and technical and agricultural assistance" was belied by documentary evidence and by the testimony of other witnesses ("Multinational Probe Hits ITT Involvement in Chile," 1974, pp. 846, 848).

Mr. Geneen defended all these activities in the following words:

> I firmly believe that fair-minded persons would agree that ITT should have tried to protect its investment in Chile in the face of a Marxist takeover and all that it implies, and that we should have sought the help of our own government ["Multinational Probe Hits ITT Involvement in Chile," 1974, p. 848].

In response to this statement, Senator Church observed that describing the interaction between ITT and the U. S. Government in terms which might be used to describe a citizen petitioning his government was, to say the least, highly misleading ("Multinational Probe Hits ITT Involvement in Chile," 1974, p. 849). The real nature of the relationship, in contrast, was accurately indicated by a question from Senator Case: "Is the CIA working for the United States or for ITT and McCone?" ("Multinational Probe Hits ITT Involvement in Chile," 1974, p. 848).

The example of cooperation between ITT and the CIA may seem to be unique only because a great deal of evidence has been accumulated about these dealings, but such relationships appear to be the norm rather than the exception. Such a pooling of information, covered by a cloak of secrecy, enabled a number of large grain dealers to make huge windfall profits on the Soviet wheat deal in 1972 (Krebs, 1975, pp. 353–372). Similarly, through access to government officials, secrecy, and perhaps even market manipulation, milk producers were able to increase their profits through a rise in price support levels in 1971 (Wright, 1971, pp. 17–21). One could cite other examples, but the conclusion is already clear: to be a participant in the information marketplace is to be in a position to exercise significant political power and to gain substantial financial rewards.

Blowing the Whistle: The Exception Which Proves the Rule

If it is instructive to examine cases where government–interest-group secrecy operates for the benefit of those involved, it is also educational to explore what happens when someone violates the rules of the information marketplace and "goes public" with privileged information. In this connection, it should first be noted that even existing legal regulations imply that the right of corporations to privacy is more important than the right of the public to know. Thus a public official "is held individually accountable under criminal statutes for releasing trade secrets or other confidential commercial information," while "the public official who illegally refuses to release information is subject to no civil or criminal penalty" (Wellford, 1974, pp. 209, 210). Furthermore, efforts to amend the Freedom of Information Act to give the courts the power to discipline civil servants who violate the law failed, although a provision was enacted which made civil servants who "capriciously or arbitrarily" withhold information from the public subject to disciplinary action by the Civil Service Commission ("Freedom of Information Veto Overridden," 1975, pp. 648–649).

What happens when an official decides that the public's right to know is being subverted and he makes information available to the public? All too often the result is the loss of his government job and blackballing by private industry. Not only was the man who revealed the cost overruns on the C5A transport plane, for example, fired on personal instructions from President Nixon, he was also unable to return to the defense consulting work he had done before his Pentagon days. In his words, "My status as a Pentagon-designated outlaw automatically made me an outcast with major institutions having an interest in getting along with the military spending complex" (Fitzgerald, 1974, p. 257). In another case, two union officials who worked on a military reservation informed members of Congress that the procurement office was accepting delivery on faulty helicopter parts. Both men were fired, and one of them was nearly beaten to death by government security officers (Fitzgerald, 1974, pp. 258–259). One final example involves an official in the Office of Economic Opportunity (OEO), who released some "confidential" information and was suspended from his job. He filed a suit under the Freedom of Information Act to obtain this same information and, even though OEO decided under threat of the law suit to release it, thus tacitly acknowledging that the information should not have been kept secret, OEO "refused to lift his suspension" (Wellford, 1974, p. 210).

Cases such as these, and more examples could be cited from both government and the private sector (see, e.g., Fitzgerald, 1974, *passim*), are the exceptions which prove the rule. Although they reveal that the web of government–interest-group secrecy can be broken, they also show the price which is exacted from the person who "blows the whistle." Those who violate the rules of the information marketplace must bear the consequences.

LIMITS TO PRIVACY

Now that our empirical examination has revealed the general nature of the conflict between privacy and open government, what can we say about legitimate limits to privacy? An essential lesson to recall in this connection is that we are not dealing simply with the rights of the individual as opposed to the rights of society. Rather, the privacy–openness conflict is most accurately portrayed as a contest between government and select interest groups, on the one hand, and the bulk of the public, on the other. The central issue to be examined here is thus whether the privacy of interest groups should be limited in order to promote the value of openness in a democracy.

Criteria for Limiting Privacy of Interest Groups

To develop criteria for making such a judgment, we must first understand the nature of the value which is served by an open democracy. A recent analysis of some major theorists of democracy makes clear that the central value promoted by the public's right to know is the protection of the power of the people to govern (Bay, 1977). Thus our basic criterion for assessing the openness–privacy issue is: *the power of the people to govern must be ensured.* Establishing a democratic process, however, does not explicitly define the ends of that process. Therefore, we must delineate a second criterion, which is assumed by the first and deals with the ends of democracy: *decisions of the polity must promote the good of the community rather than benefit the few at the expense of the many.* This second criterion, of course, poses a difficulty of its own. Even the strongest defenders of democracy worried about the possibility, in de Tocqueville's words (1882, pp. 330–345), of the "Tyranny of the Majority." Thus we would want to supplement our first two criteria with a third: *policies must promote the human rights of individual members of society.* In the sense used here, human rights include not only political freedom, but also economic freedom—including such things as access to adequate nutrition, health care, and education—which is essential if individuals are to be able to fulfill their full potential.

Does the existing equation between openness and privacy in American society serve such democratic goals? Some analysts would argue that it does. Rourke (1975), for example, writes:

> The task of striking a balance between legitimate claims for withholding information and the essential right of the public to know what is going on in their own government is largely accomplished in the American system of democracy by the interplay of competing organizations [p. 2].

Rourke argues that, although there are many pressures for secrecy, these are countered by Congress, "an increasingly influential constellation of news organizations, and reform groups with active and effective representation in Washington" (p. 2).

Prospects for a Balance in Openness–Privacy

The empircal evidence presented in this paper, however, reveals a picture, not of balance, but of overwhelming imbalance. Privileged groups in the information marketplace dominate in decisions on such matters as trade policy, the development and use of the nation's natural and agricultural resources, and the relations of this society with the peoples of other nations. Policy is made in the day-to-day contacts between government officials and those in the private sector who possess the valuable commodity of information, not in the open arena of democratic politics. The criteria outlined above, therefore, are not being met. Instead of rule by the people, there is rule by privileged interest groups. Instead of policies for the benefit of the community, in numerous instances we have seen policies for the benefit of the select few. Instead of the protection of human rights, our evidence shows a limitation of freedom both for those who are deprived of the economic necessities and for those who are coerced by social and economic pressure to comply with the rules of the information marketplace.

Actually, this empirical evidence should not surprise us, for the groups which Rourke describes as defenders of the public's right to know are often unwilling or unable to perform that role. In spite of our own examples which do show that Congressional committees can be a force for openness, congressional committees have often relied upon secrecy in their own deliberations, with the same effect as executive secrecy has had: namely, the dominance of privileged interest groups in the policymaking process (Nader, 1975, pp. xi–xxiii). In addition, the press, in spite of its recently gained reputation for investigative reporting, is largely dependent upon government sources for stories. To make bureaucrats unhappy is to be cut off from information vital to a reporter's success. The reporter's normal role, therefore, tends to be more as an adjunct to standard bureaucratic politics than as an independent force for openness in a democracy (Sigal, 1973). Finally, public interest groups, which often are supportive of the people's right to know, lack the kind of information resources and access to government policy-making which producer groups possess. Therefore, although public interest groups can have an influence on policy, particularly when up-coming elections make politicians unusually sensitive to public opinion (Beer, 1969, pp. 339–349), they are much less influential than producer groups in the day-to-day decision-making which determines the major directions of government policy.

But what of the Freedom of Information Act and the Sunshine Act—do not these laws provide solutions to the problems outlined above? Unfortunately, it seems that, up to now, such laws have done more to define the problem than to solve it. Policymaking by private groups has continued, in spite of the law. When attempts have been made to close old avenues of influence, new ones have been found. Furthermore, not only have the new legal means for obtaining information from the government proved less effective than the established routes (Galnoor, 1977a, p. vii), but the legal means which are provided are most often used, not by public interest groups, but by the private corporations themselves (Wellford, 1974, p. 196). Why have these laws been less than fully effective? The most obvious reason is that certain groups which hold the predominant power in society benefit from the existing relationships. It is not in their interest to allow changes in society's authority structure, and those who could benefit from such a change lack the power to bring it about. Thus one major conclusion must be that the problem of openness in a democracy cannot be solved simply by efforts to expose government decision-making to the light of day. The problem is deeper than this, going to the very roots of our political and economic system.

The real issue is whether, in a democracy, it is legitimate for private groups to monopolize important information and thus greatly to affect decisions fundamental to the well-being of the entire society. In essence, then, the openness–privacy debate raises basic questions about the nature of the polity itself. To the extent that one accepts the role of private groups as decision-makers for society, then the balance described by Rourke, in spite of its deficiencies, is the best which can be hoped for. Small improvements may be possible, but the central character of the process will remain unaltered. On the other hand, if one truly values democratic precepts, one must recognize the necessity of qualifying the right to privacy. If the ends of democracy are to be accomplished, the right to privacy for privileged interest groups must be substantially circumscribed. Accomplishing this goal, of course, would be exceedingly difficult. But an important first step in this direction is the recognition that such a limitation of privacy is made fully legitimate by the need for openness in a democracy, by the right of the people to know.

REFERENCES

Administrative Procedure Act. *United States Statutes at Large*, 79th Congress, 2nd session, 1946, *60*, Pt. 1, 237–244.

Amendments to the Freedom of Information Act. *United States Statutes at Large*, 93rd Congress, 2nd session, 1974, *88*, Pt. 2, 1561–1565.

Arab boycott records. *1975 Congressional Quarterly Almanac, 31.* Washington, D.C.: Congressional Quarterly, 1976.

Bathory, P. D, & McWilliams, W. C. Political theory and the people's right to know. In I. Galnoor (Ed.), *Government secrecy in democracies.* New York: Harper & Row, 1977.

Bay, C. Access to political knowledge as a human right. In I. Galnoor (Ed.), *Government secrecy in democracies.* New York: Harper & Row, 1977.

Beer, S. H. *British politics in the collectivist age.* New York: Random House, 1969.

Curzon, D. The generic secrets of government decision making. In I. Galnoor (Ed.), *Government secrecy in democracies.* New York: Harper & Row, 1977.

Export Bill killed over anti-boycott issue. *1976 Congressional Quarterly Almanac, 32.* Washington, D.C.: Congressional Quarterly, 1976.

Fitzgerald, E. Blowing the whistle on the Pentagon. In N. Dorsen & S. Gillers (Eds.), *None of your business: Government secrecy in America.* New York: Viking, 1974.

Frank, R. A. Enforcing the public's right to openness in the foreign affairs decision-making process. In T. M. Franck & E. Weisband (Eds.), *Secrecy and foreign policy.* New York: Oxford University Press, 1974.

Freedom of Information Act. *United States Statutes at Large*, 89th Congress, 2nd session, 1966, *80*, Pt. 1, 250–251.

Freedom of Information Act. *Hearings before a subcommittee of the Committee on Government Operations, House of Representatives, 93rd Congress, 1st session, on H. R. 5425 and H. R. 4960, on May 2, 7, 8, 10, and 16, 1973.* Washington, D.C.: Government Printing Office, 1973.

Freedom of Information Bill enacted. *1966 Congressional Quarterly Almanac, 22.* Washington, D.C.: Congressional Quarterly, 1967.

Freedom of Information veto overridden. *1974 Congressional Quarterly Almanac, 30.* Washington, D.C.: Congressional Quarterly, 1975.

Galnoor, I. Government secrecy: Exchanges, intermediaries, and middlemen. *Public Administration Review*, 1975, *35*, 32–42.

Galnoor, I. Editor's preface. In I. Galnoor (Ed.), *Government secrecy in democracies*. New York: Harper & Row, 1977. (a)

Galnoor, I. What do we know about government secrecy? In I. Galnoor (Ed.), *Government secrecy in democracies*. New York: Harper & Row, 1977. (b)

Government in the Sunshine Act cleared. *1976 Congressional Quarterly Almanac, 32*. Washington, D.C.: Congressional Quarterly, 1976.

Krebs, A. V. Of the grain trade, by the grain trade, and for the grain trade. In C. Lerza & M. Jacobson (Eds.), *Food for people not for profit*. New York: Ballantine Books, 1975.

Lowi, T. J. The information revolution, politics, and the prospects for an open society. In I. Galnoor (Ed.), *Government secrecy in democracies*. New York: Harper & Row, 1977.

Moss Subcommittee: Arab boycott records. *Congressional Quarterly Weekly Report*, December 13, 1975, *33*, No. 50, 2708.

Multinational probe hits ITT involvement in Chile. *1973 Congressional Quarterly Almanac, 29*. Washington, D.C.: Congressional Quarterly, 1974.

Nadel, M. V. Corporate secrecy and political accountability. *Public Administration Review*, 1975, *35*, 14–23.

Nader, R. Introduction. In R. Spohn & C. McCollum (Directors, Ralph Nader Congress Project), *The revenue committees*. New York: Grossman, 1975.

Natural gas deregulation. *1973 Congressional Quarterly Almanac, 29*. Washington, D.C.: Congressional Quarterly, 1974.

Panel cites Morton: Contempt recommendation. *Congressional Quarterly Weekly Report*, November 15, 1975, *33*, No. 46, 2490–2491.

Relyea, H. C. Opening government to public scrutiny: A decade of federal efforts. *Public Administration Review*, 1975, *35*, 3–10.

Rourke, F. E. Introduction to a symposium on administrative secrecy: A comparative perspective. *Public Administration Review*, 1975, *35*, 1–2.

Saloschin, R. L. Administering the Freedom of Information Act: An insider's view. In N. Dorsen & S. Gillers (Eds.), *None of your business: Government secrecy in America*. New York: Viking, 1974.

Saloschin, R. L. The Freedom of Information Act: A governmental perspective. *Public Administration Review*, 1975, *35*, 10–14.

Sigal, L. Bureaucratic objectives and tactical uses of the press. *Public Administration Review*, 1973, *33*, 336–345.

Tocqueville, A. de. *Democracy in America* (Vol. 1) (H. Reeve, trans.). Boston: Allyn, 1882.

U. S. policy probed: Congress studies impact of Arab boycott. *Congressional Quarterly Weekly Report*, October 18, 1975, *33*, No. 42, 2243–2245.

Wellford, H. Rights of people: The Freedom of Information Act. In N. Dorsen & S. Gillers (Eds.), *None of your business: Government secrecy in America*. New York: Viking, 1974.

Wright, F. The dairy lobby buys the cream of the Congress. *The Washington Monthly*, 1971, *3*, 17–21.

V

NON-LEGITIMATE LIMITATIONS: THE ASSAULT ON PRIVACY

Some Problems of Privacy and Surveillance in a Technological Age

JOSEPH F. KUBIS

Joseph F. Kubis received his B.A. degree from St. John's University, and his M.A. and Ph.D. degrees from Fordham University. He has been a career-long member of the Fordham faculty, where he is professor of psychology, and a past chairman of the Department. Dr. Kubis has been a consultant to NASA almost from the beginning and is the recipient of its Certificate of Excellence Award for his work on the psychological aspects of space-flights, especially long-duration flights. He is a pioneer in lie detection, both by voice analysis and polygraph methods, and his principal publications deal with these topics as well as with the psychological effects of space flights. A former president of the American Catholic Psychological Association, Dr. Kubis is a member of the American Psychological Association, the Psychometric Society, the American Mathematical Society, and the American Statistical Association.

Not so very long ago, a person who wanted to keep some information from being generally available knew how to go about it. The drawn shade and the closed door preserved the privacy of his behavior; the locked drawer contained his confidential documents; only the ear of a trusted ally heard his secrets. His techniques to forestall discovery were of the same order as, and by and large adequate to, the means which others might employ to force disclosure. Although, to be sure, groups and governments always had resources surpassing those of a single individual, essentially it was a matter of the eye, ear, and brain of one human being matched against the eyes, ears, and brains of other human beings. In that sense, and to that extent, the competition was reasonably equal.

But mankind has not rested content with the sense organs and memory which constituted its naturally given equipment. In his unceasing quest for knowledge, man has invented sensors which can pick up vibrations which he can neither see nor hear, and transform that energy into perceptible modalities, thus vastly extending the powers of his eyes and ears. He has created a crude model of his own brain, and found to his wonderment that it can compute with an accuracy and speed which he can barely imagine, and can remember with an exactitude which embarrasses human recall. While rejoicing in the benefits which these new and powerful tools have brought about, mankind has become uneasy. Human capabilities man knew and could control; unfamiliar with the capabilities of the new information technology, he perceives that its control lies exclusively in the hands of those who have specialized access to it. The individual who wishes to keep personal data to himself is no longer dealing on equal terms with his own kind; he is matched against machines. How will he restore the balance?

He must restrain the use of information-gathering, -processing, and -storing devices and techniques; that would seem the obvious solution. Yet on what grounds may he ask the legal structures of society to grant him this remedy? What right does he have? The answer being put forth with increasing force and cogency in recent years is "the right to privacy."

RECENT BACKGROUND

Thirteen years ago, Westin (1967) published a masterful exposition of the interlocking relationships existing among privacy, surveillance, and disclosure. Entitled *Privacy and Freedom*, the book presented compelling evidence that the delicate balance between privacy and surveillance was indeed being threatened by the pervasive technological advances of modern times. Miniaturized microphones and recorders, cheap but powerful transmitters, and sophisticated photographic systems sensitive to very low light levels can see and hear individuals wherever they may be, day or night, providing easy access to their most intimate moments. High-speed computers process and distribute diverse bits of information garnered from the myriads of records now available about each individual. His home, his person, and even his mind are potentially at the disposal of others' curiosity.

Despite the importance which he accords to privacy, Westin holds that an individual's right to privacy is not absolute, but is accompanied by a corresponding obligation to disclose as much information about himself as is necessary for the proper functioning of society. For its part, society has a particularly urgent need to protect itself against antisocial behavior, and hence a corresponding right to engage in information-seeking or surveillance activities. The latter are divided by Westin into three categories: physical surveillance, such as photography and wiretapping; psychological surveillance, by means of such instruments as polygraphs and personality tests; and data surveillance, exemplified by large computer systems processing and exchanging information about individuals. Westin's extensive study also included the conditions or limitations which may be placed upon the legitimate use of these classes of surveillance. His carefully documented treatise provided a strong impetus for further development of the issues which he had raised.

In 1971, Miller published his book *The Assault on Privacy*, which amplified one aspect of Westin's concern for the facility with which the right to privacy can be abrogated by modern technology. Miller described in detail the ease with which a variety of government and private agencies can gain access to giant data banks, and left no doubt that the very existence of such active storehouses of information poses a continual threat to individual privacy. That same year, the proceedings of an interdisciplinary conference on a similar topic, sponsored by the American Society for Political and Legal Philosophy, appeared in book form under the title *Privacy* (Pennock & Chapman, 1971). Meanwhile, a steady stream of legal articles continued to analyze the concept of privacy in the light of the 1965 Supreme Court decision in the case of *Griswold v. Connecticut* (Note 1). It is this decision which has been widely hailed as a landmark, in that it established a constitutional basis for the "right to privacy," thus guaranteeing its protection as a fundamental right under American law.

With these developments as a background, it is the purpose of the present paper to review some of the more recent interpretations and formulations of the privacy concept, and to examine and evaluate the state of the art in surveillance technology. Inasmuch as the defining characteristics of privacy may serve to identify the invasive aspects of surveillance, various descriptions of privacy will be considered first.

PRIVACY

Any attempt to relate privacy to surveillance encounters immediate obstacles by reason of the complexity of the privacy construct itself. Almost universally, writers on privacy have stressed the many difficulties in defining the concept, and have lamented the lack of a satisfactory unitary solution. Thus, Miller (1971) finds the notion of privacy "exasperatingly vague and evanescent" (p. 25); Gross (1967) warns that it is "infected with pernicious ambiguities" (p. 35); and Dixon (1965) complains that "few concepts [are] more vague or less amenable to definition and structured treatment than privacy" (p. 199).

Definitions of Privacy

Nevertheless, among the various definitions of privacy which have been proposed, a number of distinctive elements may be identified: access to oneself, information about the self, respect for the person or for human dignity, autonomy, and personal space. In general, these elements are not independent; the interrelation of more than one element is usually implied in any particular definition

Access to oneself. The classic Warren and Brandeis (1890) definition of the right to privacy as the "right to be let alone" clearly involves control of access to oneself. Equally succinct but more specific in its connotation is Parker's (1974) recent definition of privacy as "control over who can sense us" (p. 280). It may be noted that, although the Warren and Brandeis definition offers no explicit caveat against covert surveillance, Parker's definition specifically protects the individual against any unwanted observation. As an additional distinction, separation from society seems more total in the Warren and Brandeis expression. A potential source of difficulty in the Parker definition is the meaning to be attached to the word "sense." The effectiveness of modern surveillance techniques resides precisely in their capability of acquiring information far beyond the limits of the human sensory apparatus. It is not certain whether Parker intended to include technical sensors in his definition, although his choice of an unaccustomed usage would seem to suggest that he might well have.

Information about the self. Control of information about oneself is the essential feature of a number of definitions. Westin (1967), for example, holds that "Privacy is the claim of individuals, groups, or institutions to determine for themselves when, how, and to what extent information about them is communicated to others" (p. 7). Similarly, Miller (1971) claims that "the basic attribute of an effective right of privacy is the individual's ability to control the circulation of information relating to him" (p. 25). Lusky (1972) points out that these definitions are too broad, in that they imply an invasion of privacy whenever two neighbors discuss a third without the latter's consent. A more important defect from the point of view of the present paper is the absence of specific mention of information gathering, and of the necessity of protecting the individual against intrusive techniques. Thus, no distinction is drawn between two different types of information transfer: acquisition and dissemination. Although logically one cannot have the latter without the former, nevertheless each would seem to require its own set of regulatory principles.

In a position similar to that of Westin and of Miller, Fried (1968) considers privacy to be "that aspect of social order by which persons control access to information about themselves" (p. 493). But because privacy is "a context for respect, love, friendship and trust . . . a threat to privacy seems to threaten our very integrity as persons" (p. 477). In this formulation there is no explicit allusion to the dissemination of information, as found in Westin and in Miller. But Fried introduces the notion of a close connection between privacy and integrity of personality, and his strong emphasis on this point provides a transition to the next class of definitions: that relating privacy to an inviolate personality.

Respect for human dignity. "Respect for the person" and a "proper regard for human dignity" may usually be considered synonymous when referred to privacy. Thus Benn (1971) suggests that "a general principle of privacy might be grounded on the more general principle of respect of persons" (p. 8). He feels that violations of privacy invariably degrade the status of people to that of "objects or specimens." To be watched, as one would watch a thing or an animal, is an affront to human dignity in that it treats the person as a lesser creature, which one has the "right" to observe with impunity. Covert surveillance would seem particularly reprehensible, for to the reduction in status it adds the element of potential threat, the danger which lurks in being watched unaware.

Bloustein (1964) similarly considers privacy to be an aspect of human dignity. In a vigorous defense of the unitary nature of the "right to privacy," he equates the Warren and Brandeis (1890) principle of "an inviolate personality" with "the individual's independence, dignity, and integrity; it defines man's essence as a unique and self-determining being" (p. 971). It may be noted in passing that, as Gross (1967) indicates in a critical review of the privacy concept, Bloustein has shown why the interest being protected by privacy merits legal protection, but has not demonstrated precisely what that interest is.

Autonomy. Bloustein's introduction of the term "independence" in his formulation reveals the manner in which concepts of personal autonomy and privacy are closely interwoven in much thinking on this subject. However, a logical distinction is in order: "While an offense to privacy is an offense to autonomy, not every curtailment of autonomy is a compromise of privacy" (Gross, 1971, p. 181).

Rossiter's (1958) definition of privacy clearly identifies it with autonomy.

> Privacy is a special kind of independence, which can be understood as an attempt to secure autonomy in at least a few personal and spiritual concerns, if necessary in defiance of all the pressures of modern society. . . . It seeks to erect an unbreachable wall of dignity and reserve against the entire world [p. 17].

Beardsley's (1971) treatment is somewhat more complex. She maintains that not only autonomy, but selective disclosure as well, should be referred to in defining privacy. In fact, at the conclusion of her analysis, she restricts "the concept of privacy-violating conduct to violations of the right of selective disclosure" (p. 70). For Beardsley, then, selective disclosure is "the conceptual core of the norm of privacy"; but its moral rationale is grounded in the norm of autonomy.

Personal space. The notion of "space" or "region" has gained wide currency as an explanatory construct in various disciplines. Thus, one reads about "life spaces," "personal spaces," and even "breathing spaces," the latter a term introduced by Justice Brennan in the case of the *NAACP v. Button* (Note 2). The clearest description of privacy as a "space" is given by Konvitz (1966).

> Its [privacy's] essence is the claim that there is a sphere of space that has not been dedicated to public use or control. . . . Even when public, it is part of the inner man; it is part of his "property" . . . with respect to which its owner has delegated no power to the state [p. 279].

Van Den Haag's (1971) definition also emphasizes the spatial analogy.

> Privacy is the exclusive access of a person (or other legal entity) to a realm of his own. . . . It is an extended part of the person. . . . Privacy then refers to control over one's psychic area, with such dimensions as living space [pp. 149–150].

The dynamic character of such a region is implied in Simmel's (1971) definition of privacy as "a territory that gets to be 'our own' in an uneasy truce between ourselves and society" (pp. 82–83). As for the features belonging to such a region, Shils (1966) presents a partial enumeration.

> Intrusions on privacy are baneful because they interfere with an individual in his disposition of what belongs to him. The "social space" around an individual, the recollection of his past, his conversation, his body and its image, all *belong* to him. . . . They belong to him by virtue of his humanity and civility [p. 306].

All these conceptions of privacy as analogous to a spatial region centering in the individual directly imply the treatment of privacy as a kind of property, with its owner possessing exclusive right to dispose of it as he wishes. Though it is initially promising, the limitations of such a conception become apparent when it is considered vis-à-vis the notion of human dignity. Can an individual dispose of his personhood? Accordingly, the spirit of modern law has been moving away from the consideration of privacy as a property right to its newer status as a personal right (Dionisopoulos & Ducat, 1976). Moreover, in practical terms, the property interpretation is difficult to apply in certain situations: Miller (1971), for example, in his exposition of the danger inherent in large computerized information-processing systems, rejected the property theory as an inadequate basis for a relevant concept of privacy.

Summary. These, then, are the pervasive themes underlying the definition of privacy. The early idea of "being let alone" emphasized the aspect of freedom from interference, liberty even to the point of isolation from society. Access to information about the self, and the communication or dissemination of such information, have a modern ring, with overtones of anxiety about computer technology. Respect for the person, for human dignity, and for personal autonomy are value-oriented concepts which have inherent appeal. Finally, privacy as an inviolate retreat, a personal space belonging to the individual, has conceptual power independent of its implications for property theory. Whether any of these recent formulations has actually served to clarify the privacy construct is certainly debatable. Nevertheless, their richness and variety provide a basis for analyzing some of the problems associated with the concept.

Problems of Privacy

Research. The abundance of definitions cited might create the impression that a great deal of work has been done in the area. True, there has been a quantity of legal and paralegal thought and writing, but other disciplines are only beginning to awaken to the importance and relevance of privacy for them. Philosophers have notably neglected the topic (Negley, 1966), while anthropologists have failed to give it "the systematic attention that the subject deserves" (Roberts & Gregor, 1971, p. 200). Westin (1967) deplored the fact that "few values so fundamental to society as privacy have been left so undefined in social theory or have been the subject of such vague and confused writing by social scientists" (p. 7). "Empirical research on privacy is essentially nonexistent," says Altman (1975, p. 10). A 1977 report by the American Psychological Association's Task Force on Privacy and Confidentiality finds that research on the psychological aspects of privacy "is just beginning. Progress is hampered by the fact that such investigations still have to define the area to be studied" (Note 3, p. 21).

Law. Even the development of legal theory has been hampered by the dearth of hard evidence on the subject of privacy. In the absence of factual data, it would seem that little progress can be made in identifying the critical dimensions. In particular there has been considerable controversy over whether privacy is a unitary concept or is rather composed of several irreducible components. After an exhaustive review of a large number of cases relating to privacy, Prosser (1960) concludes that, "the law of privacy comprises four distinct kinds of invasion of four different interests of the plaintiff, which are tied together by the common name, but otherwise have almost nothing in common" (p. 389). It was in reply to Prosser that Bloustein (1964) offered his emphatic contradictory opinion, arguing (as indicated earlier in this paper) that Warren and Brandeis' (1890) concept of the "inviolate personality," understood as respect for human dignity, constituted a basic unifying principle underlying all applications of the privacy right. Bloustein (1968) responded with equal vigor to Kalven's (1966) criticism that Warren and Brandeis had made a relatively insignificant contribution in an area which is legally well defined.

Conceding that privacy in its broader aspects "obfuscates analysis," Freund (1971), following Prosser (1960), enumerates five distinct legal rights covered by the concept. Why then, Freund asks, should privacy, subsuming these different rights, be treated as a unitary concept? The answer which he gives is pragmatic rather than logical. The law needs a "large concept in order to offset an equally large rhetorical counterclaim: freedom of inquiry, the right to know, liberty of the press" (p. 193).

The difficulties surrounding the notion of privacy were not resolved by the Supreme Court in the 1965 case of *Griswold v. Connecticut* (Note 1), although this case established "privacy"—specifically, "marital privacy"—as a "new" and independent constitutional right. Rather, the intractable complexity of the concept of privacy would seem to have been reflected in the variety of opinions offered by the justices and the differing constitutional sources presented as the underpinnings of the right. Legal experts in general have tended to agree with Dixon (1965) that *Griswold* "does little, certainly, to clarify the conceptual dimensions of privacy" (p. 205). Gross (1967) is even more critical. He faults the Court for trying to create a single referent for the many dissimilar senses of the word "privacy," and for failing to see that the basic issue before the Court was one of autonomy and not privacy.

A recent unsigned review ("Constitutional right of privacy," 1974) examines the court decisions relating to privacy which have followed the *Griswold* case. The review finds that the constitutional right to privacy has been restricted to protect only the most tangible and traditional aspects of private life as exemplified in family relationships: marriage and procreation, child-rearing and education. Lower courts have been reluctant to recognize privacy rights beyond these areas. Thus, despite *Griswold*, legal recognition of the right to privacy has not advanced beyond the nineteenth century, according to the review. Moreover, it is pointed out that, in the same conservative spirit, the Court has not shown itself overly concerned with the growing tendency of governmental agencies to gather, store, and disseminate large amounts of personal data about citizens. For example, in the 1972 case of *Laird v. Tatum* (Note 4), the issue revolved around the army's right to collect personal information which could be related to civil disorder and to circulate such information to various army posts across the country. According to the review, the

Court's majority opinion, in supporting the army's position, rejected the definition of privacy proposed by Westin (1967). In general, the review is impatient with the Court's "traditional reluctance" to adapt with sufficient speed to the "new threats arising today at exponential rates" (p. 301).

Summary

From the viewpoint of the objective of this inquiry, neither the newer definitions of privacy nor the more recent court decisions involving the right to privacy have been particularly helpful, either in resolving the nature and applications of the concept, or in clarifying the role of surveillance as a counterbalancing right of the state. The decisions were restricted to a limited range of interests, within which traditional protections were available. There were occasional allusions to modern technology's posing a threat to privacy. Yet Westin's (1967) formulation of privacy, developed specifically in response to such dangers, was apparently ignored in *Laird v. Tatum.*

The next section of this paper will examine in detail some of the more recent advances in surveillance technology, particularly those which seem to have the greatest potential for abuse. Surveillance will be discussed in terms of its relation to, and effect on, privacy.

SURVEILLANCE

Surveillance, meaning literally to "watch over," or to maintain vigilance over, is an activity which is usually thought of as being conducted for the benefit of the person or group engaged in it. Yet it is well to be reminded at the outset that certain types of surveillance are instituted for the protection of the one being watched: the toddler is guarded by his parents, and the patient in an intensive-care unit is kept under constant surveillance by the medical staff. No objection can be raised to surveillance in such contexts. It is when the interests of the watcher govern the activity that conflict of rights may arise.

Different kinds of surveillance reveal the variety and complexity of the interests involved. A small primitive community may be observed continually at close hand by a resident anthropologist; a department store's operations may be studied by a nearby competitor; a suspected criminal's behavior may be watched unknown to him. In fact, despite its exotic connotations, surveillance is virtually an inescapable concomitant of social living. Neighbors observe each others' comings and goings; secretaries learn that bosses may be counted upon to be a little late; cars parked too long in one spot fall prey to vandals. The interesting observations of Goffman (1963) provide other examples. The point to be made is that, over and above deliberate surveillance, incidental or peripheral notice of human beings is always taken by others.

There are doubtless as many reasons why people engage in surveillance as there are types of surveillance activity. For some, it may be to satisfy curiosity; for others, it is to gain information, perhaps the better to understand behavior; and for still others, it is for the ultimate purpose of controlling the behavior of the target individual, for the gain or protection of the watcher. Whatever motivates it, surveillance is more often covert than overt. In this way, the observer protects himself as well as the object of regard from the embarrassment or shame which discovery would entail. Even in quite legitimate operations, unobtrusive observation is frequently considered desirable to guarantee the naturalness of the behavior of interest.

These reflections—for example, the matter of embarrassment, the question of altered behavior—point up the fact that, despite its universality or defensible purposes, the knowledge that one is being watched is an uncomfortable experience. Hidden surveillance offends the sensibilities still more. Whether overt or covert, surveillance intrudes on privacy, however that concept be understood, and poses a potential threat to individual freedom of action. Yet for mutual protection, or to advance such common goods as scientific knowledge, citizens have allocated to their social agencies the right to "intelligence." The means employed will be discussed in the three categories proposed by Westin (1967): physical surveillance, psychological surveillance, and data surveillance.

Physical Surveillance

Although observation of others, overt or covert, for the purposes of scientific experimentation does not fall within the scope of this article, subjects' privacy rights are undoubtedly matters of serious concern in such investigations. Webb, Campbell, Schwartz, and Sechrest (1966) were well aware of these issues when they published their provocative study of the use of unobtrusive measures in the social sciences. To meet some of the problems posed by the use of human participants in scientific inquiry, the various disciplines have generally adopted codes of ethics for use by their members. The specific issue of privacy as related to scientific research is treated elsewhere in this volume (McGuire, 1980) and in other sources (e.g., Ruebhausen & Brim, 1965; Committee on Federal Agency Evaluation Research, Note 5; Edsall, Note 6).

Formerly, physical surveillance required extensive personnel for the adequate observation of the target individual(s). The use of informers or undercover agents served to supplement the surveillance operation. But modern technological advances have all but eliminated the human element in the direct acquisition of information about an individual under surveillance. Evidence no longer depends upon a human witness' seeing or hearing the event in question. The behavior of the target individual can now be instrumentally observed at great distances and under very unfavorable conditions. Automatically recorded on film or tape, the behavior is totally preserved, without the associated human handicaps of selective observation and partial recall.

Technology. It would serve no useful purpose in a paper of this nature to provide an exhaustive list of the equipment and instrumentation used in surveillance operations. These techniques have been competently, even dramatically, described by Brenton (1964), Brown (1967), Long (1967), Snyder (1976), and Westin (1967). Yet some indications of relevant advances in the field are in order.

Telephoto lenses can bridge great distances, and image-intensification devices effectively permit night vision. Infra-red photography can dispense with ordinary light entirely. Miniature movie and television cameras, the size of a pack of cigarettes, can record total dynamic information. Fiber optics and holography are still more recent entrants into the field of surveillance technology.

A microphone the size of a matchhead, together with transmitter and battery, the total about an ounce in weight, can send messages over a distance of a quarter of a mile. Called "bugs," these devices can be planted anywhere: inside a telephone, in a cigarette lighter, or in a pen. Tiny radio transmitters, attached surreptitiously to the target individual (or to his car), make it possible to shadow his movements and locate his whereabouts.

Wiretapping came into existence as soon as telephones were available for public use. Of the many ways in which telephones can be tapped, the induction coil method is the most popular: it is effective, cheap, and imperceptible to the conversing parties.

The growth of electronic surveillance capability has been truly phenomenal, and the extent of its use appeared, until very recently, about to pervade all elements of society. In the private sector, eavesdropping was, until lately, almost a matter of course in industry, politics, marital affairs, and, in some instances, even scientific research. Electronic surveillance was becoming big business for the manufacturers of apparatus, and for detective agencies. Its unchecked growth was due, in the main, to inadequate and antiquated legal controls. In the public sector, a parallel boom occurred. Based on data published in 1962, Westin (1967) could report that "At least fifty different federal agencies have substantial investigative and enforcement functions, providing a corps of more than 20,000 'investigators' " (p. 119). And in a 1965 nationwide survey of state and local law enforcement agencies, it was found that approximately 80% of them used wiretapping, at least occasionally (Westin, 1967, p. 127).

Particularly in the past decade or so, surveillance devices not only have improved in scope and reliability, but have proliferated in new directions. Technological spinoffs from the space program, especially in communication, photography, and automatic control systems—all featuring miniaturization—have become available to the scientific and industrial communities.

Attempts to develop international nuclear arms control programs inevitably led to the problem of inspection, since there can be no absolute certainty that all nations, including non-signatories, will honor agreements limiting the manufacture, storage, and deployment of atomic weapons. Since on-site inspection is at present not permitted by some countries, the necessary consequence was the development of sophisticated remote sensors, some possibly integrated with orbiting satellite systems. These inventions use sensitive photographic and electromagnetic detectors to identify nuclear storage and emplacement areas and to alert the world community to the type, magnitude, and location of atomic tests being made. Although the specific design features of such surveillance devices will not be in the public domain for some time to come, the scientific and engineering principles underlying them are undoubtedly well known, and it is only a matter of time before their modification for ordinary surveillance applications will have been accomplished.

Public concern. It would seem fair to say that by and large the general public has not been unduly disturbed by the increase in the number and diversity of surveillance activities. In a politically divided world, with nuclear holocaust still an ever-present threat, the average citizen may choose to feel secure in the belief that his government is effectively engaged in maintaining external security, in particular, in finding out what its potential adversaries may be doing in the so-called arms race. Correlatively, the citizen is alert to the fact that foreign agents may be operating within his own country, trying to ferret out its secrets. Mutual espionage, with its attendant surveillance activity, seems to be accepted by most citizens as a fact of life. That such surveillance may accidentally or tangentially affect the privacy of loyal citizens is a risk which seems to be a necessary evil.

There is, in addition, another kind of threat to internal security—the depredation and assault on society by the criminal element. Close surveillance over the activities of such individuals or groups is not only readily accepted, but even demanded, by the ordinary citizen. Finally, most individuals hope for more effort at containment of civil disturbances, so that socially damaging excesses could be reduced to a minimum. In the furtherance of these societal goals, the individual tends to tolerate surveillance measures as aids toward the preservation of law and order.

From an altogether different vantage point, inherent human curiosity and crowded urban living lead to unintentional but universal eavesdropping. Worse still, there is tacit acceptance of this as a way of life, whether it be a matter of small-town gossip or the overheard arguments of the couple in the upstairs apartment.

Moreover, individual values in regard to privacy have been subject to a subtle and insidious undermining from still another source. For several decades now, the American public has been exposed to the psychoanalytically derived palliative that self-disclosure, whether on the couch or in one's dealings with others, induces a condition of mental health and well-being (Jourard, 1964, 1966). The extreme form of this doctrine eventually culminated in the group encounter movement, which attracted large numbers of people (Back, 1972). Participants were pressured into and by a confessional atmosphere in which absolute "honesty" was demanded, an uncensored revelation of what one thought about oneself and others in the group (Schutz, 1973). Stripped of his privacy and psychologically naked, the individual had nothing and no place to hide. This separation of innermost, intimate thoughts from their sanctuary in the self led, in far too many cases, to anxiety and mental distress which required psychological treatment (Lieberman, Yalom, & Miles, 1973). Even for those who had no direct personal experience with encounter groups, the climate fostered by the movement helped to create a present-day atmosphere in which individuals are made to feel defensive about their desires to keep something of themselves private. Reticence and reserve have become negative traits in a society which values "openness" and a childlike form of candor. Disclosure is deemed natural and healthy while secrecy implies guilty or asocial states of mind.

All these influences—external and internal threats to security, close living and curiosity, the philosophy of total self-disclosure—have eroded the sense of privacy and produced a consequent indifference toward surveillance.

Law. The public's tolerance of eavesdropping has been reflected in the inadequacy of legal protections against surveillance. As expressed in numerous hearings between 1934 and 1967, the attitude of Congress was generally to ban eavesdropping. Nevertheless, before 1968, there was no federal law to regulate electronic surveillance. The only operating federal statute, Section 605 of the Federal Communications Act of 1934, dealt with wiretapping only, prohibiting the "interception and divulgence" of telephone conversations. This wording proved unfortunate: it was interpreted to mean that both interception and divulgence were necessary for violation of the statute. The two conditions were seldom met in the cases brought before the courts, hence the statute was generally unenforceable. Although "surreptitious listening was widely frowned upon as an invasion of privacy and often labeled 'dirty business' " (Lapidus, 1974, p. 11), there was no effective means of preventing it.

However, in reaction to the resurgence of organized crime and increasing public attention to problems of "law and order," Congress in 1968 enacted the Omnibus Crime Control and Safe Streets Act which, under its Title III, authorized eavesdropping by law enforcement officials under specified restrictive conditions. As its name indicates, the primary purpose of the Act was to strengthen the hand of law enforcement agencies in their battle against crime, particularly organized crime. At the same time, the Act sought to protect the individual against undue violations of privacy, by prohibiting eavesdropping by individuals or non-public agencies. A court order showing "probable cause" was required before wiretapping or electronic surveillance in civil matters could be permitted, thus providing an additional safeguard to ordinary citizens.

From the beginning, Title III has been a controversial law, with some critics contending that it constitutes a threat to liberty, permits an unconstitutional invasion of privacy, and is not even particularly effective in law enforcement. Such critics further claim that it is too easily subverted for political advantage and leaves too much indiscriminate power in the hands of the executive branch of government. In large part, these objections have been aimed at the provision which allows government agencies to eavesdrop without court order. Title III permits such surveillance in two types of situation: namely, in an emergency involving conspiratorial activity (surveillance to be limited to 48 hours' duration), and by authority of the President to protect national security.

Soon after the passage of what came to be known as the Omnibus Crime Act of 1968, the Department of Justice claimed that it now had the power to conduct eavesdropping activities without court order in cases involving domestic political dissidents who used "unlawful means to attack and subvert the existing structure of government" (Lapidus, 1974, p. 96). In 1972, however, a unanimous Supreme Court decision, in *United States v. United States District Court* (Note 7), affirmed an appellate court ruling which denied the government the right to wiretap domestic radicals, as long as their activities were independent of any foreign power or its agents. By this decision, the abuse of federal surveillance authority in the purported interest of "law and order" was averted.

Eight years after the enactment of Title III, the National Commission for the Review of Federal and State Laws Relating to Wiretapping and Electronic Surveillance (1976) prepared an evaluative study of the operation of Title III in the first six years of its existence. In its report, the Commission pointed out that Title III had represented a compromise of two opposing views: that of those who "believed that a total ban on electronic surveillance was necessary for the protection of individual privacy" and that of those "who hesitated to limit the use of a technique claimed by many to be a vital tool in fighting crime, particularly organized crime" (p. xiii). The report itself concluded that electronic surveillance was indispensable and effective in the war against organized crime, but that such surveillance should be permitted only when authorized and supervised by court order and only in certain major types of crime and offenses. The Commission further advised that court-authorized surveillance requests be required to show "some special reason for extending the surveillance" beyond its original time limit (p. xvii). It was also recommended that the emergency provision be amended "to require oral notification of a judge prior to installation of the emergency tap" (p. xvii). Where surreptitious entry was necessary to install a bugging device, "court orders should include express authorization to enter upon premises" (p. xvii). However, in consensual surveillance, where the permission of one of the parties must be obtained before operations can begin, no court authorization need be required.

The general conclusion of the "National Wiretap Commission" was that the procedures legislated by Title III "served to protect the privacy not only of innocent individuals but also of the persons who are the subjects of the investigation" (p. xvi). The commissioners considered one of their most heartening findings to be the reduction in illegal surveillance in police, industrial, political, and marital investigations which followed upon Title III regulation of the manufacture and sale of bugging devices. With the publication of the commission's detailed and carefully prepared report, it is now up to the Congress to decide what changes, if any, it will make in the Title III provisions.

Psychological Surveillance

> Under psychological surveillance are grouped those scientific and technological methods that seek to extract information from an individual which he does not want to reveal or does not know he is revealing or is led to reveal without a mature awareness of its significance for his privacy. The heart of the privacy issue in psychological surveillance lies in polygraph and personality testing [Westin, 1967, p. 133].

Of the two procedures mentioned by Westin, special attention will be given to polygraph testing ("lie detection") and to some recent innovations in the area of psychological interrogation, particularly voice analysis. Personality testing as it relates to privacy is considered in another chapter of this book (Anastasi, 1980).

Polygraph: Basic description. The name "polygraph" refers to the multiple writing units which are an immediately observable feature of the apparatus. Each pen records on moving paper tape the deflections transmitted from one of several physiological measuring devices attached to the individual being examined. In most current usage, these are blood pressure and respiration cuffs placed around the arm and chest respectively, and small metal electrodes fastened to the fingertips. Corresponding changes in the individual's blood pressure, breathing, and the electrical resistance of his skin are thereby monitored.

Over the course of time and trial, it has been found that these three physiological functions provide the most stable and usable indicators of bodily reactivity to emotional fluctuations. Among others which were explored as potential additional inputs, muscle contractions, volume changes of body parts, and electrical "brain waves" may be mentioned. Each was subsequently rejected when it failed to attain the discriminatory power of other indices, or was found to duplicate those already in the system. Originally equipped with only two pens, recording breathing and blood-pressure changes, the polygraph has now stabilized into its present three-pen structure with the addition of galvanic skin resistance (GSR) recording. It may be noted that in particular applications, especially for research purposes, only one or two of the indices may be used.

The theory of the polygraph is that these physiological changes accompany and reflect changes in emotional states induced during the psychological examination. This examination traditionally consists of questions concerning specific details of the matter (e.g., crime) under investigation, interspersed with neutral or "buffer" items of no particular emotional import. Questions are always phrased so as to elicit either a "Yes" or "No" answer; the subject is not required to provide spontaneous narration. Each "Yes" or "No" response produces great or slight deflection of the writing pens; thus, an evaluation of the pattern of physiological reactivity associated with each question and its reply enables the polygraph operator to form a judgment as to whether the test subject is lying or telling the truth. These judgments are the heart of the polygraph procedure: it is vitally important to recognize that the examiner, not the apparatus, is the "lie detector." Moreover, this final judgment phase of the proceeding is typically performed only later, with care and deliberation, by the responsible examiner. The validity of polygraph examination also depends upon the complete cooperation of the subject. The examinee must take the test voluntarily, and he must be told in advance what it is that he will be questioned about.

The polygraph, then, records several physiological changes simultaneously, and these are synchronized with the questioning. It is of interest to note that the conscious verbal responses, "Yes" and "No," are under the control of the central nervous system, often referred to as the voluntary nervous system, while the physiological responses are regulated by the autonomic nervous system, sometimes designated the involuntary nervous system. Thus the non-conscious, relatively "automatic" physiological reactions are essentially used to evaluate the truth or falsity of the "Yes" and "No" responses which are under voluntary control. One might be tempted to say that while the psychological self may lie, the body proclaims the truth (Kubis, 1953). But it would be more precise to say that lying may be inferred at those points at which the physiological responses are larger (or smaller) than they should be, or the indications of stress are greater than would normally be expected.

Polygraph and privacy. It might be well to pause at this point to inquire how personal privacy may be endangered in polygraph applications. Since the individual submits voluntarily to the polygraph test, and knows generally what he will be asked about, it could be maintained that he has wittingly sacrificed his right to privacy on the matters under investigation. (In fact, it is not unknown for persons even to insist on being tested.) On the other side, it may be argued that it is unlikely that the circumstances surrounding an ordinary investigation permit a truly free choice, or are conducive to a clear understanding of what is to take place. For example, in cases of business pilferage, when told that "everyone in the office is going to take the test," a worker who refuses may by that very act attract negative notice, if not actual suspicion. With emotions already at a high pitch, the potential testee's evaluation of the orientation instructions cannot be very discriminating either. Whether fully informed and freely given consent is possible to obtain under pressure and distress may well be doubted. In such circumstances, the individual may feel that he has no real choice but to sacrifice his privacy to protect his good name.

What he has sacrificed in this instance is, of course, access to his recorded physiological responses, which constitute a peculiarly intimate kind of data about his person. He does not know, either, exactly what information he may be asked to reveal, or what will be done with his records and the report prepared by the polygraph examiner. Important questions come to mind. Are matters other than those under investigation to be included in the report? Who will have access to it? How long will it be in the files? Moreover, despite the skill and experience of the polygrapher, not every question may be perfectly phrased: there is a chance that some may have been vague and/or misinterpreted by the test subject. In the usual interrogation, the examinee does not have much of an opportunity to "correct" or explain any mistaken impressions he may have given without feeling on the defensive. Not only has he relinquished control over an intimate physiological "picture" of himself, but over its interpretation and ultimate disposition as well.

Accuracy of polygraph results. The polygraph examiner can arrive at any one of three decisions: the subject is truthful, he is lying, or his records are not conclusive. Since the proportion of "inconclusive" decisions depends on the technique used, the criteria adopted, and even on the personality of the examiner, the range may be expected to be fairly wide; and it can reach as high as 35%, even among experts (Barland, 1975). In view of the indefinite boundaries of the "inconclusive" category, accuracy percentages reported in the literature correspondingly differ, depending upon whether inconclusive decisions are included or excluded from the total. (No convention in this regard has been established.) Accuracy percentages must also differ because examiners differ—in experience, ability, and in such relevant personality variables as tendencies toward risk-taking and impulsivity/caution.

It should give no scandal that a certain proportion of polygraph decisions are inconclusive. Lie detection is a human endeavor, the success of which depends upon a delicate synchrony of mechanical, physiological, and psychological variables. Ambiguous records may result, for example, from less than optimal cuff pressure; the subject's physiological reactivity may be low; or excessive anxiety may tend to obliterate an easily readable differential between deflections at critical and non-critical questions.

Even when relatively clear-cut records have been obtained, the decision process is always complicated by the necessity of integrating readings from the three different physiological indicators used. It would indeed be a very pleasant surprise to find all of them agreeing with each other at every point of the examination. This can scarcely ever occur for several reasons, the most important being that individuals characteristically manifest distress in different ways. For some, emotional strain is revealed predominantly in respiration, for others in perspiration, or in cardiovascular reactivity. For still others, the stress may be more generally pervasive, affecting several physiological functions. For their part, polygraph examiners too have individual preferences for certain physiological indices rather than others: in evaluating charts, some examiners may tend to resolve the complex integration problem by relying most heavily on that measure in which they personally have come to have the greatest confidence. Whether the measure of each one's choice is indeed superior is debatable on other evidence; but that polygraphers do rate some indices as possessing greater reliability than others is well established (Barland, 1975).

The polygraph examiner, nevertheless, is taught to combine the information provided by each index at critical points in the questioning. How he does so is not a matter of standard practice. It is conceivable that (especially for research purposes) an examiner might assign numerical weights derived from reliability ratings to each physiological index, and then combine these three differentially weighted units mathematically for each critical question and for the final decision. More typically, perhaps, the examiner makes a kind of intuitive integration of the three components of a reading, in which case, of course, his subjectively preferred index may "unconsciously" be given greater weight.

However performed, the process yields an essentially statistical outcome which depends upon the degree of agreement calculated or perceived among three differentially weighted units at critical points in the record. If the statistical criterion is high (i.e., absolute agreement at a preponderance of points), the number of inconclusive findings will be large; if the criterion is low, the "inconclusives" will be correspondingly few. When all is said and done, it is apparent that the polygraph decision is the "negotiated" end point of a complex interplay of many factors. That published accuracy scores have varied thus becomes less remarkable than that they agree as well as they do.

In fact, as experience with polygraph techniques has developed and grown more sophisticated, there are increasing reports of a uniformly high standard of polygraph accuracy's being attained. The consensus of the literature now seems to be that, under well-controlled conditions, expert polygraphers can operate at about a 90% accuracy level (Raskin, Barland, & Podlesny, 1977). Yet it would seem reasonable to assume that of the many examiners in the field, there are not too many experts who consistently maintain 90% accuracy. Over the long run, the average examiner may be expected to fall well below this level, especially if he is operating in a "real world" situation rather than in a scientific laboratory. Given the unsettling personal, official, and temporal pressures associated with a real crime, the conditions under which the test is formulated and conducted are rarely under the complete control of the polygrapher; nor are they likely to be optimal for examination. On the basis of such considerations, an accuracy level of 80% would seem to be more realistic for the run-of-the-mill practitioner. Romig (1972) went so far as to claim that "a margin of error as high as 30% could be expected in some examinations where the accuracy of the instrument and the competence of the examiner are questionable" (p. 129).

Risk to the examinee. With the reasonably conservative figure of 80% accuracy, it follows that 20% of the decisions will be in error, characterizing either the innocent as guilty or the guilty as innocent. Moreover, it is safe to assume that these two types of error occur with approximately equal frequency. Although the published data do vary somewhat as to the proportion of these errors (Raskin, Barland, & Podlesny, 1977; Kubis, Note 8), the differences are not sufficiently divergent to challenge the assumption of a 50–50 proportion. On the average, then, among ordinary polygraphers, an innocent individual will be judged guilty 10% of the time and the guilty individual will be judged innocent at the same rate. What does this imply? It surely means that "equal protection" is not operating in the lie detection situation, for the innocent individual always stands some chance of being judged guilty (with grievous consequences), while the guilty individual always stands a chance of being judged innocent (often with complete but unjust exoneration). The message is clear. An innocent person should never volunteer for polygraph examination, since he is always exposed to serious risk and in this sense can only lose. On the other hand, the genuinely guilty should not hesitate to be tested since, as he is already suspected, the additional risk of a negative finding is of lesser import to his case and, moreover, he even stands a good chance of being reported innocent.

What particular consequences does polygraph accuracy have for privacy? One should expect that, in return for relinquishing some aspects of his privacy, the innocent individual would gain some benefits, such as relief from inner tension and the suspicion of others. But are the accuracy figures high enough to justify the risk of false report? This is a question which the innocent person must resolve for himself before volunteering. But the guilty party, by permitting some invasion of privacy, has a real but undeserved opportunity for gain: namely, personal freedom and a whitewashed reputation.

A further privacy issue is involved in the following question: Is the physiological "picture" of the individual, relatively uncontrolled by him, to supersede the verbal "picture" which he has authorized as "official"? Does an individual fully realize that this is apt to happen once he voluntarily takes a polygraph test? Moreover, if the polygraph operator should give a report of "inconclusive," what sort of "picture" of the individual remains? If innocent, the person is marked with a stigma—"possibly guilty"—for the rest of his life. If actually guilty, the individual—"possibly innocent"—has been given a decided advantage in evading justice.

Uses of polygraph examinations. Polygraphs are used extensively by state and local law enforcement agencies, by business and industrial organizations, by detective agencies, and by private practitioners. Contrary to a popular impression linking lie detection primarily to police work, by far the greatest use of polygraphs is in the private sector, mainly in personnel situations. Polygraphs are used to expedite pre-employment screening and in promotion decisions; they are used as a deterrent against theft and on a periodical basis to check on losses. Banking institutions, for example, are understandably hesitant about hiring an individual with a history of petty theft. Companies engaged in classified or proprietary operations use polygraphs to establish security checks and to discourage security risks from applying. Gambling, drinking, and drug use are some of the other habits deemed incompatible with the work responsibilities of many occupations.

Until about 1964, the polygraph was used fairly routinely even in the federal government for pre-employment screening. Congressional hearings held in that year were particularly critical of this practice. As a result, ten years later, during a new round of congressional hearings on the polygraph, David Cooke, Deputy Assistant Secretary of Defense, was able to report (1974):

> The Civil Service Commission has limited the use of the polygraph for pre-employment screening of prospective competitive service employees

> to those agencies which have a highly sensitive intelligence or counter-intelligence mission directly affecting national security [p. 270].

However, the virtual elimination of polygraphic pre-employment screening in the federal government has had no corresponding effect on the private sector. As a matter of fact, the use of the polygraph for pre-employment screening in business and industry is a growing and lucrative practice. Nevertheless, its heyday may be drawing to a close. Cautions are already being issued.

> A more sensitive area is use of the polygraph to screen employment applicants. The professional body of polygraph examiners risk very substantial opposition from influential sectors of public opinion if indiscriminate use of the polygraph for profit is widely carried on [George, 1974, p. 96].

This opposition from public opinion is to be understood as eventuating in legal action, and George (1974) warns that judicial acceptance of the polygraph for pre-employment screening may not be readily forthcoming. He indicates a number of caveats for practitioners wishing to avoid or successfully to defend actions which may be brought against them. George's article is thoughtful and essentially sympathetic; but the tenor of opinion from certain academics is much more critical. Lykken's (1974) radical rejection of the practice is not atypical: "The general use of the lie detector in employee screening cannot be justified, however, and psychologists have a professional responsibility to oppose this growing practice" (p. 738).

Westin (1967) raised rather serious objections to the use of polygraph examinations, questioning in particular the extent to which the individual can truly have a "mature awareness of its significance for his privacy." It was the use of lie detection in employment screening that Westin was primarily concerned about. Such procedures "attempt to penetrate the 'inner domain' of individual belief" (p. 238). They also interfere "with the individual's sense of personal autonomy and reserve" (p. 238). Finally, the impressive trappings and dramatic character of such examinations confer on the authorities giving the test "increased psychological power over individuals" (p. 238).

The right to privacy may also be violated if the polygraph examiner includes questions which are highly personal. Matters, for example, of personal practice in sex, religion, politics, child care, or illness in the family are extremely private, and questioning about them is especially intrusive if these behaviors are not relevant to the job—and it would seem that the burden of proof should be on the employer to show conclusively that they are so.

Very often, too, attitudes and opinions—as distinguished from facts of behavior—about race, religion, politics, and specific persons and organizations are queried in the polygraph examination. Invasive of privacy as they undoubtedly are, such questions are totally inappropriate for another reason. Whatever accuracy the polygraph has derives from its use in matters of fact. Attitudes and opinions, by contrast, fluctuate in intensity from one time to another, and thus cannot be definitively explored by the lie detection technique.

Privacy may also be considered to have been violated if the operator uses a procedure other than the one permitted by the individual under test. A nice question arises here: the individual may have agreed in good faith to take the polygraph test because he believed a highly reliable instrument was going to be used—one which does not make mistakes. But, as has been seen, the polygraph examiner does make mistakes, often in a substantial proportion of cases. In this sense, then, it is not the procedure the individual agreed to be tested by. Polygraphers—or the companies contracting for their services—thus have an obligation to acquaint prospective examinees with the risk factor, in a non-technical manner which they can comprehend.

Voice analysis: Background. Voice analysis has a long research history to which, as might be expected, the laboratories affiliated with the telephone system have made significant contributions. Speech, in particular, is a highly complex acoustic phenomenon and its electronic resolution into visible wave patterns yields a very complicated spectrum. Analysis of the speech spectrum has been used in voice identification and, more recently, in lie detection. Both uses of the voice modality are a kind of surveillance and, as such, may infringe on the right to privacy.

When employed for identification purposes, the voice records are called "voiceprints," by analogy to fingerprints. These two identification techniques, however, are based upon different stability principles. Fingerprint identification depends upon anatomical structural stability; voiceprint identification assumes a dynamic stability in the patterns of sounds produced by an individual's speech apparatus.

Voice identification and verification. In a paper presented before the Acoustical Society of America in 1962, Kersta of the Bell Telephone Laboratories (Note 9) compared voiceprints and fingerprints in the following way.

> Closely analogous to fingerprint identification, voiceprint identification uses, instead of the uniqueness in people's fingerprints, the unique features found in their utterances. Fingerprinting uses the inked impressions of the ten fingers; voiceprints use the spectrographic impressions of the utterances of ten frequently used English words [p. 1].

Kersta showed that young high school girls with minimal training could identify unknown prints correctly with an accuracy of 99%. Among the problems Kersta foresaw as needing ultimate resolution were the use of automated detection techniques and the potential ability of mimics to confuse the automatic devices.

Ten years later, progress in those areas was reported by Lummis (1972) from the same laboratories. He and his co-workers developed a speaker verification system which could lead, for example, to a "checkless" society in which people conduct their banking business by telephone. Using a computer to analyze six speech characteristics, and to determine whether an "unknown" voice matched the standard, they found an error rate of only 1%. When human subjects made the same verification, the error rate was 4.2%. In particular, human subjects found it difficult to distinguish the voices of identical twins.

There is, however, at least one caveat. Working under optimal conditions, outstanding professional mimics could reproduce a person's voice with such fidelity that the computer made errors at a rate as high as 27%. This unusual situation excepted, the computer approach to voice verification appears basically sound. The National Institute of Law Enforcement and Criminal Justice (1975) has been sponsoring considerable research in this area. They feel confident that the results obtained "may enable police officers to identify the human voice as routinely as they now identify fingerprints" (p. 23).

Voice analysis in lie detection. The fact that the voice is an expressive indicator of emotions has led some investigators to the natural conclusion that the speech spectrum might be potentially useful in lie detection. Research results in this area, however, have so far not been too promising. Thus, Myers and Merluzzi (Note 10) stated: "Progress is being made in relating complex physical characteristics of speech to emotions and to emotional stress . . . but using only physical characteristics of speech as a determination of emotions or stress is still unreliable" (p. 4). In a current review of the experimental literature, Simonov and Frolov (1977) warned that "the determination of human states through speech analysis is a very complicated problem. It is far from being solved" (p. 24).

Despite the present rudimentary state of scientific knowledge about speech-spectrum analysis as related to stress or emotional states, a version of this technique already forms the basis of two recent commercially marketed devices which purport to measure "voice stress" and "psychological stress," but are used by their purchasers predominantly as lie detectors. These instruments, the Voice Stress Analyzer (VSA) and the Psychological Stress Evaluator (PSE) make use of the output of an ordinary tape recorder. Despite the claims made for them, an extensive research study (Kubis, 1974) of the lie detection capabilities of the VSA and the PSE revealed that neither device performed above chance level. The polygraph, however, used in conjunction with these instruments, significantly differentiated the three types of suspect (thief, lookout, innocent) who were tested in an experimental lie detection situation. The report of this investigation concluded that "neither of the presently existing voice analysis instruments may be accepted as valid 'lie detectors' within the constraints of an experimental paradigm" (p. 40). In testimony before the 1974 Congressional Hearings on the Polygraph, David Cooke, Deputy Assistant Secretary of Defense, stated: "Our evaluations indicated that the Psychological Stress Evaluator was not of sufficient reliability in its present state of development" (Cooke, 1974, p. 271).

Voice analysis and privacy. The fundamental problem which voice analysis poses for privacy is that, like the polygraph, it takes a physiological "picture" of an individual—in this case, a sample of his speech patterns—over which he has little control. Moreover, unlike the polygraph, the recording of voice requires no apparatus attachment to the person, and consequently can be made without the speaker's knowledge.

It would appear that Title III of the Omnibus Crime Control Act of 1968 is pertinent in this situation, for although perhaps not explicitly mentioned as a prohibited technique, voice spectrum recording clearly entails a kind of electronic surveillance, very likely in the acquisition, and certainly in the analysis, of speech. From this point of view, the activity is at present clearly illegal, unless it is carried out with permission of a court or the speaking party.

As with the polygraph, matters of accuracy are fundamental to the problem of privacy in voice analysis, for if the technique is unreliable, the question of privacy violation becomes moot. When a procedure is to acquire and disseminate information about an individual, there is an obligation that permission be obtained first, and that the information be accurate and not distorted. This is the condition and expectation under which a person permits the partial loss of privacy. If, contrary to the individual's belief, the procedure is inaccurate and yields distorted information about him, the acquisition of such information and its dissemination before it can be corrected clearly constitute violations of justice as well as of the right to privacy.

In public circumstances, such as a television appearance, a requirement for prior permission to record would be unenforceable; and the absence of restrictions has led to the uncomfortable situation of politicians having their speech monitored and analyzed for lie detection purposes. One can readily imagine the chilling effect such operations could have on ordinary speech were the devices known to be highly accurate in detecting lies. The freedom to express oneself could be strongly inhibited by the thought that somewhere out there a tape recorder might be spinning—spinning the threads from which a fabric of lies might be woven. More seriously, because speech is involved, voice analysis technology potentially threatens not only the right to privacy, but the right to free speech as protected by the First Amendment to the Constitution. However, challenges to veracity arising from speech-spectrum analysis may be a somewhat different issue, such challenges possibly being more akin to critiques offered by journalistic commentators from their analysis of a speech's semantic content, opinions which themselves are protected by the First Amendment.

One final problem relating to voiceprints bears comment. The potential use of the voiceprint as a citizen identifier involves the same difficulties for privacy as the ill-advised concept of universal fingerprinting, or the more recently proposed use of the Social Security number as a national identifying number. In a free society, to be tagged for tracking has totalitarian implications strongly resisted by citizens. It is even a point to consider when and if "telephone banking," or similar personal-business conveniences utilizing voiceprints, are offered to the public. To place on file an ineradicable and unalterable attribute of oneself, by which one's identity can be uniquely determined forever after, is to give up that aspect of privacy which is sometimes called "anonymity," and which preserves to the citizen the right to participate in society only to the extent to which he freely chooses.

Other lie detection techniques. Brief mention must be made of attempts to devise instruments which monitor the physiological reactions of an individual without requiring attachments, and hence, potentially at least, without his awareness. For example, there already exists a remote sensing device which can record an individual's respiration and cardiovascular activity. These physiological functions are, of course, two of the measures used in traditional lie detection. Whether lying is more easily detected when the subject knows that he is taking a lie detector test or when he is unaware that such an examination is being conducted has yet to be decided on the basis of research data, since the remote-sensing equipment is still too new to have been widely available for testing.

Based on their experience with the conventional apparatus, polygraphers generally hold that a deliberate attempt to control one's behavior when telling a lie during a polygraph test tends to enhance the physiological reactions indicative of lying (Kubis, Note 8). Thus a person who knows he is being tested may be more apt to be caught in a lie. In any case, covert lie detection devices are direct assaults on privacy, since information is being extracted from an individual without his knowledge and without his permission. It is, as it were, a "second-order" type of eavesdropping, inasmuch as the data obtained (i.e., the physiological record) must be interpreted before it can yield an inference about the mental state (lying or truthful) of the individual.

Since ancient times the proverb *In vino veritas* has epitomized man's belief in the relation between drug-induced reduction of voluntary control of conscious mental activity and revelation of the truth. Though wine-induced veracity is no longer a professionally sanctioned technique, the emergence of "truth serums" in modern times reflects man's continuing fascination with the phenomenon. Such disinhibiting drugs, which supposedly enable the individual to talk more freely about repressed or suppressed experiences and feelings, have been proposed from time to time for lie-detection purposes. Results with such drugs have been mixed, and there are many problems associated with their use in lie detection (Kubis, 1957). At best, they may serve as ancillary to the traditional polygraph examination, providing, perhaps, additional bits of information which require further verification.

It should be realized that coherent, specifically relevant narration is not characteristic of narcosis. The drugged individual typically rambles, often vaguely and confusedly, touching upon many areas of his life or the lives of others which have no bearing on the matter at hand. It is precisely the gathering of this nonspecific and nonrelevant information, from an individual in a state of reduced responsibility, which constitutes the problem for privacy in a drug interview. The technique facilitates indiscriminate "eavesdropping" on the communication of material which the drugged individual would ordinarily consider highly sensitive, and which he would doubtless withhold were he in condition to control the flow of his mental activity. In law enforcement investigations, self-incrimination may also be at issue.

An analogous position may be taken with respect to the use of hypnosis in lie detection. Although more in control than the individual under a drug, the hypnotized person also may reveal irrelevant personal material which he had no prior intention of disclosing. Moreover, the temptation to indiscriminate eavesdropping is even greater in hypnosis, since hypnosis is often employed precisely with the objective of uncovering information tangential to the matter being investigated, but which may be helpful in resolving the problem. Although cooperating in the hypnosis, the subject is not at all aware of the nature and extent of what will be discussed with him, and he may unwittingly violate his own privacy.

Although privacy may thus be regarded as seriously jeopardized by narcotic or hypnotic interrogation, it is perhaps a saving feature of such techniques that the material communicated is frequently only slightly less garbled and incomplete than that produced by a person talking in his sleep. As a consequence, interpretation has been difficult and guarded. Furthermore, research to explore and develop these procedures has been limited by the requirement of its being legally performed only under medical supervision.

With regard to any of these reduced-control techniques, a word of caution is in order. It must not be forgotten that the ultimate objective of most surveillance is to exert control over the person being observed. Chemical agents in particular would seem to be tools par excellence for the attainment of such an objective. In point of fact, the medical goal of techniques such as narcosynthesis, even when used therapeutically, is to regulate and redirect the mental state of the patient, so that he may again think, feel, and behave as he did before becoming ill. The same may also be said of medications such as tranquilizers and mood elevators, but these drugs do not have revelatory communication as their primary purpose. Of more concern are the less benign drugs which now exist, which have the capability of putting the mental faculties in disarray, obliterating memories of lived experiences, and dissociating behavior from voluntary control. The ominous possibilities of such drugs scarcely need elaboration. Medical and pharmacological research may well alleviate the ills of mankind, but, at the same time, it may also produce for the unscrupulous the means to modify and control the behavior of others for selfish and antisocial ends.

Data Surveillance

The rapid development of the modern computer has created a technological revolution of unprecedented proportions, affecting every aspect of society. Working at unbelievable speeds and processing mountains of data with unerring accuracy and at relatively low cost, the computer has become one of the great benefactors of mankind. But its very capabilities seem somehow to threaten the distinctiveness of the individual person. Being forced to deal with a rigid system rather than with a fellow human being who can adjust to his individuality, the average citizen tends to feel helpless, demeaned, and dehumanized in his communications with the computer. Moreover, as general public familiarity with computers and the uses which can be made of them grows, people have become increasingly aware of the implications of computers' tremendous information-storage capacity. They have begun to realize that personal information about themselves can now be readily preserved in computerized form. As the computer advances on his private data, the individual senses himself about to be swallowed up "bit-by-bit."

The problem of records. From the day of his birth to months, sometimes years, after his death, the citizen of a modern bureaucratic society fills out, or has filled out for him, innumerable forms providing information about himself and those about him. Westin's (1967) enumeration is an impressive one.

> To help himself, to help science, and to help society run efficiently, the individual now pours a constantly flowing stream of information about himself into the record files—birth and marriage records, public-school records, census data, military records, passport data, government and private employment records, public-health records, civil-defense records, income tax returns, social-security returns, land and housing records, insurance records, bank records, business reporting forms to government, licensing applications, financial declarations required by law, charitable

> contributions, credit applications and records, automobile registration records, post-office records, telephone records, psychological and psychiatric records, scholarship and research-grant records, church records —and on and on. New forms of financial operations have produced the credit card, which records the where, when, and how-much of many once-unrecorded purchasing, travel, and entertainment transactions of the individual's life [p. 159].

In the past, no one was particularly concerned about providing this enormous quantity of data about himself, for the information was scattered about in various agencies and organizations which seemed to operate in isolation. Such independence in record-keeping was less a matter of management policy than of practical and economic considerations. Thirty years ago, it would have been a monumental task to accumulate and store such a mass of data on an individual. The collection of even a few of the records into one place was prohibitive in terms of staff and cost. Even within a single organization, long-term continuity of record-keeping was all but impossible because of storage limitations, with older records periodically having to be destroyed. Thus, bits and pieces of an individual may have been known here and there, but never a total composite "picture" all in one location. Moreover, there was a much greater prevalence of handwritten material which was not easily duplicated. As a consequence, informational privacy, or privacy of records, was not a matter of much practical concern except in a few isolated cases.

With the appearance of the computer on the scene, all that has changed. Gone are the bulky folders crammed with perishable papers requiring arrays of file cabinets and warehousing rooms to hold them. A strip of small magnetic tape preserves all the relevant information. Gone are the scribes and, to a lesser extent, even the typists; the keypunch operator now prepares the data for processing, and the personal letter is supplanted by the seemingly all-too-reproducible printout in many large-scale businesses and other organizations and agencies. It has become a relatively simple matter to accumulate and store vast quantities of information.

As the drive for efficiency continues, computers will become bigger and better, replacing the smaller and less reliable ones, and incorporating additional features and capabilities. Even now, computers can transmit information directly and automatically to other computers. Thus a relatively small computer may be given access to a vastly larger central data bank; and "shared memories" may be allocated among several intercommunicating computers. Widespread dissemination of personal data is not only possible; it is already occurring.

Thus, it is not the mere recording of numerous items of fact about an individual which is the crux of the threat to privacy. It is, rather, that the new information technology has made it increasingly less likely that such records will remain, as heretofore, dispersed among various agency files.

The computer has made the assemblage of all this information into one centrally maintained personal dossier an entirely feasible prospect; and it is this unified locus of control which jeopardizes privacy.

There are other aspects of computerized records which have serious implications for personal privacy. As has already been suggested, one of the most obvious is the relative permanence of such records. Once established, a file on an individual may follow him throughout his days, possibly to his embarrassment. Thus childish trespasses, long suppressed and all but forgotten by an individual and his family, may surface again at times when they should no longer be relevant. Traits, opinions, associations, and activities may have drastically altered in the course of a lifetime, but to the computer nothing has changed. Charitable human forgetting is replaced by inexorable total recall. The computer hoards every bit; it does not forgive or forget.

What is even more damaging, the data in the dossier may be inaccurate or distorted. Moreover, no one today knows what files have been prepared on him, what sources have been tapped, or how the information has been compiled. Where is the file located? Who maintains it? Not privy to such facts about his own records, the individual has little if any opportunity to review and correct them. And even if the information is accurate and pertinent, what persons or organizations have access to it? How can the individual be sure that it is being used for the purpose for which it was intended? These questions pose very real problems for privacy.

The essence of the uneasiness which the individual feels may lie less in his fear of damage to particular interests of his (e.g., his credit rating in the commercial community) than in his recognition that his true self has been superseded by an assembled man whom he does not know, might not recognize, and in whose development he took no part. No longer he himself, but the computer, tells his fellows who he is. He has lost control over his own identity.

The ability of the computer printout to provide, not only an overall picture of an individual sketched over a number of years, but an "instantaneous" snapshot of an individual's activities over a limited period of time, adds another foreboding dimension to the invasion of his privacy. For example, the credit card follows its user from morning until night, providing a faithful and incontrovertible log of his movements: gasoline purchase, parking in city, lunch, bar, dinner, theater, and after. Physical surveillance could not have equalled this performance.

Of course, it is not the computer per se, but its capability, especially in uncertain hands, which poses the real threat to privacy. Like any technology, the computer provides the means, not the motive. The extraordinary power of those means, however, and their unprecedented nature in the experience of mankind, require a concerted effort on the part of societal institutions to create structures and expectations for computer use which are conformable to deeply held values. Managers of information systems should be the executors, not the dictators, of the people's will. Opportunities for unethical exploitation of the new information technology must be restricted by legal and other sanctions (such as codes of professional practice).

Information privacy and the law. All kinds of organizations—government agencies, institutions, businesses—have been quick to see the usefulness to their operations of getting increased information from the private citizen. Frequently, though, it seems that the actual need for specific items of data sought has not been well justified. This mechanized version of "knowledge for its own sake" could easily have led to such requests' becoming routinized and accepted as the status quo, with little incentive or opportunity for necessary changes later on. However, the imposition of multiple requests for additional facts from people, coupled with fears of an unchecked computer "takeover," aroused informed public opinion, which in turn ultimately influenced the deliberations of Congress. The work of Westin (1967) and of Miller (1971) helped to crystallize the growing concern, emphasize the immediacy of the problem, and at the same time suggest procedures for effective solution.

Chronologically considered, the decisive response to the computer threat to privacy began in the mid-1960s with reaction to the proposal to establish a National Data Center (McCarty, 1976). Strong antagonism from the public and the press caused this federal proposal to be withdrawn. In 1971, the Fair Credit Reporting Act required any consumer-reporting agency to let an individual know the character of the information about him which it had in its files, and to give him an opportunity to correct this information.

A report of the Project on Computer Databanks sponsored by the Computer Science and Engineering Board of the National Academy of Sciences (Westin & Baker, 1972) kept the privacy issue squarely before the public and the scientific community. The project surveyed the computerized record systems of more than 500 government and private organizations, with on-site visits to 55 of those with the most advanced computer systems. The report found that, contrary to the dire predictions of many critics, the introduction of highly advanced and sophisticated computerization had not, as of that time at least, led organizations "to collect more detailed and intrusive personal information about individuals; to consolidate confidential information from previously separate files; and to share confidential personal data with government agencies and private organizations that had not received it before" (Westin, 1976, p. 119).

Most agencies and organizations continued the same policies on the collection and sharing of data as they had before computerization. Nevertheless, the report recommended legislation specifying the individual's right of access and challenge to files about him, the development of explicit rules for data sharing, the limitation or exclusion of intimate personal information from records, the implementation of confidentiality safeguards and policies within the computer industry, and, finally, a drastic curtailment of the use of the Social Security number as a "national identifier."

A correlative report entitled *Records, Computers, and the Rights of Citizens*, prepared by the Department of Health, Education, and Welfare (1973), was also devoted to the record-keeping practices of government and private organizations. It considered privacy in terms of mutuality: "The organization that holds personal data must not have complete control over it and, conversely, neither may the data subject—each has a stake in seeing that the information is used properly" (Ware, 1976, p. 113). The report also advanced a set of fundamental principles which serve to define "fair information practice."

> There must be no personal-data record-keeping systems whose very existence is secret.
>
> There must be a way for an individual to find out what information about him is in the record and how it is used.
>
> There must be a way for an individual to prevent information about him obtained for one purpose from being used or made available for other purposes without his consent.
>
> There must be a way for an individual to correct or amend a record of identifiable information about him [Ware, 1976, p. 113].

Also proposed were a number of safeguard requirements by which fair information practices could be implemented. The Health, Education, and Welfare Department's report concurred with that of Westin and Baker (1972) in insisting that the use of the Social Security number should be strictly limited to those instances in which it is mandated by law.

The privacy issue with regard to computerized information systems, then, has been a matter of public study and debate for a number of years. Within that time, the ideas relating personal information, data banks, and privacy had developed and crystallized sufficiently for the 93rd Congress to debate and act upon several of the many privacy bills which had been introduced. As a result of these congressional deliberations, two major bills were passed: the Family Education Rights and Privacy Act of 1974, and the Privacy Act of 1974.

The Family Educational Rights and Privacy Act, or the "Buckley Amendment," as it is more popularly called, has had the wider publicity. It permits parents access to the school records of their children. This right is also available to students over 18 years of age. Correspondingly, disclosure or dissemination of school records to outside sources is drastically curtailed.

The Privacy Act of 1974 specifically acknowledged that the development and use of sophisticated computers, though essential for modern society, posed a threat to individual privacy. As a consequence, it became necessary "for the Congress to regulate the collection, maintenance, use, and dissemination of information by such [federal] agencies" (Note 11, Section 2, a, 5). This law applies exclusively to the management of federal records. Its avowed purpose is "to safeguard individual privacy from the misuse of Federal records, to provide that individuals be granted access to records concerning them which are maintained by Federal agencies, to establish a Privacy Protection Study Commission, and for other purposes" (Note 11, Section 1).

The safeguards against invasion of privacy consist of the principles defining "fair information practice." The 1974 Privacy Act places the disclosure of records about an individual under his control and, in most cases, requires an accurate accounting of any disclosures. Each federal agency is to "maintain in its records only such information about an individual as is relevant and necessary to accomplish" (Note 11, Section 3, e, 1) its lawful purpose and to "make reasonable efforts to assure that such records are accurate, complete, timely, and relevant for agency purposes" (Note 11, Section 3, e, 5). Further, "appropriate administrative, technical, and physical safeguards [should be established] to insure the security and confidentiality of records" (Note 11, Section 3, e, 10). Every agency which maintains records on individuals is required to publish annually a descriptive notice of the systems which it controls. Disclosure of an individual's Social Security number is discouraged.

The Privacy Protection Study Commission established by the Act was empowered to review and analyze the complex interrelation of privacy and record-keeping both by government agencies and by private organizations and to "report on [such] legislative recommendations as it may determine to be necessary to protect the privacy of individuals while meeting the legitimate needs of government and society for information" (Note 11, Section 5, b, 2).

The final report of the Privacy Protection Study Commission has just been published (1977). Its recommendations stress the responsibilities of private organizations in regard to files and dossiers on individual citizens. Not surprisingly, these recommendations have a familiar ring, paralleling as they do those of the Privacy Act of 1974. Information privacy, whether in government agencies or in private organizations, has basically the same requirements. Some of the recommendations follow. Private organizations, such as insurance companies, credit bureaus, and private investigators should inform individuals when records or dossiers are kept on them; individuals should be permitted to see such records and to correct them if they are in error; the individual's permission is necessary before the organization can disseminate any records about him;

companies such as banks and credit card firms should not turn over information to government agencies without a court order; only information relevant to the individual's problem and the needs of the organization should be collected; and old information should be destroyed or updated after a reasonable period of time. The ultimate goal of these recommendations would seem to be the application of uniform standards for the maintaining, processing, and sharing of private records, whether in government agencies or in private organizations.

CONCLUDING COMMENTS

Perhaps the most striking outcome of this inquiry into the contemporary relations between privacy and surveillance is the recency of definitive legislation in the field: 1968 for electronic surveillance (Title III) and 1974 for data surveillance (Privacy Act). There is as yet no corresponding legislation covering psychological surveillance. But Senator Birch Bayh of Indiana has recently introduced a Polygraph Control Act which would ban the use of the polygraph in pre-employment screening or as a condition of continued employment, as he disclosed in a letter to the Editor of *The New York Times* (Bayh, 1977, p. 28). In his letter, Senator Bayh observes that such legislation is one of the recommendations of the Privacy Protection Study Commission report.

The question arises, naturally enough, as to why the legislation is so late and why it has been compressed within so short a time frame. The problems related to physical surveillance have been around for a long time, those associated with psychological surveillance (as lie detection) have been known since about 1930, and those concerned with data surveillance began to surface somewhere around 1960. Apparently, the legal basis of privacy was not considered broad or powerful enough to unify the various interests subsumed under the common name. Although the concept of a right to privacy had been discussed and debated in the legal literature for approximately three-quarters of a century, its emergence as an important individual right of citizens was not fully established until 1965, when the Supreme Court's *Griswold* opinion founded the right to privacy on constitutional grounds. The ensuing debate in legal circles about the *Griswold* case has kept the notion of privacy clearly in the forefront of popular and legal attention.

From another vantage point, the enactment of laws regulating physical and data surveillance was undoubtedly stimulated by the unprecedented technological advances in electronic detection and computer sophistication. The rapid development of these technologies produced a situation in which the balance between society's right to know and the individual's right to privacy was being tipped against the individual. Technological growth was accelerating so rapidly that an immediate response was necessary to protect the dignity and autonomy of the person. On the other hand, the absence of technical advances in the field of lie detection may help to explain why legislation in this area was not forthcoming. The standard instrumentation employed in the polygraph is no further advanced in principle than it was in the 1930s. As for voice analysis, as has been seen, a great deal of basic research is needed before this technique can begin to be considered as a competitor to the polygraph. In either case, the transition from physiological reactivity to the complex mental state described in words as "lying" or "truthful" is not direct; nor is it an easy one to infer. Thus, no immediate threat to privacy, instrumental or procedural, is envisioned which has not existed heretofore; and the proposed legislation to be introduced by Senator Bayh will address the only application of lie detection, employment screening, which has so far been objected to as an abuse of privacy.

All issues involving surveillance and privacy are complex and difficult to resolve in practice. Any balancing of opposing rights is a delicate matter, all the more so in the case of so ill-defined a right as that of privacy. Illegitimate surveillance, too, is less easy to identify in particular instances than might be imagined. As a current example, the recently reported electronic eavesdropping by the Soviet Union on microwave radio transmission in the United States presents a problem with no facile solution. If the messages being transmitted by microwave radio are easily picked up by anyone having the appropriate apparatus, and if no particular effort seems to have been made to make these communications reasonably secure, then it may be assumed that the sender is not very much concerned about the content or recipients of his message. The situation may be compared to that of two people talking to each other in the presence of a stranger. If they really desire their conversation to be private, they could converse in a language the stranger does not understand, or they could remove themselves from his presence and thus deprive him of the opportunity of listening in on them. An analogous procedure will undoubtedly be employed eventually with regard to long-distance telephone messages which are transmitted by microwave radio. In other words, an attempt will be made to limit the opportunity of the Soviet Union to "tune in" on such communications.

As observed in the analysis of the many definitions of privacy, it is difficult to find a unitary core underlying the concept which would be acceptable to all. Similarly, the division of surveillance into physical, psychological, and data components serves to emphasize the complexity and broad denotation of the concept. It may be that the identification of the modern idea of "information" with the concepts of privacy and surveillance will function to unify any discussion about the problems associated with both. Thus, the "loss of control over information about oneself" would seem to be a pragmatic description of the loss of privacy, and one which helps to clarify the connection between the concepts of surveillance and privacy.

REFERENCE NOTES

1. *Griswold v. Connecticut, 381* U. S. 479, 85 S. Ct. 1678, 14 L.Ed. 2d 510 (1965).
2. *NAACP v. Button, 371* U. S. 415 (1963).
3. American Psychological Association. *Final Report: Task force on privacy and confidentiality.* Unpublished manuscript, 1977. (Available from American Psychological Association, 1200 Seventeenth St., N. W., Washington, D.C. 20036.)
4. *Laird v. Tatum, 408* U. S. 1, 92 S. Ct. 2318, 33 L.Ed. 2d 154 (1972).
5. Committee on Federal Agency Evaluation Research, Assembly of Behavioral and Social Sciences, National Research Council. *Protecting individual privacy in evaluation research.* Washington, D.C.: National Academy of Sciences, 1975.
6. Edsall, J. T. *Scientific freedom and responsibility* (A Report of the American Association for the Advancement of Science Committee on Scientific Freedom and Responsibility). Washington, D.C.: American Association for the Advancement of Science, 1975.
7. *United States v. United States District Court, 407* U. S. 297, 92 S. Ct. 2125, 32 L.Ed. 2d 752 (1972).
8. Kubis, J. F. *Studies in lie detection* (RADC-TR 62–205). Rome, N.Y.: U. S. Air Force Rome Air Development Center, June 1962.
9. Kersta, L. G. *Voice print identification.* Paper presented at the meeting of The Acoustical Society of America, University Park, Pennsylvania, May 1962.
10. Myers, L. B., & Merluzzi, T. V. *Lie detection by voice analysis: A literature survey* (Report No. LWL 0529-100). Columbus, Ohio: Battelle Memorial Institute, 1971.
11. Public Law 93–579, December 31, 1974.

REFERENCES

Altman, I. *The environment and social behavior.* Monterey, Cal.: Brooks/Cole, 1975.

Anastasi, A. Psychological testing and privacy. In W. C. Bier (S.J.) (Ed.), *Privacy: A vanishing value?* New York: Fordham University Press, 1980.

Back, K. W. *Beyond words.* New York: Russell Sage Foundation, 1972.

Barland, G. H. The reliability of polygraph chart evaluations. In N. Ansley (Ed.), *Legal admissibility of the polygraph.* Springfield, Ill.: Thomas, 1975.

Bayh, B. Letter to the editor. *The New York Times,* August 30, 1977.

Beardsley, E. L. Privacy: Autonomy and selective disclosure. In J. R. Pennock & J. W. Chapman (Eds.), *Privacy* (Nomos XIII: Yearbook of the American Society for Political and Legal Philosophy). New York: Atherton, 1971.

Benn, S. I. Privacy, freedom, and respect for persons. In J. R. Pennock & J. W. Chapman (Eds.), *Privacy* (Nomos XIII: Yearbook of the American Society for Political and Legal Philosophy). New York: Atherton, 1971.

Bloustein, E. J. Privacy as an aspect of human dignity: An answer to Dean Prosser. *New York University Law Review,* 1964, *39,* 962–1007.

Bloustein, E. J. Privacy, tort law, and the constitution: Is Warren and Brandeis' tort petty and unconstitutional as well? *Texas Law Review,* 1968, *46,* 611–629.

Brenton, M. *The privacy invaders.* New York: Coward McCann, 1964.

Brown, R. M. *The electronic invasion.* New York: Rider, 1967.

Constitutional right of privacy. *Northwestern University Law Review*, 1974, *69*, 263–301.
Cooke, D. O. Defense Department statement on the polygraph. *Polygraph*, 1974, *3*, 269–271.
Dionisopoulos, P. A., & Ducat, C. R. *The right to privacy*. St. Paul: West, 1976.
Dixon, R. G., Jr. The *Griswold* penumbra: Constitutional charter for an expanded law of privacy? *Michigan Law Review*, 1965, *64*, 197–218.
Freund, P. A. Privacy: One concept or many? In J. R. Pennock & J. W. Chapman (Eds.), *Privacy* (Nomos XIII: Yearbook of the American Society for Political and Legal Philosophy). New York: Atherton, 1971.
Fried, C. Privacy. *Yale Law Journal*, 1968, *77*, 457–493.
George, B. J., Jr. Essential considerations toward judicial acceptance. *Polygraph*, 1974, *3*, 90–99.
Goffman, E. *Behavior in public places*. New York: Free Press, 1963.
Gross, H. The concept of privacy. *New York University Law Review*, 1967, *42*, 34–54.
Gross, H. Privacy and autonomy. In J. R. Pennock & J. W. Chapman (Eds.), *Privacy* (Nomos XIII: Yearbook of the American Society for Political and Legal Philosophy). New York: Atherton, 1971.
Jourard, S. M. *The transparent self*. New York: Van Nostrand Reinhold, 1964.
Jourard, S. M. Some psychological aspects of privacy. *Law and Contemporary Problems*, 1966, *31*, 307–318.
Kalven, H., Jr. Privacy in tort law—Were Warren and Brandeis wrong? *Law and Contemporary Problems*, 1966, *31*, 326–341.
Konvitz, M. R. Privacy and the law: A philosophical prelude. *Law and Contemporary Problems*, 1966, *31*, 273–280.
Kubis, J. F. Lie detection: Recent developments and persistent problems. *Transactions of The New York Academy of Sciences*, 1953, *16*, 34–38.
Kubis, J. F. Instrumental, chemical, and psychological aids in the interrogation of witnesses. *Journal of Social Issues*, 1957, *13*, 40–49.
Kubis, J. F. Comparison of voice analysis and polygraph as lie detection procedures. *Polygraph*, 1974, *3*, 1–47.
Lapidus, E. J. *Eavesdropping on trial*. Rochelle Park, N.J.: Hayden, 1974.
Lieberman, M. A., Yalom, I. D., & Miles, M. B. *Encounter groups: First facts*. New York: Basic Books, 1973.
Long, E. V. *The intruders: The invasion of privacy by government and industry*. New York: Praeger, 1967.
Lummis, R. C. Speaker verification: A step toward the "checkless" society. *Bell Laboratories Record*, 1972, *50*, 254–259.
Lusky, L. Invasion of privacy: A clarification of concepts. *Columbia Law Review*, 1972, *72*, 693–710.
Lykken, D. T. Psychology and the lie detector industry. *American Psychologist*, 1974, *29*, 725–739.
McCarty, A. Privacy—A perspective. In K. S. Larsen (Ed.), *Privacy, a public concern: A resource document*. Washington, D.C.: Government Printing Office, 1976.
McGuire, W. J. The value of privacy vs. the researcher's need to know. In W. C. Bier (S.J.) (Ed.), *Privacy: A vanishing value?* New York: Fordham University Press, 1980.
Miller, A. R. *The assault on privacy: Computers, databanks, and dossiers*. Ann Arbor: The University of Michigan Press, 1971.
National Commission for the Review of Federal and State Laws Relating to Wiretapping and Electronic Surveillance. *Electronic surveillance* (Final Report of the Commission). Washington, D.C.: Government Printing Office, 1976.

National Institute of Law Enforcement and Criminal Justice, Law Enforcement Assistance Administration, U. S. Department of Justice. *First Annual Report: Fiscal Year 1974*. Washington, D.C.: Government Printing Office, 1975.

Negley, G. Philosophical views on the value of privacy. *Law and Contemporary Problems*, 1966, *31*, 319–325.

Parker, R. B. A definition of privacy. *Rutgers Law Review*, 1974, *27*, 275–296.

Pennock, J. R., & Chapman, J. W. (Eds.). *Privacy* (Nomos XIII: Yearbook of the American Society for Political and Legal Philosophy). New York: Atherton, 1971.

Privacy Protection Study Commission. *Personal privacy in an information society* (Final Report of the Commission). Washington, D.C.: Government Printing Office, 1977.

Prosser, W. L. Privacy. *California Law Review*, 1960, *48*, 383–423.

Raskin, D. C., Barland, G. H., & Podlesny, J. A. Validity and reliability of detection of deception, *Polygraph*, 1977, *6*, 1–39.

Roberts, J. M., & Gregor, T. Privacy: A cultural view. In J. R. Pennock & J. W. Chapman (Eds.), *Privacy* (Nomos XIII: Yearbook of the American Society for Political and Legal Philosophy). New York: Atherton, 1971.

Romig, C. H. The dilemma of the admissibility of polygraph evidence. *Polygraph*, 1972, *1*, 125–135.

Rossiter, C. The pattern of liberty. In M. R. Konvitz & C. Rossiter (Eds.), *Aspects of liberty*. Ithaca, N.Y.: Cornell University Press, 1958.

Ruebhausen, O. M., & Brim, O. G., Jr. Privacy and behavioral research. *Columbia Law Review*, 1965, *65*, 1184–1211.

Schutz, W. C. *Elements of encounter*. Big Sur, Cal.: Joy Press, 1973.

Shils, E. Privacy: Its constitution and vicissitudes. *Law and Contemporary Problems*, 1966, *31*, 281–306.

Simmel, A. Privacy is not an isolated freedom. In J. R. Pennock & J. W. Chapman (Eds.), *Privacy* (Nomos XIII: Yearbook of the American Society for Political and Legal Philosophy). New York: Atherton, 1971.

Simonov, P. V., & Frolov, M. V. Analysis of the human voice as a method of controlling emotional state: Achievements and goals. *Aviation, Space, and Environmental Medicine*, 1977, *48*, 23–25.

Snyder, G. S. *The right to be let alone* (Rev. ed.). New York: Julian Messner, 1976.

U. S. Department of Health, Education, and Welfare. *Records, computers, and the rights of citizens: Report of the Secretary's Advisory Committee on Automated Personal Data Systems*. Washington, D.C.: Government Printing Office, 1973.

Van Den Haag, E. On privacy. In J. R. Pennock & J. W. Chapman (Eds.), *Privacy* (Nomos XIII: Yearbook of the American Society for Political and Legal Philosophy). New York: Atherton, 1971.

Ware, W. H. Records, computers, and the rights of citizens. In K. S. Larsen (Ed.), *Privacy, a public concern: A resource document*. Washington, D.C.: Government Printing Office, 1976.

Warren, S. D., & Brandeis, L. D. The right to privacy. *Harvard Law Review*, 1890, *4*, 193–220.

Webb, E. J., Campbell, D. T., Schwartz, R. D., & Sechrest, L. *Unobtrusive measures: Nonreactive research in the social sciences*. Chicago: Rand McNally, 1966.

Westin, A. F. *Privacy and freedom*. New York: Atheneum, 1967.

Westin, A. F. Databanks in a free society: A summary of the project on computer databanks. In K. S. Larsen (Ed.), *Privacy, a public concern: A resource document*. Washington, D.C.: Government Printing Office, 1976.

Westin, A. F., & Baker, M. A. *Databanks in a free society: Computers, recordkeeping, and privacy*. New York: Quadrangle, 1972.

Privacy and the Communications Media: Public Events, Private Lives

THOMAS POWERS

Thomas Powers, who has a B.A. degree from Yale University, is a journalist and writer. He was a general assignment reporter for United Press International from 1967 to 1970, and in 1971 won a Pulitzer Prize for National Reporting. In addition to his newspaper reporting and writing, Mr. Powers is the author of two books: Diana: The making of a terrorist *(1971), and* The war at home *(1973).*

THE LURE OF PUBLIC EVENTS

Well, what do you know? There he is again: the boy with the big ears, standing just the other side of the police barricade on a hot June night in 1968. An odd-looking boy in his late teens, with mossy teeth, big ears, freckles, curly hair piled on top of his long head. He reminded me of somebody the first time I saw him and finally I remembered who it was: Howdy Doody. Not the Howdy Doody most people remember, the round-faced, freckle-cheeked kid with the slicked-down hair and cowboy bandanna around his neck, but the first Howdy Doody with big ears and curly hair piled on top of his long head. And here he is again, in his accustomed place in the very first row behind the police barricade, up in the South Bronx—not an easy place to get to—on a hot June night. There is a strange, excited grin on his face.

Public events attract crowds. Not just gala movie premieres, inaugurations, ribbon cuttings, and Polish Day parades, which are deliberately orchestrated to attract crowds, but almost any kind of public event, as long as cameras are around. I live in New York, where they have been shooting a lot of movies of late, and no sooner do the police barricades go up than a crowd begins to collect. People stand in the winter snow or the summer heat for hours, watching the grips put up the big reflectors and camera scaffolding, waiting for the moment when shooting begins. If a well-known actor or actress is expected, the crowds can grow to astonishing size. You might pass them on the way to an appointment in the morning, and then return by the same route in late afternoon, and they are all still there, pressed up against the barricades, as patient and wondering as cows.

I think it must be the cameras. New York University has a film school and the students can often be found setting up their tripods and ancient Bolexes in Washington Square Park, with half-a-dozen people standing around, watching. There is something fatally attractive about the camera, even a Leica in the hands of some skinny fellow in tight jeans, shirt open halfway to his navel, squatting on the ground to photograph a model in a leather coat. People stand and watch, with the same blankness in their faces. If you live in New York, you see this sort of thing frequently, perhaps two or three times a month.

But if you work as a reporter you see it every day. As soon as the television crews arrive, the crowd begins to gather. When the lights go on, a kind of electricity passes through the crowd. If there is no barricade, the crowd inches forward on the sidewalk, closing in around the crew and the reporter. Later you see them on the six o'clock news, businessmen and giggling schoolgirls and women with shopping carts in the background, looking at the camera with expressions which range from blank wonder to ineffable longing. Sometimes they wave at the camera, little tentative, embarrassed waves, the hand going back and forth as if they were trying to catch the attention of a baby. If you were watching the local New York news back in 1968 and for a couple of years thereafter, and perhaps even if you were watching the national news in Iowa or Arizona, you probably saw the boy with the big ears. More than once. Because the boy with the big ears was a true media freak. He showed up everywhere, always in the front row, pressed up against the barricades, the same excited grin revealing his mossy teeth. The romance of public events had not simply invaded his life; it had taken him over altogether.

PUBLIC FIGURES AND THE RIGHT TO PRIVACY

We live in a world of unprecedented intimacy with the great, the powerful, and the merely famous. To get an idea of what I mean take a look at Horace Walpole's (1845/1894) *Memoirs of the Reign of King George the Third*. He was an interesting figure, perhaps the last British king who was really a king and a man whose increasing madness was carefully hidden from the public. Walpole, of course, was one of the wittiest men of his age, an indefatigable letter-writer with an insatiable appetite for news and an eye for the nuances of character, a fact which makes his *Memoirs of the Reign of King George the Third* all the more puzzling. They are flat and flavorless, an endless series of tableaux and set pieces: George III greeting his courtiers, climbing into his carriage, presiding at meetings of state. Walpole describes what he wore, how he looked, the timbre of his voice. After awhile you realize he is describing the man for those who have never seen him, who do not know the least human fact about him, not even his height.

Searchlight on Richard Nixon

We are accustomed to a greater intimacy with the men and women of power. We know very well what they look like, what sort of clothes they wear, how they tell a joke, the sound of their voices, their range of expression. A man like Richard Nixon revealed much of himself through the medium of television: the nervous stumbling over words, the pugnacious assertion of innocence, the restless eyes, the nervous patting of sweat from his upper lip, the odd dissonance between word and gesture. He was a strangely tense and driven man, at once secretive and transparent, and television made him as familiar as a neighbor. In a way, we almost *knew* him.

This fact has had some odd effects. For one thing it has sharpened our appetite for knowledge of the people who capture our interest. Photographs "at home" will no longer suffice. Carl Bernstein's and Bob Woodward's (1976) history of Nixon's fall, *The Final Days*, is filled with the sort of human detail which Suetonius would not have dared to publish about the Roman emperors until after they were safely dead. The fact, for example, that Nixon did not sleep with his wife. Or Mrs. Nixon's drinking. Or the awkward, unsettling scene where the President and Henry Kissinger both get down on their knees to pray.

At the time of its publication the book was widely criticized as an outrageous intrusion upon the Nixons' privacy. What did such details have to do with the legitimate affairs of state? They were purely salacious, a kind of disguised gloating over the destruction of a much-hated man. Whatever Nixon the President may have done, it was said, Nixon the man had a right to his own inner privacy. If he lied about Watergate, well, all right, expose his lies; but there is something indecent about squeezing in after him when he retires with his anguish into his own bedroom.

There is something in this, but the point raised strikes me as properly a moral one, a matter for the writer to decide in communion with his own conscience. I have been writing a biography of a man whose public career is of considerable interest; in the course of my research an astonishing number of people suggested that I talk to his first wife. She was described as a bitter woman with a great deal to say. Now you know as much about their life together as I do. I confess to a certain curiosity about what she might have told me, but in the end I decided against it. Divorces are notoriously acrimonious; how would I confirm, or even judge, what she had to say? What relevance did it have to the man's public career? The whole idea seemed unfair, vindictive, and wrong, an illegitimate invasion of the man's privacy.

Is Richard Nixon a Special Case?

But the case of Nixon was something else again. I would have done just as Bernstein and Woodward did. Never was a man's character so completely his fate. He was, and presumably still is, a strange mixture of intelligence and insecurity, awkward in public, in private sometimes able and resolute, sometimes suspicious, devious, vacillating, and vindictive. What happened to him was of his own doing, and there is no way to explain it without reference to his character.

Besides, the world is a harsh place. As Harry Truman once said, if you can't stand the heat, get out of the kitchen. Nixon himself seems to have understood this. He told David Frost, "I gave them a sword. And they stuck it in. And they twisted it with relish. And, I guess, if I'd been in their position I'd have done the same thing." The losers of great public contests tend to lose everything, not just power and place but the respect of their enemies and the reticence of their friends. They are as defenseless as the dead, and indeed one has to remind oneself not to write of Nixon in the past tense.

It is not the license of the press which explains the merciless scrutiny of Richard Nixon, but rather the character of the man and the nature of the world he inhabits along with the rest of us. Even without the First Amendment as an obstacle, there would be no way to legislate a rule of reticence dividing the public from the private Nixon. John F. Kennedy, not a "greater" man, exactly, but certainly a better-loved one, was for years the beneficiary of a kind of public indulgence, but even his defenses have begun to crumble. The private councils of his government were the first to be invaded, by memoirists like Arthur Schlesinger, Jr. (1971) and reporters like David Halberstam (1969), but the intrusion did not stop there; we have been into his bedroom, too, and no doubt we can expect to be visiting it again in the future. There is something in us which wants to know the truth about such men, not just the truth as they hoped it would appear, but the truth as it was. Cromwell without his warts is no Cromwell.

Does the Case of Oliver Sipple Raise a Different Issue?

But what about the private men who stumble into the public eye through no fault of their own? A man like Oliver Sipple, for example, an ex-Marine living in San Francisco who may have saved the life of Gerald Ford when he deflected the aim of a woman who fired a shot at the President in the late summer of 1975. Sipple acted purely on instinct; he was not trying to force his way into Truman's kitchen, just to save a man's life. But saving the President made him a "hero" in spite of himself. The press busied itself to find out who he was, and in short order discovered, and published, the fact that Sipple was a homosexual, something he had been at pains to hide from his family. Sipple was furious, and went to court claiming civil damages for the invasion of his privacy. Does the press have the right to "publish and be damned," when its target is a man who has committed no crime—far from it!—and cultivates his own anonymity?

It depends on what you mean by a "right." The First Amendment certainly gives the press a right to publish, but whether it has a "right" to immunity from damages even where damage has occurred is a legal question, still undecided, in the ballooning realm of privacy law. I am not a lawyer, so my opinion in this matter does not count for much, but it strikes me that giving Sipple relief—that is, a large sum of money to compensate for his "mental anguish"—would be a bad idea. For one thing, I am against paying people for mental anguish unless the intent is also exemplary and punitive. Money and suffering are apples and oranges; the attempt to compensate the one with the other is morally corrosive. We are mercenary enough as it is, and do not need encouragement. The only good argument for damages when a parent loses a child, or a man his reputation, is that it might persuade the responsible party to be more careful in the future.

But in the case of Oliver Sipple, it is precisely that admonitory effect which we ought to be most careful to avoid. No one has suggested that press reports of Sipple's homosexuality were either false or malicious; his whole case, in fact, depends on his claim that he has suffered because they were true. Who, besides Sipple, stands to gain if the press is warned in this instance to be wary of the truth? What happened to Sipple was unique and fortuitous, one of the accidents of life, and it does not make sense to impose a psychology of restraint on a fundamental institution of our society in order to protect the occasional individual from the equivalent of a bolt of lightning.

The really unique thing in Sipple's case is the fact that an entirely private man suddenly found himself in the fierce light of public consciousness. This rarely happens. Very rarely. Very *very* rarely. The attentions of the press are more narrowly focused. When you consider that there are perhaps 220 million Americans, the cast in the public drama begins to seem small. In a year we might draw up a reasonably accurate list from a handful of sources: the people columns in *The New York Times*, *The Washington Post*, *Time*, and *Newsweek*; the magazines *People* and *Us*; page six of the *New York Post*; *Women's Wear Daily*; *Forbes*; the guests on the big television talk shows; the Ear column in the *Washington Star*; *TV Guide*. There might be a couple of thousand names in all, one in 200,000 Americans. It would not be a list of the important people in American life, just of the public ones, the people who generate interest and attract attention (frequently with the aid of highly-paid press agents), and whose lives are sometimes probed by the press in minute detail.

THE CAST IN THE DRAMA OF PUBLIC EVENTS

A "Mixed Bag" of Personalities

Who is on the list? Present and past incumbents of the White House, first of all, and some (but not all, despite their efforts) of those who have got their eye on it. The Kennedys. Athletes by the score. Gore Vidal, Truman Capote, and Norman Mailer. A very small number of generals, businessmen, and scientists. Movie stars who get a million dollars a picture, plus some who used to, and some who would like to. Close relatives of the Kennedys. Billy Carter. Women who spend a great deal of money on clothes. Men who escort Jacqueline Bouvier Kennedy Onassis in public. At least one author of a diet book. Television "personalities." Distant relatives of the Kennedys. At least one representative from the women's, environmental, consumer, and gay rights movements. William F. Buckley. Television anchorpersons. An evangelical. John Kenneth Galbraith. Anwar Sadat. A painter or two. Jerry Brown. Somebody with a vast sum of money. And so on. A mixed bag of the durable and the fleeting, a handful of heavyweights and a battalion of lightweights. The point is not that we—I guess it has to be we—are so absorbed by the trivial, but that this small group, this precious few, is the cast of our public drama. We know as much about some of them as we do about our friends, a fact which begins to seem odd when you consider that *they* know nothing about *us*.

The Pathological not Excluded

Sometimes this has pathological results. It is well known that Presidents tend to get a zillion birthday cards, that rock musicians get love letters from teenagers, that celebrated murderers get offers of marriage, that public figures who cross the public are sometimes the target of extraordinary anonymous abuse. These are symptoms of the extent to which public figures enter private lives. Of course the public figures do not generally become public through inadvertence; they must storm the citadel of fame, and for every individual who squeezes inside, there must be a thousand more striving in perfect seriousness to join them. But even though public figures know something about anonymity, having fought so hard to shed it, I do not think they often anticipate the neurotic intensity of the response which they can elicit in the anonymous multitudes who know all about *them*.

I think something like this must have been at work in the life of Lee Harvey Oswald. No doubt he had his "reasons" for killing John F. Kennedy (setting aside for the moment—I wish it were forever—the possibility that Oswald did not act alone) but it is hard to see how they could have been sufficient without an element of personal resentment, anger, and hate. Oswald was a lonely, proud, brooding man, resentful of those who dismissed his "ideas," and fired with desire to make himself count. After he moved to Texas with his Russian wife, Marina, he failed at everything he attempted, rebuffed the friendships which were offered him, turned obsessively inward. But at the same time he was fascinated by Kennedy, and Marina describes him watching Kennedy on television, hanging on every word, clipping stories about him from the papers, arguing about him with the occasional visitor.

So much for what we know. What we do not know, but which I suspect, was that in Oswald's imagination he became an intimate of Kennedy's. The press and television brought him close, and Oswald completed the process, giving himself a fantasy role at Kennedy's side. I suspect that he argued with Kennedy in his mind, perhaps warned him against advisers like McGeorge Bundy, grew eloquent in defense of his "ideas." I suspect that in his own mind Oswald never shone brighter than he did when he was "with" Kennedy.

But Kennedy would not listen. He ignored Oswald's advice. He refused to soften his policy toward Cuba. Their intimacy was all in one direction. Oswald might grow emotional, even tearful, warn Kennedy against his mistakes in words which would soften a stone. But Kennedy would not listen. His eyes were always slightly averted. He acted as if Oswald did not even exist. At that point, I think, Oswald's lover's gift of himself began to turn toward hate.

I do not want to make too much of this; it is only a theory. Perhaps it did not happen that way at all. But there is no longer much question in my mind that in bringing public figures close, the media—television with its intimacy, the press with its detail—have created a psychic chasm between the precious few and everybody else. Far from threatening the privacy of the people, the media have banished them to it. The public drama has a rich cast in its hermetic way; every human type seems to be represented, but it is witnessed across a chasm far greater than could ever be created by footlights alone. The vast majority of the people are imprisoned in their privacy, locked out of the "real" world, and they gaze across the chasm with ineffable longing.

THE URGE TO BARTER AWAY PRIVACY

Evidence of this is all around us, but it is not of the sort a mathematician might marshal to prove a theorem. It does not add up, but only suggests. A friend who used to work for *Newsweek* once told me of a trip he took to Fort Riley, Kansas, back in the mid-1960s to do a story about soldiers leaving for Vietnam. A reporter for a local paper learned he was in town and asked for an interview. My friend was amazed and embarrassed in equal measure: why did the reporter want to interview *him*? He was not anybody. But the local reporter saw it quite differently; my friend worked for *Newsweek*, a national magazine, and he lived in New York. Between the lines of the reporter's story could be read an unmistakable yearning for the real world of the precious few.

Almost every reporter can tell stories of this sort. They may consider themselves inky wretches, with reason, but once they get out of New York and Washington they find themselves figures of unexpected glamour for the simple reason that they are associated with, even part of, the world of the precious few. I have watched it myself in Texas, Mississippi, Florida, Illinois, and New Hampshire, and it is unsettling. People do not seem to regard a meeting with a writer or reporter as an ordinary encounter. They may be engaged in the most serious sort of work themselves, may even have a low regard for the press as biased, frivolous, and wrongheaded; but some part of them wilts all the same, and a moment generally comes when they express a longing for the "real" world of those who talk and are talked about.

I am not making this up; the yearning is really there. You can see it in the audiences of television shows, where adults wave at the camera—look! it's me! !—and squirm like children if the camera should be directed for a moment at *them*. A famous face will do it without fail; Elliot Gould in a restaurant, say. Perfectly sensible people cannot take their eyes off him. Even economists at a convention will lose the thread of learned conversation when John Kenneth Galbraith enters the room. It is especially apparent in academic communities, where intellectual fires grow cold in the daily round, and professors of literature and political science think wistfully of the "real" worlds of writing and politics. They feel cut off, isolated, and anonymous, and wonder uneasily if they have made bad bargains in trading the dangers of the "real" world for the security of careers and curriculum committees. Their wives seem to sense the chasm more keenly still. They hang Käthe Kollwitz prints and Guatemalan bolas on their walls, serve wine and exotic cheeses at parties, subscribe to *New York* magazine and the Sunday *Times*, read hardback novels. They are heroically *au courant*. But ten minutes of conversation can reveal a frightening intensity of longing for the electricity of the "real" world they have read about, and know is there, but can never reach.

Of course, some of this is just life; summer never quite lives up to the promise of spring, and every life is touched with regret. But even when you have taken that into account there remains the yearning of those who live in a media-saturated world for something of the magic of the precious few. Not in everybody all the time, but astonishingly close to everybody at least some of the time. The press talks without ceasing, but it never talks about them; their privacy is inviolate, and it takes some of the salt out of a life to feel so utterly neglected.

Perhaps it could be no other way. The press defines the world, but while the world has been growing larger, the press is growing smaller. The London of Samuel Johnson had as many newspapers as a man could read, doing nothing else. New York once had a dozen newspapers, then five, then three. We live in a big country, but the barriers of region have been going down. There may be 1,762 daily newspapers, but they all subscribe to the same two wire services. There are three national newsmagazines, two in New York and one in Washington. There are three television networks, all headquartered in New York. It is not exactly a rich diversity of voices for 220 million people. Small wonder that the cast in the public drama is so small, and that the rest of us must live on the far side of the chasm.

And there he is again: the boy with the big ears. Someone has shot and killed two boys, both Puerto Ricans: not much of a story under normal circumstances, but Bobby Kennedy was murdered only a few days before, they are talking of gun control in Washington, and snipers are news. So the press is out in force: three or four television crews, setting up their lights in the late June evening; half-a-dozen radio reporters with their Sonys; at least a dozen reporters.

The police are searching a building for the sniper. The bodies are over there on the sidewalk, covered with a tarpaulin. A foot sticks out from under the edge of the canvas; I can see that the shoe is untied. A pool of blood, dark and thick as motor oil, slowly spreads out into the street. Off to one side the police are holding back some weeping women; they must be the mothers of the boys.

But the boy with the big ears is not paying attention to all that. He is pressed up against the barricade, his eye for the cameras, straining to emerge from his anonymity.

REFERENCES

Bernstein, C., & Woodward, B. *The final days.* New York: Simon & Schuster, 1976.

Halberstam, B. *The unfinished odyssey of Robert Kennedy.* New York: Random House, 1969.

Schlesinger, A. M., Jr. *A thousand days: John F. Kennedy in the White House.* Boston: Houghton Mifflin, 1971.

Walpole, H. *Memoirs of the reign of King George the Third* (4 vols.) (G. F. Russell Barker, Ed.). London: Lawrence & Bullen, 1894. (Originally published, 1845).

The Assault on Privacy by the Agencies of Government

ATHAN G. THEOHARIS

Athan G. Theoharis earned his academic degrees at the University of Chicago: A.B. in 1956; M.A. in 1959; and Ph.D. in 1965. He taught at Texas A. & M. University, Wayne State, and CUNY (Staten Island) before coming to Marquette University where he is currently Professor of History. Dr. Theoharis has been consultant, U. S. Senate Select Committee on Intelligence Activities (the so-called Church Committee); consultant, Subcommittee on Government Information and Individual Rights of the House Government Operations Committee; consultant on wiretapping legislation, staff of U. S. Senator Gaylord Nelson. Dr. Theoharis is the author of The Yalta myths *(1970) and* Seeds of repression *(1971); co-author of* Anatomy of anti-communism *(1969) and* U. S. in the twentieth century *(1978); and co-editor of* The specter: Original essays on the Cold War and the origins of McCarthyism *(1974).*

Of necessity, organized government requires that governmental agencies impose some restrictions on individual privacy. To concede this, however, is not to concede that government officials have unrestricted authority to circumscribe personal privacy. Not only must there be a legitimate administrative and legislative need for such restrictions but, more important, under the American political system these agencies must comply with the specific requirements of the U. S. Constitution and statutory authority.

CONSTITUTIONAL AND LEGAL GUARANTEES

For the purpose of this paper's focus on federal intelligence agencies, the most relevant provisions of the Constitution are the first, fourth, and fifth amendments. These amendments indirectly ensure a right to privacy not by positively conferring such a right to the individual but by sharply confining governmental powers. Thus, the First Amendment stipulates that

> Congress shall make no law respecting an establishment of religion, or prohibiting the free exercise thereof; or abridging the freedom of speech, or of the press; or the right of the people peaceably to assemble, and to petition the Government for a redress of grievances.

The Fourth Amendment establishes that

> The right of the people to be secure in their persons, houses, papers, and effects, against unreasonable searches and seizures, shall not be violated, and no Warrants shall issue, but upon probable cause, supported by Oath or affirmation, and particularly describing the place to be searched, and the persons or things to be seized.

Finally, the Fifth Amendment provides that

> No person shall be . . . compelled in any criminal case to be a witness against himself, nor be deprived of life, liberty, or property without due process of law.

To these constitutional safeguards the Congress has directly or indirectly imposed additional restrictions upon governmental agencies: directly by specifying limits to these agencies' powers and indirectly by limiting the authority of federal law enforcement agencies to investigate only violations or suspected violations of federal law.

These legal and constitutional limitations, accordingly, broadly define the privacy rights of American citizens. The First Amendment recognizes explicitly the right of the individual to dissent and to organize to effect change, and implicitly the right to discuss and organize privately—as long as these activities do not violate federal law. The Fourth Amendment prohibits government agents from seizing the papers (and, given recent technological developments, statements) of individuals unless these agents first obtain warrants and thereby specify to an independent authority (a federal judge) the papers sought and the particular violations of law which justify such invasions of personal privacy. The Fifth Amendment establishes the individual's right to remain silent and not to testify to his or her guilt of specific crime. In sum, then, these amendments ensure privacy rights by defining the permissible authority of governmental agents. They are based on definite premisses and principles: namely, that the United States is a government of laws and not of men, that the authority of executive officials must be tightly defined and reined in to prevent them from abusing such potentially vast power, and that law enforcement officials in the course of prosecuting citizens for violating the law cannot in the process violate the law. The Founding Fathers might not have been libertarians; they did place a high value on order and security. Nonetheless, they feared that unchecked and non-accountable authority would threaten individual freedom—hence, their concern for privacy.

RECENT INFRINGEMENTS BY GOVERNMENT AGENCIES

It is ironic, then, that we have recently learned that these carefully formulated constraints have neither ensured privacy nor minimized government intrusions into individual privacy. This knowledge has come from a number of sources, but notably the recent hearings and reports of the House and Senate select committees on intelligence activities, the requests of individual citizens utilizing provisions of the Freedom of Information Act of 1966 (as amended in 1974) for the files which the Federal Bureau of Investigation (FBI) and the Central Intelligence Agency (CIA) had compiled on their past political activities, and lawsuits (totaling, as of May 1977, 143) for damages filed against government agencies by the Socialist Workers Party, the National Lawyers Guild, and countless individuals.* As a result, we now know that for roughly 40 years government agencies (without legal authority in some cases and in clear violation of the U. S. Constitution in others) assaulted privacy rights of U. S. citizens. In addition, these high-level intelligence officials knowingly authorized violations of the law and the Constitution in order to acquire information which they intended to use for political and not for prosecutive purposes: in the words of an August 25, 1967, memorandum from FBI Director J. Edgar Hoover to all FBI Special Agents in Charge to "expose, disrupt, misdirect, discredit, or otherwise neutralize" organizations which Bureau officials had concluded threatened the national security.

An analysis of the activities of government agencies (and this paper will detail certain historical practices of four federal agencies—the Federal Bureau of Investigation, the Central Intelligence Agency, the National Security Agency, and the Internal Revenue Service) offers insights into the scope of this assault on privacy, the underlying causes for these developments, and the future prospects for individual privacy in our society.

* These suits are compiled in a May 6, 1977 report of the Comptroller General of the United States, Elmer Steats, to the House Subcommittee on Government Information and Individual Rights.

OPERATIONS OF FEDERAL BUREAU OF INVESTIGATION

Established in 1908 by executive order as the investigative division of the Department of Justice, the Bureau of Investigation (formally identified as the Federal Bureau of Investigation in 1934) had authority to investigate only violations of interstate commerce law. At the time, moreover, Attorney General Charles Bonaparte assured concerned congressmen that the Bureau would not investigate political activities or beliefs. But concerns over "national security" and "subversion," which surfaced during World War I and in the postwar scare of 1919–1920, soon led the Bureau to investigate extensively dissident political activities.

Early Expansion of FBI Surveillance

The scope of the Bureau's surveillance of American citizens' legitimate political dissent, investigations which began in 1917 and continued after the end of the war until 1924, and the illegality of some of these practices (which included mail covers, break-ins, and wiretaps of congressmen investigating the Teapot Dome scandal) were publicized during the early 1920s. Responding to these revelations of the Bureau's abuses of power, in 1924 Attorney General Harlan Fiske Stone issued an executive order instituting a series of reforms. One of these was to ban FBI political surveillance: the Bureau's authority was restricted to investigating violations of federal statutes (Countryman, 1973, pp. 33–49; Theoharis, 1976, pp. 71–72).

But Stone's ban on FBI political surveillance proved to be temporary. Concerned over the radicalization of American politics during the 1930s, and convinced that many American radicals and political extremists were either Soviet or German agents, FBI Director J. Edgar Hoover sought presidential authorization empowering the FBI to investigate "subversive activities." First in 1936 and again in 1939 by exploiting President Franklin D. Roosevelt's concerns about possible foreign direction to dissident political activities and, then, in 1950 and 1953 by exploiting both the Cold War concerns of Presidents Harry S Truman and Dwight D. Eisenhower and their ignorance of Roosevelt's earlier directives, Director Hoover succeeded in securing presidential authorization for the FBI to investigate dissident political organizations and individuals (Theoharis, 1976–1977, pp. 649–672).

Having obtained this authority (if by questionable means), FBI Director Hoover sought to ensure continued presidential approval. He did so first by servicing specific presidential requests (whether from Roosevelt, Truman, Eisenhower, Kennedy, Johnson, or Nixon) for information on that administration's political critics and then by independently and regularly forwarding to key White House staff members reports detailing the planned activities of their critics. Begun during Franklin Roosevelt's presidency, this FBI reporting practice continued through succeeding administrations.

During Richard M. Nixon's presidency, in 1969, moreover, this reporting role was regularized and rationalized—and was given a formal name, the Inlet program—by FBI Director Hoover. Included among the subjects of these Bureau reports, which ranged from derogatory highly personal information to detailed accounts of the political strategies of opponents of these administrations, were: critics of the Roosevelt Administration's lend–lease proposal, the Henry Wallace Progressive Party campaign of 1948, the John Birch Society and other right-wing critics of the Eisenhower Administration, congressmen and lobbyists seeking to enact an alternative sugar-quota bill to that supported by the Kennedy Administration, the strategy of civil rights groups at the 1964 Democratic National Convention, and key foreign policy advisers to Democratic Senator Edmund Muskie, an aspirant for his party's 1972 presidential nomination (Sullivan, 1974, p. 95; U. S. Senate Select Committee, 1975, Vol. 6, pp. 368–369, 452–454, 495–510, 623–638, 642–644, 683, 713–717, 721–724; U. S. Senate Select Committee, 1976, Bk. 2, pp. 7–9, 48–52, 64–66, 81, 105, 117–118, 175, 180, 201, 227–230, 232–234, 237–239, 251; U. S. Senate Select Committee, 1976, Bk. 3, pp. 123, 245–246, 313–314, 324–326, 328–330, 335, 337, 343, 345–348, 350–351, 457, 483–485, 532–533, 551).

Although inadequate executive oversight had permitted the FBI director to define the scope of the Bureau's investigative authority, Hoover's decisions to respond to presidential requests for information about political opponents and further to volunteer similar information ensured that the Bureau need not be concerned that presidents would attempt to curb these activities. Nonetheless, because the Bureau's broad investigative effort had no prosecutive purpose and thereby lacked legal authorization, these investigative activities potentially entailed major political risks for the Bureau. Disclosure of the FBI's role in servicing the political interests of various presidents could precipitate an adverse anti-FBI reaction. This made it imperative that the Bureau ensure that these activities could not become publicly known. Accordingly, beginning in 1940 FBI Director Hoover and other Bureau officials devised (and then refined) elaborate file-keeping procedures.

The Bureau's File-Keeping Procedures

Because it was the Department of Justice's investigative agency, the FBI had to devise an efficient, comprehensive file-keeping system. Such a system was essential: (1) to ensure that responsible officials could have ready and complete access to all FBI investigative reports when preparing indictments, grand jury presentations, and prosecutions; and (2) to enable government attorneys to comply with court-ordered disclosure requirements for all information (if any) of illegal governmental activities. To meet these needs, Bureau officials devised a centralized filing system in which all documents submitted from FBI field offices to the Washington Bureau headquarters were given a serial number and were organized by subject and legal area so that they could be both cross-filed and readily retrieved.

These filing procedures posed certain problems for the post-1936 Bureau. Court-mandated disclosure requirements, for one, could expose the extent and nature of FBI investigations of the political, and non-criminal, activities of American dissidents. Moreover, the possibility of disclosure through leaks or court proceedings of the FBI's responsiveness to presidential requests for name checks of individuals critical of administration policy and then Director Hoover's periodic and independent volunteering of political information about political critics of these administrations could prove embarrassing or actually damaging to the Bureau's image and authority. To avert these possibilities, in memoranda of 1940, 1941, 1942, and 1943, FBI Director Hoover informed Bureau officials of the procedures which they should employ when they were preparing memoranda which should not be retained and filed in the FBI's general files.

One purpose for these procedures was to minimize unnecessary paper work. But an additional purpose was to ensure that FBI field offices could submit sensitive information in writing to the FBI director and to other high-level Washington Bureau officials with the assurances that the information could be kept confidential and could not be retrieved through normal filing procedures. A March 1, 1942, memorandum from FBI Director Hoover to all Bureau officials underscores this purpose. Hoover specifically identified memoranda to be so submitted (on pink paper, distinguishing these memoranda from those others which were to be prepared on white paper and would then be serialized and filed) as those "prepared solely for the benefit of the Director and other officials and eventually be returned to the dictator [of the memorandum] to be destroyed or retained in the Director's office."

Having thereby resolved the disclosure problem, in an October 1, 1941, "informative memorandum—not to be sent to Files Section" (the procedure developed in 1940 and refined in 1941), the FBI director advised Bureau officials of his decision to maintain a "confidential file" in the office of his personal secretary, Helen Gandy. This file, Hoover emphasized, would "be restricted to items of a more or less personal nature of the Director's and items which I might have occasion to call for from time to time" (U. S. House Subcommittee, 1975, pp. 96–99, 103–104, 116–118, 123–146, 154–170, 173).

FBI's "Confidential Files" and "No-File" Systems

As Bureau officials and former Attorney General Edward Levi later conceded, included in Hoover's "confidential files" were potentially embarrassing information concerning prominent individuals (House Subcommittee, 1975, pp. 87–88, 97, 139–140). The creation of the "confidential files" and the devising of this not-to-be-filed procedure would enable Bureau officials subsequently to forward derogatory and political information which the FBI director or other Washington Bureau officials could then leak to "friendly" news reporters,* White House officials, or prominent personalities.† That the Bureau was violating privacy rights and exceeding its legal authority no longer need be a concern: effective measures had been devised to preclude the risk of exposure.

If not inevitable, it was not wholly unexpected that the Bureau would adopt similar file-keeping procedures when initiating "clearly illegal" activities. One such involved the decision by the FBI director to authorize break-ins by FBI agents. Only through break-ins, Washington Bureau officials recognized, could FBI agents install microphones (bugs) or obtain membership, mailing, contributor, or similar lists identifying members, supporters, or proposed strategies of those organizations which these officials deemed "subversive." Accordingly, in 1942 the FBI leadership devised an elaborate "Do Not File" procedure to enable agents to conduct break-ins, subject to close supervision from FBI headquarters in Washington, but at the same time without creating a retrievable written record which could be disclosed during court proceedings (U. S. Senate Select Committee, 1976, Bk. 3, pp. 355–371). This procedure was fully de-

* One such reporter was the conservative *Chicago Tribune* Washington correspondent Walter Trohan. See Memo, Marvin Watson to President Lyndon Johnson, July 10, 1967, WHCF FG135A/2, FG 135-6 1/14/67-6/30/68, Lyndon Baines Johnson Library. See also the extensive correspondence between FBI Director Hoover and Trohan in the Walter Trohan Papers, J. Edgar Hoover File, Herbert C. Hoover Library.

† On February 27, 1946, the head of the FBI's Intelligence Division, D. M. Ladd, proposed that the Bureau release "educational material" through "available channels" to influence "public opinion" (Senate Select Committee, 1976, Bk. 2, p. 66). Rev. John F. Cronin was one recipient of this FBI educational campaign. When preparing a report for the American Catholic Bishops on Communism in the United States in 1945 and another report on this same subject for the U. S. Chamber of Commerce in 1946, Father Cronin had privileged access to FBI investigative files. Then, in August 1948, Father Cronin acted as an intermediary between FBI agent Ed Hummer and Republican Congressman Richard Nixon, forwarding to the congressman on a daily basis the latest results of the FBI investigation of Alger Hiss (Wills, 1971, pp. 36–37; Irons, 1974, pp. 79–82).

scribed in a July 19, 1966, memorandum from the head of the FBI's Intelligence Division, William Sullivan, to Assistant FBI Director Cartha DeLoach.‡ Sullivan began by noting that authorization could not be obtained "from outside the Bureau" (i.e., from the attorney general). He then emphasized:

> The present procedure followed in the use of this technique calls for the Special Agent in Charge of a field office to make this request for the use of this technique to the appropriate Assistant Director. The Special Agent in Charge must completely justify the need for the use of the technique and at the same time assure that it can be safely used without any danger or embarrassment to the Bureau. The facts are incorporated in a memorandum which, in accordance with the [FBI] Director's instructions is sent to [Assistant FBI Director] Mr. Tolson or to the Director for approval. Subsequently, this memorandum is filed in the Assistant Director's office under a "Do Not File" procedure.
>
> In the field, the Special Agent in Charge prepares an informal memorandum showing that he obtained Bureau authority and this memorandum is filed in his safe until the next inspection by Bureau inspectors, at which time it is destroyed [U.S. Senate Select Committee 1975, Vol. 2, pp. 273–275].

In 1975 congressional testimony, former Assistant FBI Director Charles Brennan conceded that this "Do Not File" procedure ensured that break-in requests and authorizations would not be serialized, thereby making it possible for Bureau officials to destroy these documents without having left a record of having done so. Brennan further conceded that the "Do Not File" procedure also enabled the Bureau to comply with any future court disclosure orders and to affirm that a search of FBI records uncovered no evidence of illegal governmental activities (U. S. Senate Select Committee, 1975, Vol. 2, pp. 98, 129–131).

Counter-intelligence Surveillance Extended to Dissidents

Having resolved the disclosure problem and neutralized meaningful executive oversight of FBI investigative activities, it was only natural that the Bureau would formalize and refine its political efforts to undermine the influence of dissident groups. Beginning in 1956, accordingly, the FBI devised a series of so-called counter-intelligence programs—identified in Bureau documents as COINTELPRO. The 1956 program was directed

‡ In 1965, a Senate subcommittee had begun an investigation of illegal or questionable activities by federal intelligence agencies, focusing on the Internal Revenue Service. Concerned over the political impact of this investigation, FBI Director Hoover requested that Washington Bureau officials review FBI practices. This July 1966 memorandum followed from this request and detailed how the FBI conducted break-ins and the safeguards adopted to avert disclosure.

against the Communist Party. Similar programs were instituted involving the Socialist Workers Party (in 1961), so-called White Hate–Extremist groups (in 1964), so-called Black Nationalist–Extremist groups (in 1967), and the New Left (in 1968). These programs did not have as their purpose to acquire evidence of illegal or treasonous activities; indeed, the Bureau already possessed extensive information about the activities of members of these organizations which it could not use for prosecutive purposes because the information either had been illegally obtained or revealed no violation of any federal statute. Rather, the rationale for and impetus to these COINTELPROs was to obtain and disseminate information in order to "expose, disrupt, misdirect, discredit, or otherwise neutralize" these organizations.

FBI activities under these programs included: (1) attempts to break up marriages; (2) the dissemination of derogatory information (personal as well as political) to the media, employers, and public officials; (3) efforts to ensure Internal Revenue Service tax audits of individuals who were prominent members of these groups; and (4) attempts to prevent the election or appointment of, or to have public officials or private employers fire, members of these groups. All these COINTELPROs, moreover, were initiated without the prior consent or knowledge of various attorneys general (let alone presidents). In addition, elaborate procedures were devised to ensure that Bureau involvement in the activities which the FBI director had authorized under these programs could not be traced to the FBI (Blackstock, 1976, pp. 27–192; Wise, 1976, pp. 148, 279, 281, 314–320; U. S. Senate Select Committee, 1975, Vol. 6, pp. 372–407, 432–442, 762–817; U. S. Senate Select Committee, 1975, Vol. 3, pp. 45–47; U. S. Senate Select Committee, 1976, Bk. 3, pp. 3–72, 81–184, 187–223, 839, 845, 847–859).

Nor was the FBI the sole federal agency illegally assaulting individual privacy rights, and for non–law-enforcement purposes. Other agencies—notably, the Central Intelligence Agency, the National Security Agency, and the Internal Revenue Service—similarly investigated or harassed American citizens because of their dissident political beliefs. Sensitive to the illegality of these investigative activities, these agencies also devised procedures to minimize the risk of exposure.

National Security Agency and its procedures

In 1952, President Harry S Truman established by executive order the National Security Agency (NSA) within the Department of Defense. The NSA's responsibility was to intercept international electronic communications essential for military defense and for foreign policy planning. Responding to requests from other intelligence agencies, however, in 1967 the NSA began to intercept the international communications of targeted American citizens and organizations. In the interim, because of the development of more sophisticated technology, the NSA had developed the capability to intercept virtually all international messages sent from the United States. It thus became essential that the Agency be able to identify particularly desired messages.

This posed no problem for interception of defense-related signals. To employ this technology toward dissidents, however, required that the NSA be provided with a list of specific names or code words. In 1967, the FBI and CIA forwarded such a list of American citizens and organizations to the NSA, a so-called Watch List. Sensitive to the illegality of this activity (because it was directed against American citizens in violation of the Fourth Amendment and of the provisions of the Federal Communications Act of 1934), in 1969 the NSA devised formal procedures to ensure that its involvement in this warrantless electronic surveillance of American citizens could not be discovered. To conceal that the NSA was the source of this information, reports produced under this interception program were not given NSA serial numbers, were not filed with other NSA reports, and were disseminated "For Background Use Only." Agencies receiving these NSA reports were directed either to destroy or to return them to the NSA within two weeks. Lastly, these reports were hand-delivered and only to those officials having knowledge of the NSA's servicing role. This program's formal charter, under the code name MINARET, outlined its procedures and objectives:

> 1. MINARET (C) is established for the purpose of providing more restrictive control and security of sensitive information derived from communications as processed [deleted] which contain . . . (b) information on U.S. organizations or individuals who are engaged in activities which may result in civil disturbances or otherwise subvert the national security of the U.S. An equally important aspect of MINARET will be to restrict the knowledge that such information is being collected and processed by the National Security Agency.
> 2. MINARET specifically includes communications concerning individuals or organizations involved in civil disturbance, anti-war movements/demonstrations and military deserters involved in anti-war movements [U. S. Senate Select Committee, 1975, Vol. 5, p. 150].

The object of the NSA's MINARET program was to uncover information about possible foreign influence on or control of dissident political activities. Its purpose was thus distinctly political: this information could then be used by administration officials to discredit these activities as "subversive." Though they were willing to violate the law, the first concern of these federal intelligence officials was to ensure that the NSA's involvement in this illegal effort would not become publicly known. It is not surprising, then, that risk of exposure and not concern over illegality or violations of privacy rights led to this program's termination in 1973.

During pre-trial hearings in a federal court case, *U. S. v. Ayres*, Federal District Judge Damon Keith ordered specified federal agencies (including the NSA) to submit affidavits disclosing whether they had engaged in illegal activities directed at any of the defendants in the case. After first attempting to narrow the scope of the judge's ruling, and then after lengthy and troubled intra-administration discussions whether to comply with the judge's order, the government eventually decided to drop prosecution of the case rather than risk disclosure of this NSA program. This ruling, moreover, led NSA and Justice Department officials to terminate MINARET (U. S. Senate Select Committee, 1976, Bk. 3, pp. 736–764, 781–782; U. S. Senate Select Committee, 1975, Vol. 5, pp. 7–24, 31–33, 145–163; Theoharis, 1974, pp. 140–141).

Special Service Staff of Internal Revenue Service

Furthermore, on June 25, 1969, the Internal Revenue Service created a special division, the Special Service Staff (SSS), to focus IRS field-office tax-audit investigations on particular individuals and organizations. Those who were targeted by the SSS were not suspected of having violated federal tax law. These individuals/organizations were targeted because they opposed administration policy. Thus, when informing FBI Director Hoover in August 1969 that this new division had been established, an Assistant IRS Commissioner (Compliance) identified the purpose of this effort as "to gather data and recommend actions to be taken within the Internal Revenue Service relating to various organizations of predominantly dissident or extremist nature and/or people predominantly identified with these organizations." The assistant commissioner requested that the Bureau include this IRS division on its "dissemination list" of dissident organizations and individuals. The FBI readily complied.

Through its own investigations and the lists provided by the FBI, the SSS developed information on particular activists and organizations, analyzed the information to ascertain whether a tax issue was involved, and then forwarded the information to IRS field offices. Though it could not direct field offices to initiate a tax audit, the SSS's activities did unbalance IRS tax-audit investigations and ensured that disproportionate attention would be given to these targeted dissidents. Because of the political nature of this project, IRS officials sought to confine knowledge of the SSS to those having a "need to know." An unsigned July 24, 1969 memorandum highlighted this exclusive concern over political embarrassment:

> We certainly must not open the door to widespread notoriety that would embarrass the Administration or any elected officials. This is one of the reasons why we are not publicizing this Committee [the SSS] except as such publicity may be necessary within the [Internal Revenue] Service

[U. S. Senate Select Committee, 1975, Vol. 3, pp. 2–4, 9, 14, 29–35, 39–44, 50–52, 96–101; U. S. Senate Select Committee, 1975, Vol. 2, pp. 309–312, 395; U. S. Senate Select Committee, 1976. Bk. 3, pp. 837–838, 842–844, 848, 850, 854–855, 857, 858, 876–920].

EXPANSION OF CIA SURVEILLANCE

The National Security Act of 1947 authorized the creation of a Central Intelligence Agency (CIA) to improve the flow and quality of intelligence information to the White House, information deemed essential for foreign policy and defense planning. This statute, moreover, specifically banned the CIA from engaging in domestic surveillance investigations. But within six years the CIA had ignored the ban. In 1952, the CIA instituted a mail-cover project in New York City, reading envelopes and recording the names of those corresponding with or receiving mail from the Soviet Union, ostensibly to collect foreign intelligence information. Shortly thereafter, the CIA began opening this mail of American citizens and after 1958 forwarded to the FBI information obtained through this mail-intercept program. CIA documents of the 1960s disclose an awareness that this program was illegal. Because they were confident that the agency's involvement could be safeguarded without risk of disclosure, however, CIA officials concluded that there was no reason to discontinue this program. The CIA's mail program was finally terminated in 1973, not because CIA officials were belatedly sensitive to legal considerations, but because they had concluded that continuance of the program was too risky politically in the post-Watergate atmosphere, given the more assertive position adopted by members of Congress (U. S. Senate Select Committee, 1976, Bk. 3, pp. 561–636; U. S. Senate Select Committee, 1975, Vol. 4, pp. 4–7, 16–17, 24, 31, 34–38, 45–49, 60–61, 71–75, 80–95, 113–114, 119–129, 148–150, 154–156, 167–168, 175–183, 189, 192, 195–196, 199–205, 219–223, 245–248; Presidential Commission on CIA, 1975, pp. 20–21, 102–106, 110–114).

Then, in 1967 and again in defiance of the National Security Act's domestic surveillance ban, the CIA instituted a series of programs (code-named CHAOS, MERRIMAC, and RESISTANCE) focusing on the dissident political activities of American citizens. Ostensibly, the purpose of these programs was to ascertain foreign influence or control (if any) over domestic dissident activities and organizations. Almost immediately, however, CIA agents began to gather information about domestic dissent, and their findings were incorporated in reports which were then sent to the White House. Moreover, when CIA reports of 1969 and 1970 emphasized that no evidence of foreign influence or control had been uncovered, the Nixon White House refused to accept these conclusions. Instead, the White House first broadened the definition of foreign "control" to include any form of influence or contact and then pressured Agency officials to continue and to intensify this investigative effort. Clearly, the administration's concern was political: if possible to uncover information which it could then use to discredit its critics. Again because they recognized the "sensitivity" (i.e., illegality) of these programs, the CIA officials disseminating these reports urged Nixon White House personnel to safeguard closely that the CIA was the source of this information. In a February 18, 1969, memorandum to President Nixon's national security adviser Henry Kissinger, CIA Director Richard Helms starkly affirmed:

> In an effort to round out our discussion, we have included a section on American students. This is an area not within the charter of this Agency, so I need not emphasize how extremely sensitive this makes this paper. Should anyone learn of its existence it would prove most embarrassing for all concerned [U. S. Senate Select Committee, 1975, Vol. 2, p. 401].

Helms's sole concern over embarrassment, and not legality, also determined the decision of his successor as CIA director to terminate this program. As with the NSA's MINARET program and the CIA's mail cover/intercept program, 1973 proved to be the terminal year. The reason again was political: the Senate Watergate Committee hearings and the attendant questions raised about possible CIA involvement in the Watergate break-in and cover-up had led Agency officials to conclude that continuance was simply too risky (Presidential Commission on CIA, 1975, pp. 22–24, 26–27, 117–138, 144–148, 152–154; U. S. Senate Select Committee, 1976, Bk. 2, pp. 96–105; U. S. Senate Select Committee, 1976, Bk. 3, pp. 681–732).

THE AFTERMATH OF WATERGATE: IS ABUSE OF POWER NOW UNDER CONTROL?

The duration of these various programs (one for more than 40 years), the refinement and extension of these violations of privacy rights by federal intelligence agencies, and federal intelligence officials' arrogant disdain for legal and constitutional restrictions when authorizing what they recognized to be illegal or unconstitutional activities dramatically expose the fragility of privacy rights in our society. Federal intelligence officials, moreover, not only had authorized what they recognized to be clearly illegal activities, but had sought to avert disclosure by devising elaborate file-keeping procedures. In addition, these officials terminated these programs only when they had concluded that their continuance was politically risky. Accordingly, we are confronted with the troublesome recognition that legal and constitutional restrictions, and the underlying principles governing the American political system, have proven ineffective. Rather than celebrating the workability of our constitutional system, as we did in 1974 during the course of the congressional impeachment proceedings, we might better recognize the starker, more unpleasant reality that in fact the system had not worked and that only fortuitous circumstances resulted in the disclosures of the extent of past abuses of power.

Disclosure of Illegal Abuse was Fortuitous

Furthermore, we cannot derive solace that these violations of privacy rights either were done in the past or were recently exposed. We cannot, for one, because these violations lasted over a long period of time transcending the tenure of six different presidents, and further because extremely unusual circumstances led to our knowledge of these past abuses. It was only the bungled Watergate break-in, the bungled cover-up, and, most important, the forthright stand adopted by two principled individuals—Federal Judge John Sirica and U. S. Senator Sam Ervin—which led vulnerable White House aides and federal intelligence officials to decide to leak or to release formerly highly classified information disclosing these activities. There is no assurance that this combination of circumstances will be repeated or that future congresses and/or presidents will be more zealous in meeting their oversight responsibilities.

We cannot be optimistic, furthermore, in view of the contrasting positions of recent political leaders, whether Joint Chiefs of Staff Chairman George S. Brown or President Jimmy Carter. On the one hand, Chairman Brown (in May 1976 remarks before an assembly of the National War College, remarks which were not released until March 1977) characterized congressional investigations as an irresponsible infringement on military authority and as causing "a wreck" in U. S. foreign relations. Brown further dismissed complaints about violations of privacy rights (the intelligence agencies' opening the mail and their use of informers to report on the activities of American citizens) as a concern confined to "subversives." As the Chairman of the Joint Chiefs of Staff rather crudely contended: those who oppose federal intelligence agencies' reading their mail or using informers should have their mail read and their meetings observed because they obviously have something to hide. For Brown, no constitutional issues were involved: congressmen are "kibitzers" and Congress should have no oversight function; only subversives can be concerned about and insist upon privacy rights or that investigations conducted by federal agencies should be confined to the use of legal and constitutional means.

Conversely, whereas candidate Carter had campaigned against CIA abuses and excessive secrecy and had pledged to institute an open administration and to expose security abuses, President Carter recently expressed his opposition to the public disclosure of questionable CIA past activities, sought to limit the number of administration officials having access to "security" classified information in order to reduce the prospect of leaks, and tacitly supported the efforts of those congressmen who have proposed legislation to impose criminal penalties on federal employees who disclose without proper authority "classified" information (regardless of whether the information warranted being classified or whether such classification had precluded public knowledge about federal officials' abuses of power and/or illegality).

National Security Mentality Prefers Secrecy over Disclosure

If it is not surprising that federal officials prefer secrecy to disclosure—for if knowledge is a source of power, then, too, ignorance by the press, the public, and the Congress enhances executive power—we must nonetheless recognize that this concern for secrecy is not confined exclusively to the executive branch. It is ironic that in the aftermath of the revelations of 1975 and 1976 both of far-ranging abuses of power by the intelligence community and of the way secrecy permitted and encouraged these abuses, the Congress' recent responses have been either to preserve secrecy or to curb disclosures. Thus, in January 1976 the House voted to suppress the report of the House Select Intelligence Committee (the so-called Pike Committee) on the premiss that this report should remain classified in order to prevent the disclosure of "national security" information. Moreover, in the spring of 1977 the Senate Special Intelligence Committee (created in May 1976 to supervise the intelligence agencies) focused principally on drafting legislation to impose criminal penalties for the unauthorized disclosure of classified information.

These congressional actions do not bespeak a major concern over privacy rights or a desire to preclude abuses of power by federal agencies, abuses which we only recently learned were neither exceptional nor narrowly confined. We are left with the disturbing question as to why neither the Congress nor the public shares a commitment to safeguard privacy rights.

One explanation is the impact of the Cold War on popular values and national priorities. The emergence of a "national security" consensus, formalized in the 1950s, underlay the conviction that the privacy and constitutional rights of the individual would have to be sacrificed in order to preserve the internal security, and that the objective of a realistic internal security policy should be absolute security. In turn, these convictions underpinned acceptance of policies and techniques (a far-reaching federal employee security program, extensive use of wiretapping, plans for the emergency detention of "dangerous" persons) justified as "preventive." The principal internal security problem was the "potentially" disloyal, and the underlying premiss was that in the future these individuals "might" harm the national security. By these standards, the potential threat posed by so-called subversive groups and foreign agents required secrecy, on the one hand, and far-ranging surveillance to compile lists of "subversive" individuals and organizations, on the other.

If Joint Chiefs of Staff Chairman Brown put the issue crudely in May 1976, his private comments aptly capture this conviction that an excessive concern for privacy and congressional oversight could only aid foreign powers and undermine the internal security. The Chairman of the Joint Chiefs of Staff's other point also provides a further insight into why this has occurred: the conviction that certain matters should not be publicly debated but should best be handled by experts. That insistence on deference to self-proclaimed experts, and the underlying conviction that considerations of security and order should take precedence over liberty and dissent, highlight what have become unquestioned priorities of most Americans. These preferences for more efficient, rationalized procedures confirm an uneasiness with democratic principles of open debate, mass participation, and the full airing and testing of all manner of ideas and beliefs. For Americans today do not expect policy to be based on clearly-defined principles, are less confident and secure about the future, and prefer immediate results and order.

Given these preferences, it is not surprising that federal intelligence officials acted surreptitiously to circumscribe privacy rights. These officials, it must be conceded, did so because they sincerely believed that the nation was threatened from within, were further convinced that they knew what was best in the national interest (the royal prerogative?), and yet were unwilling to base their objectives and techniques on specific legal authority (after all the public might not understand and thus might deny requests for such authority). Our recently acquired knowledge of the past abuses of power by federal intelligence agencies, therefore, scarcely warrants the optimistic conclusion that these assaults on privacy were either aberrations or a past historical problem. Perhaps the sole hope we retain is that the grosser abuses of the past can be curbed and/or prevented. There is little basis for optimism that respect for privacy rights, or for the law and the Constitution, for that matter, will determine the future policies and practices of federal intelligence agencies.

REFERENCES

Blackstock, N. *COINTELPRO: The FBI's secret war on political freedom.* New York: Vintage, 1976.

Countryman, V. The history of the FBI: Democracy's development of a secret police. In P. Watters & S. Gillers (Eds.), *Investigating the FBI.* Garden City, N.Y.: Doubleday, 1973.

Irons, P. American business and the origins of McCarthyism: The Cold War crusade of the United States Chamber of Commerce. In R. Griffith & A. Theoharis

(Eds.), *The specter: Original essays on the Cold War and the origins of McCarthyism.* New York: New Viewpoints, 1974.

Presidential Commission on CIA Activities Within the United States. *Report to the President.* Washington, D.C.: Government Printing Office, 1975.

Sullivan, W. Personal observations and recommendations on privacy. In *Privacy in a free society.* Cambridge: Roscoe Pound–American Trial Lawyers Foundation, 1974.

Theoharis, A. Illegal surveillance: Will Congress stop the snooping? *The Nation,* 1974, *218,* 138–142.

Theoharis, A. Executive orders—reform or cover-up? The origins of FBI political surveillance authority. *Intellect,* 1976, *105,* 71–73.

Theoharis, A. The FBI's stretching of presidential directives, 1936–1953. *Political Science Quarterly,* 1976–1977, *91,* 649–672.

U. S. House, Committee on Government Operations, Subcommittee on Government Information and Individual Rights. *Hearing on inquiry into the destruction of former FBI Director J. Edgar Hoover's files and FBI recordkeeping,* 94th Congress, 1st session, 1975.

U. S. Senate, Select Committee to Study Governmental Operations with Respect to Intelligence Activities. *Hearings on intelligence activities,* Vol. 2: *The Huston plan,* 94th Congress, 1st session, 1975.

U. S. Senate, Select Committee to Study Governmental Operations with Respect to Intelligence Activities. *Hearings on intelligence activities,* Vol. 3: *Internal Revenue Service,* 94th Congress, 1st session, 1975.

U. S. Senate, Select Committee to Study Governmental Operations with Respect to Intelligence Activities. *Hearings on intelligence activities,* Vol. 4: *Mail Opening,* 94th Congress, 1st session, 1975.

U. S. Senate, Select Committee to Study Governmental Operations with Respect to Intelligence Activities. *Hearings on intelligence activities,* Vol. 5: *The National Security Agency and Fourth Amendment rights,* 94th Congress, 1st session, 1975.

U. S. Senate, Select Committee to Study Governmental Operations with Respect to Intelligence Activities. *Hearings on intelligence activities,* Vol. 6: *Federal Bureau of Investigation,* 94th Congress, 1st session, 1975.

U. S. Senate, Select Committee to Study Governmental Operations with Respect to Intelligence Activities. Final report, *Intelligence activities and the rights of Americans,* Bk. 2, 94th Congress, 2nd session, 1976.

U. S. Senate, Select Committee to Study Governmental Operations with Respect to Intelligence Activities. Final report, *Supplementary detailed staff reports on intelligence activities and the rights of Americans,* Bk. 3, 94th Congress, 2nd session, 1976.

Wills, G. *Nixon Agonistes: The crisis of the self-made man.* New York: New American Library, 1971.

Wise, D. *The American police state: The government against the people.* New York: Random House, 1976.

VI
IN PASTORALLY RELATED AREAS

Homosexuality: A Purely Private Issue?

PAUL R. GASTONGUAY

Paul Robert Gastonguay received a B.S. degree from Bates College, Lewiston, Maine, in 1958, and an M.S. degree from Rivier College, Nashua, New Hampshire, in 1967. From 1962 to 1969 he was on the faculty of St. Joseph's College, North Windham, Maine. In 1969 he transferred to Stonehill College, North Easton, Massachusetts, where he currently is Associate Professor of Biology. Mr. Gastonguay is the author of the book Evolution for everyone *(1974). He is particularly interested in the relationship of science and religion, and is a frequent contributor on this and other subjects to such periodicals as* The Catholic World, America, Linacre Quarterly, *and* Liguorian.

The Western male often experiences a powerful urge to dominate his environment, and to display his physical prowess and superiority to all who care to observe. He stands square-shouldered, and in the absence of such, shoulder padding may suffice—not unlike a cat ruffling its fur in order to appear larger than it really is. He is often depicted walking westward, with a musket in one hand and a cigarette in the other. In his quest for self-esteem, and the safeguarding of such (for it is often quite fragile), he has expanded his social territory to maximal dimensions, allowing only those closest to him to penetrate its invisible perimeter.

In an age of sexual competition and overstress, he must "perform" or not be a man; he must "swear like a man" in order to substitute for the bull ring, lion's den, or pistol duel of ages past; and he must never cry, or display any emotion deemed to be "feminine." Western man must not touch another man, or smile too sincerely at him. The Eastern male becomes a threat, for his social distance is much less. The Westerner moves away. I am reminded of my own unrelenting uneasiness when holding another man's hand in my first squaredancing lessons some years ago; the secret was never to relinquish the superior hand position.

Similarly is the Western female maladjusted. Thin at all cost, tanned, and often trapped, she feels a strong social pressure to evoke a sexual appeal. As a result, her status teeters perilously between self-fulfillment and self-sacrifice.

Within this context of sexual differentiation mainly for the purpose of sexuality, with an extreme emphasis on inter-gender relationships, it is little wonder that homosexuality has become repugnant to most heterosexuals. In addition, those who attempt to serve this minority group on a pastoral level are often held in disrepute, chastised, and at times even threatened professionally or physically. For some elusive, but real, reason, which many have experienced, there arises a feeling of frustration, distaste, even anger, for the person who counsels homosexual men or women. In his book, Oraison (1977) relates one such experience: "I recall that before a conference on homosexual problems, letters and phone calls threatened me with the worst reprisals if I attended, and warned of 'commandos' " (p. 57).

Indeed, the following point is quite interesting. I must confess an urge to stress my *hetero*sexuality in a presentation on the subject of homosexuality. What are the forces which lead me to emphasize the fact that I am a "Kinsey zero" (totally heterosexual), whereas were I to write a paper on black civil rights I would not feel compelled to stress my "whiteness"? The answer could be crucially important to the analysis of most aspects of homosexuality. To what extent my Western upbringing has seeded this compulsion is, of course, speculative; but it certainly has seeded it. You will note my deliberate attempt to refer to "they" in this paper, as well as to assure my readers that I am not one of "them." It has become imperative that all heterosexuals evaluate the roots of such a severe and un-Christian form of sexism, of isolationism—a phenomenon for which I admit as much culpability as others.

Is homosexuality a private issue? Or are there some elements which invite social and public scrutiny, regulation, or discipline? What *is* homosexuality? Are there various forms and causes? Are current attempts to ban the homosexual from certain types of employment directed to all homosexuals, or only to professed homosexuals, or only to that small segment of the homosexual community which displays effeminate (in males) or masculine (in females) behavior? This paper attempts some answers.

THE PHENOMENON OF HUMAN SEXUALITY

All living things can be divided into three categories, according to their mode of reproduction. Some reproduce asexually, others sexually, and a number of organisms are capable of either mode, depending on the status of their environment. "Sex" is the term generally applied to refer to the interrelation of structures (anatomy), functions (physiology), and behaviors (ethology and psychology) which enable and direct sexual reproduction between male and female organisms. According to Lorenz (1967, p. 85), the complex mechanisms which drive an organism toward sex are but one of the four basic drives with which all such organisms are endowed; the other three are the "hunger," "aggression," and "flight" (or survival) drives. Gastonguay (1975) later related these to the human social condition.

In the course of evolutionary development, the animal kingdom has displayed an increasingly complex sexual biology and sociology, with its greatest complexity being evident in the human species. In our species, "sex" has taken on roles other than the reproductive as mankind has learned to direct and control more and more of the application of its sex drive. Technologically speaking, we now can determine with a high degree of efficiency when we will have children—indeed the jargon refers to "making babies"—and we are becoming quite proficient in determining what kinds of babies we will have, by instituting quality-control programs of prenatal detection and abortion (Milunsky, 1975). Psychologically speaking, the new dimensions of human sexuality have created their share of negative feedback effects, by causing what appears to be an increasing frequency of clinical cases of anxiety and/or anxiety-neuroses—one must belong, must partake, must be comparable, before the drive ebbs into retirement. Peer pressure is perhaps at its greatest in the sphere of human sexuality.

As a result of these human interventions, the sexual perspective of man now includes psychosocial as well as reproductive functions. Sexuality has evolved, and is continuing to evolve, a dual status. As could have been anticipated, this has become the focus of much concern, debate, and legislation. If sex is not solely for reproduction, in which other directions may society allow its expression? To what extent is "victimless" sex ethical or legally permissible? To what extent are one's sexual drive, and its psychosocial dimensions, a private issue? These are crucial questions, for it is conceivable that human sexuality will continue its shift toward a greater and greater psychosocial status, with a corresponding decrease in its need to produce children. With the very real feasibility of producing babies by means other than the conventional (test tube fertilization, nine-month artificial incubation outside the womb, etc.), there may come a time when human sexuality may be totally a psychosocial phenomenon. Therefore, the directions now being molded by ethical and social guidelines may very well serve as the steppingstones to the future role of our sexual component.

There are three distinct levels of human sexuality, each with a corresponding anatomy, physiology, and ethology/psychology: (1) gender assignment, (2) sexual drive, and (3) sexual preference. It appears that although the first two have rather extensive biological roots and are less responsive to environmental influence, the third may be more amenable to environmental influence.

The Assignment of Gender

One's gender is generally predetermined by one's genetic endowment. But there are other elements of gender assignment in addition to the "genetic": namely, "embryonic" (or developmental) assignment and "cultural" assignment.

Of the 46 chromosomes in human body cells, two are referred to as the "sex chromosomes" since a substantial number of the genes on these two chromosomes relate to the development of the primary and secondary sex characteristics. If an embryo's cells contain two X chromosomes, the embryo is destined to differentiate into a female. If the sex chromosome constitution, on the other hand, is XY, then the presence of the genes on the Y chromosome will yield maleness. As long as a Y chromosome is present, no matter how many X's (some pathological cases display XXY, XXXY, etc. chromosomal pictures), the person is male, albeit possibly sterile or incompletely developed.

For approximately six weeks, the embryo remains sexually neutral and undifferentiated. By the seventh week after conception, the Y genes have begun to cause the production of testosterone, the most abundant male sex hormone. The presence of testosterone then causes a regression of the potentially female structures, and a rapid development of the male structures. Therefore, we are all destined to become female unless something happens to alter that fact; i.e., unless testosterone is secreted in the proper quantity and at the proper time. This time has been called the Critical Period of sexual differentiation (Gadpaille, 1972). Several abnormal conditions can prevent the expression of the Y genes and the development of maleness, such as an unresponsiveness of the developing embryo to testosterone, even if it is being produced, or a defect called Testicular Feminization in which the embryo's testosterone is not converted chemically into the active, or usable, form—and consequently the testes never descend into the scrotal sacs, but remain hidden in the abdomen. In such cases, a genetic male offspring may be reared as a female and even subsequently marry a man. There are several other abnormalities of biological sexual development, such as hermaphroditism and various forms of partial or complete sterility. But, generally, by the twelfth week of embryonic development, the fetus has been assigned a gender.

Such an assignment, it has been found, is not restricted to the reproductive organs, but extends to specific brain centers as well. A region called the hypothalamus is known to differentiate into a male or female orientation (Levine, 1966). Since all body systems must necessarily be interrelated for health and survival, it is not surprising that sexual differentiation occurs in other systems besides the reproductive. Indeed, many other regions of the nervous system and the hormone-producing glands (the endocrine system) appear to develop differently in the male from the way they develop in the female.

In addition to the genetic and embryonic gender assignments described above, there is a third component of assignment, as stated earlier, and it is theorized that it may be just as difficult to reverse its effect as it is for the first two components of assignment. This is the "cultural," or postnatal, assignment of gender. Studies have shown (Gadpaille, 1972) that no matter what the genetic gender of a child (XX or XY), the gender in which it is reared determines the gender with which it will later identify. Gadpaille has stated (1972): "It is . . . clear that gender of assignment and rearing predictably takes precedence over and overrides all contradictory determinants: chromosomes, hormones, gonads, internal and external sexual morphology, and secondary pubertal changes" (p. 200). He estimated that the Critical Period of cultural gender assignment may be between 12 and 18 months of age, and that "after about 2 to 2½ years of age, shift of core gender identity cannot take place, even when all sexual determinants are those of the other sex" (p. 200).

To a considerable extent, therefore, there is evidence to suggest that one's gender, and the gender to which one believes one belongs, is the result of biological and environmental influence, and that there is little choice in the matter.

The Sexual Drive

Studies in the sexuality of mammals closely related to our species (monkey, rat, guinea pig, etc.) have shown that specific regions of the hypothalamus and of an area associated with it and overlapping it—namely, the limbic system—are directly related to the sex drive. Muller, Roeder, and Orthner (1973) have provided adequate evidence that it is the nucleus of Cajal which is mainly involved in the control of sexual behavior (p. 114). Earlier, McCleary and Moore (1965) had shown that the destruction of this specialized area of the hypothalamus caused a decrease, or even a complete loss, of sexual drive in the human. In fact,

Muller claims to have caused "proper sexual adjustment," or a reduction in sex-drive pressure, in 15 male sexual deviates by destroying the nucleus of Cajal on one side of the brain by psychosurgery.

These studies and others seem to substantiate the claim that the sexual drive, of itself, has a strong biological component; hence, it may be subject to some degree of genetic predetermination. However, one must remember that man has brain elements above the vegetative lower brain. He has mind, and thus has the ability to overcome his biological being, to a greater or lesser extent. I shall return to this point.

Sexual Preference

Although recent studies have indicated that one has little choice in one's gender assignment, and in the fact of having a sexual drive, there is much less empirical evidence to suggest a similar predetermination in the preference for people of the opposite or of the same gender. Yet perhaps all of us can attest to the fact that we gradually came to prefer one gender or the other *without* any conscious attempt to do so. Although no definite biological correlate has yet been found, it does seem safe to assume that we do not plan our sexual preference; we "naturally" come to prefer males or females.

One investigator has attempted to prove a correlation between human biochemistry and sexual preference. Margolese (1970) has reported finding a relationship between the ratio of two chemical substances in human blood and the gender of choice. Although most investigators of hormonal correlates to homosexuality concentrate on testosterone levels in homosexual males, Margolese studied the levels of the by-products of testosterone breakdown in the human liver. The liver breaks testosterone down into two components: androsterone and etiocholanolone. Margolese claimed that the relative concentrations (the ratios) of these two compounds may determine one's choice of gender, or at least be related to it. He has hypothesized that "a relatively high androsterone value [is related to] sexual preference for females by either sex, whereas a relatively low androsterone value is associated with sexual preference for males by either sex" (p. 154).

In relation to such studies, two points must be stressed. First, although one may find relationships between the amounts of specific blood or urinary substances and one's sexual preference, it is entirely possible that it is the preference which yields the chemical changes, not the reverse. Current knowledge of the relation between mind and body (between thought and vegetative functions) indicates a mutual relationship, so that mental activity can cause bodily responses as well as be caused by bodily activity. If one detects correlations between blood chemistry and mental states, one can seldom be certain of the direction of cause and effect.

Secondly, one may possibly accept a biological, and/or environmental, role in the determination of gender, drive, and preference, while still believing that all three (to varying degrees) of these components of human sexuality are also subject to conscious control or alteration. Man has a biological makeup, but by virtue of being man he also has some ability to overpower his "biology." It seems that we have little choice in the selection of gender, or in the fact of *having* a sexual drive and preference. But the activation or suppression of drive and preference is certainly under one's conscious and deliberate control. Unless a person is mentally abnormal, even temporarily, that person has the conscious mental capability of directing the outputs of drive pressure and of choice pressure.

In a sense, human sexuality is "vectorial," having magnitude and direction. Accepting the evidence from current research, I tend to believe that the three components of human sexuality are largely predetermined. Yet I also believe that the pathways along which one allows such forces to be activated can be consciously assigned in accordance with the free will of the individual.

In a word: the preferred targets of one's sexual drive may be predetermined, but the realization, the activation, of such drives can be controlled by the normal human mind. Therefore, the homosexual probably has no choice in being a homosexual, but does have a choice to manifest his or her homosexuality or to suppress the sex drive. I am not, at this time, evaluating the moral or psychological implications of suppression or activation of sexual pressure, but merely stating that such suppression is possible. In other words, the homosexual person has a choice whether to become sexually active or not. He or she is not an automaton.

SEXUAL ORIENTATIONS CLASSIFIED

The majority of human beings are heterosexual. Approximately 4% (with estimates ranging as high as 10%) of adult males and 1% of adult females are considered to be homosexual, according to statistics from the United States. In addition, approximately 25% to 30% of adults have had at least one homosexual encounter.

What is homosexuality? It it a frame of mind, or a form of sexual expression, or both? If a prisoner, for example, is normally heterosexual, but performs homosexual acts while in prison, is he then in fact a homosexual? Can one be temporarily homosexual? Further, what extent of like-gender preference must one harbor mentally, or display by actual sexual expression, to be considered homosexual? Gadpaille (1972) defines homosexuality as "the preferred or exclusive choice of a same-sex object as the source of genital sexual excitation and gratification in overt behavior or fantasy" (p. 193). Cavanagh (1976) further differentiates between "overt" and "latent" homosexuality, the latter assumed to be a repressed, yet still dynamic, drive. He claims that "Latent, masked, or unconscious homosexuality is a definite clinical entity" (p. 145).

To account for, and differentiate among, the wide spectrum of gender preference which they found in their studies, Kinsey et al. (1948) designed the following scale (p. 638):

Rating	*Designation*
0	Exclusively heterosexual
1	Predominantly heterosexual, only incidentally homosexual
2	Predominantly heterosexual, more than incidentally homosexual
3	Equally heterosexual and homosexual
4	Predominantly homosexual, more than incidentally heterosexual
5	Predominantly homosexual, only incidentally heterosexual
6	Exclusively homosexual.

This scale often serves as a basis for studies which attempt to relate one's sexual preference to the amount of sperm production, of blood, or urinary sex hormone levels, and so on.

It can be quite difficult to determine a person's sexual preference unless (*a*) his or her lifestyle becomes an obvious indication of such preference, (*b*) he or she freely divulges such, or (*c*) precise psychological testing is performed. Several methods for determining one's "psycho-sexual-social" history have been adopted. In this regard, a very perilous assumption has been circulating through human circles for centuries. Some assume that effeminate males prefer males, and masculine females prefer females. Several studies have shown that this assumption is totally unwarranted; in fact, the vast majority of effeminate males have been found to be heterosexual.

Some studies have attempted to prove a correlation, instead, between the degree of masculinity of males, or of femininity of females, and the ratio of androgens to estrogens in the blood (to which must be added a substantial susceptibility to environmental and cultural influence). Androgens are the "male sex hormones," the most predominant being testosterone; and estrogens, the "female sex hormones." Males produce both sets of hormones, but more androgens than estrogens. The situation is reversed in females. The hypothesis states that the greater the androgen/estrogen ratio in males, the greater the degree of masculinity; conversely, the higher the estrogen/androgen ratio in females, the greater the degree of femininity. But there exists very little substantiating evidence to support this hypothesis; hence, it must be regarded as totally speculative at this time.

Consequently, it is generally believed that the homosexual cannot be detected by his extent of femininity (or by her extent of masculinity). I accept this notion without reservation. However, I do find some difficulty with the reported statistics. Studies have reported that only 2/1000, or

0.2%, of the homosexual population consists of effeminate males or mannish females. The vast majority of effeminate males, therefore, are heterosexual. But if we assume a current adult male population in the United States of approximately 147,000,000 and further assume a 4% rate of homosexuality, we can presume a male homosexual population of nearly 6 million. Assuming further a 0.2% rate of effeminacy among male homosexuals, we would derive a figure of 12,000 male, effeminate homosexuals in the country. General knowledge would seem to weaken the logic of this assumption.

To return to the classification of sexual preference: a final note is in order. The *Diagnostic and Statistical Manual of Mental Disorders* of the American Psychiatric Association (1968) went through six printings of the second edition before its trustees voted, in December 1973, to eliminate homosexuality from its list of mental disorders. In its seventh printing, in 1974, the Association substituted a new category, "Sexual Orientation Disturbance," upon the approval of "a substantial majority" of its voting membership. The publication stresses that the new category "is distinguished from homosexuality which by itself does not constitute a psychiatric disorder. Homosexuality per se is one form of sexual behavior. . . ." However, it is not clear why transvestitism, pedophilia, sadism, etc., are still considered "sexual deviations" by the Association when homosexuality is not. One might argue that these are also "forms of sexual behavior." The Association states that homosexuality, and some "other forms of sexual behavior [the latter not being specified] are not by themselves psychiatric disorders," but it does not indicate the reasoning behind this shift in attitude.

"CAUSE" AND "CURE" OF HOMOSEXUALITY

As one might expect, the analysis of any complex human behavior, such as that related to the sexuality of Homo sapiens, will yield conflicting and confusing data. The more complex are the biological and cultural roots of a behavior pattern, the more amenable it is to varied interpretations. And when such a behavior or frame of mind is also subject to personal, conscious, and voluntary imposition, the difficulty of assigning cause–effect relationships becomes staggering.

All attempts to find a "cause" of homosexuality have uncovered more exceptions than confirmations. Yet from the maze of data there is beginning to arise some statistically significant (but still only weakly so) information. I shall summarize briefly the two major schools of thought regarding the origin of a homosexual tendency, latent or overt. These two schools profess the Organogenic Theory and the Psychogenic Theory, respectively. Of course, in accordance with my previously stated belief that a person's basic preference is largely predetermined, whether it be homosexual or heterosexual, one would expect me to assume some causation, or an intermingling of causations. And I so assume such, while accepting the notion that whatever one's preference, it is subject to conscious and voluntary control and restraint by the mentally normal person.

Organogenic Viewpoint

Several investigators have attempted to determine if one's testosterone levels, in blood or urine, are related to one's Kinsey rating. Kolodny, Masters, Hendryx, and Toro (1971) have reported finding a direct correlation in young homosexual males, as shown below. The "normal" value of blood testosterone in males is about 800mg/100 ml of blood (and in non-ovulating females it is about 36, rising to 135 during ovulation).

Kinsey Rating	*Mean Blood Testosterone Level* (Males)
2	775 mg/100 ml
3	681
4	569
5	372
6	264

However, several factors must be considered in the attempt to interpret such data. (*a*) Testosterone levels have been found to drop sharply when a person is under stress. One study (Kreuz, Rose, & Jennings, 1972) reported a drop, in heterosexuals, from 822 to 548 mg/100 ml. (*b*) Other investigators have found results which differ substantially from those of Kolodny and his associates. Some have reported levels of testosterone higher in homosexuals than in heterosexuals; and others, levels which were nearly equal in the two groups. (*c*) In most such studies each subject is tested but once, yet it is known that testosterone levels fluctuate from day to day, with cyclical variations during the day (although in the Kolodny study all subjects were sampled between 7:30 A.M. and 10:00 A.M.). (*d*) Of Kolodny's subjects, 43% smoked marijuana at least once a week, yet in a later paper (Kolodny, Masters, Kolodner, & Toro, 1974) it was claimed that marijuana tends to reduce testosterone levels by as much as 44% (from 742 to 416 mg/100 ml) if used at least four times a week. Therefore, one must assume another variable in the equation: namely, the use of marijuana to any extent. (*e*) As stated earlier, even if we could verify a correlation between blood testosterone levels and Kinsey rating, it would still remain uncertain whether the reduced levels caused homosexuality, or the homosexuality caused a reduction of testosterone. One could still not assert that a person becomes a homosexual because that person produces less testosterone.

Psychogenic Theories

The psychogenic theories of homosexual causation can be divided into two groups: familial and societal. Many investigators have reported finding greater or lesser correlations with family situations in early upbringing. Bieber (1962) has proposed a Parental Influence Theory whereby it is assumed that the combination of a close-binding, intimate, or domineering mother and a detached, indifferent, or hostile father yields a greater potential for the development of homosexual tendencies in male offspring. However, Bieber's data and procedures have been questioned quite extensively, and the reliability of his conclusions correspondingly weakened.

On a societal level, there has arisen the Psychoanalytic Instinct Theory. The child, it is believed, passes through basic stages of psychosexual development, and each stage must fall in place and complement the others if normal development is to occur. Gadpaille (1972) writes: "The child's development [proceeds] through a series of phases representing partial instincts which must ultimately become integrated harmoniously for adult sexual functioning" (p. 193). If an adverse environmental stimulus interferes with this normal chain of events, according to the theory, the child's final stage of sexual maturity will never be achieved, or will be deviant.

Also on a societal level are the theories which attempt to relate the social awareness, and acceptance or rejection, of homosexuality to the degree to which a society is patriarchal or matriarchal. If, it is believed, a society emphasizes male supremacy, then it is less likely to condone homosexuality, and, hence, more likely to have a relatively low frequency of homosexuality. Taylor (1973) points out that in those societies "where fathers are upgraded, women will be downgraded" (p. 30). He believes that in patrist societies the deity is considered to be male; in matrist societies the reverse is true. As fatherhood is downgraded, he says, there arises greater sexual freedom and permissiveness. "Possession" of a female is no longer the norm. Divorce, wife-swapping, promiscuity (and the rates of venereal disease) all rise in popularity. He observes that "It is noticeable that patrist societies are much shocked by homosexuality, whereas matrist societies are tolerant of homosexuality but alarmed by incest" (p. 31); and adds: "When we look at the contemporary scene, we can see very easily that we are moving toward matrism" (p. 32).

If the psychoanalytic theories have any validity, then the current male preoccupation for "moonlighting" and for competing could certainly weaken further the father image, due to a substantial absence from the home scene—with a subsequent increase in homosexual development. Assuming for a moment that such a possibility does exist: there could arise a catastrophe of unknown proportion if the reduction in father-influence is not offset by an increase in mother-influence. Currently, our society is attempting to correct a wrong and an injustice which it has imposed on its women; it is attempting to render an equal opportunity to them. But, in this context, if the male within a family unit does not assume the responsibilities previously assigned (often involuntarily) to the female, if both parents adopt careers which are exceedingly demanding in time and thought, if both parents adopt a perennial detachment, might there result a perilous inability to identify with either sex? What might be the effect of this historically innovative venture upon the psychosexual development of society's children? Total disinterest in sexuality? Increases in sexual disorientations, abuses, and/or sexual criminality? If Taylor is even partially correct, what would be the sexual climate in a society which is *neither* patriarchal nor matriarchal? We are sorely in need of research on the subject.

Diversity of "Cures"

In summary, for all human behaviors which are as complex as sexual behavior, it is virtually impossible to assign universal cause–effect relationships. The interplay of genetic, developmental, nervous, hormonal, familial, societal, and personal elements is so varied and complex as to preclude any universal explanation. Some homosexual tendencies may have hormonal causes; others, familial, etc. Most of these tendencies, however, probably arise from some complex summation of the various factors—hence, the conflicting theories.

Since it is virtually impossible to assign a specific and universally applicable cause of homosexuality, it is equally impossible to convert the homosexual into a heterosexual by means equally successful in all cases. Of course, the homosexual who denies that he or she is "ill" resents the reference to a "cure"—one must be ill in order to be cured. Nevertheless, for a variety of reasons, many homosexuals request such a change. The means employed range from classical conditioning (such as the use of electric shock while showing homosexual movies, or the stimulation of the limbic system's "pleasure center" while showing stag movies) to psychosurgery. Only in the latter method, in which the brain sites specifically related to sexual activity are destroyed, has the alteration been nearly consistently successful. However, one must ask here the same questions about the ethical propriety of invading a person's brain, and modifying it permanently, as one asks when such an invasion is done to alter any other manifestation of personality—such as psychosurgery performed on overactive children, difficult prisoners, or depressed housewives.

IS HOMOSEXUALITY "NATURAL"?

In order to answer this question, one must, of course, define "natural." There are several options. (*a*) It could imply those conditions which were existent in nature, and in the animal kingdom, prior to the alteration of such conditions by the human mind or hand. (*b*) It could imply the traditional human way of doing things, such a tradition being the product of a very gradual cultural evolution from the time of man's origin. (*c*) It could imply the influence which basic human instincts have upon human behavior.

Natural? Not the Crucial Issue

I shall propose one option, and hope that the readership will agree with me. I wish to define a "natural action" as one which is predetermined by genetic, developmental, and/or environmental stimulation; i.e., one which is rooted in our biological being. Whether it became rooted there as a result of animal evolution or as a result of human history is inconsequential in the present context. Secondly, and consequently, I wish to define a "human action" as one which derives from conscious, free, and deliberate choice. For example, hunger, aggressiveness, the sexual drive, and the survival drive are all basic, "natural" components of our being, but the manner in which we exercise or activate them is a matter of free choice, a matter of truly "human" activity. Being human means, in part, being capable of conscious and rational decision-making, capable of overcoming our basic biological instincts. Being human implies an ability to overcome nature, to prevent micro-organisms from killing us, to extend our lifespan far beyond the limits previously imposed by nature, etc. Consequently, the phrase "I am only human," used to imply a sense of involuntarism, should be "I am only animal," for it is precisely the "human" element of our being which allows us to overcome the "animal," the "natural," in us.

I maintain that heterosexuality is natural for the heterosexual, and that homosexuality is natural for the homosexual. However, the fact that a state of thought or of action is "natural" does not ensure that it is morally proper. The sphere of morality does not apply to our genes or our hormones. What I am stressing is this: it is not sufficient to determine whether homosexuality is "natural" or not. That has no bearing on its ethical status.

Further, it is useless to attempt to determine whether homosexuality is "normal" or "abnormal." Normalcy is based on the concept of averages. What is "normal" is so because it is more common. An IQ of 200 is abnormal, as is one of 50. A heterosexual preference is normal, because it is far more common. Therefore, homosexuality is abnormal. That does not mean that the homosexual is ill; it means only that he or she is in the minority. Homosexuality is a deviant form of sexual expression, for it deviates from that form which is far more common in our society. It follows that celibacy as well is abnormal. In each case, however, the abnormality per se does not imply an unethical status.

Is It Pathological?

Instead of evaluating the naturalness or the normalcy of homosexuality, we need to determine if it is pathological. A "pathological condition," be it found in the functioning of an organ or of a behavior pattern, is one which impedes or prevents that organ or behavior from enhancing the survival of an organism. A disease uncured or uncorrected can lead to the death or severe impairment of a patient. Unfortunately, it is much simpler to determine if an organ's function is pathological than it is to determine if a complex behavior pattern (such as homosexuality) is pathological. The behavior may secondarily become pathological if, in an adverse environment, it yields a level of stress or anxiety which approximates levels indicative of neurotic states. In such a case, it is not the behavior per se which is pathological, but the state of mind which results from the stress imposed by society against such behavior.

I believe that homosexuality is (*a*) secondarily pathological, for the heterosexual society has imposed such restraints, legal, religious, and implied, upon the homosexual as to render that person largely incapable of truly free and guiltless sexual expression; (*b*) natural, because, as I stated earlier, none of us voluntarily chooses whether we will come to prefer girls or boys—it just happens; and (*c*) abnormal, for 90% to 96% of the population are heterosexual.

There is a fourth perspective to be assessed. Because homosexuality is a deviant form of sexual desire and/or expression, does it follow that it is a "perversion"? I believe that a perversion of sexual expression is one which is (*a*) unnatural, (*b*) socially detrimental, (*c*) detrimental to the victim, whether willing or not, or (*d*) detrimental to a person with whom a sincere and close relationship has been established. In light of this, I would assert that homosexuality per se is not a perversion. But there are perverted homosexuals, as there are perverted heterosexuals. A few examples of sexual perversions follow:

(1) at the level of mind–state: erotic pedophilia (sexual perversion toward children) and fetishism (erotic desire for inanimate objects);
(2) at the level of activation: masturbation or self-abuse (if these interfere with the normal sexual relation between spouses), infidelity, incest, rape, and bestiality.

In summary, it is my contention that homosexuality within our society is natural, abnormal, secondarily pathological, and not a perversion in itself.

IS HOMOSEXUALITY A PRIVATE ISSUE?

Numerous elements of our society have taken a deep interest in this issue, with a resulting polarization which is as immovable as that which emanated from the abortion debate. It is possible that the social and moral stigmas which we have placed upon homosexuality have created a climate which encourages homosexual perversions, that is, perverted acts by those few homosexuals who do engage in such, just as the sexual revolution undoubtedly is responsible for the rapid increase in heterosexual perversions. In a sense, one might conclude that homosexuality is not a private issue largely because society has prevented it from becoming so.

There are several areas in which homosexuality is a public issue. Two such areas are outlined below.

Threat to Family Stability

A society has an inherent right to ensure its stability and continuity. If a society is based largely upon the family unit, it has an obligation to ensure the continuation of this unit. It also has the obligation to ensure the continuation of the species. Therefore, if, in such a society the majority sincerely believes that a behavior pattern poses a threat to stability and/or survival, it is natural, and quite understandable, for that element to ban such behavior—unless and until it becomes proven that the behavior poses no threat to the social structure.

But this responsibility does not grant a society the right to enslave, imprison, or deny the civil rights of existing homosexuals, any more than it has the right to deny the civil rights of prostitutes, prisoners, the mentally incompetent, or children. But society does have the right to restrict certain rights of those individuals (*a*) who may be detrimental to the social structure, or (*b*) who may be personally harmed if given complete freedom. In the first category belong the prostitute, the prisoner, and some of the mentally incompetent; in the second category I would include others among the mentally incompetent and children. The question to be asked, then, is whether the homosexual belongs to either category. As long as the majority of the people believes that he or she does belong to either one, it has the ethical right to "protect" itself; however, should it be shown that its fears are unjustified, then it has the equally ethical duty to abandon its discrimination. Let us analyze this last point.

The fact that our society has chastised the homosexual community has caused that community to become increasingly protective and militant. There are the "screamers" who have come out of the closet, and there are the "discovered" who have been pulled out of the closet; and, of course, there are the undiscovered. It would appear that the screamers are increasing in number. They defend themselves (which is a natural reaction, and a human one as well, to any attempt to disenfranchise a group), promote their goals, enlist membership—if only by increasing their exposure. As a consequence, polarization becomes more severe, some social elements come to fear the repercussions of such exposure on the society's children, and there arise calls for the denial of certain civil rights even in a nation increasingly devoted to the equalization of such rights. Communities may admit the constitutional rights of homosexuals, but deny them access to certain positions—in education, for instance. Spokesmen from each side quote biblical passages in support of their positions.

In an attempt to formulate a position on the advisability of employing the homosexual in the educational process, various fronts arise, based on varying premisses. My own analysis is based on two points. First, it must be recognized that our social structure has a nearly total dependence upon the family unit; although this unit is more transitory than ever before, because of increasing divorce rates, divorcees still seek to remarry, still seek a substitute family unit. As a consequence, it is a justifiable position to seek to retain all social parameters which promote the stability of this unit. Secondly, the general educational process requires a level of expertise conducive to the optimal transfer of information, guidelines, and systems of thought and analysis from teacher to student.

With these two thoughts in mind, I must reluctantly adopt the following position, knowing that it will enrage a segment of the readership. Society has the right to deny elementary and secondary educational roles to certain factions, such as the untrained, the sexually harmful (such as prostitutes and sexual perverts), the criminal unless rehabilitated, the mentally subnormal, and the homosexual. I do not mean to relate these five categories in any way. My only contention is that since the society, the heterosexual society, has caused such conviction and militancy to arise within the homosexual community, there is increasing evidence to suggest that the homosexual tends to render acceptable, or to glamorize, this sexual abnormality (even if subconsciously or by his or her mere presence) in the sympathetic, vulnerable, and liberal eyes of youngsters who by their very nature tend to reject a certain portion of their culturally imposed knowledge, and to seek out new vistas, new horizons. It seems undeniable that such exposure tends to create a general acceptance for the teacher's lifestyle, hence tends to increase the probability that borderline adolescents will adopt such a lifestyle.

When a professed homosexual seeks and obtains public employment in a position of exposure, his or her presence in such a position becomes a constant reminder of the manner by which that person achieves sexual satisfaction. I admit that such a state has arisen directly from the stigma placed upon homosexuality by the heterosexual community. Nevertheless, it is a current state to recognize. In the classroom, for example, that person's presence does not remind the student of the teacher's eating habits, hobbies, academic skills, etc., but of his or her sexual habits. It is unlikely that this constant reminder exists for the heterosexual teacher, or for the "unannounced" teacher. By virtue of declaring his or her homosexual state, a person is announcing to the world his or her means of attaining climax. It is of little wonder that the heterosexual community objects. I admit that such objections are unjust, perhaps immoral, certainly unconstitutional. But, in fact, they will persist as long as does the militancy of the homosexual community. Solution? Corrective measures will have to be targeted to other areas of constitutional freedom—quite unfortunately.

Injury to Another Person

A second perspective on privacy involves a person's right to refrain from divulging, or having divulged, his or her homosexual tendencies. Does a prospective spouse have the right to know that his or her betrothed is a homosexual? This raises two related questions. Should homosexuality, latent or overt, be sufficient grounds for marriage annulment? Should a physician who knows that a future spouse is homosexual tell the betrothed, thereby breaking the contract of confidentiality between physician and patient?

Cavanagh (1976) believes that "ecclesiastical authorities should give thought to making homosexuality, whether latent or overt, an impediment to marriage" (p. 145). He offers some debatable reasons, however, such as: "Homosexual love is always selfish love, a sensual love" (p. 142), and "The homosexual cannot experience true love" (p. 143). Harvey (1976) adds: ". . . the vast majority of homosexuals do not desire and do not seek this kind of union" (p. 175). He also insists that "chastity is mandatory for the homosexual" (p. 177). But before making such a claim or insistence, one must remember that the support systems available to the celibate clergy are not equally available to the homosexual.

Although there may be some truth to the belief that the homosexual does not truly fall in love (a statement vigorously disputed by the homosexual and the pastoral counselor), I would feel more comfortable seeing corroborative data. Nevertheless, if it be true that homosexual "affairs" are mainly transient, such a state could well be the result of a social rejection and isolation. I believe that, in the realm of heterosexual marriage, it is immoral for one partner to refrain from divulging a homosexual trend; here homosexuality loses its element of privacy.

With regard to the duty of the physician to inform others who may be imperiled, the *Hastings Center Report* recently published a case study in which a woman blamed her physician for failing to inform her that her potential husband was homosexual (Kuschner, Callahan, Cassell, & Veatch, 1977). There are three comments on the case. Callahan maintained that one major exception to the right of confidentiality arises when a private condition has a significant public implication. He concluded that "the physician would have acted in an honorable way" (p. 16) if he had broken the confidence, provided he informed the man beforehand that he was doing so, and provided he was willing to face the lawsuit which might result. Also, the physician could have hinted to the woman about the need to know more about her future husband. Cassell (pp. 16–17) commented that the physician should have tried everything to allow the woman to know, short of breaching the confidence. Veatch gave two choices: first, the physician should have tried to convince the man to tell his fiancée; secondly, he could have faked a heavy schedule and have referred both parties, or one, to another physician. He maintained that "breaking the relationship is preferable to continuing in a relationship that must be based on trust without disclosing" (p. 17). I doubt if Veatch's last option properly answers the problem.

This and other similar reports have pointed out the difficulty in assessing a person's right to privacy. I contend that if the withholding of this information (either by the homosexual person or by another party professionally related to that person, except in the perspective of confession) creates a significant probability of injuring another person known or unknown, then the information enters the realm of public, albeit restricted, property. This position, I must stress, would allow the unannounced homosexual the right to seek public employment, as in education, with no moral obligation to inform a prospective employer of his sexual state—unless he personally is aware that he could pose a danger to others, if that be the case.

In summary, if a democratic society decides that some, perhaps small, segment of the homosexual community poses a potential threat to the continued survival of that society's way of life, or if a person is likely to be affected adversely from not knowing of the homosexual status of another person, then homosexuality becomes a public issue.

Similarly, if a homosexual person is truly confident that his or her status cannot injure others, whether in a state of employ or of matrimony, or of other personal interactions, then that person is entitled to the privacy of such a state. That does not imply that the person is acting morally within that state, only that he or she is entitled to privacy in the matter.

ON THE MORALITY OF HOMOSEXUALITY

In the pamphlet entitled *Principles to Guide Confessors in Questions of Homosexuality*, the National Conference of Catholic Bishops (1973) attended to several points relating to the sinfulness of homosexuality. In the opening paragraph of the guide the bishops declared: "Our concern is with the individual whose attraction to his own sex has made him aware of a moral problem, namely, whether the genital expression of his inclinations is seriously sinful for him; and, if it is, what viable ways of living are open to him" (p. 3). This statement implies that homosexual expression may not always be seriously sinful ("if it is"). Stating further that "one cannot pinpoint precisely the decisive factors in the history of any homosexual" (p. 7) and that "Homosexuals vary in the degree of freedom which they possess in controlling their sexual desires" (p. 8)—as, I believe, heterosexuals do as well—the document differentiates between the subjective and the objective morality of sexual acts. It attempts to be compassionate, and encourages the pastoral counselor to assist the homosexual in seeking "to form stable friendships among both homosexuals and heterosexuals" (p. 11). But it adds: "The confessor, however, should provide the person with a viable alternative, however difficult the chaste life may be" (p. 15).

I suspect that there is little resistance to the belief that the utilization of any person's body solely for sexual purposes is inherently and always immoral. The mechanization of sex, in the absence of commitment, love, and respect, destroys people; it destroys societies. The following, for some examples, are perilously deranging the moral order of sexual development in youngsters, as they are accelerating the engineering and dehumanizing of sexuality: (*a*) reciprocal masturbation in public washrooms, or other isolated areas; (*b*) adult molestation of young children (which, it is reported, occurs 12 times more frequently between adult males and young girls than between adult males and young boys); (*c*) the bed-hopping of adolescents; and (*d*) the "turn-on" gimmickry of films and magazines so prevalent today.

I expect greater resistance, however, to the contention that homosexual satisfaction is inherently and always immoral if achieved by the mentally sound person. I disagree with Curran's (1976) "Principle of Compromise" which assumes a subjectivity in the homosexual union. Either masturbating another person outside the marriage union is morally right, or it is not. There can be no subjectivity. The Sacred Congregation for the Doctrine of the Faith (1976) in its "Declaration on Certain Questions Concerning Sexual Ethics," issued with papal approval on January 15, 1976, stated that masturbation is intrinsically wrong. Yet the Confessor's Guide of the bishops implies that the homosexual experience may not always be sinful and even advises the confessor to recommend to the homosexual some stable relationships with other homosexuals.

If we allow for the possibility that the homosexual act is moral in some cases, then we are in fact stating that hand–genital masturbation between two men, or two women, is a "human" thing to do in some cases. If we dare to include within the sphere of psychosocial sexual gratification the moral right to cause another to attain climax by means other than vaginal impregnation, and outside the marriage bond, then we would need to allow for these other deviant forms of sexual behavior as well, in some cases. (And I am assuming for each case mentioned that the parties are adult, mentally sound, capable of "human" imposition upon the "natural" instincts, and, finally, willing participants.) The cases would be: (1) the allowance of a third party in the ritual; (2) oral impregnation; (3) the use of animals or inanimate objects; and (4) the reliance on pain, urination, or other totally unnatural as well as inhuman forms of sexual mechanization. The illogic of the above must be obvious. If we assess the morality of homosexuality, we are in fact assessing the morality of the homosexual act.

I am not an ethicist or a theologian. I do not wish to convey the notion that I am developing a thesis in support of the immorality of the homosexual act. I am only stating that if we allow for a moral status in homosexual behavior, we would then, it seems, also have to allow for a moral status in several other kinds of behaviors in which the parties are adult, mentally sound, capable of human imposition upon the natural instincts, and willing participants. I submit that the ethicist or theologian would find it difficult to justify the first while denying the second.

SUMMARY

I contend that homosexuality is intrinsically: (1) natural; (2) abnormal; (3) secondarily pathological; (4) not a perversion; (5) usually a private, but at times a public, issue; and (6) immoral.

But I hope to have provided a basis for the contention that society, heterosexual society, must begin to respect the plight of the homosexual. If he or she "comes out of the closet," a massive social stigma arises; if he or she remains hidden, the fear of discovery is constant. Each and every standard of Christian ethics and of democratic law and practice implies an equality for all peoples. Yet clergy, laity, and various professional groups have traditionally distorted this principle when relating it to the homosexual, or to one who attempts to counsel the homosexual.

Heterosexual society cannot be blamed too severely for the rejection, but it must temper it. Homosexual society must recognize the reasons for the rejection. Conditions will improve only when both elements learn to speak with each other, making no excessive demands, yielding no reasonable rights.

The usually private nature of a person's homosexuality has been stressed here. Yet the nature of homosexuality as a social phenomenon can be described only as public at this time in our history, for the homosexual community (at least a small segment thereof) has chosen to make it public. I sincerely hope that there will never result a polarization as deep and as painful as that which has arisen from the issues of abortion and euthanasia.

REFERENCES

American Psychiatric Association. *Diagnostic and statistical manual of mental disorders.* Washington, D.C.: Author, 1968.

Bieber, I., et al. *Homosexuality: A psychoanalytic study.* New York: Basic Books, 1962.

Cavanagh, J. R. Latent homosexuality as a cause of marital discord. *Linacre Quarterly*, 1976, *43*, 138–146.

Curran, C. E. Sexual ethics: Reaction and critique. *Linacre Quarterly*, 1976, *43*, 147–164.

Gadpaille, W. Research into the physiology of maleness and femaleness. *Archives of General Psychiatry*, 1972, *26*, 193–206.

Gastonguay, P. R. A sociobiology of man. *American Biology Teacher*, 1975, *37*, 481–485.

Harvey, J. F. A critique of John McNeill, S.J. and Gregory Baum, O.S.A. on the subject of homosexuality. *Linacre Quarterly*, 1976, *43*, 165–178.

Kinsey, A. C., Pomeroy, W. R., & Martin, C. E. *Sexual behavior in the human male.* Philadelphia: Saunders, 1948.

Kolodny, R., Masters, W., Hendryx, J., & Toro, G. Plasma testosterone and semen analysis in male homosexuals. *New England Journal of Medicine*, 1971, *285*, 1170–1174.

Kolodny, R., Masters, W., Kolodner, R., & Toro, G. Depression of plasma testosterone levels after chronic intensive marijuana use. *New England Journal of Medicine*, 1974, *290*, 872–874.

Kreuz, L. C., Rose, R. M., & Jennings, J. R. Suppression of plasma testosterone levels and psychological stress. *Archives of General Psychiatry*, 1972, *26*, 479–482.

Kuschner, H., Callahan, D., Cassell, E. J., & Veatch, R. M. The homosexual husband and physician confidentiality. *Hastings Center Report*, 1977, *7* (2), 15–17.

Levine, S. Sex differences in the brain. *Scientific American*, 1966, *214*, 84–90.

Lorenz, K. *On aggression.* New York: Bantam Books, 1967.

Margolese, M. S. Homosexuality: A new endocrine correlate. *Hormones and Behavior*, 1970, *1*, 151–154.

McCleary, R. A., & Moore, R. Y. *Subcortical mechanisms of behavior: The psychological functions of primitive parts of the brain.* New York: Basic Books, 1965.

Milunsky, A. *The prevention of genetic disease and mental retardation.* Philadelphia: Saunders, 1975.

Muller, D., Roeder, F., & Orthner, H. Further results of stereotaxis in the human

hypothalamus in sexual deviations. First use of this operation in addiction to drugs. *Neurochirurgia*, 1973, *16*, 113–126.
National Conference of Catholic Bishops. *Principles to guide confessors in questions of homosexuality*. Washington, D.C.: Author, 1973.
Oraison, M. *The homosexual question*. New York: Harper & Row, 1977.
Sacred Congregation for the Doctrine of the Faith. Declaration on certain questions concerning sexual ethics. *Catholic Mind*, 1976, *74* (April, no. 1302), 52–64.
Taylor, G. R. *Rethink: A Paraprimitive solution*. New York: Dutton, 1973.

Abortion:
A Purely Private Issue?

JAMES J. DIAMOND

James J. Diamond, a practicing physician in Reading, Pennsylvania, obtained his M.D. degree from Temple University Medical School in 1948. He is a diplomate, certified by the American Board of Surgery, and he is an Attending Surgeon at St. Joseph's Hospital in Reading. Apart from contributions to medical journals, Dr. Diamond has written on abortion and related issues in such periodicals as America *and* Theological Studies.

It is not considered "cricket" to read the last page of a mystery novel before plowing through the details of the crime and its investigation, but there is enough of the ghost of Chesterton in the abortion issue that a glaring paradox be cited at the start: in our attempt to privatize abortion by law we have publicized it beyond the wildest dreams of all but the most sophisticated of observers.

INTRODUCTORY BACKDROP

Any perceptive observer of the American abortion scene has by now come to realize that there is no such thing as a purely private abortion. This is not merely because there is no such thing as a purely private act of any kind, but because the utter non-privacy of abortion necessarily involves the public-ness of fundamental judicial decisions which sweep far beyond mere abortion.

The general tone of the abortion debate was chaotic, particularly among the citizens. The debate ranged through population control, public health, the medical aspects of abortion and pregnancy, separation of church and state, sexual freedom, sexual privacy and the like to a final resting point: namely, the freedom to choose to bear or slay the child one has begotten. For public relations purposes this is adroitly shortened to "freedom of choice" because everyone is in favor of the flag, mom, apple pie, and freedom of choice. Specifically, what was sought was a private freedom to decide whether to accept the responsibility and all the consequences, both private and public, of what one had brought about freely. Against this was pitched the notion that the unborn child is a public victim when he is slain by abortion; hence, abortion is not a private matter. The Supreme Court said—by simple unexplored dictum or fiat—that the unborn child is not a public victim and that, therefore, abortion is a private victimless act beyond the interests of the state.

It was the Court's development of the imperatives of privacy which proved to be most troublesome. It reached out for this notion in the *Griswold* case* where it ruled that the practice of contraception was a private bedroom matter between a man and a woman and thus beyond the interests of the state. Two points are noteworthy here. First, the Court acknowledged that parenthood is a personal burden resulting from a private act; there, couples can act privately to defend themselves from personal, private burdens. The second point is curiously ambiguous: much of the commentary and argumentation in *Griswold* centered upon the holding that the begetting of a child was both a private and a public matter because impregnation resulted in the genesis of a member of the polis—i.e., an unborn child who depended upon society in many ways, not the least mentioned way being the use of tax monies for prenatal care when the mother is indigent.

Appellate courts employ the practice of asking "What was the intent of the legislature?" or "What was the intent of the framers?" when they work toward answers. Yet in *Griswold* no one raised the question "What is the logical extent of the intent of those pleading the unconstitutionality of the laws overturned by *Griswold*?" Here lies a second paradox: the Court, which demands from individuals before the bar a duty to take into account the intent of an antagonist, rejects that duty in its own workings.

The courts have no difficulty in imposing upon the "self-defending" killer the duty of demonstrating that he carried out reasonable measures to determine the answers to many basic questions: why are you pointing that gun at me, what sort of gun is it, is it loaded, do you really intend to pull the trigger, what happens to me if the trigger is pulled, what are you really trying to do with that gun, etc. This is such common fare down at

* *Griswold v. Connecticut, 381,* U.S. 479 (1965). In a 7–2 decision the Supreme Court invalidated a Connecticut law forbidding the dissemination of birth control information as a violation of a right to marital privacy.—Ed.

the level where law intersects with individual lives that one can only wonder why the "constitutional" pleaders in *Griswold* were not similarly interrogated by the highest Court in the land. Why was "privacy" not explored in *Griswold* when every perceptive reader of *Griswold*'s "privacy" knew immediately that it would serve in both principle and precedent to permit abortion?

I shall hazard an answer. I do not believe that it is just an instance of the Court's, as is its practice, saying no more than is needed to resolve the case before it. I believe that the answer lies elsewhere. The answer, as I see it, lies in the fact that our society today is such that we are served by courts not with a *system* of deciding but with a *method* of deciding. We are in an age of *ad hoc*-ism. In matters of welfare we solve problems by throwing money and regulations at them. Courts solve problems by throwing *dicta* at them. Whence the slogan: "The Constitution says what we say that it says."

The problem in a government of laws, rather than of men, is that in laying down laws on central matters we are forced to acknowledge the content of principle and precedent in a law. As the revered legist Roscoe Pound has gravely warned us, the awesome burden of the appellate court is to recognize that it is called upon to enuntiate principles and precedents in cases where no precedental experience exists and the logical extensions of the principles must be fully explored because of unanticipated extensions. This is because in high law an idea is precedentally valid to the full extent of its intrinsic logic. The Court thus entrapped itself in *Griswold*, not just vis-à-vis the forthcoming *Roe v. Wade* decision,* but also vis-à-vis many other extremely public matters currently before it and inevitably destined to come before it in the future. It is within this sense that we have publicized abortion extravagantly.

TWO SETS OF PUBLIC MATTERS

The Non-Private Side of Abortion

In a paper of this brevity I must limit myself to the more salient of the public effects or parallels of abortion. At the start, I must emphasize that I personally consider it to be an enormously public matter that we snuff out more than 1,000,000 lives each year in this country with the blessing, encouragement, and subsidization of the state. I do not give this point

* *Roe v. Wade, 410*, U.S., 113 (1973). On January 22, 1973, in a 7–2 decision the Supreme Court ruled the laws of Texas and Georgia restricting the practice of abortion unconstitutional. In doing so, the Court held that the right of privacy encompasses a woman's decision to terminate pregnancy, and that the life of an unborn child is not to be considered of any compelling value prior to viability, i.e., during the first six or seven months of pregnancy.—Ed.

short shrift by citing it only briefly here; it is just that we are not called upon to argue the personhood of the unborn.

First, it is of public interest that we identify clearly how we got to *Roe v. Wade*. The architectonic abortion mentality in the United States does not lie in the Supreme Court, or even in the 1961 Model Penal Code of the American Bar Association (ABA). These two are merely the vehicle used to carry the legal load. The public matter of interest here is that the idea is very much alive among American power brokers that society ought to act so that only the healthy, wealthy, wise, and wanted individuals in that society are free to live.

What is of major public interest is this. When some lawyers opposed the ABA proposal because of the "all-or-none" problem, they were drowned out by those who argued that a state could validly break the all-or-none rule by specific legislation. Yet in *Roe v. Wade* the Supreme Court zeroed in on this precise point in the Texas law which it overturned because Texas did provide for life-saving abortions, and thus violated the "all-or-none" rule. It was bad enough, that so many of the nation's top legal minds were blind to this problem, but what followed was worse. The drowning-out voice then moved into really treacherous thinking, for it argued that limited abortion would not lead to abortion-on-demand because the public ethical marketplace would not let it do so. It was held that there is necessarily some sort of dynamic tension built into society and its individuals whereby excesses are automatically avoided. According to this reasoning, there is a valid human cry for permission to do some abortions in a certain set of devastating circumstances; this provides one source of tension.

Against this is poised the innate goodness of a society, its love for children, its anxiety to maintain family life, its natural proclivity to protect the defenseless young as frequently as possible, its ineradicable abhorrence of abortion-on-demand, even its enduring grasp upon the precept "Thou shalt not kill." All these notions were proposed as promising to be of such permanent influence that the modest ABA proposals contained absolutely no danger of moving into abortion-on-demand. One wonders whatever became of *The Federalist Papers* (Fairfield, 1788/1966), especially nos. 15 and 51, where we based our democratic principles precisely upon the fact that citizens are not naturally inclined to make themselves good. Whatever happened to Madison's warnings about powerful factions; whatever happened to Hamilton's warning that powerful factions naturally tend to undercut the powerless?

What all the above comes down to is not a set of public matters caused by abortion but rather a set of public matters which operated in the open as we moved toward abortion and will operate in the open as enormous matters in bio-ethics finally move into the public forum and into the appellate courts of our land. I would now like to move to a second set of public matters: namely those matters which arose because of *Roe v. Wade* and because of the way in which their effects are inevitably destined to affect the lives of all of us sooner or later.

The Public Consequences of Roe v. Wade

Our Constitution was constructed by a group of deists who were speaking from a mindset which differs radically from the public mindset of today. It is a tritism to observe that one cannot talk about rights unless one also talks about the other side of the coin, that is, about duties. The Bill of Rights is exactly what it purports to be, a list of rights held by the people over and against the government. Nowhere is there described a bill of duties or a bill of responsibilities. This is because at the time of the framing of the Constitution there was a homogeneity to the people. The polis of the time contained the best and the worst of individuals, subject to all the virtues and vices of human nature. Yet all its members knew well from family exposure, socio-cultural exposure, daily experience, schooling, tradition, heritage, and peer pressure just what their duties were. Not everyone did his duty or fulfilled his responsibilities, but when individuals failed in this manner they knew that they were failing. Given this homogeneity of the people, it is no wonder that the early decades of our history were ones in which the Supreme Court rarely made actual contact with individuals, dealing mainly with the government itself.

Eighty years into our country's life, in 1857, on the eve of one of our greatest constitutional crises, Thomas Babington Macaulay wrote his famous letter to an American friend, a letter in which he describes our Constitution as being "all sail and no anchor." He asked what would happen when, as was inevitable, there would emerge a large enough group of citizens bent upon what they perceive to be their rights, even though negligent of their duties, able to bring voting pressure to bear upon elected representatives anxious not to be voted out of office. Macaulay gave as his bitterest example the case in which the right involved was that of the hungry to have food. Yet his vision was larger, for he knew that people march upon the government for many reasons; and he foresaw the day when issues would be converted from sociological issues into "rights" issues and be carried to the doors of legislatures and courts. This is precisely what has occurred among our people. We are a litigious people, so much so that it is becoming difficult to imagine a human situation which cannot be dressed up in the clothing of a "right" to be pleaded before the appellate ladder. In another day myriad matters were handled by social groups, local political organizations, private charities, and personal solutions, and a host of matters were thus handled which today are the stuff of major court cases, taken all the way through the appeals system until the Supreme Court is forced to rule. We have now even seen the development of a willingness to go beyond the Court, to the point even of crying out for impeachment of justices who displease us. One wonders just how far we are from the assassination of justices who displease us.

As I noted, the earlier homogeneity of our people was such that a Bill of Rights could be written while the theoretical "Bill of Duties" was understood by the people, so much so that even when the people did not do their duty they at least knew that they were not doing it. Just about the worst thing which a representative, a senator, or a judge can do is to legislate or adjudicate that duty be done, for then he is—as the saying goes—legislating morality. It is as though justice and morality were two different things. Thus it came about that our litigious society, converting sociological issues into "rights" issues, and lacking any way of addressing itself to duties, has forced the Court into a corner, so much so that every argument to which the Court responded in *Roe v. Wade* can be laid down for infanticide, euthanasia of undesirables, and senicide. Since I believe that there is still a fair amount of time before serious campaigns are launched for these other forms of social killing, I will confine myself here to an examination of what happened when an *ad hoc* Court, trying to make a social problem go away and interpreting a Constitution which is "all sail and no anchor," wove a nexus of contradictory ideas, all of which are of public significance.

The Court listened to a welter of empirical testimony derived from the physical sciences which delineated the facts of abortion as homicide in the biological order. It then stated that it was unable to rule upon the legal applicability of these facts because theologians were not in agreement upon the applicability. This is an astounding judicial holding. On what major issue of justice are theologians ever in agreement? In a fit of whimsy one might muse that perhaps things have come full circle and that the Court is reinstituting theology as queen of the sciences, so that when the servants of the queen are in disagreement the mere facts adduced by the scientific handmaidens to the queen cannot be permitted to decide a case. Of all the things which the Court might cite, "theological disagreement" is most certainly the worst.

No one has yet figured out just what the Court meant when it used the term "meaningful existence" as it groped—unsuccessfully—for a definition of the word "person" as contained in the fifth and fourteenth amendments. Yet this is the term which most concerns observers of the Court. When one employs the word "meaningful," one is also saying "valuable." This points up the fact that one of the great fulcra of ethical jurisprudence is *intrinsicism* vs. *extrinsicism* in values. Is human value something which a man possesses no matter how few of his fellows subscribe to it, or is human value something which is ascribed to a man by his fellows? The Judaeo-Christian heritage, as expressed in legal codes of Western man, was intrinsicist in its derivation of human rights. As Ramsey (1962) has observed, it is small wonder that human rights are disappearing when we no longer know how to derive them.

As I noted above, one of the traditional approaches of the Court is to limit itself to saying only enough to resolve the issue before it. That is, in general, a laudable prudence, for it allows the Court future flexibility whereby future cases which any dynamic society will engender can be handled on their merits. But *Roe v. Wade* was a categorically central case, one which literally screamed out for a fundamental anchor statement by the Court. In any systematic approach to central issues, there is a hierarchy of principles to be discerned. The more primal the principle, the more it reaches out beyond its most immediate extensions into other areas of the superstructure of which it is a part. In *Roe v. Wade*, Mr. Justice Douglas used his concurring opinion to overextend the majority decision in a most devastating way; this is a case of one man's view, garbed in royal purple, empowered by judicial authority.

The "right" to abortion was derived by the Court from a right to privacy which it found within the Ninth Amendment. This right surfaced in *Griswold* where the Court found private bedroom activity about birth control to be beyond state interests. Court observers immediately wondered whether *Roe v. Wade* would take the same tack, for this would represent a categorical leap from personal matters to enormous spectra of fundamental bio-ethical matters far beyond mere abortion. Never given to taciturnity, Mr. Justice Douglas lost patience with his fellows and overextended the decision. He gratuitously added that the state has no interest over and against what works for the personal happiness of the citizen; he used the word "health" in *Roe v. Wade*, but then defined "health" in limitlessly broad terms, in such a way that "health" means "happiness" in the Aristotelian sense of *eudaimonia*, but without Aristotle's dissections.

ABORTION AS IT AFFECTS NATIONAL INTERESTS

Looking to the future, can we see other reasonably anticipatable Court decisions? I think we can. What is more, I believe that we can see the social forces which will give backdrop to the decisions. I have special reference to just a few areas of court activity.

Fiscal Status of Welfare

Our national fiscal status is already such that we are near to a state of imbalance between money sources for welfare and money allocations for the same. The drastic lowering of our national birth rate and the progressive increase in the number of the aged have already forced us to dip into general revenues to shore up the Social Security program. Fewer and fewer wage earners are providing the taxes which subsidize more and more receivers of tax benefits. There is a certain point beyond which a government cannot raise taxes. I do not know just where that point is or just how close we are to it, but I suspect that the point has been passed when wage earners are forced to limit their children to milk every second day so that tax beneficiaries can have milk every day, or when a laborer must deny a college education of his choice to his children so that tax-subsidized scholarships can go to others, or when the workingman who earns $15,000 a year and can barely afford a modest home is taxed to build $55,000 housing units for his tax-benefited neighbors.

The vast bulk of welfare dollars now go to provide aid for dependent children (ADC), usually in fatherless families. There are two points of importance here: first, I believe that we are not ever going to get to the point where we will make children pay the price by denying them support; and, secondly, this topic is "raw nerve" material because it largely refers to children of minority-group persons. Shall we soon see laws which hold that, although a woman has a right to reproduce, she does not have the right *ad libitum* when her children must go to the tax trough for support? Only compulsory sterilization or compulsory abortion can control the segment of our welfare expenditures for aid to dependent children.

If I have read correctly the statements of the government family planning agencies, our planners do not believe that they have the time or the ability to teach the poor and the unsophisticated to a point of voluntary family limitation. There is also the likelihood that cries of "genocide" and "racism" will be raised in such a situation. If its logic is extensible, *Roe v. Wade* can stretch to the point where the Court could rule that no one has the right to protect an unborn, constitutionally non-existent person over and against the tax interests of society. It will be interesting to see how the Court faces this problem, especially if the majority of taxpayers are white and the majority of ADC tax beneficiaries are not. The average American citizen has within him enough liberality to grant his neighbor freedom. But he also has a few reservations about how his neighbor exercises that freedom; in general, the old frontier mentality still obtains: "Do what you please, but don't frighten my horses or send me the bill for your pleasure." Marx maintained that the "bottom line" of the morality calculus is eventually expressed in terms of cash for toil performed. I believe that the American people—hence, their representatives and their non-representative courts—will in time, if pushed far enough, arrive at the same "bottom line."

National Health Insurance

The second matter is already taking form. We are currently in the throes of formulating a National Health Insurance (NHI). As many observers have noted, all NHI plans also have a "bottom line" tenet, one which in this case says "This many dollars for health care and no more." Undeterred by the historical inability of the governmental bureaucracy to deliver on time and at level cost the mail, railroad passengers, or defense items, we have now said "This much money for health and no more."

It is common knowledge that the vast bulk of abortions are performed for reasons of convenience and not because the pregnancy threatens the physical health or life of the mother. For purposes of developing a later point, we can note here that vasectomies, tubal ligations, and sterilizing hysterectomies can be, and most often are, done for the same reason. Just in the matter of abortions, our direct costs are running at about a half-billion dollars annually and our indirect costs at perhaps three times that much. Enter now the Douglas precedental dictum that "health equals happiness." Any physician (and any thoughtful patient) will tell you that many medications, treatments, office visits, surgeries, and hospitalizations are done wholly or partly for reasons which promote patient "happiness" though not necessarily patient health. If our nation's health industry were limited exclusively to the control of above-average physical pain and actual threats to life and limb, fully one-half of our doctors, nurses, paramedical personnel, hospitals, drug industries, and nursing homes would be out of business.

Within my profession's current scrutiny of itself are emerging significant studies showing that much "health" care is really "convenience" care. The upcoming question is: "Is a 'convenience' abortion really a 'health' abortion?" I believe that the Court's earliest decision on this will provide for "convenience" abortions even though it might rule against "convenience" doses of librium for nervousness.

Future National Interest

Depending upon how one looks at it, we are either blessed or cursed by a sense of nationalism. I, for one, do not sense that we, as a people, accept limited expectations for ourselves. I suspect that we have not really learned much from the Spanish-American War, two World Wars, and the Vietnam fiasco. I suspect that we are learning precious little from the ongoing nuclear arms race. We are as nationalistic as have been the best and the worst nations of history. There is a point to be made of this. Are we really different from those nations in Europe which have now banned abortion because of the "national" interest? Are we really different from, let us say, the rabbinate of Israel which pleads for the abandonment of abortion lest the Jewish faith, state, and people decimate itself into oblivion? Are we really different from nations such as Canada and Italy where pro-natalist campaigns have actually been launched because of the "national" interest? Are we really different from the editors of *Pravda* who urge the Eastern European satellites to start having large families so that the "people's ideology" can be assured of survival in the geo-politics of tomorrow? In all these cases the state begins to legislate in the interests of the state. For this reason I believe that we can safely prophesy that in time Mr. Justice Douglas' dictum will be ruled out of existence, but in the true tradition of the Court it will be ruled out for the wrong reason, i.e., the interest of the state.

How proximate is that time when our population status might raise the specter of "national interest"? It is dreadfully difficult to plow through a maze of demographic inquiries into this area. A few undebatable facts are available. We still bear more than we bury; hence, we are still growing numerically at a minimal pace. However, by one calculation we have been in negative reproduction for about two years because we have not reproduced 2.11 children for each childbearer. What is more significant is that the better part of a generation has passed since we last relatively replicated the preceding generation. If, for purposes of explanation, we posit that a generation on the average reproduces itself every 25 years, we can measure absolute generational replication by simply noting the number of births this year as compared with the number of births 25 years ago. Relative generational replication became negative about 13 years ago; this is measured in terms of births per fertile woman (on a national level). But of even greater importance is the way in which we determine our national concern or lack of concern about our population. No sound Wall Street broker, whose business it is not to lose money, would do money-things the way we do population-things. The master investor does not look either at the Dow-Jones average of the day or the direction in which it is moving today. No flood forecaster works by measuring the river height and flow today; he wants to know how much snow the winter dropped upon the mountains upstream. The broker is interested in what he calls "leading economic indicators." In the matter of the American population, as we survey the snow depth up in the mountains, it is by now unmistakably clear that there is at present not one social, cultural, economic, or political factor working for the long-term sustaining of our people. Every measurable factor is now negative; what is more important, their degree of negativity is increasing. I mention all this not to call it good or bad or indifferent. The facts are just there and they all possess downward momentum, with no visible governmentally endorsable reversal mechanism.

SUPRANATIONAL DIMENSIONS OF ABORTION

Personal and Public Health Effects

Before I pass to the supranational matters involved in abortion, a note is in order concerning an area of reflection which this paper more or less ignores, i.e., the personal health and public health effects of abortion. It is certainly of indirect public health interest that over 50,000 women are rendering themselves sterile each year by aborting a first pregnancy in their youth. We simply do not now know how many cases of venereal disease are emerging from the promiscuity which abortion availability permits. We do not know the long-term psychological effects on a woman when she arrives at middle age or at the menopausal "empty nest" stage of life and has the occasion to reflect upon what she has done to the children she might have allowed to live. Which of us has ever met a woman in her later years who really lamented that she had had too many children? Have not most—if not all—of us known women who in their later years have lamented their having too few children or none at all?

Although I am a physician, I am deliberately not going into these purely medical matters here because they belong in another literature. But there are two "personal health" matters which I must mention because of their bearing on my larger view. The first of these has to do with what Hauerwas (1972) has described as the ethics of character. By slaying her child a woman contributes to the formation of her ethical character and actually changes herself for the next time her character will face an ethical issue.

The second matter is related to the first. As Dorothy Day has observed regarding abortion, "It is simply not in the nature of a woman to slay the child she has begotten."* I believe that this is so simple a truth that it just is not going to go away no matter how many millions of abortions history records throughout the centuries past and future. Every woman, no matter what the Supreme Court identifies in her womb, knows with a knowledge given only to women exactly what is in her womb. And so does the father of the child. They also know how the child got there. All these knowledges just do not get up and walk away simply because of the sense of relief which an abortion produces.

Threat to Western Democracy

We all have read Toynbee (1962) and understand his thesis of rise to power, plateau effect, decline, and fall. Is social cyclicism the true faith? If so, are the truths of this faith now ripening for the democratic West in general and for the American democratic experiment in particular, perhaps even for democracy itself? This is quite a leap for our line of thought to make, i.e., from the private little abortion legalized in America to the collapse of the sky. The truth is that no one living today will ever know for sure that there will be such a thing as this nation some few generations from now; yet there is something in the human spirit of us all which wonders about our survivability among the nations.

* Address before the 41st International Eucharistic Congress, Philadelphia, Pa. August, 1976.

The growth phase and power-plateau phases of civilizations are characterized by taboos about sex and taboos about abortion. Both these notions crop up throughout history as ongoing distillations of the wisdom of the past. No matter how often individuals broke the taboos privately, the taboos clung to something which endured beyond the individual private acts. An anthropologist might look upon this in a sense which few others would discern. As evolving man passed from the "oestrus" type of sexual inclination (i.e., periodic "heat" among females) to circadian sexual inclination, to what degree was the teleological purpose of sexual inclination lost? Is the basic purpose of libido the guaranteeing—as best possible—of the continuation of the species? Was libido absolutely necessary to guarantee this survival because without libido the propagation of self by the members of the species would not occur if ever there emerged a good reason, sufficiently compelling to rationally free men, not to reproduce? Did nature instill libido because nature does not instill an irresistible desire to have children? These are interesting questions to ask at a time when we see emerging a heightening disparity between an increasingly libidinous culture and an increasingly childless culture. This is a matter to explore more deeply elsewhere, and I will limit myself here to three observations.

First, every argument for *Roe v. Wade* to which the Court responded in its derivations of the right to privacy is logically applicable to "neonaticide" and infanticide. Both these forms of privacy-seeking have been used in the past and are today being recommended in this country.

Secondly, the Zero Population Growth (ZPG) figure of 2.11 children per female in order to maintain a steady population is no longer applicable. The figure really should be slightly higher, as a matter of fact, perhaps as high as 2.15 children per woman. However, when a society is in numerical decline, it cannot count upon those women who are sterilized by abortion and those women who are sterilized by venereal disease (gonorrhea) induced by unrestricted expression of libido. Neither can it count upon those women who are driven by economic forces to have themselves sterilized into childlessness or to choose other forms of access to the childless life. Add to this the speculation that homosexuality (which can and often does cause the election of childlessness) might be increasing not just in its visibility but also in its incidence, and that homosexuality might be a natural force built into societies to help to bring about the declining phase of societal cyclism. Even if just a few of the above are true, we are probably already dealing with a situation where our society—in calculating ZPG—might have to point only to those women who can have children physically, can have children psychologically, and can afford children economically. Among these women, each one at present must have about 3.5 children; how many of us can look around and see families of this size in any significant numbers?

Thirdly, any enduring willingness of our people to abort children *ad libitum* will sooner or later have geo-political and geo-economic effects. When high level meetings are held among world population planners, they always include representatives from the United States government which is currently wrestling with the question: "Should we send foreign aid to Third World peoples who will not restrict their population growth?" To which the Third World nations respond that, just as the United States had its opportunity to grow and flourish, the nations and peoples of the emerging world also want that opportunity, even though the United States wants to stop growing. Is this a restatement of "a baby today is a world power tomorrow"?

CONCLUSION

When one has in fact done one's homework on the privacy and non-privacy of abortion, I should like to believe that one necessarily arrives at a resting point close to the one on which I shall conclude.

Just as abortion has been with us for countless centuries, so also its proscriptions. Man was not born yesterday. From the beginning man has had to deal with libido, sexuality, love, lust, passion, and the reproductivity of sex. Biologically, the purpose of the individual member of a species is to reproduce the species; given the reasons for which an individual member may choose not to reproduce, this dictum is naturally alterable into a paraphrase: the purpose of a species is to reproduce itself. This has been true throughout the nomadic, agricultural, and industrial ages of emerging man. For reasons appropriate to each age, each age has by some sort of distillation of the facts come to the conclusion that both individual sexuality and individual reproduction—"private" abortions, if you will—must be surrounded with some sort of public cover. It does no good whatsoever to refer to this cover as a taboo, as an archaic law, as a religious interdiction, or as male chauvinism. For any of a variety of reasons man has, in all his ages, finally agreed that sexuality must be contained despite the privacy claims of individuals, and that abortion must be restrained despite the privacy claims of individuals. Given the cyclicity of time, we are now in an age—as compared with all other ages—in which both sexuality and abortion (perhaps linked with a general contraceptive mentality) are up for redistillation. We have never lived in other ages; we have lived only in this age; we would be foolish to believe that we live in an age in which either sexuality or abortion is a unique problem.

I would suggest that we are in one of those cyclically recurrent ages in which we have lost grasp of the nature of sexuality. I am referring not to the effects of sexuality, but to the cause of sexuality. I subscribe unreservedly to theism. Were I God I would not be the least nervous about abortion. I would reflect upon man—"you very badly need a lesson about both sexuality and abortion; but my purposes, being timeless, have no inviolable relationship with your current attitudes toward abortion." To take a cue from Teilhard de Chardin (1965, 1971): man cannot bounce upward from one of his downward phases until he has hit bottom. I would submit that in order to persuade a truly stubborn man that he cannot swim, it is sometimes necessary to let him jump into water over his head. Can we see something going on in the public phenomenon of abortion which can otherwise escape us? Sexuality has always been capable of privacy in performance, but because of the public effects of privately consummated sex man's societies threw up whatever perimeters they could about private sex. Now that most of the restraining perimeters are no longer effective, the public effects of sex (still privately consummated) are running loose across the societal landscape. Man is seeking new perimeters to the effects of sex which invade the commonweal; his perimeter this time is abortion considered in itself and as a running mate of contraception. But the setting up of this legistic abortion perimeter has caused man to go against many other ingrained concepts of himself, concepts woven into his very warp and woof: i.e., that sex cannot be a free-for-all, that families are the stuff of culture, that killing is wrong, that the logic of jurisprudence must approach internal homogeneity, etc.

I should therefore like to close with one observation. Abortion is so little a private matter and so much a public matter that perhaps we might be seeing in motion the dynamics of an often-told tale being taught once again. It would not be the first, and probably not the last, time that stubborn man learned how to swim by diving into water over his head. This brings me to my last loose end, i.e., what I see as the final resting place of abortion as we relearn how to swim. I believe that the ethics and jurisprudence of abortion might one day reside within a single concept: abortion is to be permitted only under circumstances and on grounds whereby we would consent to legal and moral killing of ourselves or our loved ones. Abortion is fundamentally a lack of love of the unborn child; we will not get out of abortion until we, as a people, are agreed upon why it is wrong for me to kill you or your loved ones. If we learn this by diving into water over our heads, it just might—in the long run—be worth the dive. In the meantime, it is the poor and the minorities who will have to figure out for themselves why abortion "rights" were the only rights they did not have to drag out from the wealthy and non-minority power-brokers in the land. Every other right was gotten only by tooth-and-nail struggle. This disparity is of public interest.

REFERENCES

Fairfield, R. P. (Ed.). *The Federalist papers: A collection of essays written in support of the Constitution of the United States* (2nd ed.). Garden City, N.Y.: Doubleday, 1966. (Originally published, 1788.)

Hauerwas, S. Toward an ethics of character. *Theological Studies*, 1972, *33*, 698–715.
Ramsey, P. *Nine modern moralists.* Englewood Cliffs, N.J.: Prentice-Hall, 1962.
Teilhard de Chardin, P. (S.J.). *Building the earth.* Wilkes-Barre, Pa.: Dimension Books, 1965.
Teilhard de Chardin, P. (S.J.). *Christianity and evolution.* New York: Harcourt Brace Jovanovich, 1971.
Toynbee, A. J. *A study of history*. New York: Oxford University Press, 1962.

Dying:
A Purely Private Issue?

ROBERT M. VEATCH

Robert M. Veatch received his B.S. degree from Purdue University (1961), and M.S. from the University of California Medical Center (1962), and then a series of degrees from Harvard University: B.D. in 1967, M.A. in 1970, and Ph.D. in 1971, the graduate degrees with a specialization in medical ethics. He was a Research Associate in Medicine at Columbia University, 1971–1972, and he is currently Senior Associate, and Staff Director of the Research Group on Death and Dying, at the Institute of Society, Ethics and the Life Sciences at The Hastings Center, Hastings-on-Hudson, New York. Dr. Veatch is the author of the following two books: Death, dying, and the biological revolution *(1976), and* Case studies in medical ethics *(1977). He is also editor or co-editor of half-a-dozen other books, and author or co-author of approximately 50 journal articles dealing principally with various aspects of medical ethics.*

Though privacy may be a dying issue in some spheres, it certainly is not in the area of dying. The right to die, in fact, to die with dignity, is becoming so fashionable that it has become a major movement. Since the passage of the California Natural Death Act in 1976, at least 40 states have considered legislation purporting to grant the right to die, and several states have passed such bills in one form or another. The underpinnings of this legislation and this movement is the notion of privacy. The

California bill claims that "The Legislature finds that adult persons have the fundamental right to control the decisions relating to the rendering of their own medical care, including the decision to have life-sustaining procedures withheld or withdrawn in instances of a terminal condition" (Note 1). It makes the claim in the name of the concepts of "dignity and privacy." Historically, however, privacy has not always been the foundation of an ethic of death and dying. Traditional physician ethics has had a very small place for the notion of privacy.

First, I should like to examine the limits on privacy in death and dying decisions involving the competent patient, looking at the traditional physician ethic, the evolution of the doctrine of privacy, and the conflict between privacy and the public health ethic in order. I shall close the first section by examining the necessarily public dimensions to death and dying for even the competent patient.

In the second part, I shall examine privacy and the incompetent patient where a thoroughgoing commitment to privacy is much harder to maintain even for the committed libertarian. After examining the important impact of the *Quinlan* decision for the evolution of the doctrine of privacy for decisions involving the incompetent patient, I shall explore the idea of "familial privacy" which may be emerging, and the limits of familial autonomy. The outcome, as we shall see, is one in which privacy and the underlying principles of self-determination and autonomy are much more central than the medical profession has been willing to concede, but nevertheless subject to severe moral constraints. Patterns of dying are appropriately set by individuals exercising their right of privacy, yet, at the same time, dying can never be a purely private issue.

THE CHALLENGE TO PRIVATE DYING FOR COMPETENT PATIENTS

The Traditional Physician Ethic

Wherever the thrust for increased privacy in choices related to dying has come from, it has not been primarily from the tradition of the physician. Not that the notion of privacy and the principles of freedom and autonomy are totally alien to physician history, but they have played an extremely limited role. The Hippocratic Oath, the most dominant compilation of medical ethics for physicians, is an appropriate place to begin. It had its origins as a code for an apparently Pythagorean cult having many of the qualities of a mystery religion (Edelstein, 1967, pp. 3–63). While of minor importance among the competing philosophical schools of medicine of the day, it has emerged under Judaeo-Christian influence as the summary of the ethical tradition of the modern medical cult. To be sure, it is not always followed faithfully by the medical practitioner—he may not have read it or heard it since leaving medical school, but it does accurately summarize the contemporary as well as the traditional norms or ideals of physician practice.

The closest hint of a notion of privacy or a theory of autonomy found in the Oath is the commitment to secrecy. It appears in two forms. There is a lukewarm pledge to confidentiality: the physician will not disclose to others those things which ought not to be "spread abroad" (leaving open the question of what ought to be spread abroad). More basically, the Oath begins as a pledge of secrecy and loyalty. The physician will teach the art of medicine to his teacher's offspring, his own children, and "those who have signed the covenant" but to no one else. The secrets of the cult are private matters, not to be entrusted to strangers. This seems to be the forerunner to the American medical claim to physician freedom from governmental and other non-professional control and the claimed right of the physician to control his own practice, fees, and style.

There is no hint of a doctrine of privacy for the dying patient, however. The physician's duty is to do what he thinks will benefit his patient, "keeping him from harm and injustice." Should the physician feel that the patient would benefit from open disclosure and patient choice, this would be acceptable, but it is derivative from the overarching moral commitment to paternalistic concern for patient benefit. This is the moral foundation for the physician's non-disclosure of a terminal diagnosis—information which would be necessary for the patient to play an active role in decisions about his own care. Patient privacy in the sense of the patients' being able to make decisions autonomously—the right to control the decisions relating to the rendering of their own medical care in the terms of the California statute—is totally absent.

The Principle of Privacy

Contemporary American physicians may not unequivocally ignore patient autonomy and patients' rights. As human beings who are more than representatives of the traditional physician ethic, they are also part of the American heritage and its radically different political philosophy. Certainly the constitutional basis for the right of privacy in American law is somewhat uncertain. Since the *Griswold* decision (Note 2), and, more recently, the Supreme Court abortion decisions (Notes 3 and 4), there has been much debate over that basis. Defenders of the constitutional right to privacy have based their argument on several principles, including "emendations" from the Bill of Rights, the Fourteenth Amendment right not to be denied liberty without due process, and the Ninth Amendment provision for the people's retention of other rights not enumerated in the Constitution (see Notes 3 and 5; Henkin, 1974; Baker, 1974; Greenawalt, 1974, 1976). The problem is made more difficult by the embarrassing lack of reference to the principle of privacy in the Constitution. The underlying principle of liberty, however, is present in the legal tradition not only in the Fourteenth Amendment, but in the Preamble and Declaration of Independence as well.

When one steps back from the question of constitutional law to examine the place of privacy more generally in contemporary Western political philosophy, there can be no doubt that in contrast to the professional medical tradition, freedom, liberty, autonomy, self-determination, and, by implication, privacy are central (Adler, 1973; Bay, 1970; Berlin, 1958). The emphasis reached its zenith in the nineteenth century in Mill's *On Liberty* where it is apparently argued that the individual is not accountable to society for his actions except when they are prejudicial to the interests of others (Mill, 1859/1956, p. 114). In fact, Mill himself seems to have placed some other limits on liberty. He argues that an individual should not be permitted to sell himself into slavery even if he believes that he would be happier because of it. He argues:

> By selling himself as a slave, he abdicates his liberty; he forgoes any future use of it beyond that single act. He therefore defeats, in his own case, the very purpose which is the justification for allowing him to dispose of himself. . . . The principle of freedom cannot require that he should be free not to be free. It is not freedom to be allowed to alienate his freedom [p. 125].

Thus even within the tradition of liberty there are the seeds of the principle's own limits. It is precisely in the realm of choosing a course which would hasten dying that it could be plausibly argued that one is surrendering one's own liberty. Even Mill seems to hold that there is a duty over and above the protection of the interests of others: the preservation of one's own possibility of future liberty.

Be that as it may, the tradition of liberty is firmly rooted in the tradition outside the professional medical arena and is reflected in the legal and ethical traditions regarding the rights of the competent patient to refuse medical treatments. The legal cases are myriad. At first they seem to be a chaotic mixture of conflicting opinions, but analysis reveals a rather simple set of rules. No competent patient has ever been forced by American law to undergo medical treatment which is proposed for the individual's own good.* Children have had treatments ordered for them for their own good, but they are not considered legally competent. A parent is not given unlimited authority to refuse medical treatments. There are limits to how foolish or malicious or unreasonable the judgment may be. Adults have had treatments ordered for them for their own good, but always after a declaration that they are not mentally competent. The most

* For a full analysis of the cases supporting this conclusion, see Veatch, 1976, pp. 116–163.

obvious examples of exceptions to the legal right of self-determination to refuse medical treatment are made in the name of the protection of others —the exception granted by Mill and all other libertarians. This exception is the basis of what might be called the "public health ethic."

The Public Health Ethic

One of the cases often cited as the exception to the rule that adults may refuse medical treatment is that of Mrs. Jesse E. Jones (Note 6). Mrs. Jones was in need of an emergency blood transfusion, having lost two-thirds of her blood from a ruptured ulcer. She was 25, and the mother of a 7-month-old child. She refused the blood apparently on the grounds of religious objection. The hospital sought a court order to have the blood administered. After an initial denial, the request was appealed to Judge J. Skelly Wright of the United States Court of Appeals. In a complicated and confusing decision Judge Wright ordered the transfusion. He offered five reasons for the order, including the belief that she was not competent to decide. Since she was a known Jehovah's Witness with long-standing beliefs on the subject, this argument is questionable. But he also argued that Mrs. Jones "had a responsibility to the community of care for her infant." He concluded, "The people have an interest in preserving the life of this woman." The treatment was being ordered, not for her own good (or at least that alone), but for the good of her child. But treatments offered because they are in the interests of another form a potential category of exception to the privacy principle.

That this basis for overriding the right of privacy is limited is seen in the case of Charles Osborne, a competent adult Jehovah's Witness who desperately needed a transfusion because of internal bleeding resulting from an accident (Note 7). He had two young children. The court considered the argument that the transfusion be ordered because it was in the interests of the children, but was swayed by the wife's supporting testimony that she and her husband's brother could run the family business and take care of the children—"As far as money-wise, everybody is all right," she said. "We have money saved up. Everything will be all right. If anything ever happens, I have a big enough family and the family is prepared to care for the children." The court was persuaded and did not intervene.

The argument that privacy in the right to refuse medical treatment for the competent adult should be limited in the name of the good of others is more often and more plausibly introduced in cases where the interests of the community, especially the health interests, are at stake. The public health movement introduces a new ethic into the medical context. In contrast to the individualistic, patient-benefiting ethic of the traditional medical professional, the public health movement sees the community, as a whole, as the relevant group to whom the public health officer is responsible. Invasions of autonomy and even of privacy are justified according to this ethic for purposes of sanitation inspections, vaccination in an epidemic, the maintenance of public health records, and quarantine. In public health, medical matters are decidedly more than matters of patient benefit. They are also more than matters of personal privacy, and the limitation on personal freedom seems to be acceptable.

Most of these limitations on freedom in the area of death and dying are not in direct conflict with the public welfare. But one contemporary area has begun to receive attention where privacy in one's dying would appear to be limited by the public health ethic. Mass immunization has received new public attention through the recent efforts to promote swine flu immunization. It is just the latest of a series of immunization efforts designed to protect "the public" by increasing the level of immunity in the population sufficiently that the probability of disease transmission is significantly decreased. Anyone who can remember horrors of the fear of poliomyelitis before the possibility of immunization recognizes the real public benefits coming from such efforts.

With the swine flu campaign the question arose whether an individual should have the moral right to refuse the immunization. The problem is structurally similar to more isolated efforts to resist polio, measles, and other immunizations. For the time being, consider only the case of an adult refuser. The right of privacy of the individual to refuse the immunization is an example of permitting privacy in one's own dying (in the assumption that the immunization refusal leads to an increased death risk). At first it appears to pit the privacy principle squarely against the public health ethic in the realm of death and dying. The individual in refusing an inoculation not only runs the risk that he himself will get the disease and perhaps die. If that were all that were at stake, then, à la Mill, the public would have no overriding interest. The public health concern is that the individual refusal of immunization decreases the level of protection of the population, and increases the chance that one will not only get the disease, but also transmit it to others. The result would be increased morbidity and mortality rates in the population as a whole and elimination of "herd immunity."

Yet the conflict between the public health concern and the principle of privacy is not as direct as it at first appears. To be sure, if I refuse an immunization, get a disease, and die, the national mortality rate increases, but it is hardly reasonable to say that that constitutes a public health interest. The real concern growing out of the public welfare exclusion to the principle of privacy must be the benefits to others in the society rather than the benefits to "the public" expressed in the gross statistical indicators. In a case where the public health statistics, such as the mortality rate, increase but only the individual who was exercising his right of privacy is affected, it is hardly a real "public" harm.

The defender of the public health ethic will go on, however, to point out that it is not only the individual himself who refuses the immunization whose risk of morbidity and mortality increases, but also others whose likelihood of exposure increases because of increased exposure. That, they claim, is where the real *public* health dimension arises. But that cannot be an adequate opposition to the principle of privacy by itself. Among those who could be at increased risk are those who had the immunization and those who are fellow-refusers. The fellow-refusers acting under the principle of privacy are (except in special cases to be mentioned momentarily) no more a *public* health concern than the refuser himself. That means that the only real conflict is the case where the acceptor of immunization is somehow put at risk because of the non-acceptor. That, however, is the group which is protected and therefore generally not at risk.

There are some qualifications to this argument against the public health ethic as a limitation to the principle of privacy in treatment refusal. In the first place there are special cases where the acceptor is put at risk because of the non-acceptor. Immunity is not perfect even for those inoculated. The public health argument would work if significant additional protection of the well-meaning, but unsuspecting inoculated one is safeguarded by the forced inoculation of an individual trying to refuse. The risk to the inoculated ones and the number of principled refusers are both so small, however, that it is hard to justify invasion of privacy on public health grounds on this basis.

The more interesting case is when benefit in the form of protection from communicable disease will come to non-inoculated ones who have some justifiable grounds for not being inoculated. One case might be when children (who cannot be principled refusers because they are not competent to refuse) would benefit from the herd immunity generated by forced inoculation. The alternative, however, is a better compulsory immunization program for those children whose parents have not had the initiative, conviction, or the resources to get them inoculated. The general benefits to non-inoculated incompetents then seem hardly to be the grounds for the violation of the right of privacy even for communicable disease.

A more subtle case might provide that justification. If it were the case that some group (such as the elderly) were at risk for a disease such as swine flu, but they were also at high risk for serious side effects from the immunization process itself (as the elderly apparently were for swine flu), then one might argue that this group would constitute a group of justifiably non-inoculated people who deserved protection by invading the privacy of principled refusers. That kind of special, peculiar circumstance, and that kind alone, would seem to be a real case of a conflict between the health interests of the community and the principle of privacy in a case where an individual was attempting to refuse a medical treatment in a manner which increases his risk of death. I find the conditions to be much more constraining than originally anticipated. In fact, the cases where forcing medical treatment, such as immunization, on a competent person against his will will produce significant protection to those who have a justifiable claim to be protected and could not be protected in some other way without the invasion of privacy are probably so rare that the public health arguments against the invasion of privacy as a whole must be very suspect. Even public health concern is unlikely to provide a rationale for limitations on the right of competent adults to refuse medical treatment. This is so not because, in principle, the public benefit is not an acceptable limiting counter claim, but because, in fact, the number of cases where benefits will accrue to those who have a justifiable claim is so small that the situation will hardly ever arise. In contrast, the opposition to the principle of privacy in cases where specific others to whom one is responsible (such as one's children) will benefit seems much more plausible. Even that is a very limited principle. We are left with the conclusion that only in the rarest and most exceptional circumstances would the legal limitation on the right of privacy for individual choices related to one's own dying ever be justified.

The Public Dimension to the Ethical Imperative

Before turning to the more complicated question of the right of privacy in dying for the incompetent patient, we must explore some limits of privacy even for the competent one. What has gone before seems to establish a nearly absolute legal right of privacy for competent patients to refuse medical treatment offered for their own good and even when offered for the purported good of others. But what is ethical is always more than what is legal, and ethics is never a merely private matter. If the question of dying is viewed ethically rather than legally, the public dimension becomes more important. First, an individual, to be moral, must take into account the impact on others of his actions. Occasionally this will have legal ramifications, as when Mrs. Jones is ordered to undergo medical treatment for the good of her daughter. Much more often, however, there will be impacts on others of our actions which do not command the attention of the law. The dying patient may decide that the game is not worth the candle, that the time for the end is at hand, but then realize that he has familial obligations yet to be fulfilled. A patient once refused to have information transmitted about his terminal diagnosis, exercising his right not to be informed. But he was a business speculator with teenage children whose futures were at stake. Dying for him was not a purely private matter even if he had the legal right not to know.

Even if there are not specific others whose lives will be affected by one's dying, there are general social considerations which may be relevant. One may decide to volunteer for an experimental drug protocol for the benefit of others as one is dying. One may be concerned about the economic and social costs of the dying process. It would be crass to make economic costs of dying a conscious part of the legal regulation of dying. Although at the level of general policy this cannot be avoided, normally it need not be forced upon a specific patient. At the same time, it seems morally noble for the individual who is dying to take it upon himself to reflect on some of the public impact of his dying. In this sense dying cannot be a purely private matter.

At a more basic ethical level, dying is not an entirely private matter. If we focus on the ethics of dying, the significant question is "What *ought* I to do?" and not necessarily "What does the law require of me?" or "What would satisfy my personal taste?" Though dying may be purely a private matter for competent adults as far as the law is concerned, at the level of ethics there is a public dimension which contrasts with the private quality of questions of taste. Some are led to the conclusion that ethics is, after all, nothing more than personal preference. If that were the case, then the ethics of dying might also be merely a private matter. But the argument against ethical relativism is so overwhelming that the conclusion is inescapable that ethics is something quite separate from privately derived preferences or tastes (Brandt, 1959; Frankena, 1973; and Dyck, 1977, pp. 114–134). It is part of the meaning of ethical language that propositions making use of that language are meant to refer to something beyond the personal or even the socially relative. Whether ethical statements are reflections of the natural law, the decree of the godhead, objectively localized perceptions of reality, accounts of the "moral facts," or even summaries of behaviors approved of by one's society, they have a public dimension. In this sense, ethics refers beyond the private. For most people it refers beyond the culture-boundedness of one's groups. If ethics is not a purely private matter, then the ethics of dying cannot be purely private. Knowing that one is free by law to refuse a medical treatment cannot end the matter.

PRIVACY AND INCOMPETENT PATIENTS

Although the principle of privacy gives great latitude for the choices about one's dying for the competent patient at the level of law, that same individual is pushed beyond the realm of the private when he considers the impact of his choices on others. He is also pushed beyond the private realm when he strains to make ethical choice about the morally appropriate way for him to die. When we turn to the incompetent person, the question of privacy becomes even more complex. By definition, the incompetent person does not have the same rights as others to exercise competently the right of privacy in making free and rational choices about his own dying. At the same time the principle of privacy may still be extremely important.

The issue has been brought to focus by the case of Karen Quinlan. The court decision in her case explicitly extended the principle of privacy to the incompetent patient. In the second part of this paper I will explore the development of the principle of privacy in the *Quinlan* decision, examine the concept of familial privacy, and the relationship between the individual's right to privacy and the role of the family in making decisions about the incompetent one, and finally explore the limits of familial integrity and autonomy.

Privacy and the Quinlan Case

In the case of Karen Quinlan, a number of arguments were considered by the court as grounds for granting the father's request to be appointed guardian for the purposes of refusing medical treatment (Note 8). Karen Quinlan, a 22-year-old young woman, with no reasonable hope of ever recovering to what was called a "cognitive, sapient state" because of brain damage from an overdose of drugs and alcohol, clearly could not, herself, exercise the right of privacy. The court considered the possibility that the continued treatment was cruel and unusual punishment. This was rejected on the grounds that cruel and unusual punishment was a constitutional principle dealing with incarceration, not the treatment of seriously ill patients. The court considered the argument based on religious freedom. It rejected this (as it should have been rejected) on the grounds that although freedom of religious belief may be absolute, there has never been an unqualified freedom to act upon those beliefs. To hold otherwise would permit risking the lives of innocent parties through snake-handling rituals. It would also permit the Jehovah's Witness parent to refuse the blood transfusion for the young child who would be restored to a normal life with the transfusion, but would die without it. Clearly there are reasonable limits on guardian discretion to act upon religious conviction when the lives of innocent incompetents are in the balance. The fact that the Quinlans were Catholics articulating well-developed convictions based in Catholic moral theology and were supported by their pastor in the effort cannot be definitive in justifying the right of the parents to refuse the treatment on behalf of their child.

Though all these arguments were rejected, the court turned to the principle of privacy and found in it an adequate basis for authorizing the parental refusal of the treatment in this case even though the refusal was expected to hasten the death of their daughter. The New Jersey Supreme Court said "It is the issue of privacy that has given us most concern . . ." (Note 8).

The question of privacy arose over against two other interests: those of the medical profession and those of the state. The interests and responsibilities of the state are clearly the more decisive. The court dealt with those first before turning to what it called "the medical factor."

The court, acknowledging the ambiguous position of the right of privacy in constitutional history, nevertheless found an "unwritten constitutional right of privacy to exist." It based its opinion on this right to privacy, beginning as we have done by considering such a right in the case of the competent patient:

> We have no doubt, in these unhappy circumstances, that if Karen were herself miraculously lucid for an interval (not altering the existing prognosis of the condition to which she would soon return) and perceptive of her irreversible condition, she could effectively decide upon discontinuance of the life-support apparatus, even if it meant the prospect of natural death. . . . We have no hesitancy in deciding . . . that no external compelling interest of the State could compel Karen to endure the unendurable, only to vegetate a few measurable months with no realistic possibility of returning to any semblance of cognitive or sapient life [Note 8, pp. 34–35].

Carefully limiting itself to the special circumstances where intervention cannot cure and at best can only prolong an inevitable slow deterioration and death, the court went on to develop the concept of privacy in such circumstances. While for competent patients the right of privacy may be much broader and may not be qualified by the special conditions of the patient, for the incompetent one, the principle of privacy was developed by the New Jersey Supreme Court only for the particularly limited special conditions. For such cases the court concluded:

> We think that the State's interest *contra* weakens and the individual's right of privacy grows as the degree of bodily invasion increases and the prognosis dims. Ultimately there comes a point at which the individual's rights overcome the State's interest [p. 37].

The court at this point faced the most difficult question of whether this right to privacy could be exercised on her behalf by someone else. It concluded that it could be. "Nevertheless we have concluded that Karen's right of privacy may be asserted on her behalf by her guardian under the peculiar circumstances here present" (p. 38). The implications are radical, perhaps confusing in some of the unfortunate terminology, but, I think, fundamentally sound. Some of the specifics of the position have been seriously questioned. Why, for instance, privacy is related to the degree of invasion as bodily invasion increases is not clear. Does this imply that Karen's right of privacy, say, related to her medical records, is lost when she becomes incompetent? If reporters wanted access to her medical records, one would hope that her right of privacy would remain absolute even though getting the records does not involve any bodily invasion.

Perhaps the most subtle and confusing part of the argument is over whether it is Karen's right of privacy which is being exercised by her father or whether the family's right of privacy is being exercised, and, if it is hers, how it is possible for that privacy to be exercised by another. The problem is one of the relationship between individual and familial privacy.

In the case of a formerly competent adult (such as Karen Quinlan), it makes sense to speak of her continuing right of privacy even though she is now apparently permanently unconscious. Expressions of that right exercised while competent should not be lost simply because the patient is no longer competent, indeed is unconscious. If I had refused, while competent, on grounds of privacy, to donate my organs for transplantation or to turn over my medical records for research, it would seem that that right remains though I am no longer conscious.

For the never-competent or the formerly competent person who had never expressed any wishes on the subject, however, the doctrine of substituted privacy is more difficult to comprehend. There may well be certain areas where there should be a presumption of privacy. A child's medical and financial records should perhaps be treated as private matters even if the child has never been competent to insist on that privacy. Yet if there are matters for which there is a presumption of privacy, it is questionable whether the surrogate should be given discretion in waiving that privacy. At the same time we find it plausible that a parent should be permitted to let a child's medical record be examined for research purposes not directly benefiting the child. If the parent were to object, our intuition is that the record should be kept confidential, but parental permission seems adequate to waive the claims of privacy on behalf of the child.

What is at stake is much more a theory of familial autonomy and integrity than individual privacy. The question is: In cases where there is no basis for implementing decisions on the foundations of individual privacy of the never-competent or formerly competent patient, is familial privacy or integrity an adequate basis?

An Appeal to Familial Privacy

It is clear that there is an important difference between the family using its own values to make a choice in difficult cases, where termination of treatment is an option, and the family making a choice by knowing or estimating the patient's own values. The principle of individual choice should, it seems to me, take precedence. Whenever the person's wishes or the values held by the patient are known, these should be the basis of the decision-making. The only problem is selecting the agent for the patient. The most obvious candidate for this task is normally the family of the patient—the group with a general commitment to the interests and welfare of the individual and a long-term knowledge of the individual's values and lifestyle. Of course, in special cases this conclusion would not be valid. Provisions need to be made to let competent patients select their agent in advance in cases where the person would prefer someone else or when there are conflicts within the family in interpreting the person's values (see Veatch, 1976, pp. 184–186). Beyond this, the courts have routinely been used to override the presumption of guardianship in cases where the natural or designated guardian is being foolish, malicious, or otherwise unreasonable.

But what of those cases where there are no adequate instructions or knowledge of values of the formerly competent person? At that point, familial responsibility seems appropriate and must be rooted in a doctrine of familial integrity or autonomy or privacy. Within limits which must be spelled out carefully, the family is and should be given discretion in making value choices about the children of the family, about the interest of other incompetents, and about the pattern of the family as a whole. We permit parents wide latitude in choosing technically deviant (that is minority) school systems, church affiliation, reading material, television viewing, and values to be inculcated. We permit a parent to choose to teach a child authoritarianism, radical libertarianism, collectivism, or virtually any other belief system. We permit a Jehovah's Witness parent to teach a child a belief in the refusal of a blood transfusion even if the refusal will mean death and even though we do not permit the parent to refuse the blood for the child. Within certain limits the parents have the obligation of doing what is in the interests of their ward, but they are given considerable discretion in deciding what is in the child's interests. The principle of reasonable limits of guardian refusal of life-saving medical treatment seems to follow from this commitment to familial autonomy. Death and dying decisions for the incompetent one are, in this sense, more than matters of individual privacy; they become, within restriction, matters of familial privacy, autonomy, and integrity.

The Limits of Familial Privacy

The limits placed on familial privacy will be crucial if the principle is not to lead to devastating violations of the interests (not necessarily the privacy) of the incompetent members of the family. Some of these limits are drawn from the principle that the family's responsibility is to do what is in the interest of the incompetent member. Some extend beyond it. If we begin, in a case where the individual cannot express his own wishes about privacy, with the principle that the family's right and responsibility is to do what it thinks is best in the interest of the incompetent one, it is clear that this principle is limited by the necessity of responsible determination of what is in the individual's interest.

Clearly, the family need not do the thing which is most plausibly in the individual's interest. If that were the case, the New Jersey Supreme Court would not have given Karen Quinlan's father discretion, but would have told him to continue or to stop the treatment (depending upon what it considered the most reasonable course). No, the society gives to the family in its guardian capacity discretion to choose privately among many courses of action and to base the choice on a wide range of values and beliefs. The only limit is that the family in its guardian capacity cannot exceed the limits of what society can tolerate as being reasonably in the incompetent one's interests. Karen Quinlan's respirator may be refused, a blood transfusion which would restore a patient to normal health may not be, although both are life-extending procedures. Society cannot tolerate too much suspicion of conflict of interest in cases where the conflict seems to have clouded the actual decision made. Society cannot tolerate too much implausibility in the belief system upon which the choice is made. For this reason, the rationally coherent Jehovah's Witness parental blood refusal is rejected.

The criteria for the limits of reasonableness will look remarkably similar to the debate over what constitutes an "extraordinary" means. In fact, that debate is more appropriately characterized as one over what constitutes a reasonable refusal. Treatments which are gravely burdensome or are useless, given the patient's condition, are to be seen as expendable. When there is debate about whether the treatment is really useless or burdensome, the reasonableness standard will be applied, making only those treatments required when the judgment about usefulness and burdensomeness made by the family is so radically implausible that it cannot be tolerated.

There will also be other limits placed on familial integrity in making death and dying decisions for incompetent ones. The cases where these limits will arise will be very limited and very different in nature from the ones which we have already considered. Though familial integrity in deciding what is reasonably in the interest of the person will be the basis for most decisions about incompetent ones, occasionally a family may decide that it is within the best interests of the person to have, say, an extremely expensive treatment with a very small probability of success. Or the family may decide that something as extreme as full-time bedside psychotherapy would be beneficial for a dying member. At a certain point, principles of justice in the allocation of resources must place limits on what the family can be permitted to choose even if they have plausibly argued that the intervention would be in the patient's interest. A full-blown normative ethical theory for society must include more than the principles of familial autonomy and the duty of the family to do what it thinks will benefit the incompetent one. Justice may require setting policies which do not permit providing the fulfillment of certain judgments about what could reasonably be in the incompetent one's interests.

There may be other principled limits on familial privacy as well. There may be cases where social utility as well as justice or other right-making characteristics place some limits on marginal care even for incompetents. To include such a public principle as a limit on privacy in addition to the principle of justice is terribly risky. It could justify infringements on the rights and welfare of the incompetent one, but probably the duty to do good (the duty of beneficence) is as firmly rooted as any normative ethical principle. It is conceivable that there will be cases where it is pitted against the rights of the individual, the principle of justice in distribution, and other norms, and reasonably carries the day. Normally these limits on familial autonomy in deciding what is reasonably in the interest of the incompetent one should be determined at the general level of policy, not at the bedside for each individual case. Excluding normal cosmetic surgery, podiatry, or even certain levels of psychotherapy as a matter of policy is a more even-handed way of setting limits than *ad hoc* bedside exclusion. Of course, there will have to be mechanisms for exception. Cosmetic surgery for an accident victim may not be the same as for the simply vain parent. But limits of this sort to familial as well as individual privacy are simply a moral necessity.

CONCLUSION

The principle of privacy is more complex than it at first appears to be. For questions of legal rights when we are dealing with competent patients, it is fair to say that dying is, or should be, an almost purely private issue. But, even for the competent person, dying becomes much more than that when attention shifts to what is ethical rather than what is legal. If one wants to know "What should I do about my dying now that I have the legal right to decide?" then one must go beyond privacy. One must consider the impacts of one's choices on others. One must consider moral claims which have a rootedness beyond the individual's private realm of tastes and preferences. The choice made by the patient, even the competent one, is never private in that sense.

When the individual is formerly competent, dying may be a private issue, but there is a potential conflict between individual and familial privacy. The individual's wishes expressed while competent would seem to take precedence. Furthermore, if the individual has expressed no wishes, but has communicated a consistent set of values, those too would seem to take precedence over the values of other familial members. If an incompetent accident victim was known to have held values radically different from the other members of the family, we might still give the family the critical role in deciding what ought to be done, but we should insist that the judgment be made on the basis of the patient's values, not the family's. If that is too difficult a role for the family, then a new guardian capable of carrying out this task should be appointed.

In cases of the never-competent family member or the formerly competent family member who had not while competent given any signals of what should be done, familial integrity, autonomy, or privacy becomes a much more central factor. There are limits on the familial privacy in making such choices on behalf of the incompetent member. Their judgment about what is in the interests of that person must not exceed the limits of reasonableness. Beyond that, there may be limits on familial privacy rooted in other moral norms such as justice and social utility. Normally the limits on familial privacy need not, and should not, come into play. The cases where the family will be so unreasonable that society cannot tolerate it, and the cases where justice and social utility will, on balance, be so overriding that the rights of the individual are compromised, will be so rare that the safer policy is to operate under the rule that familial privacy is the basis of such decisions. Only in cases where the courts or society acting publicly in the policy-making process have placed limits on the resources available for certain types of treatments and treatment refusals will familial privacy be compromised. Dying is not a purely private issue. It cannot be. But for matters of law and public policy it may often be better to behave as if it were.

REFERENCE NOTES

1. *California Natural Death Act.* AB 3060, 1976.
2. *Griswold v. Connecticut.* U.S., 1965, *381*, 479.
3. *Roe v. Wade.* 93 Sup. Ct. 705; U.S., 1973, *410*, 113.
4. *Doe v. Bolton.* U.S., 1973, *410*, 179.
5. *Paris Adult Theatre I v. Slaton.* 93 Sup. Ct. 2628; U.S., 1973, *413*, 66.
6. *Application of the president and directors of Georgetown College, Inc.* 331 F. 2d. 1000, D. C. Cir., 1974.
7. *In the matter of Charles P. Osborne.* 294 A. 2d. 372, D.C. Cir., 1972.
8. *In re Quinlan.* N.J., 1976, *70*, 10, 355. A. 2d.

REFERENCES

Adler, M. J. *The idea of freedom* (Rev. ed.; 2 vols.) Westport: Greenwood, 1973.

Baker, T. Does privacy have a principle? *Stanford Law Review*, 1974, *26*, 1161–1189.

Bay, C. *The structure of freedom.* Stanford: Stanford University Press, 1970.

Berlin, I. *Two concepts of liberty*. New York: Oxford University Press, 1958.
Brandt, R. B. *Ethical theory*. Englewood Cliffs, N.J.: Prentice-Hall, 1959.
Dyck, A. *On human care: An introduction to ethics*. Nashville: Abingdon, 1977.
Edelstein, L. *Ancient medicine: Selected papers of Ludwig Edelstein* (O. Temkin & C. L. Temkin [Eds.]). Baltimore: The Johns Hopkins University Press, 1967.
Frankena, W. K. *Ethics* (2nd ed.) New York: Macmillan, 1973.
Greenawalt, K. Privacy and its legal protections. *Hastings Center Studies*, 1974, *2* (September), 45–68.
Greenawalt, K. The Burger court and claims of privacy. *Hastings Center Report*, 1976, *6* (4), 19–20.
Henkin, L. Privacy and autonomy. *Columbia Law Review*, 1974, *74*, 1410–1433.
Mill, J. S. *On liberty*. New York: Liberal Arts Press, 1956. (Originally published, 1859.)
Veatch, R. M. *Death, dying, and the biological revolution*. New Haven: Yale University Press, 1976.

VII
IN EDUCATIONAL AND PROFESSIONAL AREAS

Privacy in Academe: Student and Faculty Rights

MICHAEL R. LANZARONE

Michael R. Lanzarone received his A.B. degree from Fordham College in 1958, and his LL.B. from the Fordham University School of Law in 1961. New York University Law School awarded him the LL.M. degree in 1973. Professor Lanzarone is a member of the New York Bar and was in the private practice of law from 1961 to 1969. In 1969 he joined the faculty of the Fordham University School of Law where he currently is professor of Law.

STUDENT RECORDS

Universities, as part of their normal operation, collect data about their student bodies. The process begins with a student's application. That document may contain a complete history of the applicant's high school career. It undoubtedly will include a transcript of course grades and a listing of extracurricular activities. It may require disclosure of an arrest or criminal conviction. The institution may seek evaluations from the applicant's teachers and ask the applicant to supply letters from other references. If the applicant seeks financial aid, the school will request a record of the family's financial condition. The student's score on the standard college admission tests will likewise become a matter of record.

Once the applicant is admitted, the process will continue. The college will have a complete record of the student's courses and grades. The records may contain a listing of college activities, and any disciplinary matters involving the college administration or local law enforcement authorities. Individual teachers or departments may record impressions of the student's work and character. If the student desires to pursue graduate or professional education, the process will be repeated for a second time.

Most information gathered by colleges and universities is relevant to the educational task they perform. It is difficult to disagree with the proposition that an institution should receive data on the academic achievements and character of its applicants. Yet the relevance of a specific item may be less clear, and it obviously is impossible for a student to know what data may be revealed by even a friendly reference.

There is, likewise, no assurance that all the information will be correct. Honest mistakes do happen. The student and his family may have little objection (or choice) in giving information to the school; but neither one may want anyone outside the school to know about the family's finances, the student's grades, a parent's occupation, a prior divorce, or an arrest for possession of drugs. In short, they may believe that even correct information about them is no one else's business.

INADEQUACY OF PRIOR REGULATION OF DISCLOSURE

Until the passage of the Family Educational Rights and Privacy Act of 1974 (Note 1), there was little legal protection of the confidentiality of student records. The law of defamation offered some relief for the release of false derogatory information about a student. But the common law rules of defamation do not afford relief for the release of accurate information and often do not afford relief if false information is released in good faith to one who had some legitimate reason to seek the data (Prosser, 1971, pp. 737–780).

A common law or statutory cause of action for invasion of privacy does not exist in many states. In other jurisdictions, the cause of action is limited to the use of another's name or likeness for advertising purposes or to the unwarranted intrusion into an individual's private affairs. Only a few jurisdictions recognize a cause of action for the truthful public disclosure of embarrassing private facts. The plaintiff in such a case must show that private information was communicated to the public at large. In many instances, the information disclosed about students may not be embarrassing, and disclosure to a government investigator, a potential employer, a credit agency, or an insurance company may not be disclosure to the public at large (Prosser, 1971, pp. 802–818). Nevertheless, the student may not want the information disclosed.

FAMILY EDUCATIONAL RIGHTS AND PRIVACY ACT OF 1974

The Privacy Act of 1974 does not make improper disclosure of student records a federal crime. Nor does it create a new private cause of action (Note 2). Its sanction is a monetary one. Educational institutions which do not comply with the statute risk the loss of federal funds from programs administered by the U.S. Commissioner of Education. On the post-secondary level (Note 3), the Act gives students access to most of their records and requires educational institutions to enact procedures for challenges to the accuracy of such records and the correction or deletion of inaccurate, misleading, or otherwise inappropriate data.

Defining Improper Disclosure

The most relevant portion of the statute for our purposes is the provision which seeks to protect the privacy of student records. In this respect the Act provides that no funds from programs administered by the U. S. Commissioner of Education shall be made available "to any educational agency or institution which has a policy or practice of permitting the release of education records (or personally indentifiable information contained therein . . .) of students without . . . written consent" (sec. 1232 g (b)).

The Act defines education records as those records, files, documents, and other materials which "(i) contain information directly related to a student; and (ii) are maintained by an educational agency or institution or by a person acting for such agency or institution" (Privacy Act, sec. 1232 g (a) (4) (A)). The definition encompasses all the typical information which institutions maintain concerning their students, including grades and class ranking, personality profiles or test results, teacher evaluations, comments of counselors, information on admissions applications, and much more. It is, in fact, quite difficult to exclude from the definition any information normally maintained by an institution about its students.

Perhaps in recognition of the broad scope of the definition, the statute sets out a limited number of exclusions. Educational records do not include records maintained with respect to employees (Privacy Act, sec. 1232 g (a) (4) (B) (iii)) unless the job results from the individual's status as a student (Note 4). Thus, records concerning faculty and other professional and non-professional staff are not covered by the act if they relate to the individual's status as an employee. If a faculty member or non-professional employee should take a course, the records concerning the course would be covered by the Act. Also excluded from the definition are records containing only information about a person *after* that person is no longer a student (Note 4, subsec. 5). Typical alumni records, therefore, are excluded from the definition.

In most cases the institution must obtain written consent from the student before releasing educational records. The one exception involves the publication of "directory information." That term includes "the student's name, address, telephone listing, date and place of birth, major field of study, participation in officially recognized activities and sports, weight and height of members of athletic teams, dates of attendance, degrees and awards received, and the most recent previous educational agency or institution attended by the student" (Privacy Act, sec. 1232 g (a) (5) (A)). An educational institution which desires to disclose directory information must give "public notice of the categories of information which it has designated" as directory information and allow a "reasonable period of time" (Privacy Act, sec. 1232 g (a) (5) (B)) after such notice for any student to inform the institution that any or all such information about him should not be released without prior written consent.

Some Problems of Interpretation

It is reasonable to presume that records maintained by a college registrar, a dean's office, a director of admissions, and similar administrative offices of a university will meet the statutory definition of education records if the records concern students. Clearly, if an individual professor is asked his opinion about a student, he may not check the files in the dean's office and then inform a prospective employer or government investigator that the student was 90th out of 270 students and had been suspended for three days for painting the campus bell tower, because the statute forbids the disclosure, not only of "education records," but also of "personally identifiable information *contained therein*" (Privacy Act, sec. 1232 g (b) (1)).

But suppose a professor knows that a particular student obtained a grade of 95 in his biology course because the professor submitted that grade to the registrar. That information, contained in the student's education records, may not be revealed in answer to a telephone inquiry from a potential employer, even though the professor remembers the grade, has no personal record, and does not consult the office transcript. Once again, the reason for this result is that the information is "contained" in the education record. Presumably, the professor's impressions that the student worked hard, did well in class, and showed an aptitude for scientific investigation can be revealed because no such information is contained in the "education records."

If the professor himself has placed information in a student's education record, there is little problem in concluding that he may not later disclose the data. But suppose the professor knows a student's grade in another course because the student disclosed the information during an informal chat at the professor's home. May the professor disclose this information? Suppose further that our mythical senior student was suspended for two weeks in freshman year for "occupying" the dean's office during a campus demonstration. May the professor, who learned of the incident from the college newspaper, disclose this information?

The statute itself is somewhat ambiguous. It proscribes the "release of . . . personally identifiable information contained" (Privacy Act, sec. 1232 g (b) (1)) in education records. The student's course grade and prior suspension are so recorded, and disclosure may be forbidden. A review of the Department of Health, Education, and Welfare (HEW) regulations, however, suggests a different result. In dealing with the need for student consent prior to the release of information, HEW Rule 99.30 refers to the release of "personally identifiable information from the education records . . ." (Note 4). The professor's information is arguably not "from the education records," and its disclosure is permitted.

The solution is a comfortable one and may be correct. But the answer is simply not that clear. Suppose that the professor who knows this information was the student's adviser and learned the information in confidence. The legal issues are the same. The operative language of the statute and of the rule is unchanged, but we are probably less comfortable with the conclusion that the statute does not forbid disclosure.

I would suggest that we should be less comfortable with that conclusion. Legal questions aside, is the student's performance at school anyone else's business? Should a professor disclose grades or disciplinary actions without the student's consent? The question is a basic one. Educational institutions collect information about students in order to do a better job educationally. But should the student not decide whether anyone should disclose personally identifiable information about his performance at a given institution? The starting point should be a presumption against disclosure of this information to those outside the institution and to those inside the institution who have no reason to know the information. Neither the statute nor the rules give us a clear legal answer to the questions raised. The statute's wording and its policy in favor of privacy support the conclusion that disclosure of information in education records is a violation even though the professor learned the data from other sources. In some situations, this result is reasonable. In other cases, it is not.

The statute itself denies funds to institutions which have a "policy or practice" (Privacy Act, sec. 1232 g (b) (1)) of permitting the release of education records or personally identifiable information contained therein. The ambiguities surrounding the problem previously discussed would suggest that isolated instances of disclosure (even if ultimately deemed improper) should not result in a loss of funding. Nevertheless, it might be appropriate to advise faculty of the legal issues and to seek clarification from HEW.

Exceptions Recognized by the Statute

The statute recognizes that any policy of non-disclosure must have some exceptions. For example, it permits disclosure of education records within the institution itself to school officials with legitimate educational interests. Disclosure is also permitted in connection with applications for financial aid or enrollment in other educational institutions. There are likewise exceptions for disclosure to certain governmental officials (primarily those involved in education) and accrediting organizations (Privacy Act, sec. 1232 g (b) (1) (A) (B) (C) (D) (G)). These exceptions are fairly limited. Moreover, they do not mandate disclosure; they simply do not forbid it.

The Privacy Act's prohibitions against disclosure are also made inapplicable to "information . . . furnished in compliance with judicial order, or pursuant to any lawfully issued subpoena . . ." (sec. 1232 g (b) (2) (B)). The Act, however, does require that the student be "notified of all such orders or subpoenas in advance of the compliance therewith . . ." (sec. 1232 g (b) (2) (B)). Presumably, this provision is not absolute and simply requires reasonable effort to notify the student in advance of compliance (Note 4, sec. 99.31a). At the very least, notification permits the student to contest the subpoena.

It is likely that any plaintiff suing an educational institution will use judicial process to obtain relevant records. This should cause no problem with the Act. It is also likely that the educational institution which is defending the suit will wish to introduce relevant evidence to support its position. A memorandum of The Association of American Law Schools suggests that the school request a court order authorizing it to produce any personally identifiable information or education records which it believes will support its position (Note 5, p. 20).

Neither the statute nor the rules provide guidance for every situation which might occur. Perhaps the most troubling omission involves the ability of a school to confirm or deny information supplied to others by the student. Suppose a student informs a potential employer that he ranks in the top 10% of the graduating class. May the school confirm or deny the accuracy of the information? HEW officials have stated that "the practice of confirming or denying the accuracy of information given by the student to the potential employer" is permitted because it "does not result in the disclosure of personally identifiable information from the education records, but, rather, confirms or denies the accuracy of information which the student himself has disclosed" (Note 5, p. 17). The letter also states that if the student has given inaccurate information, the school may not disclose the accurate information without the student's consent.

The interpretation offers little problem if the student states that he was class president or the winner of a varsity sports letter. Informing the potential employer that the information is inaccurate is probably all that is required. But suppose the student who said he was in the top 10% actually ranks 15th in a class of 149.

If the school administration believes that it must deny the accuracy of the student's representation, may it disclose the numbers? The HEW letter says "no." But suppose the school tells the potential employer, "If Mr. X ranked one place higher, he would be in the top 10%." I would argue that in this case the disclosure of the additional information was necessary to confirm or deny the data given by the student without at the same time misleading the potential employer. But perhaps there is a technical violation of the statute.

In any common law case involving privacy, a court should find that the student consented to the release of the information by making the representation to the employer. But the statute, which requires written consent, may not track the common law or common sense in every instance. The difficult cases which can (and will) arise may not result in a loss of federal funding, but they do suggest the advisability of obtaining advance student consent for the release of information. This is particularly true in the case of potential employers who may not appreciate the school's failure to make disclosure.

To Which Records May a Student Have Access?

In addition to protecting the confidentiality of education records, the Privacy Act also grants each student the right "to inspect and review [his] education records" (sec. 1232 g (a) (1) (A)). It likewise requires that schools provide the student an opportunity for a hearing, in accordance with regulations of the Secretary of HEW, to "challenge the content of such student's education records, in order to insure that the records are not inaccurate, misleading, or otherwise in violation of the privacy or other rights of students . . ." (sec. 1232 g (a) (2)). The school must provide the student an opportunity to correct the records and "to insert into such records a written explanation . . . respecting the content of such records" (sec. 1232 g (a) (2)).

The Privacy Act does not mandate student access to every education record which is protected against public disclosure. Students may not inspect parents' financial records, for example, and may waive access to confidential recommendations respecting admission, receipt of honors, or employment applications (sec. 1232 g (a) (1) (B)).

The statute likewise accords special treatment to personal notes or records maintained by individual professors. It is probably not unusual for a university professor to keep notations about a student's writing ability, progress on a research project, or general class performance. Although this information may meet the statutory definition of an "education record," the Privacy Act exempts such records from student access. Specifically, it exempts "records of instructional, supervisory, and administrative personnel and educational personnel ancillary thereto which are in the sole possession of the maker thereof and which are not accessible or revealed to any other except a substitute" (sec. 1232 g (a) (4) (B) (i)). In order to qualify for the exemption, the record about the student must be available only to the individual professor or a substitute. Disclosure to other faculty members, department chairmen, or administrators loses the exemption.

Law Enforcement Records of Educational Institutions

Many post-secondary schools employ personnel with law enforcement functions such as campus security personnel and their administrative supervisors. Records maintained by such personnel might include data on past incidents involving students, information obtained from local police, and reports from other university employees about potential "trouble makers." The Act does not grant students access to these records if they are segregated from other data, maintained only for law enforcement purposes, and not made available to persons other than "law enforcement officials of the same jurisdiction" (sec. 1232 g (a) (4) (B) (ii)). In addition, university law enforcement personnel must not have access to any education records.

The memorandum of The Association of American Law Schools points out that the chief executive officer of a university and perhaps other administrators have law enforcement responsibilities in a university. They also may have educational, financial, or other responsibilities. As a result, they should have access to both law enforcement and general education records. The memorandum reports that HEW officials have recognized the administrative necessity for some persons to have access to both types of records and have indicated that access by a university president to law enforcement records will not destroy the exemption so long as "the arrangement is tightly controlled" (Note 5, p. 8). The text of the statute supports this result. It requires that "personnel of a law enforcement unit" have no access to education records, and that law enforcement records not be available to persons other than "law enforcement officials of the same jurisdiction" (Privacy Act, sec. 1232 g (a) (4) (B) (ii)). Presumably, the president of a university can be a "law enforcement official" without being one of the "personnel of a law enforcement unit" who can have no access to education records. The same reasoning should apply to some subordinate administrative officials, but neither the statute nor the regulations provide additional guidance.

The memorandum further suggests that, to take full advantage of this exemption and to provide the necessary safeguards, institutions consider the adoption of a rule which assigns law enforcement supervisory responsibilities to designated officials, provides that they are not personnel of the law enforcement unit, and directs them not to disclose law enforcement records to other than law enforcement personnel nor to disclose education records to law enforcement personnel (Note 5, p. 8).

Medical Records of Educational Institutions

University infirmaries often provide medical care to students. On occasion, it is important for a school to be informed about a student's special medical problems. This type of record meets the Privacy Act's general definition of an education record. Nevertheless, medical records created or maintained by physicians or other medical professionals or paraprofessionals are exempted from direct student access, provided they are created, maintained, or used solely in connection with the treatment of the student. Medical records retain this status only if they are not disclosed to anyone other than those providing treatment (sec. 1232 g (a) (4) (B) (iv)). "Treatment" probably refers to medical treatment, but neither the statute nor the regulations define this term, except by excluding from the definition "remedial educational activities or activities which are part of the program of instruction" (Note 4). Though they are not available for student review, medical records may be reviewed by "a physician or other appropriate professional of the student's choice" (sec. 1232 g (a) (4) (B) (iv)).

If medical records are disclosed to those not involved with the treatment of the student, they are then treated in the same manner as other educational records. The student has a right of access, and the more general non-disclosure provisions of the statute are applicable.

The Privacy Act has raised, and will continue to raise, numerous legal questions. Its provisions for student access and correction of records may present possibilities for abuse; but unless this occurs, I see little problem in allowing students the right to review and to attempt to correct their records. More importantly, the basic goals of the statute with respect to the privacy of student records are sound. Though the school administrator and his counsel might wish for greater clarity, a policy of non-disclosure in the absence of student consent is both legally safe and ethically proper.

GOVERNMENT INQUIRY AND PRIVACY

Privacy on the campus is affected, not only by the information gathering and disclosures of educational institutions, but also by the amount and type of information which government may demand either as a condition of its largesse or (more probably) in the exercise of its functions under various statutes.

A state civil rights agency may demand data about the age, race, and sex of faculty members and students. It may seek to determine whether a university discriminates against minorities in student admissions or faculty hiring and promotion. The federal Equal Employment Opportunity Commission, having charged a university with failure to award tenure to Professor X because he is black, may seek to examine the records of the school's tenure and promotion committees, as well as the employment records of other faculty members.

Compliance with these and other requests for information may require substantial expenditure of time and money. Moreover, some of the data may be viewed as confidential. University statutes usually provide that the deliberations of tenure and promotion committees be kept secret. Such a procedure arguably helps to ensure candor by both the decisionmakers and those who are asked for information. In short, the university and some of its faculty and students may believe that the data are "nobody's business." That the demand is made by government suggests a new and unwanted interference with educational institutions.

Judicial Precedents

Traditionally, administrative agencies charged with investigatory and enforcement tasks have enjoyed broad authority to obtain information. The courts have required only a minimal showing before enforcing agency subpoenas. The agency seeking to enforce a subpoena must show that it is authorized to investigate or decide the matter about which it seeks the information. The material sought must be relevant to the inquiry. The subpoena must adequately specify the material sought, and the request may not be unreasonably burdensome. Finally, the administrative agency may not ignore the applicable privileges such as the Fifth Amendment privilege against self-incrimination and the attorney–client privilege (Note 6).

The Supreme Court set out these guidelines more than 30 years ago in a series of cases ending with *Endicott Johnson Corp. v. Perkins* (Note 7) and *Oklahoma Press Publishing Co. v. Walling* (Note 8). The initial question, of course, is whether the administrative agency has the statutory authority to conduct the investigation in question. *Oklahoma Press* involved an investigation by the Administrator of the Wage and Hour Division of the Department of Labor to determine whether the company was violating The Fair Labor Standards Act. The subpoena sought specified records to determine whether the company was covered by the statute and whether it was violating the Act. The Court concluded that the statute expressly authorized the Administrator to obtain records for such purposes.

A second question is whether the records sought are relevant to the authorized inquiry. In enforcing the subpoena in *Endicott Johnson*, the Supreme Court pointed out that "the evidence sought by the subpoena was not plainly incompetent or irrelevant to any lawful purpose of the

Secretary [of Labor] . . ." (Note 7, p. 509). This opinion and many others thereafter demonstrate the difficulty in attacking a subpoena on the ground that the documents sought are irrelevant.

The courts also agree that a subpoena must adequately specify the documents sought. The reason for such a requirement is obvious: an individual must know what documents are sought before he can be expected to comply with the request. Likewise, a court must know what is sought before it can decide whether to enforce the demand. But it is not necessary to list each individual document. A court would and should enforce a subpoena which called for "all the letters written by Jones during November 1976" or "all documents sent by the company to its ten largest customers during the previous two years." Both requests are sufficiently specific. Finally, the disclosure sought should not be unreasonable. This requirement "cannot be reduced to formula; for relevancy and adequacy or excess in the breadth of the subpoena are matters variable in relation to the nature, purposes and scope of the inquiry" (Note 8, p. 208).

The agency making the demand and the recipient of its process are likely to disagree on what constitutes a demand for an unreasonable number of documents. In *Civil Aeronautics Board v. Hermann* (Note 9), the Supreme Court upheld a subpoena which called for the production of virtually all the records of an airline for a period of more than three years. In *Cudmore v. Bowles* (Note 10), the District of Columbia Circuit enforced an agency subpoena which called for the production of 20,000 documents. Clearly, compliance with a subpoena may be both expensive and inconvenient. At least one commentator has summarized the attitude of state and federal courts as follows:

> If it appears to the court on the whole record that the purpose of the subpoena is to "annoy and embarrass" rather than to "discover and reveal," the court may deny enforcement. It is noteworthy that in most of the cases where a court has relied on the undue burden imposed by a subpoena in declining application for enforcement, there is a strong suggestion that the subpoena was issued for improper purposes [Cooper, 1965, p. 304, citing *Winn & Lovett Grocery Co. v. National Labor Relations Board* (Note 11)].

Companies in regulated industries and private industry in general have been subject to the demands of government agencies for many years. Lawyers experienced with the discovery procedures in the federal courts are at least familiar with broad demands for information from an adversary. But educational institutions have only recently felt the impact of a series of federal laws. Faculty collective bargaining under the National Labor Relations Act is a relatively new phenomenon. HEW regulations with respect to handicapped persons are less than two years old.

The Civil Rights Act prohibitions against discrimination in employment, student admissions, and various other aspects of university life likewise provide a relatively new mechanism for what some might view as an unnecessary intrusion of government into the affairs of educational institutions. Private institutions have enjoyed almost total discretion with respect to student admissions and faculty hiring, tenure, and promotion. The Civil Rights Act limits that discretion. And it is not unusual for a professor whose contract has not been renewed to charge that the reason for non-renewal was illegal discrimination. That professor's civil lawsuit can result in broad discovery demands which may be difficult to resist, but it is also possible that federal or state agencies may investigate the claim and demand that the university provide extensive data considered confidential by the university and its students or faculty.

Examination of a Specific Court Case

Perhaps the best actual example of governmental demands for information involved the dismissal of a professor by the University of New Mexico (Note 12). In January 1971, the Dean of the College of Engineering of the University of New Mexico notified Professor Jovan Djuric that he was recommending the institution of proceedings to terminate the professor's services. In January 1972, the chairman of Dr. Djuric's department wrote to him, setting forth 12 specific statements or charges "of lack of minimum professional standards" (Note 12, p. 1299) in his performance as a staff member during the 1971 fall semester. Termination proceedings began in May 1972. In September 1972, Dr. Djuric filed a charge with the federal Equal Employment Opportunity Commission (EEOC) alleging a violation of the Civil Rights Act in that he was being terminated "because of my national origin, Yugoslav" and in retaliation for filing a charge with the state Human Rights Commission.* During the EEOC investigation, the University supplied the EEOC with requested information including:

> (a) records or lists of all terminations which occurred at the College of Engineering from September 1, 1970 to the present, revealing race or national origin, position hired into, date of hire, starting salary, ending salary, date of termination and reason for termination; (b) copies of memorandums or letters that any other terminated employees received if any terminations were for the same reason as Dr. Djuric's; (c) a complete copy of Dr. Djuric's personnel file; (d) all records or minutes held by the Engineeering Department which led to the decision to terminate Dr. Djuric's services; and (e) a statement as to why the decision was made in May of 1972 to terminate Dr. Djuric [Note 12, p. 1299].

* The state dismissed the discrimination charges in May 1973. The federal EEOC did not investigate the retaliation charge.

Thereafter, in order to conduct a more "thorough and complete investigation of the charge," the EEOC requested additional information. The University refused to comply with the EEOC subpoena which requested:

> 1. Copies of personnel files of those faculty members terminated from the College of Engineering from January 1970, to May 14, 1973.
> 2. Copies of personnel files of all faculty members in the College of Engineering as of May 14, 1973 [Note 12, p. 1299].

When the EEOC sought court enforcement of the subpoena, the University contended that: (1) the subpoenaed information was not relevant and was overbroad and unreasonable in light of the evidence already presented that Dr. Djuric's termination was solely the result of poor job performance; (2) the subpoenaed information was not sufficiently identified to protect University personnel from disclosure of confidential information and must be modified, if enforceable at all, to describe the information sought with particularity; and (3) the subpoena violated the Fourth Amendment prohibition against unreasonable searches because the EEOC, prior to its issuance, did not have probable cause to believe that the University had discriminated against Dr. Djuric.

The Court of Appeals for the Tenth Circuit rejected these contentions and affirmed the district court's order that the University comply with the subpoena. The court first examined the statutory provisions relating to EEOC investigations of discrimination charges. Under the statute the information sought must be "relevant" to or "relate to any matter" under investigation (Note 12, p. 1301). The EEOC argued that the personnel files would provide comparative data so that it could see how the employer treated faculty members of different national origins in comparable situations. It is difficult to disagree with this contention. If faculty members with poorer credentials than Dr. Djuric's had been tenured, promoted, and retained, this would support the possibility that the expressed reasons for the University's action were a pretext. But if the credentials and performance of the remaining faculty members were superior, this would tend to disprove the discrimination charge. Faculty personnel files should contain relevant data with respect to this issue.

The court concluded that the statute did not require "probable cause" for the enforcement of a subpoena and that "administrative subpoenas may be enforced for investigative purposes unless they are plainly incompetent or irrelevant to any lawful purpose" (Note 12, p. 1303). It would likewise seem clear under existing case law that the subpoena adequately specified the documents sought and that the numbers of documents requested did not make the subpoena burdensome.

The University did not seriously question the relevance of the subpoena; nor did it argue that the number of documents sought made the subpoena burdensome. It argued, rather, that the information already furnished clearly supported its allegation of Dr. Djuric's poor job performance so that there was no need for the EEOC to investigate or inquire further. Nevertheless, the EEOC convinced the court that it should have the personnel files to "ascertain whether any of the transgressions attributed to Dr. Djuric have been committed by other employees" and whether they "have been treated in the same manner as Djuric" (Note 12, p. 1301).

The Tenth Circuit in effect applied the general criteria for the enforcement of administrative subpoenas. It found that the statute authorized the EEOC investigation, that the records sought were adequately specified, and that they were relevant to the matter under investigation. Nevertheless, the decision raises some troublesome issues. Prior to this decision, there was no recorded case in which the EEOC expressly demanded the production of personnel files (Madsen, 1975, p. 266). Moreover, the University pointed out that the subpoenaed faculty personnel files "involve a myriad of matters, much of which is personal, private, and confidential." Both parties stipulated that the files and records were "confidential and extremely sensitive." The Tenth Circuit case thus raises the potential conflict between the privacy of confidential records and the necessity to investigate and prevent employment discrimination or other illegal activities.

There is no question that personnel files often contain confidential and personal information (Mironi, 1974, pp. 270–272). The data may include performance evaluations, salary information, police data, disciplinary actions, family information, and written tests relating to intelligence, aptitude, emotional traits, moral values, and character traits. If some of this information is not relevant, the administrative agency should not insist on its production, and the court should not require it. But the University made no attempt to argue that specific data within the files were not relevant. It argued, rather, that no files should be produced because they contained confidential information. It seems clear that some of the information which one would expect to find in a faculty personnel file—i.e., evaluations and applications for promotion or tenure—would be relevant to the investigation of a charge that a particular employee was dismissed for an illegal reason. If the files also contained data which were "plainly incompetent or irrelevant," the University should have attempted to make such a showing. It should have been able to resist production of medical records, for example, or of any other plainly irrelevant material if it sought to have such information exempted from the subpoena. Nevertheless, a court will and should require production of all information relevant to an investigation, even if it is "confidential and extremely sensitive." And the case law correctly places the burden on the recipient of the subpoena to show that specific information is "plainly incompetent or irrelevant to any lawful purpose."

CONCLUSION

Government agencies must be given the means to enforce the laws against discrimination. Although there are and must be limits to the government's ability to obtain information, I would suggest that the traditional confidentiality surrounding faculty personnel decisions should not prevent an agency such as the EEOC from obtaining production of this type of information any more than it should prevent the university from using the material if it would be helpful in establishing the university's defense of the charges. Moreover, the courts have not hesitated to limit the scope of EEOC subpoenas where they considered the requests to be irrelevant or otherwise impermissibly broad or vague (Madsen, 1975, pp. 266–268). But in the *University of New Mexico* case (Note 12), the demand for data was a reasonable one, and the court was correct to enforce the subpoena. The records sought were clearly identified, and there was apparently no undue burden in producing the documents. Although the University made a strong showing that it had sufficient reason to dismiss Dr. Djuric, there was no evidence that the EEOC was attempting to harass the institution or was acting in bad faith. In short, the existing law with respect to the enforcement of administrative subpoenas appears adequate to prevent excesses on the part of administrative agencies.

Discussion of privacy on the campus would not be complete without noting some differences which now exist in the treatment of student and faculty records. The Privacy Act mandates that educational institutions protect the privacy of student records, give students access to their education records, and provide a means for the correction of errors in such records. Congress has enacted no such requirements with respect to faculty records. Some collective bargaining agreements provide for employee access to personnel records, and legislation exists in two or three states (Note 13, p. 1); but, in general, educational institutions are free to deny faculty any access to their personnel records.

The Privacy Act also requires that educational institutions make reasonable efforts to notify students before surrendering educational records in compliance with a court order or subpoena. No such requirement exists with respect to faculty records. The faculty member may be willing or may be required to provide information to his employer, but he may not be willing to have his employer disclose that information. Thus, it might be appropriate for an educational institution to notify a faculty member before it discloses information from his personnel file in order to comply with a subpoena.

REFERENCE NOTES

1. Family Educational Rights and Privacy Act of 1974. *U.S. Code*, 1974, *20*, sec. 123 g. This Act is frequently referred to as "The Buckley Amendment." For the sake of brevity it will be referred to throughout the remainder of the paper as: Privacy Act.
2. *Girardier v. Webster College*. 8th Circuit Court, 1977, *563*, F. 2d., 1928.
3. The statute grants rights to parents of students, but section 1232 g (d) provides that "whenever a student has attained eighteen years of age or is attending an institution of postsecondary education the permission or consent required of and the rights accorded to the parents of the student shall thereafter only be required of and accorded to the student."
4. *Code of Federal Regulations*, 1976, *45*, sec. 99.3 (3).
5. Association of American Law Schools. "Buckley Amendment" (Memorandum), September 23, 1976.
6. *Adams v. Federal Trade Commission*. 8th Circuit Court, 1961, *296*, F. 2d., 861.
7. *Endicott Johnson Corp. v. Perkins*. U. S., 1943, *317*, 501.
8. *Oklahoma Press Publishing Co. v. Walling*. U.S., 1946, *327*, 186.
9. *Civil Aeronautics Board v. Hermann*. U.S., 1947, *353*, 322.
10. *Cudmore v. Bowles*. D. C. Circuit Court, 1944, *145*, F. 2d., 697.
11. *Winn & Lovett Grocery Co. v. National Labor Relations Board*. 5th Circuit Court, 1954, *213*, F. 2d., 785.
12. *Equal Employment Opportunity Commission v. University of New Mexico*. 10th Circuit Court, 1974, *504*, F. 2d., 1296–1304.
13. *Wall Street Journal*, December 20, 1977.

REFERENCES

Cooper, F. *State administrative law*. Indianapolis: Bobbs-Merrill, 1965.

Madsen, R. Comment: *EEOC v. University of New Mexico*: Production of employee personnel files in EEOC investigations. *Utah Law Review*, 1975, Spring, 264–278.

Mironi, M. The confidentiality of personnel records: A legal and ethical view. *Labor Law Journal*, 1974, *25*, 270–295.

Prosser, W. L. *Handbook of the law of torts* (4th ed.). St. Paul: West, 1971.

Privacy vs. the Goals of the Researcher

William J. McGuire

William J. McGuire received his A.B. (1949) and his M.A. (1950) degrees from Fordham University, with his Ph.D. coming from Yale University in 1954. From 1955 to 1958 he taught at Yale University, and then at the University of Illinois, Columbia University, and the University of California at San Diego before returning to Yale University in 1970, where he currently is Professor of Psychology. Dr. McGuire is a Fellow of the American Psychological Association, a former member of its Council of Representatives, Board of Scientific Affairs, and President (1972–1973) of the Division of Personality and Social Psychology. From 1967 to 1970 he served as editor of the Journal of Personality and Social Psychology. *Dr. McGuire is the author, or in a few cases, the co-author, of upwards of 50 articles in professional journals, principally in the area of his specialty, which is Social Psychology.*

We intellectuals—readers and writers of books—are a very private people, cherishing our own privacy and solicitous after that of others. But the intellectual vocation or predilection catches us up in an intrinsic contradiction on this issue: at the same time as we are advocating constitutional protection for the privacy of the individual, we are engaged in

The writing of this paper was facilitated by support received from the National Science Foundation, Division of Social and Developmental Psychology, via Grant BNS 73–05401.

the zealous search for truth, for making known the hidden things of this world. Anyone with the personal conviction that deprivation of privacy is a form of enslavement and with a professional life based on the premiss that the truth will make us free is functioning on the edge of a contradiction which may either lead to confusion and evasion or provide the impetus for a higher evolution of one's value system.

In this paper I shall confront the researcher's conflict of values between privacy and knowledge in the hopes of arriving at a resolution which will yield a deeper appreciation of each of its terms. I shall discuss first the most specific issue, the researcher's obligation to safeguard the privacy of the individuals who participate in his or her research. I shall then turn to the broader question of the researcher's responsibility for preserving the confidentiality of the participant's valued reference groups, what I term the "categorical" privacy issue. Finally, I shall take up the more transcendental question of the inherent privacy rights of humanity which may impose limits on the researcher's right and duty to investigate and report on any aspect of humans, their culture, and their environment.

PROTECTING THE PRIVACY OF PARTICIPANTS IN RESEARCH

The *Ethical Principles in the Conduct of Research with Human Participants*, published by the American Psychological Association (APA) in 1973 (Cook et al., 1973), presents a code of ethics to guide researchers in protecting the interests of the human beings who participate in their studies. In discussing here the problems and possibilities of protecting the privacy of research participants, I shall draw heavily on the APA code not only because it is quite recent, has taken into account previous thinking on the topic, and is based on a considerable amount of work by many and diverse people, but also because I was one of the committee of six primarily responsible for developing it. The method used to produce the code is itself of considerable interest to a pastoral psychology symposium—indeed, it may be more interesting in its peculiar method than in its predictable results—so I shall describe the odd procedures of its production before I discuss its substantive conclusions on the issue of privacy.

A Peculiar Procedure for Constructing an Ethical Code

The 1973 ethical code was not the first one published by the APA. In 1953 a slim volume (Hobbs, 1953) was issued to provide ethical guidelines for those engaged in psychological work; it dealt largely with professional services provided by psychologists, only 11 of its 171 pages being devoted to the treatment of participants in research. Only later, notably since the mid-1960s, have the ethical concerns expressed regarding psychological work focused increasingly on the treatment accorded the human beings who participate in the research. Observers both within and without the psychological profession have complained that participants were being coerced into taking part or were not accorded full information before giving their consent; or that during their participation they were exposed to unacceptable levels of physical or psychological discomfort, stress, or risk; or that after participation the confidentiality of the data and participant's privacy were not sufficiently safeguarded, etc. In this atmosphere the APA in the late-1960s directed a committee to develop a fuller code of ethics for the treatment of participants in research (Cook et al., 1973). The two guiding ideas underlying the method used in developing this code, inductive empiricism and participatory democracy, are working principles which most of us would grant have their honorable parts to play in human endeavors, but which might seem to many of us somewhat out of place in the development of an ethical code. Because of their controversiality as modes of developing an ethical code, these two working procedures will be described before I discuss the more substantive issue of what conclusions one can draw from this new APA code and other sources regarding the protection of the privacy of the participants in research.

An inductive ethics. The committee established to develop the code, rather than starting with an explicit set of principles, elected to proceed inductively by eliciting a sample of ethically worrisome incidents. After we made a pilot survey of 1,000 of the APA's 35,000 members to try out formats for eliciting descriptions of ethically significant incidents encountered in research, a revised questionnaire was developed and sent to a 9,000-member sample asking for detailed descriptions of such ethically questionable research incidents. In response we received descriptions of about 2,000 incidents, which were mulled over and classified to sketch out a preliminary list of issues.

The questionnaire was then revised and sent to a second sample of 9,000 APA members; this time attention focused somewhat on members of divisions especially involved with sensitive procedures (e.g., research on children) or on topics (such as pain research or hypnosis) where additional incidents seemed particularly needed. This second survey elicited another 3,000 incidents, giving us a data base of about 5,000 research incidents which seemed to the respondents to raise some ethical issue regarding the treatment of participants.

These incidents were sorted among numerous non-exclusive categories (e.g., informed consent, psychological stress, physical pain, use of retarded or incapacitated subjects, invasion of privacy). Each batch was analyzed by at least two members of the committee to tease out the various issues involved and, after group discussion, to write up preliminary drafts to provide guidelines on the issue. Each draft was read and discussed by the other members and then rotated to new members for revision, the recycling being repeated until the section draft was generally acceptable to all committee members. The general format used in writing each section was to state the issues which were involved in the area, present a series of incidents which showed how these issues arose, and then provide guidelines for the way the ethical problems might best be handled.

Participatory democracy. The second noteworthy working method used in evolving this ethical code was obtaining the maximum feasible participation by constituencies inside and outside the research profession. The committee members, chaired by Stuart W. Cook, worked as equals and with overlapping responsibilities. The body of incidents which served as points of departure for our cogitations and illustrations for our conclusions came from circularizing 20,000 psychologists, 5,000 of whom responded. In addition, lists were also drawn up of five kinds of people judged to be particularly acquainted with the problem area—journal editors, writers on research ethics, staff members of research review panels, etc.—and the people on these lists were asked via mail and by face-to-face interviews for their views on the issues with which we were wrestling and for their suggestions for additional issues. When a preliminary draft was available, it was sent to a wide variety of organized groups, including not only psychology and other social and behavioral science professional associations, but also relevant non-research groups, with the request that it be called to the attention of the organization's members and that we be given a report on any reactions elicited. Replies were received from 120 of these groups. An intermediate draft of the code was then circulated to the 35,000 members of the APA in 1971, and on the basis of the critiques received it was very extensively revised.

The drastically revised version was circulated to the entire APA membership in May 1972, and to other critics as well. Although the 1971 and earlier drafts had received a great deal of criticism—usually that the guidelines were too restrictive on the researcher—the 1972 draft received considerably fewer critical comments—and mostly that it was too permissive.

This May 1972 draft was then given a final revision into ten principles, a preamble, and an extensive discussion of the principles. These principles were subsequently adopted by the Council of Representatives of the APA and in 1973 distributed for their guidance to all members of the association. The guidelines for safeguarding the privacy of participants in research are given primarily in principle 10, and pages 87–94 of the code (Cook et al., 1973) discuss the privacy issues in detail.

Ideology Behind the Code's Methodology

Those who approach the task of constructing an ethical code as philosophers or theologians may regard the empirical and consensus procedures which our committee used with feelings ranging from amusement through incredulity to indignation. One might argue that in the moral order one should proceed normatively and deductively rather than by induction and consensus. But it should be recognized that the membership of the APA and especially of its ruling elites is not made up wholly or holily of people whose communions make them familiar with or sympathetic to these alternative approaches. I have noted during my own striding through the corridors of power in the scientific circles how seldom do the people I greet respond with our secret handshake. Our colleagues in the scientific elite have less often recognized and returned our secret handshake than they have asked me to reveal it (but have no fear, I have respected its privacy). Leaving aside the normative approaches as too foreign to the APA elites, I shall mention briefly several more secular approaches the neglect of which in the formulation of this code is more surprising.

Legal positivism. In our aspiration to elicit from researchers a large number of ethically significant issues to serve as our starting point and then to tailor our conclusion to evoke consensus from a wide variety of constituencies, our committee was implicitly proceeding on the "legal positivism" (or "American legal realism") philosophy which derives from such philosophers as John Austin and Jeremy Bentham and has received a classic statement in Hart's *The Concept of Law* (1961). This philosophy dominated the American judicial scene during the early part of the twentieth century, with such articulate spokespersons from the bench as Oliver Wendell Homes, Felix Frankfurter, and Learned Hand. The legal positivist would regard participants in research as having rights insofar as these rights have been created by explicit political decisions or by social conventions and practices, the existence of which can be discovered by studying at what point and against what procedures social pressure or political power is likely to intervene.

Utilitarianism. To a lesser extent our methodology in developing this code reflects the currently more popular legal philosophy which might be termed "utilitarianism," and which stems from such philosophers as John Stuart Mill, a philosophy now so dominant in judicial circles in the United States that spokespersons need hardly be singled out. A stricter adherence to this judicially more up-to-date philosophy would have had us developing the APA code by determining what regulations would be justified by their serving the public good (or, more parochially, the long-term interests of psychologists). To some extent this utilitarian philosophy was reflected in the initial pragmatic decision to have researchers draw up the code of restrictions. Admittedly, an initial vote among researchers without regard to political sophistication might have revealed a consensus against imposing any additional restrictions upon ourselves (except perhaps in the extreme cases of the exploitation of participants or the imposition of notable risks or discomforts upon them). But the more politically sophisticated researchers would probably have admitted the wisdom of our profession's undertaking this self-regulation rather than leaving the task to be carried out by non-researchers, less sympathetic to and less familiar with the needs of research. The utilitarian legal philosophy was likewise reflected in our frequent adverting to the need for empirical research to determine whether certain ethically questioned treatments of participants in research (e.g., deceiving them regarding the purpose of the research) were indeed harmful to the participants.

Relevance of moral principles. In view of the cultural lag between fields, it should not be surprising that our committee followed the older fashion of legal positivism and to a lesser extent the legal philosopher's current orthodoxy of utilitarianism, while paying little explicit attention to re-emerging legal philosophies which take as the starting point principles in their own right rather than abstracting them from precedents or from the current consensus, or positing them insofar as they serve the public good. This view re-emerging in both Britain and the United States (see Dworkin, 1977) did receive some implicit recognition in the development of the APA code insofar as we accepted as given such principles as the "benefits/cost" axiom that a necessary condition for a research procedure's acceptability is that its benefits to society, to the participants, to the researcher, etc., should exceed the costs which it imposes on these various constituencies.

Logical empiricism. Most surprising about our methodology in developing this code is that we steadfastly avoided any mention of the implications of the logical empiricism which probably constituted the modal methodological philosophy of the committee and the psychological constituency for which they worked. In spite of the fact that one often does not practice what one preaches, it is surprising that we did not exhibit some slight embarrassment for ignoring the logical empiricist approach, which would have called for our starting with a theory, a set of ethical principles regarding the treatment of participants, and the theorems derived from them, and only then collecting data to test them. As believers in this philosophy, we should have tried to generate such a theory in the form of a set of broad postulates about the treatment of participants in research, deducing from these postulates a series of hypotheses dealing with more specific issues, such as the preservation of the participant's privacy, and only then devising procedures for collecting data which bear on the hypotheses, revising the hypotheses and the principles from which they were drawn insofar as was necessary in the light of the data collected. I am here less criticizing than expressing surprise that the psychological researchers not only failed to follow the tenets of logical empiricism but even seemed boastful of the "dustbowl empiricism" of their procedure. In our psychology methods courses, we logical empiricists often caution our students that one's suppositions guide one's observations and interpretations, if not explicitly then implicitly. Hence, we should formulate our postulates and their derivations in advance of data collection so that we know what principles are guiding us rather than being unconsciously controlled by them. But we who produced this 1973 code actually seemed proud of violating our own logical empiricist philosophy in purportedly plowing through vast fields of data without setting up *a priori* hypotheses to test, thus letting our unstated preconceptions preconsciously control our interpretations, as we purported to induce the issues and their resolutions from the incidents.

But rather than continuing to describe, or to express surprise or regret at, the procedures which produced the 1973 code, I might note that one of its philosophical underpinnings is a situational ethics stance such that, written into the document itself, is the provision that the code should be revised at five- or ten-year intervals, as the problems change or the criteria of acceptability change. Perhaps the next time the APA group will adopt some kind of a logical empiricist or other axiomatic approach.

Conclusions Regarding Privacy Protection in the 1973 Code

The APA's report on ethical principles in conducting research with humans (Cook et al., 1973) fills more than 100 pages; the principles themselves boil down to a two-page decalogue, the statement on privacy being the last of these ten commandments. It reads:

> Information obtained about the research participants during the course of an investigation is confidential. When the possibility exists that others may gain access to such information, ethical research practice requires that this possibility, together with the plans for protecting confidentiality, be explained to the participants as part of the procedure for obtaining informed consent [p. 89].

This sparse statement is expounded in 11 pages of text (pp. 87–97). The code asserts (in guaranteeing oblivion to the purportedly inductive nature of the code) that this principle arises from the "widely accepted rule of human conduct . . . that every person has a right to privacy . . ." (p. 87). I shall now describe and discuss the code's commentary on the privacy principle.

It is recognized that there are various mitigating specifics, such as that some people feel a greater need for privacy than do others and that some kinds of information are more appropriately kept private than others.

Still, since one seldom has detailed information about the participant's feelings in the matter, the researcher must take a conservative stance, keeping private anything learned about the participant which any reasonable person might consider sensitive in addition to any explicit requests or promises of privacy. And where there is any foreseeable possibility of objectionable disclosure, the researcher is obligated to tell the person prior to participation of the possible disclosures as part of the informed-consent procedure.

Special problems. Other parties in the research situation may regard themselves as having a right to be given the information learned about the participants. If one's research involves measuring the abilities of young students, for example, and one appropriately seeks the informed consent of the child, the child's parents, and, where appropriate, the child's teacher, one might find the parent and/or teacher requesting information about the child's score on the abilities test. In clinical research, one might do an in-depth study of a person, and later (particularly when the research had been done in an institutional setting) the person's therapist may request a look at the patient's interview or projective technique response protocol. Or one might obtain data on drug use from the participants in one's research and later receive a request from a participant's physician regarding a patient's use of drugs. In all these cases the third party's motivation for requesting such privileged information is purportedly in the participant's own best interest. The recommendations in the code imply that in situations where such requests for privileged information about the participants can be foreseen (as in a school or hospital setting or where a parent's consent is required) if one intends to disclose the information when it is requested, then this possibility should be announced to the participant in advance as part of the informed-consent procedure. Without either advance permission or retroactively obtained permission under free and informed consent, the stated or implied privacy guarantee to the participant makes it inappropriate for the researcher to divulge the information in response to such requests, however awkward for the researcher reticence may be.

In some cases, however, the need to provide help for some participant may be so critical that the researcher will judge it necessary to sacrifice the participant's privacy in his or her own best interest. In other cases the researcher may be pressured to violate the privacy of the participants for reasons other than the participants' own good, and may at times even run into conflict with the legal code in protecting the participants' privacy. For example, the researcher who investigates the drug use of a set of respondents may have a personal dilemma in deciding whether or not to disclose drug-use responses to the physician who is endeavoring to treat one of the participants; but if the request for information comes from the courts, the researcher has no legal option but to divulge the information.

Likewise, the researcher who happens to have collected some depth-interview material during research may later be faced with a subpoena to supply the protocol to the courts should a participant be involved in a criminal trial or even in a civil suit. Whenever information which might put a participant in jeopardy is collected, the researcher is obligated to make it clear to that participant that there is no legal protection for such information should it be subpoenaed.

Inadvertent disclosure. Research procedures themselves sometimes jeopardize the privacy of the participants. For example, researchers typically file the scores and other responses obtained from participants along with the participants' identification in low security locations which are quite accessible to other researchers, clerical personnel, students, etc. Researchers are obligated to recognize potential disclosure dangers and to take security measures which will safeguard the privacy of the participants, even at the risk of inconveniencing themselves or their co-workers or of antagonizing colleagues by their reticence or seeming suspiciousness. There are additional technological risks when one's research involves a data bank of information on participants in a longitudinal design, where a person's identity must be kept associated with past information so that new information can be filed appropriately at a later date. Special care must then be taken to preserve the participants' privacy by disassociating their identity from the data, even though doing so may necessitate more tedious and costly linking procedures later.

The privacy involved is sometimes that of a third party about whom the participant reveals some information of a delicate nature to the researcher. Does the researcher have an obligation to respect the privacy of these third parties as well as that of the participant who is directly involved in the research? It would seem so, since one must respect the privacy of other people whether one has incurred any special obligation to them through their volunteered participation in one's research or not. Furthermore, the researcher has an obligation to the participant to preserve this other party's privacy since the information was given in confidence.

Obligations to violate privacy commitments. Thus far I have been discussing the researcher's obligation regarding the confidentiality of information obtained about the participant as if the only value to be considered were the need to maintain the participant's privacy. But in some cases the researcher may find that other moral considerations permit or even compel the violation even of an explicit promise of confidentiality. A researcher in conducting an intimate interview may, by an explicit assurance that all information will be kept confidential, elicit sensitive information of impending self-destructive or socially dangerous behavior, or of past misdeeds which are causing continuing suffering to others, etc., discoveries which seem to cry out for disclosure by the researcher.

The "ethical incidents" elicited from researchers in the survey carried out in constructing this code contained a number of poignant cases of this type, where guilt-ridden researchers report keeping silent about worrisome indications revealed by participants who later committed suicide, or molested and murdered children, etc. Typically, the situation was morally ambiguous, with the researcher's detecting some worrisome signs that the participant may have been contemplating behavior destructive to self or others which the researcher felt some pressure to disclose to physicians or significant others in the person's life or even to legal authorities; but, typically, the researcher decided that the worrisome indications were not sufficiently clear to warrant violation of the participant's privacy, especially in view of the explicit promise of confidentiality. Even those researchers who collect information of a more casual type will, in the course of a long research career, come upon participants from time to time who seem to be in need of help or to be potentially dangerous. Typically, in such cases, one concludes that the clear-cut promise of privacy protection outweighs the ambiguous suggestion of need for disclosure. These incidents are "hard cases" which the researcher must decide on an *ad hoc* basis. In reaching a decision one should remind oneself that the decision not to disclose should probably be re-examined more closely in recognition that since it happens to be the most convenient one, it must stand scrutiny that it was not selected as the researcher's easiest escape from risk and responsibility.

Techniques for safeguarding privacy. One of the most effective means for safeguarding the privacy of the participant is to keep the participant's identity from becoming known even to the researcher and not to record it when collecting the participant's data. Wherever possible, the researcher should collect and store the data without any explicit identification or even circumstantial information which could later link them to a specific individual. Quite unacceptable is the reverse procedure of collecting the data under the guise of anonymity but making some surreptitious marks by which the researcher can identify the respondent. Such surreptitious marking is objectionable, not only because it provides the possibility of later betrayal of privacy (even if this is not the researcher's intent), but also because it violates the principle of informed consent.

Where it is necessary to keep the respondent's identity linked to the data (for example, in a longitudinal panel study where other data will be collected from the same participants and needs to be paired with the earlier data), then the researcher has the obligation to practice security measures regarding the data storage even if such measures are atypical to the research setting and are personally awkward (in that colleagues could take them as a sign that their integrity is being questioned). Where there is any appreciable chance that the data could be subpoenaed by the legal authorities, the researcher might deposit the linking data outside the jurisdiction of the court. (For example, in one major panel study of United

States college students, the identification information is stored in Canada where it presumably cannot be subpoenaed by American courts.) This may lay the researcher open to contempt charges and he or she must be willing to go to jail to safeguard the privacy of the respondent if such a procedure is to be an effective safeguard. However, the researcher may well find him- or herself in a moral dilemma between protecting the privacy promised to the participant *vs.* obeying a lawful order from the judiciary—and perhaps in a proceeding where the researcher personally agrees that society has a right to know.

Where it is necessary to record the participant's identity at the time the data are collected, then the researcher should discard the identification as soon as the linkage is made. Discarding the identifying information is costly to the researcher both because it is often tedious to remove all the identifying information from the protocol and because it forecloses future opportunities to use the data for other, unanticipated, purposes. However, the researcher should be willing to incur these losses to ensure the privacy of the participant. Keeping the information about the participant's identity "just in case it might be needed" is not easily justified.

The researcher has the responsibility to foresee situations both exceptional and quotidian which may require disclosure of data collected, in violation of one's promise to the participant to protect her or his privacy. Such eventualities must be described adequately to the participant and be part of the free and informed consent under which the person agrees to participate in the research.

INVASIONS OF CATEGORICAL PRIVACY IN RESEARCH

Extension of Principle of Informed Consent

The privacy responsibility which most obviously falls on the researcher is to protect the personal privacy of those who participate in the research, the responsibility which I have just been discussing. Now I shall turn to a slightly more impersonal type of privacy and shall discuss the extent to which the researcher must respect the participant's privacy, not only as an individual, but also in a categorical sense as a member of a group. Need the researcher be concerned about publishing results which use the participants' data to reveal things, not about themselves as individuals, but about their membership group which they might prefer to keep private?

Hypothetical Example of the Problem

An example serves to illustrate the problem. Suppose the researcher has the hypothesis that attending parochial schools makes people more anti-

Semitic and otherwise ethnically prejudiced than attending the public schools. The researcher therefore draws a random sample of people including Catholics and non-Catholics, with the Catholics including those who attended parochial school and those who attended the public school and those who divided their attendance between the two. All people in the sample are then measured in terms of the independent variables of type of school attended and the dependent variable of amount of hostility to Jews and other ethnic groups. Let us suppose for a moment that the study reveals that Catholics are more anti-Jewish than non-Catholics; and that, among the Catholics, those who attended parochial school are more anti-Jewish than those who attended public school. A scrupulous researcher who has just read the APA code might wonder if publishing such results would raise a violation of privacy issue insofar as the Catholic respondents might not have wanted to reveal their (hypothetical) anti-Semitism and those who attended parochial school might not want to have exposed their (hypothetical) particularly intense anti-Jewish feeling. One might reasonably suspect that had the Catholic respondents foreseen such a revelation, they might not have agreed to participate. The researcher obviously feels that the question under study is of such interest and social importance that the results deserve publication (though motivation is somewhat ambiguous in that it also serves the researcher's self-interest). But does the researcher have the right to publish this "categorical" violation of the participants' privacy when the researcher did not make clear to the respondents in advance that such an (anticipated) revelation might be made, and suspects that had this advanced mention been made, people might have refused to participate?

Before I discuss the researcher's ethical dilemma in such a situation, I should make it clear, to avoid perpetuation of misinformation and to facilitate dispassionate analysis of the issue, that my example is not only hypothetical but contrary to fact. Greeley (1977) reports on the basis of a dozen National Opinion Research Council national samples totaling about 10,000 respondents that the data indicate that Catholics are less racist than comparable non-Catholic samples (and are less anti-Jewish than Jews are anti-Catholic); that Catholics who attended parochial school are less racist and less anti-Jewish than Catholics who attended public school; and that the longer they attended parochial school, the lower their anti-Jewish and other racist feelings. I have chosen this example because it coincides sufficiently with an *a priori* prejudice of many researchers to give a note of poignant verisimilitude to the discussion, and because it has been so clearly disproved that it need not be offensive.

Researcher's ethical dilemma. The researcher's moral dilemma in situations like this hypothetical one constitutes the "hard core" which in judicial proceedings facilitates the evolution of the law. It is not hard to understand why a social science researcher might feel that determining the relationship between parochial school attendance and intergroup hostility deserves investigation and publication. It is equally plausible that the researcher might suspect that if the results had (contrary to fact) indicated that the parochial school attenders were more prejudiced, they might prefer that their racism not be revealed. The APA code in its informed-consent principle requires that the participants be informed in advance of any aspect of the study which might affect their willingness to participate, and clearly the fact that the study was designed to investigate the relationship between parochial school attendance and prejudice and that it might reveal parochial school attenders to be more prejudiced are such deterring aspects. The APA privacy principle requires that such revelations are permissible only if the participant is informed of their possibility in advance. Rather than forgo a socially important investigation the researcher could, in keeping with the informed-consent and privacy principles, reveal to the participants in advance the issue under study and the possibly embarrassing outcome, thus allowing those who do not wish to have such racist feelings revealed to decline to participate in the study.

Disadvantages in each option. Unfortunately, such an informed-consent approach would risk artifactual distortions which might make the results of the study uninterpretable. For one thing, the forewarning is likely to result in selective refusal to participate which would make it hard to determine what population is represented by the sample who do participate; in addition, for those who do agree to participate, the forewarning is likely to cause a "social desirability" sensitization which might distort the answers of whatever sample does participate.

In this dilemma, the researcher might decide that society's need to know justifies a violation of the informed-consent and privacy principles. In putting these conflicting values together in a cost/benefit ratio, the researcher might decide that, happily for one's own research desires, one has the right to proceed. One might argue that the issue is an important one (since prejudice is a socially significant phenomenon and the research promises to identify a possible cause of it), and that one is violating the participant's privacy without permission only in a categorical fashion not on an individual basis. The researcher might assert that, if respondents are ashamed of such racist feelings, rather than hide them they should change them. But one purpose of having an explicit ethical code is to give us pause when our initial decision in a moral dilemma is so in accord with our preferences and self-interest. A little reflection with substitute examples reveals that often participants might want to keep concealed a characteristic of their group, not out of shame, but out of fear that exposure might subject the participants and their group to economic pressures, political persecution, etc., which it is their privilege to want to avoid.

The principle of informed consent implies that it is the participants' privilege to decide which aspect of the research is relevant to their decision whether or not to participate and to be informed of this aspect, even if it be a mere side issue (in the researcher's view) such as who is sponsoring the research, what is being investigated, or what use is going to be made of the results. The privacy principle also implies that the researcher ought to respect the confidentiality of any information supplied by the respondent which that respondent feels should be kept private. Perhaps no moral principle is absolute, and it is always possible that in this imperfect world one will have to violate any one principle to avoid committing a worse moral wrong. The fundamental dilemma regarding what we have the right (or even the duty) to reveal can perhaps be better discussed in the final section of this paper where I consider the intrinsic violation of privacy entailed by the researcher's vocation to lay bare the hidden things of this world.

RESEARCH AS INTRINSICALLY REDUCING THE DOMAIN OF THE PRIVATE

Behavioral Research as an Encroachment on Privacy

The social function of research is to make known what was previously hidden about significant aspects of people and their environment. Research is the attempt to analyze the universe and to describe the interrelations of its parts so as to make it understandable to the human intellect and perhaps also predictable and even controllable. In any uncovering of the previously unknown, there is an inevitable reduction of the realm of the private. In the case of the social and behavioral sciences, whose subject matter is the person and human culture, research inevitably lays bare aspects of ourselves and our society which had previously not been revealed. To the extent that privacy is valued above revelation, we should oppose social and behavioral science research, not only (or even primarily) because the privacy of the few participants is put at risk, but more importantly because the privacy of us all must inevitably be violated to the extent that research is successful in its function and aim of revealing significant aspects of ourselves which were previously hidden.

Should the researcher be concerned with respecting the privacy of all creation, and are there some things which are best left unstudied? These questions might seem in this age of inquiry to have an antique sound, but Popper (1972) has reminded us that only in our own time and place (and in a few other islands of history such as the Hellenic) has human culture allowed questions to be asked even about what might now seem nonsensitive matters. Only in the last two centuries in Western Europe and perhaps in a century or two of Hellenic civilization could thinkers inquire into the nature of the universe without risking charges of impiety (and even in these few inquiring epochs of history, questioners from Thales to Spinoza to Bertrand Russell have been rebuked for their questioning). The Hebraic-Christian tradition in the second and third chapters of the Book of Genesis represents the fall of humanity as entailing mankind's acquisition of shameful knowledge. Even in science-oriented nations of our own day, such as those of Eastern Europe and China, theorizing on topics as abstract as cosmology and linguistics has been injurious to the health of the speculator. That history reveals so few inquiring societies raises the worry that research may be maladaptive to the evolution, comfort, and survival of human communities.

Western society today has so pronounced a respect for inquiry that it would be perverse to propose seriously that all things are best left unstudied, that we should respect the privacy of all creation, accepting the world as it unfolds without putting questions to nature. But while it would be absurd so to question the research enterprise in its entirety, we might still ask whether perhaps there are not a few things which are best left unstudied, particularly within the subject matter of the social and behavioral sciences. Even professional researchers in their private lives often conclude that there are some things best left ambiguous or unrevealed, preserving some benign ambiguities about their own and others' strengths and weaknesses, feelings, and fate in order to make life more bearable and human relations more harmonious. In everyday life even the professional researcher seems to feel that there are some things best left unstudied, indeed undiscussed and, if possible, unthought of.

Distinction between Ethics and Aesthetics

Perhaps I am raising here an issue of taste or aesthetics rather than of morality, a possibility suggested by the wide swings of fashion on this privacy issue. Many of us probably belong to a generation who like Conrad have seen the Heart of Darkness in some personal Congo, so that sometimes even the stately Thames reminds us that "this also has been one of the dark places of earth," and in the face of it we shudder or even pull back. But already within our own lifespan there is a generation which resonates more with Jerry Rubin and the Yippies of the 1960s with their motto of "let it all hang out." Predilections which a generation ago dared not speak their names now assault our ears with constant clamor. Aesthetic feeling, though it may be an origin or a partial test of the moral sense, constitutes a rather wavering compass.

CONCLUSION

Every person probably has difficulty on occasion in reconciling two opposing obligations: to seek the truth and to expand the domain of knowledge, on the one hand, and to avoid embarrassing revelations and to preserve those saving ambiguities and personal privacies which make life more tolerable, on the other. For the reflective person and those pursuing intellectual vocations, such conflicts arise rather often. In carrying out their professional work, researchers usually have little trouble resolving this dilemma. Having chosen an intellectual vocation, we tend to put a very high value on the discovery and communication of truth; only very rarely do we decide that there are some domains which are best left private, and if these occasions do occur, it is probably in our private relationships rather than in our professional activities. My own (admittedly prejudiced) preference is for such a resolution; I feel that in our personal lives and relationships we should allow a large domain for privacy and ambiguity, not feeling compelled to divulge everything about ourselves or to inquire into everything about our associates. But as far as research is concerned, I feel that though there are some areas which I myself could not bear to study, I would be hard put to name any topic which I feel is so intrinsically private that I would put it ethically so off limits to research that I would morally condemn those who study it (though I might question their taste).

Several principles underlie my prejudice that conflicts between discovery and privacy should almost always be resolved in favor of discovery, even when the topic concerns the person and human society (excepting investigations of specifics about individuals). One justifying principle is that truth, like goodness, is a transcendental attribute of being, and ultimately the expansion of knowledge recovers the good. Knowledge for the researcher becomes, even more than 1066 and 1776 and all that, a Good Thing defining a value system in which conflicts between the revelation and the concealment of knowledge should almost invariably be resolved in favor of discovery and communication. The researcher's dominant principle in his or her professional life is that it is best to know, at least in the long run (even granting that in the short run the truth may hurt and that in the long run we shall all be dead).

So while remaining a very private person in my non-professional life, when as a researcher I am confronted with difficult questions as to whether some things are best left uninvestigated, I am inclined to endorse (admittedly sometimes with fear and trembling) the choice of those who opt to uncover the truth. This choice of discovery over privacy is obviously tainted by professional self-interest. But, in so choosing, I also hear myself in harmony with the paeon to knowledge which is found in the Book of Wisdom and which used to appear in the liturgy, rather appropriately, as the Lesson in the Mass for Saint Thomas Aquinas:

> I sought and understanding was given to me:
> I entreated, and the spirit of wisdom came upon me.
> And I esteemed her more than scepters and thrones;

Compared to her, I held riches as nothing.
I found no jewel to be her peer,
For compared to her, all gold is a pinch of sand,
And beside her silver ranks as mud.
I loved her more than health or beauty,
I preferred her to the light,
Since her light never fails.
In her company all good things came to me,
At her hands came riches without number.
In all of these things I rejoiced, since wisdom brings them,
Even when I did not know that she was the mother of them all.
What I have learned without envy I communicate without guile;
I shall not hide her riches.
For she is an inexhaustible treasure to all,
Which those who use become the friends of God,
Commended to Him by the gifts of wisdom [Wis. 7:7–14].

REFERENCES

Cook, S. W., et al. (Eds.). *Ethical principles in the conduct of research with human participants.* Washington, D.C.: American Psychological Association, 1973.

Dworkin, R. *Taking rights seriously.* Cambridge: Harvard University Press, 1977.

Greeley, A. M. *The American Catholic: A social portrait.* New York: Basic Books, 1977.

Hart, H. L. A. *The Concept of Law.* New York: Oxford University Press, 1961.

Hobbs, N. (Ed.). *Ethical standards of psychologists.* Washington, D.C.: American Psychological Association, 1953.

Popper, K. *Conjectures and refutations: The growth of scientific knowledge.* London: Routledge & Kegan Paul, 1972.

Psychological Testing and Privacy

ANNE ANASTASI

Anne Anastasi received her B.A. degree from Barnard College and her Ph.D. from Columbia University. Since 1947 she has been on the faculty of Fordham University where she is currently Professor Emeritus of Psychology. She is the author of more than 130 journal articles, monographs, and contributed papers. Her major publications include: Differential psychology *(1939, 1949, 1958),* Psychological testing *(1954, 1961, 1968, 1976), and* Fields of applied psychology *(1964). Dr. Anastasi has had a distinguished career in professional and scholarly circles. She has been President of the Eastern Psychological Association (1946–1947), the American Psychological Foundation (1965–1967), and finally the American Psychological Association (1971–1972). She is also a member of Phi Beta Kappa, Sigma Xi, the Psychonomic Society, and the Psychometric Society.*

In a report entitled *Privacy and Behavioral Research* (1967), prepared for the Office of Science and Technology, the right to privacy was defined as "the right of the individual to decide for himself how much he will share with others his thoughts, his feelings, and the facts of his personal life" (p. 2). In examining the role of privacy in psychological testing, we need to recognize at least three distinct facets of the problem. The first—and probably the most obvious—pertains to the possible invasion of privacy by the testing process itself. This is a question of what information we should try to obtain in the first place. The second facet is that of confidentiality. To whom may test results be revealed? The third relates to the person's right to know his own test results. Here the question centers on what should be communicated to the examinee and in what form. Basically, the three facets involve disclosure to the examiner, to third parties, and to the examinee, respectively.

We shall consider each of these facets in turn. But first, by way of background, let us take a quick look at what has been done about the problem thus far. What guidelines and sources of information are available?

BACKGROUND AND AVAILABLE GUIDELINES

For several decades, psychologists have been concerned about the ethical issues involved in testing. Among these issues, that of protecting the individual's privacy has received particular attention. Over the years, a succession of committees, task forces, commissions, and conferences has examined and analyzed the problem from many angles. If no firm answers or specific rules have emerged, it is not for lack of effort. Rather, it has become clearly apparent that only broad guidelines can be properly formulated. This limitation stems from the complexity of the issues and the situational specificity of the problems encountered. By this we mean simply that there are wide gray areas in which the answer can be reached only after consideration of all the conditions characterizing the particular situation. The solution varies too often with concomitant circumstances to permit the routine application of universal rules. In dealing with individual cases, there is no substitute for the ethical sensitivity and professional judgment of the test user.

Nevertheless, broad guidelines *have* been formulated and searching analyses of the problem *have* been published. These documents serve not only to spell out acceptable procedures where clear-cut answers *are* appropriate, but also to suggest what questions need to be asked in arriving at solutions in the gray areas. Official recognition of the problem of privacy in psychological testing is found in the *Ethical Standards of Psychologists* (1977), developed by the American Psychological Association. The first version of these standards was published in 1953; the latest revision was adopted in January 1977. Guidelines pertaining to privacy in the use of psychological tests are included in two of the principles specified in these *Ethical Standards*, one dealing with confidentiality (Principle 5), the other with the utilization of assessment techniques (Principle 8).

A helpful companion publication is the *Casebook on Ethical Standards of Psychologists* (1967). To illustrate the principles summarized in the *Ethical Standards*, the casebook contains disguised reports of actual cases referred for action to the APA Committee on Scientific and Professional Ethics and Conduct, together with the decisions and recommendations of the committee.

Another pertinent source is the *Standards for Educational and Psychological Tests* (1974), also published by the American Psychological Association. Though this set of standards deals largely with technical problems of test construction, such as reliability, validity, and norms, it also contains material related to the ethics of testing. Of special interest in this connection is a section on standards for the use of tests, which was added in the 1974 edition.

Let me mention one more source, chiefly because of the provocative questions which it raises about problems in some gray areas. In 1970, the Russell Sage Foundation published a report entitled *Guidelines for the Collection, Maintenance, and Dissemination of Pupil Records*. These guidelines were the outcome of an interdisciplinary conference on the ethical and legal aspects of school record-keeping, with participants from education, psychology, sociology, philosophy, and law. As the title implies, the guidelines focus on the collection and disposition of student records in elementary and high school. However, a major and especially sensitive part of such records consists of scores obtained on aptitude and personality tests. Hence, these guidelines address an important aspect of the problem of privacy and psychological testing. I shall have occasion to cite from these various sources in later parts of my paper.

TESTS AND THE INVASION OF PRIVACY

Now we may turn to the three facets of privacy and psychological testing which I outlined at the outset. A question which has often been raised, particularly with reference to personality tests, is that of the invasion of privacy. Insofar as some tests of emotional, motivational, or attitudinal variables are necessarily disguised, the examinee may reveal characteristics in the course of such a test without realizing that he is doing so. Although there are few available tests whose approach is subtle enough to fall into this category, the implications of such indirect testing procedures need to be considered.

Indirect Testing and Its Problems

For purposes of testing effectiveness it is often necessary to keep examinees in ignorance of the specific ways in which responses to *individual* items will be scored or interpreted. Such information would tend to distort responses and invalidate scores on many personality tests. For example, if a person is told in advance that a self-report inventory will be scored on a scale for measuring dominance, his responses are likely to be influenced by stereotyped (and often erroneous) ideas which he may have about this trait, or by a false or distorted self-concept.

Although concerns about the invasion of privacy have been expressed most commonly about personality tests, they logically apply to any type of test. Certainly any intelligence, aptitude, or achievement test may reveal limitations in skills and knowledge which an individual would rather not disclose (Wolf, 1974). Moreover, any observation of an individual's behavior—as in an interview, casual conversation, or other personal encounter—may yield information about him which he would prefer to conceal and which he may reveal unwittingly. The fact that psychological tests have often been singled out in discussions of the invasion of privacy probably reflects prevalent misconceptions about tests. If all tests were recognized as measures of behavior samples, with no mysterious powers to penetrate beyond behavior, popular fears and suspicions would be lessened, and the question of privacy could be viewed in the proper perspective.

Any assessment technique represents a potential invasion of privacy. A more functional basis of classification pertains to the purpose for which assessment is conducted—whether for individual counseling, institutional decisions regarding selection and classification, or research. In *clinical or counseling situations*, the client is usually willing to reveal himself in order to obtain help with his problems. The clinician or examiner does not invade privacy where he is freely admitted. When testing is conducted for *institutional purposes*, the examinee should be fully informed as to the use which will be made of his test scores. But it is also desirable to explain to the examinee that correct assessment will benefit him. It is not to his advantage to be placed in a job or educational program where he will fail or which he will find uncongenial. The results of tests administered in a clinical or counseling situation, of course, should not be made available for institutional purposes, unless the examinee gives his consent. When tests are given for *research purposes*, anonymity and confidentiality should be preserved as fully as possible. The procedures for ensuring anonymity should be explained in advance to the participants. Moreover, individuals should be given the option of declining to participate, without embarrassment or adverse consequences of any sort.

Whatever the purposes of testing, the protection of privacy involves two key concepts: relevance and informed consent. The information which the examinee is asked to reveal must be *relevant* to the stated purposes of the testing. An important implication of this principle is that all practicable efforts should be made to ascertain the validity of tests or other assessment procedures for the particular diagnostic or predictive purposes for which they are being used. An instrument which is demonstrably valid for a given purpose is one which provides relevant information. It also behooves the examiner to make certain that test scores are correctly interpreted. A person is less likely to feel that his privacy is being invaded by a test assessing his readiness for a particular training program than by a test allegedly measuring his "innate intelligence."

Informed Consent: Research Example

The concept of *informed consent* also requires clarification. And its application in individual cases may call for the exercise of considerable judgment (*Ethical standards*, 1977; Ruebhausen & Brim, 1966). The examinee should certainly be informed about the purpose for which he is being tested, the kinds of data sought, and the use which will be made of his scores. It is not implied, however, that he should be shown the test items in advance or told how specific responses will be scored. Nor, in the case of a minor, should the test items be shown to a parent. Not only would the release of such information seriously impair the usefulness of an ability test, but it would also invalidate scores on many personality tests.

On the other hand, a simple, general explanation of how test items were selected and how scores are interpreted may be quite desirable from several points of view. This was illustrated in a study conducted with the well-known Minnesota Multiphasic Personality Inventory, commonly known as the MMPI (Fink & Butcher, 1972). Among self-report personality inventories, this test has probably been cited most often as an example of the invasion of privacy. A survey of the most common objections indicates that they generally stem from a literal interpretation of item content. It has been argued, for example, that job applicants who take the MMPI are examined in such areas as family relations, social life, and sexual and religious attitudes, which are considered too personal, and irrelevant to the testing purpose (see, e.g., Testing and public policy, 1965, especially p. 923). Actually, the items are not grouped, scored, or interpreted in terms of these apparent content areas, but in terms of empirically established behavioral correlates. Moreover, individual item responses are not part of the examinee's record and cannot be identified in the total score reported for each scale.

One way to meet individual objections to such personality test items is to tell respondents that they may omit any items which they find too personal or otherwise unacceptable. But this is not a very satisfactory solution because it tends to lower score reliability and may affect different scales unevenly (Butcher & Tellegen, 1966; Walker, 1967; Walker & Ward, 1969). Moreover, it has not been demonstrated that the options to omit items makes the test more acceptable to examinees, since they have no way of knowing how their omission of certain items will be interpreted (Fink & Butcher, 1972).

A different approach was tried in an exploratory study with 100 college students at the University of Minnesota (Fink & Butcher, 1972). While the control subjects took the MMPI with the standard instructions, the experimental subjects were given modified instructions which provided simple information on how the test was constructed. To give the general flavor of this approach, let me cite the most relevant paragraph from these experimental instructions:

> Some of the statements may seem unrelated to anything about your personality, and other items may seem too personal. A word, then, about how these items were chosen. A large list of statements was given to a group of normal people and to people suffering from many kinds of personality problems. Then the statements that were answered with different frequencies by the two groups were selected as a scale, and it was shown that people having certain kinds of personality structures will answer these items in similar ways. There may be no logical reason why, for example, an unhappy person will answer items about sex, or religion, or body functions in a certain way, but he does. So, the important thing to remember is that the test interpretation does *not* involve reading your specific responses. Scoring involves simply placing a scoring stencil over the answer sheet and counting the responses for each personality scale. This allows us to compare your total responses on each scale with the other people [Fink & Butcher, 1972, p. 634].*

Following the completion of the test, all subjects answered a brief questionnaire in which they reported how they would feel about the test if they had been asked to take it as part of the selection procedure in a job application. The results showed that the explanatory instructions significantly reduced the number of respondents who felt that the test represented an invasion of privacy or who considered some of the items offensive. At the same time, the mean score profile was not affected by the modified instructions.

This study suggests a promising avenue of research which merits further exploration. Test constructors and researchers could profitably investigate the use of similar explanatory instructions with other types of examinees, other tests, and other testing contexts. Of course, altering standard test instructions is not a procedure which a test user can initiate. It must first be demonstrated that the expanded instructions do not reduce the validity of a particular test or alter the meaning of its scores. But, with appropriate methodological safeguards, this procedure offers an open and forthright approach to the dilemma of informed consent, while at the same time promoting a clearer understanding of testing procedures.

* Quoted by permission from *Educational and Psychological Measurement.*

CONFIDENTIALITY OF TEST RESULTS

Prior Clarification of Future Disclosure

Like the protection of privacy, to which it is related, the problem of confidentiality of test data is multifaceted. The fundamental question is: Who will have access to test results? Several considerations influence the answer in particular situations. Among them are the security of test content, the hazards of misinterpreting test scores, and the need of various persons to know the results.

Discussions of the confidentiality of test results generally deal with accessibility to a third person, someone other than the individual tested and the examiner (*Ethical standards*, 1977, Principle 5; Russell Sage Foundation, 1970). The underlying principle is that such records should *not* be released without the knowledge and consent of the individual. When tests are administered in an institutional setting, as in a school system, university, court, or employment office, the examinee should be told in advance that the results will be made available to institutional personnel who have a legitimate need for them. Under these conditions, no further permission is required at the time results are used or transmitted within the institution. A different situation exists when results are requested by outsiders, as when a prospective employer or a college requests test results from a school system. In these instances, individual consent for release of the data is required. The same requirement applies when tests have been administered for counseling or for research purposes.

Communication with Parents of Minors

A special problem arises in the case of minors, in which one must also consider the parents' right of access to the child's test record. This presents a possible conflict with the child's own right to privacy, especially in the case of older children. In a classic paper, first presented at a Rockefeller University Conference on Law and the Social Role of Science, Ruebhausen and Brim wrote:

> Should not a child, even before the age of full legal responsibility, be accorded the dignity of a private personality? Considerations of healthy personal growth, buttressed with the reasons of ethics, seem to command that this be done [1966, pp. 431–432].

The previously mentioned *Guidelines* of the Russell Sage Foundation recommend that "when a student reaches the age of eighteen and no longer is attending high school or is married (whether age eighteen or not)" (1970, p. 27), he should have the right to deny parental access to his records. However, this recommendation is followed by the caution that local state laws be checked for possible legal difficulties in implementing such a policy.

Apart from these possible exceptions, the question is not *whether* to communicate test results to parents of a minor, but *how* to do so most effectively and appropriately. Parents normally have a legal right to information about their child; and it is usually desirable for them to have such information. In some cases, moreover, a child's academic or emotional difficulties may arise in part from parent–child relations. Under these conditions, the counselor's contact with the parents is of prime importance, both to fill in background data and to elicit parental cooperation. Communicating test results and other findings to parents calls for a high degree of both psychological sophistication and ethical sensitivity on the part of the counselor. Deception of any sort must be carefully avoided. For an effective counseling relationship, the counselor needs the complete trust of both child and parents. Both parties must feel free to communicate openly with the counselor without fear of adverse consequences. The child should certainly be told that there will be some communication with parents, if that is in fact the case. Beyond that, much depends on the communicating of information in such a way that it will be properly interpreted and constructively used.

In the communication of test results to parents—as well as to teachers, employers, and other appropriate persons—it is of the utmost importance to adapt the presentation to the background, needs, and interests of the recipients (Anastasi, 1976, pp. 56–57, 326–357, 487–490; *Standards*, 1974, pp. 13–14, 69–73). Technical jargon should be avoided, and adequate safeguards should be provided against common misinterpretations. The results should be presented in the form of descriptive performance levels, rather than isolated numerical scores, and should include interpretive explanations by a professionally trained person. It is also desirable to take into account the recipient's anticipated emotional response to the information. In the case of a parent or teacher, for example, personal involvement with the child may interfere with a calm and rational acceptance of factual information.

Security in Maintenance of Records

Still another problem pertains to the retention of records in institutions (*Ethical standards*, 1977, Principle 8d). On the one hand, longitudinal records can be valuable, not only for research purposes, but also for the understanding and counseling of the individual. As is so often the case, these advantages presuppose proper use and interpretation of test results. On the other, the availability of old records opens the way for such misuses as incorrect inferences from obsolete data and unauthorized access for other than the original testing purpose. To prevent such misuses, the retention and utilization of past records should be subject to careful scrutiny and control. The problems of maintenance, security, and accessibility of test results—and of all other personal data—have been magnified by the development of computerized data banks. In his preface to the *Guidelines* of the Russell Sage Foundation Ruebhausen wrote:

> Modern science has introduced a new dimension into the issue of privacy. There was a time when among the strongest allies of privacy were the inefficiency of man, the fallibility of his memory, and the healing compassion that accompanied both the passing of time and the warmth of human recollection. These allies are now being put to rout. Modern science has given us the capacity to record faithfully, to maintain permanently, to retrieve promptly, and to communicate both widely and instantly [1970, pp. 5–6].

THE INDIVIDUAL'S RIGHT TO KNOW HIS OWN TEST RESULTS

The third facet of our tripartite model of privacy and psychological testing pertains to the individual's right to know his own test results. This right is recognized explicitly in the current version of the *Ethical Standards* (1977). Principle 8, Utilization of Assessment Techniques, states in part:

> Persons examined have the right to know the results, the interpretations made, and, where appropriate, the original data on which final judgments were based. Test users avoid imparting unnecessary information which would compromise test security, but they provide requested information that explains the basis for the decisions that may adversely affect that person or that person's dependents.

Discussing test findings with the examinee, under proper conditions, may serve several purposes. In some cases, the discussion may elicit further relevant data which may alter the interpretation of test scores. For example, the same item response or test score may have a different diagnostic significance and different causal implications for persons with very diverse experiential backgrounds. From another angle, test results may pinpoint specific deficits or difficulties which can be remedied by suitable training or by special educational or therapeutic programs.

It is noteworthy that a conspicuous development in current psychological testing is the broadening of testing goals, with an increasing emphasis on the individual's own self-knowledge. More and more, tests are being used to help the individual make his own decisions about personal development, learning problems, and educational and vocational objectives. Counseling psychologists typically involve the client as an active participant in his own assessment.

When test findings are transmitted to the examinee, particular attention should be given to the previously mentioned procedures for effective communication. The results should be presented in a form which is suitable for the age, educational level, and other characteristics of the individual. Labels, such as test titles, technical trait names, and diagnostic categories, which are likely to suggest stereotyped and superficial interpretations, should be especially avoided. In general, the test report should be problem-oriented. Insofar as possible, test results should be related to the specific questions which the testing was designed to answer.

It is especially important to take cognizance of the individual's emotional reaction to information about his own assets and liabilities. When the examinee is given his own test results, not only should the data be interpreted by a properly qualified person, but facilities should also be available for the counseling of anyone who may be unduly affected by such information. For example, a college student might become seriously discouraged when he learns of his poor performance on a scholastic aptitude test. Or a severe emotional crisis may be precipitated if a disturbed person is given his score on a personality test. Such detrimental effects may occur regardless of the correctness or incorrectness of the score itself. Even when a test has been accurately administered, scored, and properly interpreted, a knowledge of such a score without the opportunity to discuss it further may be harmful.

Thus we see the other side of the coin. The individual's right to know his own test results is paralleled by his right to be protected against possible harm which may ensue from this knowledge. Such protection can in fact be provided through the method and the context of communication.

REFERENCES

Anastasi, A. *Psychological testing* (4th ed.). New York, Macmillan, 1976.

Butcher, J. N., & Tellegen, A. T. Objections to MMPI items. *Journal of Consulting Psychology*, 1966, *30*, 527–534.

Casebook on ethical standards of psychologists. Washington, D.C.: American Psychological Association, 1967.

Ethical standards of psychologists. Washington, D.C.: American Psychological Association, 1977.

Fink, A. M., & Butcher, J. N. Reducing objections to personality inventories with special instruction. *Educational and Psychological Measurement*, 1972, *32*, 631–639.

Privacy and behavioral research. Washington, D.C.: Government Printing Office, 1967.

Ruebhausen, O. M., & Brim, O. G., Jr. Privacy and behavorial research. *American Psychologist*, 1966, *21*, 423–437.

Russell Sage Foundation. *Guidelines for the collection, maintenance, and dissemination of pupil records.* New York: Author, 1970.

Standards for educational and psychological tests. Washington, D.C.: American Psychological Association, 1974.

Testing and public policy (Special issue). *American Psychologist*, 1965, *20*, 857–992.

Walker, C. E. The effect of eliminating offensive items on the reliability and validity of the MMPI. *Journal of Clinical Psychology*, 1967, *23*, 363–366.

Walker, C. E., & Ward, J. Identification and elimination of offensive items from the MMPI. *Journal of Projective Techniques and Personality Assessment*, 1969, *33*, 385–388.

Wolf, R. M. Invasion of privacy. In R. W. Tyler & R. M. Wolf (Eds.), *Crucial issues in testing*. Berkeley, Cal.: McCutchan, 1974.

VIII
TOWARD A NEW POLICY ON PRIVACY

Toward a New Policy by Government

Athan G. Theoharis

Athan G. Theoharis earned his academic degrees at the University of Chicago: B.A. in 1956; M.A. in 1959; and Ph.D. in 1965. He taught at Texas A. & M. University, Wayne State, and CUNY (Staten Island) before coming to Marquette University where he is currently Professor of History. Dr. Theoharis has been consultant, U.S. Senate Select Committee on Intelligence Activities (the so-called Church Committee); consultant, Subcommittee on Government Information and Individual Rights of the House Government Operations Committee; consultant on wiretapping legislation, staff of U. S. Senator Gaylord Nelson. Dr. Theoharis is the author of The Yalta myths *(1970) and* Seeds of repression *(1971); co-author of* Anatomy of anticommunism *(1969) and* U. S. in the twentieth century *(1978); and co-editor of* The specter: Original essays on the Cold War and the origins of McCarthyism *(1974).*

GOVERNMENT'S EXPANDING ROLE IN NATIONAL LIFE

By the 1970s, the federal government had assumed an omnipresent role in national life. Motivated by the multiple objectives of curbing the power of large impersonal corporations, alleviating poverty and socio-economic inequities, and ensuring economic growth and development, since the Progressive Era of the 1900s American reformers had introduced legislation to expand radically federal responsibilities and powers. As a consequence of their successes, federal agencies now command a central role in American life, and the scope of federal responsibilities requires an intrusive federal involvement in formerly private activities. To cite but a few examples: to enforce the income tax law the Internal Revenue Service (IRS) must obtain information about the individual taxpayer's sources of income and charitable contributions; to enforce immigration, welfare, and social security laws, the Department of Health, Education, and Welfare (HEW) or the Immigration Service must demand equally personal information whether about the particular individual's employment, sources of income, or other financial means of support; federal economic surveys necessitate knowledge of consumer spending plans and capabilities; and the enforcement of safety, stock and banking, pension, government contract compliance, and housing laws compels individuals and corporations to provide formerly secret managerial information to federal officials.

Current Need to Define Its Scope

Because of this expansion, there is a greater present need to balance privacy rights and legitimate government needs, and concomitantly to define the scope of government agencies' permissible surveillance or interrogation of the individual citizen. Since the government's legislatively-defined responsibilities are now so widespread and intrusive, the limits of its investigative role must be defined in order to minimize the loss of personal privacy. At one extreme, an Idaho plumbing contractor, Ferrol G. Barlow, has recently challenged the constitutionality of the inspection-authorization provisions of the Occupational Safety and Health Act of 1970. That Act permitted federal inspectors to enter a workplace unannounced and without a warrant to check possible safety violations. These warrantless inspections, Barlow maintains, violate the Fourth Amendment's prohibition of "unreasonable searches." Barlow's suit is currently being argued before the U. S. Supreme Court (*Milwaukee Journal*, January 9, 1978, p. 10).

In another, not wholly unrelated, issue, in the 1970s Congress and then the Supreme Court attempted to resolve the competing demands of privacy rights and law-enforcement needs when enacting in 1971 and amending in 1974 presidential campaign-reform legislation, the Federal Election Campaign Act of 1971. In Public Law No. 92–225, 86 Stat. 3 (1971), amended by Public Law No. 93–443, 88 Stat. 1263 (1974), Congress, recognizing the high costs of conducting a presidential campaign in twentieth-century America, legislated against the corrupting influence of large contributions on a democratic electoral system, imposing maximum limits on the size of individual contributions to presidential candidates and requiring a detailed reporting and disclosure system. These requirements were immediately challenged by a number of diverse individuals and organizations—notably, the New York conservative James Buckley, the independent presidential aspirant Eugene McCarthy, and the American Civil Liberties Union. On January 30, 1976, the U. S. Supreme Court in *Buckley v. Valeo* (96 U. S. 612, 1976) upheld the constitutionality of the 1974 amendments. The Court's majority conceded, however, that the Act's disclosure requirements could adversely affect the First Amendment rights of minor party candidates and organizations. Facts establishing harassment of minor party contributors, the Court emphasized, had not been presented in the case. Reserving judgment on the issue, the Court thereby posited that it remained a subject for future judicial scrutiny:

> We have long recognized that significant encroachments of First Amendment rights of the sort that compelled disclosure cannot be justified by a mere showing of some legitimate governmental interest. Since *Alabama* [1958] we have required that the subordinating interests of the State must survive exacting scrutiny. We also have insisted that there be a "relevant correlation" or "substantial relation" between the governmental interest and the information required to be disclosed [*Buckley v. Valeo*, 96 U. S. 656, 1976].

Advances in Technology Increase the Need

This expansion of federal responsibilities has occurred simultaneously with a technological revolution. Because of more sophisticated technology, federal officials today can obtain and effectively utilize information which could neither have been obtained nor readily retrieved during the nineteenth century. Thus, although the historical image (and movies and novels still convey this image) of a spy is of an individual wearing a London Fog raincoat and a battered fedora and lurking on street corners, such physical surveillance necessarily limited the information-gathering capabilities of governmental investigative agencies. Police officials could be seen, their surveillance-gathering capabilities could be frustrated, and, in any event, the information which they could intercept was rather narrowly limited. The invention of the wiretap and the bug (and the technological perfection of these devices) fundamentally altered this relationship between the citizen and the police official. One is no longer obviously under surveillance, and police officials can now intercept formerly privileged conversations. Moreover, even federal officials' ability to utilize information obtained about individuals had formerly been limited because of storage and retrievability problems.

Thus, if information was gathered in Podunk Center, Iowa, it might not be available to an official in Washington, D.C. In addition, the very increase in the amount of information gathered would concomitantly create another problem: that of retrievability and selection. Through computers and data banks, recent technological developments have provided a solution to these problems. Thus, by 1970 the Civil Service Commission could retain a subversive activities data bank containing the names of 1.5 million citizens and FBI headquarters had amassed 6.5 million files with the data retrievable through a general index consisting of over 58 million index cards. Moreover, by 1972 the various federal agencies had at their disposal 6,731 computers (U. S. Senate Constitutional Rights Subcommittee, 1971; *Milwaukee Journal*, April 19, 1970, p. 6; U. S. Senate Select Committee, 1976, Bk. 2, p. 262; Westin, 1975, p. 288).

By permitting easy storage of vast amounts of information and making it readily retrievable, computers can expedite governmental business. By the same token, this capability can result in abuses of power.

Recognition of the particular threats which computers pose to privacy rights and the public's particular sensitivity to this threat have influenced two recent and differing decisions of the Carter Administration. A sensitivity to privacy rights, accordingly, led the Carter Administration in 1978 to halt development of an $850 million processing system which would have provided the IRS with almost instantaneous access to the detailed tax records of individuals and corporations. In a contrary action, in 1977 the Carter Administration approved a controversial FBI computer project to provide both governmental officials at all levels and the public with important statistical information about crime trends. Advanced in one form or another for more than 100 years, this proposal had been vetoed as recently as 1975 by President Ford's attorney general, Edward Levi. Levi did not oppose the proposal to computerize information but concluded that to avoid possible privacy abuses approval should be contingent upon congressional action outlining standards governing the exchange of data among law enforcement authorities. The Carter Administration, however, decided to proceed with the system without awaiting congressional action (*The New York Times*, November 16, 1975, p. 3E; August 22, 1977, pp. 1, 15; *Milwaukee Journal*, June 16, 1977, Pt. 2, p. 7; January 9, 1978, Pt. 2, p. 3).

NATIONAL SECURITY AND ENLARGED EXECUTIVE POWER

But the intrusiveness of the federal surveillance role, and the ability of federal officials to acquire and utilize highly personal information about targeted citizens, were not simply the inevitable by-product of the needs of a modern complex society. Nor is the principal threat to privacy rights posed by computer or data banks. Because of their size, such information systems cannot be secretive—a fact which necessitated the Carter Administration's recent diverse public decisions. The principal privacy threat derives, instead, from not readily disclosed federal surveillance. To an extent, the increase in this federal surveillance of individual activities evolved from the changing needs and character of modern society. Far more important, the changes in popular values and federal policy resulting from the Cold War accelerated this process. In this sense, it was not inevitability but particular historical concerns which provided the catalyst to what we now recognize as a serious threat to personal privacy.

Influence of Cold War Attitudes

The fear of Soviet subversion and the quest for absolute security against Communist subversion at home and abroad resulted in popular and congressional acceptance during the 1940s and 1950s of the need both for radical expansion of federal surveillance activities and for secrecy to ensure the success of an internal security program. The exclusive impetus for the particular investigative programs, moreover, emanated from the executive branch. As a result, a far-reaching federal loyalty/security program was instituted by executive orders during the Truman–Eisenhower years to preclude the employment of individuals who might be disloyal; the investigative authority and programs of federal intelligence agencies (whether the FBI, CIA, NSA, or Defense Intelligence Agency) radically expanded during these same presidencies, again as the result of executive orders and not legislative authorization; and presidents or attorneys general tacitly condoned, and further concluded that legislative authorization was not required for, federal intelligence agencies' reliance on intrusive (at times recognizably illegal) techniques such as wiretaps, bugs, mail intercepts, and break-ins.

These programs (notably, the loyalty/security program) and techniques (notably, wiretapping) were not only recent and had no historical antecedent in nineteenth-century America but also contravened clear provisions of the law. The post-Truman loyalty/security programs contravened the ban against political criteria for federal appointments and the due process hearing requirements of the Lloyd–LaFollette Act of 1912; post-1939 FBI wiretapping was conducted in violation of the ban contained in section 605 of the Federal Communications Act of 1934; and CIA investigations of 1967–1973 of dissident individuals and organizations contravened that provision of the National Security Act of 1947 prohibiting the to-be-established agency from exercising any "police, subpoena, law enforcement powers or internal security functions." The National Security Agency, significantly, has no legislative charter and was secretly created by an executive order in 1952; until the 1960s even its existence was unknown to the public or the Congress.

Executive Privilege and Secrecy

The combination of Cold War policy preferences, but principally the impetus to guarantee absolute security and thereby to undercut effective external constraints, ensured the far-reaching invasions of personal privacy publicized in 1975 and 1976 by congressional committees and by the media. Secrecy had provided the opportunity permitting federal officials to expand their power and independent authority. Significantly, "executive privilege" claims surfaced only during the Cold War years—the term itself was formally coined in 1958 during President Eisenhower's Administration—and federal bureaucrats increasingly relied on presidential orders to classify a broad range of policy documents. By 1971, in fact, nearly 3,000 federal bureaucrats had the power to stamp "top secret" on public records, 18,000 to stamp "secret," and 55,000 to stamp "confidential." This quest for secrecy inevitably led to overuse: indeed during the 1970s a former Pentagon security official, William Florence, estimated that more than 99% of all classified military documents could be declassified with no harm to the national security (Berger, 1975, pp. 1–2; Phillips, 1975, pp. 71–72; Schlesinger, 1973, p. 344).

The quest for secrecy also led federal officials to devise elaborate procedures to safeguard from public disclosure their agency's involvement in illegal, sensitive, or embarrassing activities. Willing to violate the law, but concerned only that their illegality not be discovered, FBI, CIA, and NSA officials devised separate filing procedures to isolate documents recording illegal activities from their agency's other classified records. These "do-not-file" procedures would permit these officials to destroy documents recording their agency's involvement in illegal activities without a retrievable record's having been originally created (Theoharis, 1977, pp. 393–397).

AGENCY ABUSES HIGHLIGHT A NEED FOR REFORM

Intelligence agency officials' institution of separate filing procedures sharply highlight the magnitude of the problem of devising a new policy on privacy by the government. Though welcome as a recent development, the contemporary recognition that government agencies in the immediate past had excessively violated privacy rights is insufficient. In contrast to the late 1940s and 1950s, when the public and Congress were willing to countenance secrecy demands and far-reaching surveillance activities by federal officials, in the 1970s the public and Congress have been far less deferential and recognize that protection of personal privacy necessitates curbs on executive powers. The Supreme Court's decision in *Buckley v. Valeo* symbolizes this greater sensitivity to privacy values. Far better examples of this recent awareness—and efforts intended specifically to safeguard privacy rights—are the Privacy Act of 1974 (5 U.S.C. 552 (a)) and the 1974 amendments to the Freedom of Information Act of 1966 (5 U.S.C. 552 (b)). In combination, these legislative measures permit citizens to challenge governmental claims to deny information on "national security" grounds, to obtain their files from governmental agencies, and to expunge erroneous or illegally obtained information.

This legislation and the Supreme Court's rulings in *Buckley* and other recent cases (notably *U.S. v. U.S. District Court, U.S. v. Nixon, Tatum v. Laird*), however, do not address the more serious threat which federal agencies pose to privacy rights—namely: (1) the disdain of federal intelligence officials for legal or constitutional constraints which led them in the recent past to violate the law and then to devise filing procedures to preclude discovery; and (2) the ineffectiveness of executive overview over the federal intelligence agencies. Devising a new policy on privacy accordingly requires that we address two corollary issues as well: (1) What should the executive branch's role be in defining the scope of federal agencies' investigative authority? and (2) What procedures should Congress devise to ensure that federal agencies comply with the law and respect privacy rights?

Reliance on Executive Restraint Not Sufficient

A central issue, here, is the extent of executive powers and the wisdom of deferring to proposed reforms instituted by means of executive orders. To date, apart from the Privacy Act's and the Freedom of Information Act's disclosure requirements, the only curbs imposed upon federal agencies' investigative activities to preclude the recurrence of the recently-publicized abuses have been those which President Gerald Ford instituted on February 18, 1976, under Executive Order 11905. In effect, President Ford's order prohibited some of the more extreme activities formerly conducted by the intelligence agencies and presumably instituted a system of greater presidential control over the intelligence agencies' activities (Halperin, Berman, Borosage, & Marwick, 1976, pp. 247–253).

Yet not only are these "reforms" narrow and reflective of a greater concern to safeguard the independence of the intelligence agencies than individual rights, but they are based on the underlying premiss of executive self-restraint. To accept reform by means of executive order as sufficient to meeting the problem of threats to legitimate privacy rights would require ignoring the most compelling conclusion to be drawn from the history of past abuses: namely, that these abuses either were responsive to presidential directives or were made possible because presidents were either indifferent or incapable of providing needed overview. Presidential reform, moreover, might ensure greater administrative efficiency and is based on the premiss that past abuses were aberrational and non-institutional. Yet we have learned that one cost of efficiency has been non-accountability, and it is surely questionable whether the recently disclosed abuses were aberrational because they were the product of the actions of particular individuals, or were influenced by particular events.

In addition, reforms instituted by means of executive orders can be rescinded by the subsequent issuance of new, and secretive, executive orders. Thus, Attorney General Harlan Fiske Stone's highly publicized 1924 orders prohibiting the FBI (1) from investigating non-criminal dissident political activities, and (2) from employing wiretaps were rescinded by executive orders issued secretively during the 1930s and 1940s. The political surveillance ban was lifted by a secret and oral order of President Roosevelt in 1936, and the ban against wiretapping by secret orders of Attorney General William Mitchell in 1931 and Presidents Roosevelt in 1940 and Truman in 1946.

Over the years, moreover, presidential conceptions of their authority and their need to comply with the law have altered drastically. Most sharply and publicly during the 1960s, presidents affirmed rather expansive "inherent" powers to conduct or authorize activities on their own authority, apart from clear provisions of the Constitution or of enabling legislation. Former President Richard Nixon offered the most arrogant expression of this conviction when attempting in 1976 to justify his administration's widespread violations of individual rights. Activities which might normally be illegal, the former president claimed, were legal when conducted by the "sovereign." Specifically responding to an interrogation posed by the Senate Select Committee on Intelligence Activities, Nixon maintained that

> it is quite obvious that there are certain inherently governmental actions which if undertaken by the sovereign in protection of the nation's security are lawful, but which if undertaken by private persons are not. . . . But it is naïve to attempt to categorize activities a president might authorize as "legal" or "illegal" without reference to the circumstances under which he concludes that the activity is necessary. . . . In short, there have been —and will be in the future—circumstances in which presidents may lawfully authorize actions in the interests of security of this country, which if undertaken by other persons, or even by the president under different circumstances, would be illegal [U. S. Senate Select Committee, 1976, Bk. 4, pp. 157–158].

Recent Abuses Not Accidental or Exceptional

Richard Nixon's rather bald claim was self-serving, to be sure, and scarcely warrants being cited as representing the presidential position. Yet the underlying convictions, which resulted in his contemporary authorization of illegal activities while in office (and not the quoted 1976 rationalization), were not confined to this admittedly unique presidency. Similar expansive presidential views (although perhaps not as extreme) have determined the policy decisions of every president since Franklin Roosevelt. The recently announced plans of the Carter Administration to file a legal brief arguing that former President Nixon had not violated the law when authorizing certain wiretaps conducted between 1969 and 1971 highlight both this presidential position and its continued hold on occupants of that office. In this 1977 brief, Justice Department officials claimed that former President Nixon and all other presidents should be immune from suit in illegal wiretap cases if they acted in "good faith" based on long-standing precedent (*Detroit News*, December 24, 1977, p. 2A). That such presidential activities might always have been illegal, and that precedent alone could not establish legality seemingly did not trouble the Carter Justice Department. This legal brief, accordingly, suggests the degree to which executive officials are more sensitive to the need to circumvent legislative constraints and are committed more to ensuring administrative efficiency than to a careful consideration of the limits to their powers and authority.

THE CORE OF ANY NEW POLICY

Thus, a review both of the history of presidential conceptions of "inherent" powers and of the federal intelligence agencies' far-reaching past abuses of power confirms the need for specific legislative reforms. The core of a new policy on privacy must be that Congress specify the intelligence agencies' permissible investigative powers and create an effective overview mechanism to ensure compliance with the newly established legislative requirements. The central component of this new policy requires rejection of "inherent" presidential power claims—and specifically of open-ended and meaningless "national security" and "executive privilege" claims such as recent American presidents have advanced to justify their resort to secrecy—and the need for flexible, discretionary powers to enable the intelligence agencies to perform needed missions. Recent history confirms that all too often such "national security" and "executive privilege" claims were based on political considerations. These objectives, though not necessarily partisan, were intended to advance specific policy goals and were based on the recognition that congressional and/or public scrutiny might frustrate the attainment of these goals. Preservation of the American political system requires that these objectives and the methods employed to implement them be subject to debate and be based on legislative authorization. James Madison presciently recognized these needs in the 1790s when he wrote:

> At the foundation of our civil liberties lies the principle which denies to government officials an exceptional position before the law and which

> subjects them to the same rules of conduct that are commands to the citizen [cited in Halperin et al., 1976, p. 236].

Define by Statute Permissible Powers of Agencies

In the concluding section of this paper I intend not to offer specific reform recommendations but only to outline the principles and priorities upon which a new policy on privacy should be based. A more detailed list of recommendations is available in the conclusions offered by the staff of the Senate Select Committee on Intelligence Activities in its 1976 report (Bk. 2, pp. 289–341) and by the authors of *The Lawless State* (Halperin et al., 1976, pp. 255–279). Moreover, these general recommendations have been incorporated in a specific bill, H. R. 6051, drafted jointly by American Civil Liberties Union staff attorneys and 14 members of Congress, and introduced by Congressman Herman Badillo on April 5, 1977 (the Federal Intelligence Agencies Control Act of 1977).

Suffice it here that we outline the general assumptions underlying these proposed reforms—for no legislation will be enacted (whether the stringent limitations on the intelligence agencies which would be imposed under H. R. 6051 or the more limited changes now under consideration by the Senate Select Committee on Intelligence) unless the basic values and priorities determining Cold War politics are seriously examined and reassessed. Such a reassessment requires the rejection of secrecy and national security claims, an unwillingness to defer to presidential demands for flexibility, and an insistence on greater accountability and responsiveness to Congress and the general public by executive branch officials. The Senate Select Committee on Intelligence Activities (1976) most succinctly stated this view in its concluding assessment:

> The Committee's fundamental conclusion is that intelligence activities have undermined the constitutional rights of citizens and that they have done so primarily because checks and balances designed by the framers of the Constitution to assure accountability have not been applied [Bk. 2, p. 289].

The core of a new policy must be to define by statute the limits to the investigative authority of federal intelligence agencies. At present, these agencies either have no legislative charter (the NSA) or their charters are insufficiently precise. We have recently learned that Congress' earlier failure either to prohibit investigative activities beyond those specifically authorized by statute or to assert that intelligence agencies have no additional authority to investigate activities which violate no specific federal statute seemingly only encouraged intelligence bureaucrats (1) to act on their own authority or (2) to seek presidential authorization.

More recently, moreover, Congress has tacitly encouraged presidents and intelligence officials to believe that when dealing with perceived "national security" threats they could act on their own authority. Congress did so when enacting Title III of the Omnibus Crime Control and Safe Streets Act of 1968. Having outlined procedures requiring prior court authorization for the use of wiretaps or bugs, Congress exempted from this requirement "national security" electronic surveillance:

> Nothing contained in this statute . . . shall limit the constitutional powers of the President to take such measures as he deems necessary to protect the Nation against actual or potential attack or other hostile acts of a foreign power, to obtain foreign intelligence information deemed essential to the security of the United States, or to protect national security information against foreign intelligence activities. Nor shall anything in this chapter be deemed to limit the constitutional powers of the President to take such measures as he deems necessary to protect the United States against the overthrow of the Government by force or other unlawful means, or against any other clear and present danger to the structure or existence of the Government [Theoharis, 1971, p. 747].

We have learned that one result of congressional inaction or tolerance has been widespread abuses of power. Either presidents or attorneys general were unconcerned about the scope of the intelligence agencies' activities, automatically and without careful review issuing directives drafted by intelligence bureaucrats, or they gave directives whose broad language invited abuse. The justification offered was the need to investigate first "Communism" and "Fascism," then "subversive activities," and more recently "terrorism." The vagueness of these terms requires a more precise definition of the scope of permissible investigation to ensure that investigative activities not be motivated by political considerations, notably the personal antipathy of federal intelligence officials toward radical politics or beliefs and the tendency to blur the distinction between dissent and disloyalty. A corollary reason for relying on legislative charters has been the concomitant failure of executive officials to ensure control over the intelligence agencies. Either direct orders of executive officials were flouted (as when FBI Director Hoover ignored Attorney General Francis Biddle's 1943 order to terminate the Custodial Detention program) or intelligence officials misinformed presidents about past activities or ongoing activities—as Attorney General Clark did in 1946 when requesting President Truman's approval for an expansion of FBI wiretapping authority; as FBI and Justice Department officials did in 1948, 1950, and 1953 when seeking Presidents Truman's and Eisenhower's approval of directives authorizing FBI political surveillance investigations, or when President Nixon received recommendations from intelligence bureaucrats during the formulation of the Huston Plan (Theoharis, 1978, pp. 1014–1015; Theoharis, 1971, pp. 744–745; Theoharis, 1976–1977, pp. 661–671; U. S. Senate Select Committee, 1976, Bk. 3, pp. 926, 962–967).

Congress to Exert Vigilance Against Loopholes

Congress must also enact legislation rescinding the "national security" electronic surveillance loophole of the Omnibus Crime Control and Safe Streets Act of 1968. Congress should refuse to ratify affirmatively the existence of such inherent presidential powers and require, instead, that all uses of electronic surveillance be based on a court warrant. In addition, the claim for differing standards for so-called "foreign intelligence" electronic surveillance recently advanced by presidents and intelligence agency officials should be rejected, and such electronic surveillance should be authorized only when it involves investigations of suspected statutory violations. These requirements, moreover, should extend to NSA and CIA electronic surveillance of American citizens whether within the United States or abroad. Existing espionage legislation provides sufficient authority to permit legitimate national security electronic surveillance. (As such, I commend the intent behind S. 1566—introduced on May 18, 1977, by Senator Edward Kennedy and supported by the Carter Administration—but affirm the need for a number of major amendments to that bill.) Congress should also prohibit by statute such investigative techniques as break-ins, mail covers/intercepts, and the indiscriminate use of informers. Last, army intelligence officials should be prohibited from engaging in domestic political surveillance and IRS officials from targeting for tax audits or investigations individuals by reason of their political activism.

Establish an Effective Oversight System

Insofar as presidential orders had been ignored, or executive officials had been misinformed about ongoing illegal activities conducted by the intelligence agencies, the enactment of legislative charters specifically defining and thereby limiting the intelligence agencies' investigative authority will not in itself preclude future abuses of power or violations of privacy rights. A corollary need exists for a more effective oversight system. No longer can the self-restraint of intelligence officials or responsible executive officials be relied upon. Instead, some form of external oversight is needed. Congressional committees, empowered to investigate the activities of the intelligence agencies and having authority to subpoena the testimony of heads of these agencies and to require the production of relevant documents, and the creation of a permanent office of special prosecutor, empowered to investigate crimes committed by federal intelligence officials, can best provide this needed oversight.

Attorney General Griffin Bell's 1977 decisions not to prosecute former CIA Director Richard Helms and former FBI supervisor John Morley make the need for an independent special prosecutor all the more compelling. Related directly to this is the need to ensure that unwarrantedly classified documents cannot remain classified by laws penalizing officials who leak this information whether to congressional committees, members of Congress, or to the news media. It is significant that our recent knowledge of, first, the Nixon Administration's and, then, the intelligence agencies' abuses of power derived from the leaking to the media or members of Congress by White House or intelligence agency officials of what had been classified information. These documents were improperly classified "national security." The effect of their classification was not to safeguard the national security, but to preclude public knowledge of illegal or potentially embarrassing activities, which, if published, could have had adverse political consequences either for the administration or for the agencies. There is a need to ensure that this conduit remains open, and to guarantee thereby that classification cannot be relied upon to safeguard governmental illegality.

This problem necessarily intertwines with the general issue of secrecy. We have only recently learned that the ability to classify documents "top secret" and, beyond that, to create separate filing systems encouraged if it did not ensure abuses of power. All too often the major concern of intelligence officials in the recent past had been, not whether particular activities were legal, but whether they could be conducted safely. Political risk, not respect for the law, determined how intelligence officials operated. In his executive session testimony before the Senate Select Committee on Intelligence Activities, former FBI Associate Director William Sullivan starkly admitted to this distorted set of priorities:

> During the ten years that I was on the U. S. Intelligence Board, a Board that receives the cream of intelligence for this country from all over the world and inside the United States, never once did I hear anybody, including myself, raise the question: "Is this course of action which we have agreed upon lawful, is it legal, is it ethical or moral?" We never gave any thought to this realm of reasoning because we were just naturally pragmatists. The one thing we were concerned about was this: will this course of action work, will it get us what we want, will we reach the objective that we desire to reach [U. S. Senate Select Committee, 1976, Bk. 3, p. 968].

Moreover, when intelligence officials recognized that certain activities were illegal they responded by devising "do not file" procedures to ensure against discovery of their illegality. In addition, intelligence officials terminated illegal activities only when the political climate had changed during the 1970s and the risk of exposure of ongoing illegal activities had increased. At the minimum, then, Congress must grapple with the thorny issue of executive classification policy and move beyond the Freedom of Information Act provisions, which enable individuals to demand production of records and permit court tests when federal officials refuse on "national security" grounds to produce requested records. Congress must also define more precisely the standards to be employed when classifying documents and not permit such criteria to be established exclusively by executive officials. Congress must also enact legislation mandating that the intelligence agencies create a unitary filing system and imposing high penalties for the destruction of agency records. As importantly, there is a need to resolve the issue, which the Supreme Court effectively skirted in *U.S. v. Nixon,* of the limits to presidential "executive privilege" claims. This is imperative because of the radical expansion of the office of the presidency and the resultant subordination of the Cabinet. Today the presidency is a vast, sprawling bureaucracy—the number of White House aides having increased from the 6 of President Roosevelt's Administration and the 13 of President Truman's to the 550 of President Ford's (Donovan, 1977, p. 22).

SUMMARY

In sum, a new set of priorities and a new set of values are required to ensure against future abuses of power. Federal investigative powers admittedly must be carefully delineated; the public, more importantly, must make the difficult choice between openness and secrecy, democracy and elitism. A faith in participatory politics must be regained and the Jeffersonian belief in the ability of men to act intelligently when informed reaffirmed. Involved here is not only Madison's skepticism about the superior wisdom or exceptional status of government officials, but a rejection of Cold War alarums—wherein secrecy was justified on the grounds that publicity would aid and abet the nation's enemies. The famous English statesman William Pitt in an oft-quoted statement, made during a debate in the House of Commons in 1763, aptly defined this choice when rejecting similar "Cold War national security" arguments advanced by the British monarch. He declared: "Necessity is the plea for every infringement of human liberty. It is the argument of tyrants; it is the creed of slaves" (cited in U. S. Senate Committee on the Judiciary, 1974, p. 56). Writing during the height of the Alien and Sedition Act controversy in 1798 in our own country, one of the Founding Fathers, James Madison, as perceptively commented on the relationship between liberty and national security when writing to his fellow Virginian Thomas Jefferson: "Perhaps it is a universal truth that the loss of liberty at home is to be charged to provisions against danger, real or pretended, from abroad" (Malone, 1972, vol. 3, p. 379).

All too often, we have recently learned, the resort to secrecy was motivated by the desire to deny information not to our foreign adversaries but to the American public. The safeguards adopted by the Nixon Administration in 1969, for example, to preclude public knowledge of its decision to bomb Cambodia and then its frenzied attempts to ascertain whether contemporary news stories on the Cambodian bombing derived from Administration leaks dramatically highlight this domestic objective. In the final analysis, moreover, there can be no absolute guarantees or absolute security, and the quest for such absolutes can only ensure continuance of these recently disclosed privacy abuses. Whether that optimistic sense of our future success and internal strength and the belief in the transcendent importance and appeal of those principles, which motivated the Founding Fathers and informed their particular policy decisions when forging the Constitution, can be regained remain unanswered questions. Their resolution, however, will determine the success of any new policy to safeguard privacy rights.

REFERENCES

Berger, R. *Executive privilege: A constitutional myth.* New York: Bantam, 1975.

Donovan, R. *Conflict and crisis: The presidency of Harry S. Truman, 1945–1948.* New York: Norton, 1977.

Halperin, M., Berman, J., Borosage, R., & Marwick, C. *The lawless state: The crimes of the U. S. intelligence agencies.* New York: Penguin, 1976.

Malone, D. *Jefferson and his time.* Vol. 3. *Jefferson and the ordeal of liberty.* Boston: Little Brown, 1972.

Phillips, W. The government's classification system. In N. Dorsen & S. Gillers (Eds.), *None of your business: Government secrecy in America.* New York: Penguin, 1975.

Schlesinger, A., Jr. *The imperial presidency.* Boston: Houghton Mifflin, 1973.

Theoharis, A. Misleading the presidents: Thirty years of wiretapping. *The Nation,* 1971, *212,* 744–750.

Theoharis, A. The FBI's stretching of presidential directives, 1936–1953. *Political Science Quarterly,* 1976–1977, *91,* 649–672.

Theoharis, A. Bureaucrats above the law: Double-entry intelligence files. *The Nation,* 1977, *225,* 393–397.

Theoharis, A. The Truman administration and the decline of civil liberties: The FBI's success in securing authorization for a preventive detention program. *Journal of American History,* 1978, *64,* 1010–1030.

U. S. Senate, Committee on the Judiciary, Subcommittee on Constitutional Rights. *Hearings on federal data banks, computers and the Bill of Rights,* Pts. 1 & 2, 92nd Congress, 1st session, 1971.

U. S. Senate, Committee on the Judiciary, Subcommittee on Criminal Laws and Procedures and on Constitutional Rights. *Hearings on electronic surveillance for national security purposes,* 93rd Congress, 2nd session, 1974.

U. S. Senate, Select Committee to Study Governmental Operations with Respect to Intelligence Activities. Final report, *Intelligence activities and the rights of Americans,* Bk. 2, 94th Congress, 2nd session, 1976.

U. S. Senate, Select Committee to Study Governmental Operations with Respect to Intelligence Activities. Final report, *Supplementary detailed staff reports on intelligence activities and the rights of Americans,* Bk. 3, 94th Congress, 2nd session, 1976.

U. S. Senate, Select Committee to Study Governmental Operations with Respect to Intelligence Activities. Final report, *Supplementary detailed staff reports on foreign and military intelligence,* Bk. 4, 94th Congress, 2nd session, 1976.

Westin, A. The technology of secrecy. In N. Dorsen & S. Gillers (Eds.), *None of your business: Government secrecy in America.* New York: Penguin, 1975.

Toward a New Policy by Business

CHRISTOPHER A. BARRECA

Christopher A. Barreca has an A.A. and a J.D. degree from Boston University and an LL.M. degree from Northwestern University. Upon his graduation from law school in 1953 he joined the General Electric Company, where he currently holds the position of Labor Arbitration and Litigation Counsel. He is also counsel of the General Electric Personal Privacy Review Board. An expert in arbitration and collective bargaining, Mr. Barreca is co-chairman of the American Bar Association's Labor Relation Law Section Committee on Arbitration and the Law of Collective Bargaining Agreements. He is also a member of the Arbitration Advisory Committee of the Federal Mediation and Conciliation Service.

In a major article on personal privacy, the April 4, 1977, issue of *Business Week* ominously warned business executives: "The odds are 50–50 that your privacy will be invaded . . . and before the year is out" ("Protecting Your Privacy," 1977, pp. 103–104). A recent Harris survey revealed that 32% of the general public now feel "threatened" by having personal information about themselves in various files, compared to 23% in 1974 (Harris, 1977).

Why is this so? What has caused this recent growth in concern over personal privacy? Is this greater concern the result of public awareness of a serious problem, or is personal privacy merely the latest media superstar?

Ironically, perhaps, the right of personal privacy had its legal birth at the end of the nineteenth century as a reaction to the perceived abuse by the news media. In their classic article on the right to privacy in the *Harvard Law Review*, Warren and Brandeis (1890) wrote as follows:

> The question whether our law will recognize and protect the right to privacy in this and in other respects must soon come before our courts for consideration. Of the desirability—indeed the necessity—of some protection, there can, it is believed, be no doubt. The press is overstepping in every direction the obvious bounds of propriety and of decency. Gossip is no longer the resource of the idle and the vicious, but has become a trade, which is pursued with industry as well as effrontery [p. 196].

We are now told by the news media: "The real need today is to safeguard the immense amount of personal information stored in vast files and computer data banks" ("Protecting Your Privacy," 1977, p. 104).

There can be little doubt that the volume of information about individual citizens maintained by the federal government alone is vast. A recent report on federal agencies revealed that there were over 6,700 information systems in place which contain over 3.8 billion records on individuals (Richardson, 1976). In addition to federal, state, and other government bodies, private business also maintains a substantial number of information systems concerning employees, customers, and suppliers.

Nevertheless, few, I believe, would question the need for maintaining information systems in our society. Surely, most of us recognize that the development of more elaborate employee compensation packages and the increasing complexities of social legislation require more sophisticated record-keeping systems—just to meet the demands which the public itself has made upon both its public and its private institutions.

The question, of course, is what is the proper balance between the right to privacy and the need for information in our society today. On this difficult question, the United States Privacy Protection Study Commission, established by the Privacy Act of 1974, has been reviewing privacy practices in a number of areas, including the private sector, and, in fact, was scheduled to make its legislative recommendations to the President and to Congress in June of 1977. According to published reports, the study commission recommended only voluntary guidelines for personnel files of private employers, rather than the mandatory legislation espoused by some, to stop alleged privacy abuses ("Privacy Commission Recommends Voluntary Action to Prevent Abuses in Employee Recordkeeping," 1977). These recommendations should, of course, receive a careful study. Interestingly, more than 50 bills concerning privacy have already been introduced in the 95th Congress (McClain, 1977).

TWOFOLD PURPOSE OF KEEPING EMPLOYEE RECORDS

The General Electric Company keeps information on employees for two reasons: (1) to meet business needs, and (2) to comply with government requirements.

General Electric Privacy Review Team

Now, in order to put my topic in better perspective, I shall first discuss some of the 1976 findings of the General Electric Privacy Review Team, based upon a study of representative components, with respect to privacy problems and practices of the General Electric Company. The General Electric Company is a diversified manufacturing company with more than 268,000 employees in the United States. Business is conducted in all 50 states, the District of Columbia, and the Commonwealth of Puerto Rico. It may be of interest to my readers to learn of the magnitude and variety of files, documents, and data elements maintained by General Electric about its employees. For instance, employment and personnel records are maintained by more than 50 personnel accounting operations and by more than 200 employee relations operations. Personnel information is also maintained in more than 250 smaller facilities. A limited number of centralized files contain information about employees, such as pensions and savings plan records.

In one large component with over 37,000 employees, more than 700 unique data elements—that is, items of information related to employees—were identified. The data elements were contained in more than 450 separate files—both mechanized and manual—and more than 1,200 separate documents were involved.

In the private sector, the cost of data collection and maintenance of record systems is an important consideration. Consequently, the volume of information maintained notwithstanding, each of these files, data elements, and documents is being maintained either for compliance with regulations at all levels of government or justified as an expenditure required to meet what is believed to be an established business need.

Moreover, the area of employee-related record-keeping systems is dynamic. Compliance is a way of life, with the multiple and changing requirements of government agencies and laws; such as, the Internal Revenue Service, the Federal Insurance Contributions Act, the Federal Unemployment Tax Act, the Fair Labor Standards Act, the Equal Pay Act, Title VII of the Civil Rights Act, the Equal Employment Opportunities Commission, the Office of Federal Contract Compliance, the Occupational Safety and Health Act, the Employee Retirement Income Security Act, Wage and Hour Laws, State Unemployment Compensation

Laws, and many others. In addition to these almost overwhelming legal requirements, the needs of the business, including those related to collective bargaining agreements, are constantly changing, requiring the restructuring of information collection, processing, and dissemination.

Practices to Protect Employee Privacy

Given the scope and complexity of these record-keeping problems, what are the current General Electric practices with respect to privacy protection? First, with respect to the question of employee access to information about themselves, nearly all data record-keeping systems containing what may be described as historical personnel information are available for review by that employee, although some confidential information, such as medical opinions by physicians, would not be disclosed without the physician's specific consent.

On the other hand, business planning information, including salary forecasts and manpower planning, investigations of employee complaints, and investigations of suspected employment-related improprieties, can be misleading, misunderstood, and may involve personal information about other individuals. Therefore, such data are not available for employees to see.

When an employee has asked to see his records, these are made available to him, excluding, of course, those business planning and confidential data elements just referred to. But, to be quite frank, there have been only a minuscule number of these review requests.

Consequently, the principal source of employee-generated requests for corrections stems from data which are furnished to the employee from the output of a system—for example, paychecks and W-2 statements. Incidentally, employees have been excellent auditors in discovering errors in the output from such systems. It is in the company's interest, of course, to keep accurate records, and employees are encouraged to report any discrepancies so that appropriate action may be taken.

With respect to the disclosure of such personal information outside the company, most disclosures are generated by employees who wish to have certain information about them used to satisfy such personal needs as obtaining a mortgage or other type of loan or verifying employment. Still it is the established practice not to supply personal information to others, beyond employment verification, without the employee's consent unless there is a legal requirement to do so. Where there is a legal requirement, the practice is to advise employees of the information being supplied.

General Electric also has collective bargaining agreements with more than 200 different unions, and data record-keeping systems must be designed to provide the data mandated by those agreements. To safeguard the data in these systems, employees working with such records are periodically reminded of the confidential nature of the information involved and, in fact, are held personally responsible, as a condition of employment, for maintaining the necessary security. Moreover, employee-related record-keeping systems are segregated in separate facilities and safeguarded through the use of locked files or enclosures. Access to personal information is restricted to authorized personnel on a need-to-know basis. For example, an employee's own supervisor does not have access to medical expense-claim records.

With respect to the hiring process:

- Information supplied by prospective employees is not exchanged or made available to other organizations without the employee's consent except where required by law.
- Applications of individuals not hired are destroyed within a year in the absence of any legal requirements to maintain them.
- Testing is not widely used, and where it is used it is limited to determining skills and aptitudes for particular jobs.

On the other hand, the goal in the hiring process is to match individual and job requirements so that the right person is placed in the right job. This does require disclosures by the individual of certain information about himself or herself, and disclosure by the company of information about the job or jobs which may be available. As would be expected, the extent of the information communicated depends upon the complexity of the job and the skills involved as well as compliance with the requirements of Equal Employment Opportunity (EEO) laws and similar considerations. Little is required if the open job is relatively simple and requires little responsibility, education, training, or experience. In interviewing for jobs which require college degrees, or their equivalent, there is a greater need for information exchange.

A number of jobs in General Electric involve responsibility for valuable company assets. These jobs include, for example, cashiers and stock room attendants as well as company executives. If an individual is to be assigned to such a position, he or she is asked to complete a fidelity bond application. As part of the prescribed procedure, an investigative consumer report may be obtained to verify the information supplied by the individual in the bonding application.

MANDATORY PRIVACY LEGISLATION FOR THE PRIVATE SECTOR COULD BE COUNTERPRODUCTIVE

With this brief summary of some current problems and practices regarding personal privacy at General Electric added to the inputs previously made on the overall subject of privacy in this volume, readers may already have their own answer to the recent headline: Should government protect your job file from prying? (1977, p. 56). In my own view, there can be little doubt that personal privacy is a very legitimate matter of individual self-interest. At the same time, however, the espousal, in some quarters (Mironi, 1974; Brant, 1976; Hayden, 1976), of comprehensive personal privacy legislation, which may be suitable to the public sector, for application in the private sector has profound negative implications, I believe, for some of our basic liberties.

On this point, existing privacy legislation in the public sector has been inspired primarily by the desire of individual citizens and private institutions to block the further invasion of government agencies into their private lives. Legislation to control comprehensively the information systems of private institutions could itself constitute an invasion of privacy of potentially staggering proportions. Such legislation might well circumscribe rather than ensure personal liberty and privacy. Privacy in this sense could become a contradiction in terms.

On this question of corporate privacy, Rev. Theodore V. Purcell of the Jesuit Center for Social Studies at Georgetown University, in testimony before the Securities and Exchange Commission in 1975, on whether corporations should be required to disclose EEO-1 statistics to the general public, observed:

> Here I make a difficult decision based on the trade-offs between the limited and symbolic benefits I listed above *versus* the real and possible detriment to the advancement of minorities and women. In my judgement, the disadvantages outweigh the advantages. Therefore, while corporations may well voluntarily disclose consolidated EEO-1 data, I recommend that the Securities and Exchange Commission should not require such disclosure. My reason is the basic purpose I have had before my eyes during my years of research in this field, the better and faster participation of minorities and women at all levels of American corporate life [1975, p. 11].

Though General Electric has voluntarily made consolidated EEO-1 data available to shareowners for several years, the potential surge toward extending privacy legislation, in bulk, from the public to the private sector raises some privacy concerns in my mind.

One obvious major concern is the potential scope of personal privacy legislation. Is there not a danger here of establishing suffocating controls of almost every facet of private communication in the guise of privacy protection?

Another major concern involves the potential application to the private sector, without clarification, of the "Code of Fair Information Practice" of the Department of Health, Education, and Welfare's Advisory Committee on Automated Personal Data Systems, which is widely regarded as "one of the more significant influences" on privacy legislation (Bushkin & Schaen, 1976, p. 1). These "five basic principles" are:

1. There must be no personal data record-keeping system whose very existence is secret.
2. There must be a way for an individual to find out what information about him is in a record and how it is used.
3. There must be a way for an individual to prevent information about him obtained for one purpose from being used or made available for another purpose without his consent.
4. There must be a way for an individual to correct or amend a record of identifiable information about him.
5. Any organization creating, maintaining, using, or disseminating records of identifiable personal data must assure the reliability of the data for their intended use and must take reasonable precautions to prevent misuse of the data [Secretary's Advisory Committee on Automated Data Systems, 1973, p. 41].

Though these privacy principles are, in most respects, sound and constructive, there are significant ambiguities—particularly with respect to their application to unautomated records in the private sector. For instance, what would be the definition of a data record-keeping system in the private sector? Would it include confidential planning information pertaining, for example, to future salary increases and potential future job assignments, or would it be limited to recognized personnel files which are repositories of historical information?

What would be the definition of a "secret" record-keeping system? Would it, for example, include confidential investigative files such as those involving peculation—which may go to the very core of the conservation of private resources?

Who would determine the "reliability" of a private information system? Would the resolution of completeness, for example, open and promote yet another area for litigation in an already litigious society? In short, would the resolution of disputes under blanket personal privacy legislation in the private sector require the establishment of another elaborate agency with the potential for broad overreaching?

WHAT IS A DATED RECORD-KEEPING SYSTEM?

Because of these ambiguities and in order to come to grips with the problem of privacy protection, General Electric submitted its own definition of a data record-keeping system at the Privacy Protection Study Commission hearing on December 9, 1976. The suggested General Electric definition is the following:

> A data record-keeping system is a methodical arrangement of data elements which (1) have been collected; (2) have been entered into a mechanized or manual file; and (3) are systematically available to those who have access to the file.

Under this definition, data elements which have merely been collected do not constitute a *system* of records until the two remaining criteria have been satisfied.

For example, under this definition, a collection of time-clock registration cards is not considered a data record-keeping system. A payroll master file, into which data from such cards have been entered and from which such data can be systematically retrieved, is considered a data record-keeping system. Similarly, data elements which may be informally accumulated are not considered a data record-keeping system, while a formal personnel file into which such data have been entered, and from which information about data subjects can be systematically retrieved, is.

COST TO THE PRIVATE SECTOR OF IMPOSING UNIFORM PRIVACY REQUIREMENTS

Another major concern is the potential cost of compliance with detailed uniform requirements. Private institutions are now encumbered to such a degree with meeting the requirements of federal, state, and local governments that sizable legal, clerical, and accounting staffs, as well as a significant proportion of managerial time, must be directed exclusively to this purpose.

The inevitable cost of these requirements is a significant factor in the price of every product, and has a substantial impact on the inflationary trends of our economy. Comprehensive "privacy" legislation would represent another quantum leap, not only in the governmental regulation of business, but in the costs and, hence, the consumer prices which it imposes.

In testimony given to the Privacy Protection Study Commission on December 9, 1976, it was estimated that the start-up cost to General Electric, alone, to comply with the requirements of the Privacy Act of 1974, if its provisions were made applicable to the private sector, would be in the neighborhood of $34 million, with an ongoing annual cost of $15 million. This would create a very substantial cost burden for General Electric. We suspect that there likewise would be a very heavy cost burden for the country as a whole.

One may rightly ask why this estimated cost to General Electric is so high if General Electric is already in essential compliance with privacy principles as my earlier remarks suggested. The answer is that the myriad of files, documents, and data elements maintained by General Electric about its employees conform to no standard uniform pattern because each one was developed to meet a specific business need or government requirement. To comply with the provisions of the Privacy Act of 1974, for example, would require elaborate procedures for establishing and validating systems, handling and tracking disputes, retaining and purging data, accounting for accesses, and registering systems with the government.

Why Restrict the Use of Social Security Numbers?

Another concern relates to the suggestion which some have made to restrict the use of the Social Security number only to where and when it is legally required. The Social Security number is required by law in reporting such items as Social Security taxes; federal, state and local income tax withholdings; information returns for savings plans, pensions, and dividends; state unemployment and workmen's compensation reports, United States Savings Bond purchases; and similar purposes.

This means that a large percentage of employee-related record-keeping systems *must* include this data element. Therefore, the use of the Social Security number for other business purposes provides a unique and positive identifier in an efficient and cost-effective manner. Establishment of another identifier would simply increase costs because both identifiers would then have to be maintained on an accurate and timely basis.

Do Employees Express Unusual Concern?

In the final analysis, the big question is: Do abuses of personal privacy in the private sector justify the imposition of comprehensive government controls on private information systems? It is significant that there is very little evidence of employee concern about employer information systems, but this absence of expressed employee concern may be due to a lack of awareness or even a fear of reprisal. Yet it may also be due to the fact that employees have little reason to complain—perhaps because most employers recognize that it is simply good business voluntarily to protect the personal privacy of their employees.

VOLUNTARY PROTECTION OF INFORMATION A POSITIVE POLICY

In conclusion, I submit that the testimony of such companies as GE, IBM, Ford, and others before the Privacy Protection Study Commission, expresses a positive policy by business toward voluntary privacy protection. This voluntary action, coupled with lack of evidence of abuse or employee concern, on the one hand, and the very substantial costs to society which would be involved, coupled with concern for big brother control of all private information systems, on the other, should raise serious question as to the advisability of omnibus privacy legislation for the private sector.

Yet there may well be some situations in the private sector where personal rights of privacy have been ignored and abused to an extent which would justify legislation to correct such specific abuses. This, in fact, was done in the case of the Fair Credit Reporting Act. In my view, any mandatory privacy legislation for the private sector should likewise be targeted specifically to the correction of a well-documented and substantive body of privacy abuses. Otherwise, we all pay too high a price.

REFERENCES

Brant, J. A general introduction to privacy. *Massachusetts Law Quarterly*, 1976, *61* (1), 10–18.

Bushkin, A. A., & Schaen, S. I. *The Privacy Act of 1974: A reference manual for compliance.* McLean, Va.: Systems Development Corporation, 1976.

Harris, L. Our privacy in danger. *Harris Survey Column Subscription*, 1977.

Hayden, T. How much does the boss need to know? *Civil Liberties Review*, 1976, *3* (August/September), 23–32.

McClain, W. E., Jr. Bills in Congress. *Access Reports*, 1977, *3* (9), 11–12.

Mironi, M. The confidentiality of personnel records: A legal and ethical view. *Labor Law Journal*, 1974, *25*, 270–295.

Privacy Commission recommends voluntary action to prevent abuses in employee recordkeeping. *Daily Labor Reports*, 1977 (No. 100, C–1).

Protecting your privacy. *Business Week*, April 4, 1977, pp. 103–106.

Purcell, T. V. (S.J.). The limited value to the institutional investor of corporate EEO–1 disclosures. Testimony before the Securities and Exchange Commission, May 6, 1975 (S.E.C. File No. 57–551).

Richardson, E. Unpublished speech delivered to the National Conference on Privacy. Washington, D.C.: Department of Commerce, 1976.

Secretary's Advisory Committee on Automated Data Systems. *Records, computers, and the right of citizens.* Washington, D.C.: Department of Health, Education, and Welfare, 1973.

Should government protect your job file from prying? *U. S. News & World Report*, January 10, 1977, p. 56.

Warren, S. D., & Brandeis, L. D. The right to privacy. *Harvard Law Review*, 1890, *4*, 193–220.

Toward a New Policy for the Church

JAMES A. CORIDEN

James A. Coriden received his B.A. degree from St. Meinrad Seminary in 1954, and his theological degrees, S.T.B. in 1956, and S.T.L. in 1958, from the Gregorian University, Rome. He is a doctor both of canon law, with a J.C.D. (1961) from the Gregorian University, and of civil law, with a J.D. (1972) from the School of Law of the Catholic University of America. He has been admitted to practice before the Bar in Indiana and in the District of Columbia. After completing a variety of assignments in his native diocese of Gary, Indiana, Father Coriden joined the faculty of the Catholic University of America in 1968. From 1973 to 1975 he was chairman of the Department of Theology, and he is currently Academic Dean of the Washington Theological Coalition. Father Coriden is a frequent contributor to such journals as the Jurist, American Ecclesiastical Review, Journal of Ecumenical Studies, *and* Linacre Quarterly.

It seems strange, almost perverse, to worry about problems of privacy in a Church which is preoccupied with secrecy. Issues of personal privacy, which are real and growing, stand out in striking contrast against the larger problems of candor, openness, and accountability. For several years American canon lawyers have railed and lobbied against the monarchical mode of government, the closed processes of decision-making, and the concealment of facts, and for greater honesty, co-responsibility, and access to information (McManus, 1970, p. 258). It seems anomalous to be wrestling with the privacy question; it is a slightly uncomfortable feeling. However, privacy is truly an important issue, a value close to the dignity and integrity of the human person—and the Christian person—which is endangered on several fronts.

It is possible to distinguish at least ten different areas or situations in today's Roman Catholic Church in which privacy is an embattled value. I shall itemize these, briefly describing the nature and origins of the problem in each case, and attempting some policy suggestions to safeguard the appropriate level of privacy in each. After this enumeration I shall add a word about the serious negative consequences which can be anticipated if privacy is not effectively "shored up" and defended.

CLARIFICATION OF CERTAIN TERMS

Before addressing the specific areas or problem situations, it might be helpful to clarify briefly some of the notions which will be used.

"Privacy" is used here in the informational sense. It is the limitation of access to one's personal history, life, health, and feelings. "Privacy is the claim of individuals, groups, or institutions to determine for themselves when, how, and to what extent information about them is communicated to others" (Westin, 1967, p. 7). Privacy is not used here in the more profound sense of the right to self-determination discussed by Richard McCormick (1976) and utilized by Richard McBrien elsewhere in this volume. Rather, privacy here refers to the protective covering or screen which insulates the individual from others; privacy is based on the autonomy, selfhood, self-determination, and sacred specialness of the human person, but it is not identified with it. Apparently it is this sense of "limitation of access to the person" which the Fathers of the Second Vatican Council had in mind when, in the document on the Pastoral Constitution on the Church in the Modern World, they enumerated the right to the protection of privacy among those things "necessary for leading a life truly human" (Vatican Council II, 1966, p. 225).

It goes without saying that the right to privacy is not absolute, even though it is closely related to the identity, autonomy, and sacredness of the person. The need of the society or the community to obtain a certain amount of information about its members, certain critical or qualifying facts, balances and puts in perspective the individual's need for and right to privacy. The Roman Catholic Church is the community in question here; the parishes, seminaries, religious communities, and dioceses are the social settings which constitute the other pole of the tension with personal reserve or privacy.

The "internal forum" is the forum of conscience (*Code of Canon Law*, 1917, canon 196); it is the "place" or situation in which the individual confronts the Lord—in responsibility, guilt, sorrow, and reconciliation.

One accounts to the Lord for one's moral conduct. The internal forum is either sacramental, i.e., related to the sacrament of penance, or non-sacramental, i.e., outside that sacrament, but within the unique, radical communication of conscience. It is distinguished from the "external forum," the public arena of the Church's government. A member of the community accounts socially and juridically to the group in view of the common good (Naz, 1953, Vol. 5, cols. 871–873). A special and sacred mode of confidentiality is demanded by the nature of the communications of the internal forum.

AREAS OF LATENT THREAT TO PRIVACY

It should be pertinent to the formulation of recommendations for a new policy to discuss in brief detail selected areas of ecclesiastical and pastoral activity in the Church in which there may well lurk potential invasion of individual or group privacy. The ten potential problem areas which I shall discuss are the following:

1. *The Sacrament of Penance.* This unique and privileged moment of reconciliatory action of the Church finds new expression in our day. The self-revelatory acts of the penitent—acknowledgement of sin, sorrow, conversion, and amendment—now encounter the "power of the keys," mediated through the absolving words and gestures of the priest in different settings and in less rigid forms. For many centuries the Church has protected this sacramental forum with the closest confidentiality; the "confessional seal" represents the highest level of professional secrecy and sacred trust (*Code of Canon Law*, 1917, canons 888–890). This secrecy is respected by the civil law courts, and the conscious violation of it brings upon the revealer the most severe sanctions of canon law (*Code of Canon Law*, 1917, canon 2369). The effectiveness of this level of privacy is best attested by the legendary dependability which has grown up around it and by the confidence which believers have in it. The dark and anonymous confessional box was a very apt setting, both symbolically and really, for this kind of uniquely privileged communication.

The new Rite of Penance, promulgated on December 3, 1973 (*Ordo Paenitentiae*, 1975), provides for variant forms of the sacrament, especially the confrontational and conversational styles as well as the communal forms, which call for different physical settings and pose new problems in terms of privacy. The new "reconciliation rooms" or "confessional parlors" in churches or rectories provide for the face-to-face, more personal and dialogic form of the sacrament, but they may also give the unconscious impression to both priest and penitent of a less formal and less privileged form of communication. Especially when the sacramental confession is made in the context of a larger, wider-ranging counseling session, the special sacramental secrecy may not be adverted to or strictly observed. The more relaxed, cordial atmosphere, and even "small talk" for the sake of ease and comfort, may lead the participants to treat the material revealed for absolution with merely "ordinary confidentiality" and with something less than the highest sacred secrecy which befits the revelations of a human conscience to a forgiving God.

There are probably lesser dangers in the communal forms of penance—especially where general absolution is administered—since less is personally revealed in the group rite of reconciliation. Yet two problems are possible if care and discretion are not observed: (*a*) individuals might be encouraged and gradually led to make public revelation of specific sins before the entire group if there is an excessive "openness," a "let it all hang out" attitude, which can be contagious; or (*b*) when many confessors are located all over a church or auditorium for the "telling of faults" portion of a communal celebration of penance, the very physical proximity and unprotected setting, together with a certain hurried or perfunctory manner, could lead to a lessened concern for privacy during the confession and for confidentiality afterward.

It is fondly to be hoped that these imagined "dangers" are no more than the frettings of nervous canonists. No reports of abuses have reached us. Perhaps there are no grounds for concern. In any event the only policy we recommend is the present one: inculcate new priests with the same solemn sense of awe for the secrecy involved in the Sacrament of Penance, regardless of the form of its celebration, which priests of former generations were taught, and remind both ministers and people, carefully and frequently, of the special level of privacy which befits a sacramental forum in which sins are revealed in order to be forgiven.

2. *Spiritual Direction.* Even outside the Sacrament of Penance there exists an area of spiritual direction or Christian guidance which is also part of the *forum conscientiae* or *forum Dei* and is surrounded by a special sense and obligation of secrecy. It is the arena in which personal sins and weaknesses, strivings and failings, spiritual joys and sorrows are discussed with a trusted adviser in order to progress in the struggle toward a more perfect Christian life. For the believer the revelations are intimate and vital; they concern love, grace, sin, happiness, prayer, ascetic regimen —in short, the whole of one's life with God.

A recent development may give rise to problems with privacy in this area: the vastly increased use of spiritual directors. Thousands of believing Christians are seeking out "spiritual guides." Not only seminarians, novices, and some nuns and priests, but people from every walk of life who are serious about their vocations as followers of Christ are looking for and often finding holy and wise men and women to whom they go regularly for spiritual direction. The popular "directed retreat" is but one occasion for this kind of consultation. To my knowledge, no special attention is being given to the issue of the special level of privacy appropriate for this grave and intimate form of communication. Indeed, the quality of the persons involved in it may nearly preclude the need. However, many of those newly involved in spiritual direction, both the guides and the guided, are not professionally prepared, and they may not always advert to the need for and responsibility of strict confidentiality. This level of exchange seems to be more intimate and ultimate than "mere professional counseling" and calls for higher standards of confidentiality and trust.

3. *Internal Forum Solutions to Marriage Cases.* The relatively recent pastoral initiative to help those Catholics who are in a second marriage (following a divorce) which cannot be canonically validated is often called a "good faith" or "internal forum" solution (confer the articles in the *Jurist,* 1970, *30,* 1–74*). These involve the reconciliation to the sacraments of the couple who petition in good faith, whose present union appears stable and loving, and whose responsibilities to previous spouses or offspring are being met. No judgment or external forum decision is made about the canonical validity of their present union, often because inadequate evidence makes it impossible to reach a judgment.

Whether or not this form of pastoral action is or should be entirely a matter within the internal forum is in dispute. Some authors and some dioceses recommend that questionnaires be filled out and sent to chanceries or tribunals, documents or decrees issued, and records kept. These procedures bring the matter out of the internal forum (but they do not mitigate the danger to privacy; rather they seem to exacerbate it). Other authors and pastors urge that these "solutions" be kept within the forum of conscience; they recommend no questionnaires, referrals, decrees, or records. In either event the public nature of marriage makes this a very delicate problem in terms of privacy. The sacredness, unity, and permanence of marriage have always been important moral standards in the Christian community. A casual and informal approach to the reconciliation of the divorced and remarried could threaten those standards and weaken our witness to those values. Still it seems that those who have experienced the tragedy of divorce, repented, and remarried should have a chance for reconciliation to the sacramental life of the community without excessive self-revelation. Our view is that pastoral discretion can be trusted; the matter is best left in the internal, confidential forum.

Instead of the simple counseling situation involving the pastor and the couple, it has been recommended that these "solutions" would be better

* This section is entitled: Intolerable marriage situations: Conflict between external and internal forum. It consists of a report of a special *ad hoc* committee of the Canon Law Society of America charged to "investigate immediate internal forum solutions for deserving persons involved in canonically insoluble marriage cases." In addition to the committee report, papers submitted to the committee by theologians are also included.—Ed.

worked out in a dialogue with a local "marriage committee," i.e., persons knowledgeable in theology, psychology, and married life in addition to the pastoral person and the concerned couple. Both informed, objective, and balanced judgment and the standards of the local community would be better ensured by such a procedure. This procedure magnifies the problems of confidentiality, just as reference to the diocesan chancery does, and would call for clearly stated norms of confidentiality.

4. *Pastoral Counseling.* A wide range of human problems are brought to rectories, convents, chaplain's offices in hospitals, schools, prisons, and colleges. They are most often the "ordinary" crises of human growth and development, school adjustment, family tensions, love relationships, alienation and loneliness, conflict situations, experiences of discouragement and failure, unemployment, old age, illness, and so on. Sometimes the persons are more deeply troubled and beyond the ability of a pastoral counselor to assist. But the one who receives these people, listens to them, and tries to help—in the name of Christ and with the values of the gospel and of Christian tradition in mind—has obligations to respect and preserve the revelations made. This responsibility of confidentiality closely parallels the professional responsibility of social workers, psychologists, or psychiatrists. Even though there is often an explicitly Christian dimension to the assistance given by the pastoral counselor, as well as to his or her motivation, there does not seem to be any claim to higher standards of secrecy than that of other professional counselors. However, the standards are certainly no lower either, and the norms should be carefully observed. Indeed, the pastoral counselor should have a special sense of the sacredness of the human person and the respect and privacy which flow from it (Kuhlmann, 1970).

In the past, information from counseling sessions occasionally found its way into the casual conversations of priests. In contrast to confessional secrecy which was sedulously maintained, matters of counseling were sometimes treated rather loosely and lightly. For the past several years most candidates for the priesthood and other ministries have received some formal training in counseling during their theological studies. Presumably this training includes an ethics of confidentiality, and presumably it will be conscientiously observed in their pastoral ministry.

5. *Psychological and Vocational Testing.* Personality tests of various kinds are quite frequently administered to candidates for religious communities and for the diocesan priesthood. It is not a universal practice, but it has grown steadily in the past two decades. The care and understanding with which these tests are administered and interpreted has also improved in this time; most often very good professional consultants are employed for this purpose. The possible problems remain in the disclosure of the results, directly or indirectly, to those to whom the candidate has not authorized disclosure—and the potential misuse of the results by some

of those so informed. In some religious communities, vocational offices, and seminaries there is an informal and unprofessional sharing of such knowledge—sometimes with superiors, bishops, or faculty members—when such communication is not clearly foreseen by the candidate. Sometimes the persons informed (often in position of authority) are unaware of, or naïve about, the meaning of the test results. There is a danger to privacy in both the wide and unauthorized disclosure of personality test results and in their application by persons unequipped to interpret them properly.

Another form of testing which is becoming quite common in seminaries is achievement or proficiency measurement, like the "Readiness for Ministry" evaluation designed and controlled by the Association of Theological Schools. These sophisticated, computerized assessment instruments are used to measure the pastoral attitudes and ministerial skills which students possess when they begin theological studies and again as they prepare to leave the seminary and enter full-time active ministry. The "Readiness" program is new and still in the process of refinement. However, it poses some problems of privacy: in some schools it is mandatory, and the resulting personal profile is made available to the academic authorities. It is easy to imagine instances in which the evaluation will be made part of the decision-making process (e.g., for ordination, final profession, or pastoral assignment) by ecclesiastical superiors. It may not be entirely clear in advance to the candidates that the test will be used for this purpose; nor is it certain that the superiors will be capable of interpreting the profiles intelligently and accurately.

Personality inventories to evaluate compatibility are more and more frequently administered to couples preparing for marriage. They serve as useful indicators of values and attitudes about partner, family, sex, finances, employment, and other questions which often influence married life, and they are used to provoke discussion of such issues between the prospective partners. The tests are commonly administered by parish clergy, corrected by computers, and the scores returned to the assisting minister. The potential dangers to personal privacy are related to the mandatory nature of the evaluation in some dioceses (giving the impression of a qualifying examination which must be passed in order to marry), to the disclosure of the results to unauthorized persons, and to the interpretation of the results by untrained personnel.

Policies governing the administration of both kinds of tests, i.e., psychological and vocational, need to be clearly spelled out by the institutions using them, and the policies must be made known fully and in advance to those subject to the evaluations. The guidelines suggested by William Bier (1962) appear to be in the right direction, namely: (1) that free and informed consent be given; (2) that the reason or warrant for giving the test be proportionate and justifying; (3) that restraint be used in seeking only necessary information; (4) that confidentiality be observed regarding information obtained. To these one more might be added: namely, that those administering, interpreting, and applying the results of the tests be thoroughly and professionally trained. (For good moral analyses of these problems confer Ford, 1962, and McCormick, 1966.)

6. *Marriage Tribunal Investigations and Judgments.* In the past ten years American diocesan marriage tribunals have vastly increased the number of decisions rendered—from about 450 in 1968 to about 20,000 in 1977. There are several factors involved in the increase, both procedural and substantial, but the largest category or "ground" which accounts for the vast majority of decisions is "psychic incapacity," a general rubric which covers a range of psychological or personal developmental conditions which effectively prevent valid matrimonial consent. It includes radical forms of mental incompetence and relatively mild cases of immaturity and incompatibility. When such conditions are alleged as the basis for an invalid marriage, there exists a special need for care and confidentiality because of the serious and sensitive personality characteristics involved (a similar delicacy has been recognized in dealing with the more traditional but rarer ground of sexual impotence). Sometimes the psychological allegation about a party to marriage is revealed to a witness when he or she is questioned in an effort to obtain supporting testimony. Sometimes the psychic condition is indirectly revealed when a permission for another marriage in the Church is issued by the tribunal which finds the incapacitating condition. In either event the partner accused can be thoroughly outraged at the revelation, and some have proceeded to sue the former partner and the tribunal for slander.

As long as the Church continues to engage in this type of matrimonial adjudication, the dangers of disclosure will remain. But they can be minimized by the use of great discretion in interviewing and questioning (e.g., asking for observed behavior and attitudes only, and avoiding suggestions or implications of psychological disturbances).

7. *Team-structured Personnel, Formation, and Grievance Boards.* The post–Vatican II trends toward greater "collegiality" or "co-responsibility" in Church government have greatly affected the areas of personnel management, religious formation, and conflict-solving. These sensitive and critical functions, in both dioceses and religious communities, now are often controlled and sometimes even administered by committees or boards rather than by individuals. Formerly they were some of the most difficult tasks which bishops or provincials or chancellors had to perform. Now they are responsibilities more widely shared, often with partially elected committees whose membership rotates by means of periodic replacement. To the obvious advantages of this more representative and responsive system must be added the considerably increased dangers of

disclosure. When an entire board or committee has knowledge of the personal weaknesses, indiscretions, or flagrant failings of priests, nuns, seminarians, and novices, then the likelihood that those problems will become more widely known is significantly increased. In smaller dioceses or communities personal failings which once were known only to the bishop or provincial and their trusted advisers are now known to a wider group which is gradually enlarged by elected replacements. (The context for religious subjects is insightfully studied by McCool, 1971.)

This development of these collegial structures is not to be lamented—the benefits are obvious, and the level of professionalism among personnel and formation staffs is rising—but personal privacy is in need of special protection in the new situations. A code of confidentiality needs to be carefully articulated, made known to all those in these areas of work, and rigorously observed. The persons on such boards should be selected with care, small in number, with relatively long terms of service, and frequently reminded of their obligations of secrecy.

8. *Publication of Research Results and Marriage Tribunal Decisions.* As the Church utilizes social research more widely and shares the benefits of those studies in reports and publications, and as its marriage courts establish a living jurisprudence by publishing selected decisions, there may arise new problems of confidentiality. These threats to personal privacy are not different from those faced by social scientists or court reporters generally in the "secular" world, but they are not always adequately attended to when the Church ventures into areas in which recent experience is slim. In addition, the Christian community should be especially sensitive to and defensive of the dignity, autonomy, and privacy of the human person. Our standards in these matters should be the highest, not the lowest. Is anonymity always adequately safeguarded when a survey of religious attitudes is made in a small community of religious men or women? Is the identity of persons sufficiently concealed when a marriage case is published within a few months of its trial and decision? There do not appear to be widespread or flagrant abuses at present, but perhaps a review of our policies and a closer adherence to them is in order. (Consult, for instance, the Code of Ethics of the American Sociological Association.*) An injury to the reputation of one person or an unwarranted disclosure of his or her conscience is a very serious failure and needs to be guarded against.

9. *Prayer, Sharing, and Support Groups.* In the past ten years we have witnessed a grand proliferation of small groups gathered for prayer, for mutual support, and for sharing of religious experiences. This entire development seems to be a genuine manifestation of the Holy Spirit; it includes the charismatic movement, "Jesu Caritas," "Genesis II," group

* Adopted, September 1, 1971, and available from the American Sociological Association, 1722 N Street, N.W., Washington, D.C. 20036.—Ed.

spiritual direction and discernment, group retreats, and similar encounters. Though these forms of spiritual renewal and mutual assistance are healthy and welcome, they do pose some problems related to personal privacy. These small groups, when they are stable and their members are comfortable and confident with one another, often lead to a very deep sharing and self-revelation. Personal religious experiences, problems, and failings are freely communicated. And, of course, the personal experiences during the group's own prayers are observed by all the members. These sometimes include such extraordinary manifestations as speaking in tongues, prophecy, healing, being "slain in the Spirit," and so forth. Needless to say, these religious experiences, attitudes, and faith convictions are intimate expressions of grace and the human personality; they are often close to the very core of our conscious being. As such, they must be accorded profound respect, and their disclosure must be in a context of the utmost discretion and trust.

Two problems related to confidentiality may arise. The first is that some members of such groups may be led into intimate self-disclosures almost unwillingly. They can be swept along by the mood and exchanges within the group to levels of self-revelation which they had not suspected or anticipated. This can amount to an almost coercive intrusion, even though the group may be quite unconscious of its happening. Older, experienced members of such groups or movements should fully advise new members of the expectations of the group, and gently warn them in advance about the levels of self-disclosure which are customary and acceptable.

The second problem is the communication to others outside the group of what is said or done by the group members. Sometimes the obligations of confidentiality and extreme discretion which are owed in such situations are not mentioned or are only touched upon quite generally and implicitly. Consequently some more naïve, neophyte, or imprudent members quite casually relate matters to third parties which are intensely personal and private. Some serious and explicit "ground rules" of trust and confidentiality should be formulated or accepted by the group, mutually agreed upon, frequently referred to, and repeated whenever new members are brought into the group. A conscious attitude of respect and privacy can be created and maintained, but it cannot be simply presumed.

10. *Parish Sacramental Records.* The baptismal and matrimonial registers, maintained in every Catholic parish, contain some information of keen sensitivity and personal importance in addition to the routine records of sacramental events (*Code of Canon Law*, 1917, canons 470, 777, 1103, 2383). The fact of illegitimacy, an unknown parent, the fact of adoption, the identity of adoptive or natural parents, the fact of a previous marriage, the reason for its annulment, prior religious profession, or ordination to ministry all may be noted in the registers of baptism or marriage.

Sometimes this personal background information is a well-guarded secret, and its disclosure could cause embarrassment, anguish, open conflict, or trauma. Access to the parish records, and the dissemination of facts and issuance of certificates from them, are usually monitored carefully and conscientiously. But occasionally there is negligence in custody of the records or facile issuance of information without authorization. The canonical safeguards and diocesan regulations (e.g., from Catholic Charities regarding adoptions) should be sedulously observed, and more than ordinary prudence is called for. It is irresponsible, for example, to turn over complete control of the parish sacramental registers to clerical employees who are not aware of the full implications of the more sensitive information contained in them.

IMPORTANCE OF SAFEGUARDS FOR COMMUNITY OF FAITH

After this brief examination of ten areas of possible problems for personal privacy, a final few words should be said about the unhappy consequences which may befall the Church if a sense of privacy is eroded. Our whole American society is troubled by the question—witness the whole spate of legislation (e.g., the Privacy Act of 1974, the Buckley Amendment) and literature (e.g., Raines, 1974; the new *Privacy Journal*;* and the recent report of the Privacy Protection Study Commission, July 1977). And well it might be; the prospect of life in an electronically surveyed and computer-monitored society is not a pleasant one. But for a community of faith the problem is especially sensitive—for two reasons: it is essentially a voluntary association, and it must witness to the freedom and dignity of the human person.

Unlike citizens or even employees, debtors, or welfare recipients, members of the Church freely choose to affiliate, and they can also opt out. They may imperil themselves by cutting ties to a community of grace and salvation, but they are free to do so—and thousands do. A climate of distrust, gossip, indiscreet disclosure, and lack of sensitivity in matters of personal intimacy can cause disenchantment and alienation. A sense of trust and personal worth is right at the heart of life within a community of faith and love.

Since its inception, the Church has prized the singular sacredness of the human person. Its witness to personal values, and the primacy of conscience in particular, has been flawed and erratic, but the Church has returned repeatedly to take its stand for the integrity and autonomy of the person. For this reason the standards of privacy and confidentiality must be high in the Church, models to the world around—not poor and pale imitations of the norms arrived at in federal courts or national legislation.

* A monthly which began publication in 1974; address: Box 8844, Washington, D.C. 20003.—Ed.

When it comes to respecting the person and the privacy surrounding the person, the Church should lead, not follow. A compromise with these standards, or a serious failure in this leadership, amounts to a betrayal of a central point of Christian witness.

REFERENCES

Bier, W. C. (S.J.). Psychological tests and psychic privacy. *Proceedings of the Catholic Theological Society of America*, 1962, *17*, 161–179.

Code of Canon Law. Codex juris canonici, Benedicti Papae XV autoritate promulgatus. Rome: Vatican Polyglot Press, 1917.

Ford, J. C. (S.J.). Religious superiors, subjects, and psychiatrists. *Proceedings of the Catholic Theological Society of America*, 1962, *17*, 65–129.

Kuhlmann, F. L. Communications to clergymen: When are they privileged. *Journal of Pastoral Care*, 1970, *24*, 30–46.

McCool, G. A. (S.J.). The conscience of the religious subject. In W. C. Bier (S.J.) (Ed.), *Conscience: Its freedom and limitations*. New York: Fordham University Press, 1971.

McCormick, R. A. (S.J.). The polygraph in business and industry. *Theological Studies*, 1966, *27*, 421–433.

McCormick, R. A. (S.J.). The moral right to privacy. *Hospital Progress*, 1976, *57*, 38–42.

McManus, F. R. The internal forum. *Acta conventus internationalis canonistarum*. Rome: Vatican Polyglot Press, 1970.

Naz, R. For. *Dictionnaire de droit canonique*. Paris: Letouzey et Ané, 1953.

Ordo Paenitentiae. The rite of penance: English translation prepared by the International Commission on English in the Liturgy. New York: Catholic Book Publishing Company, 1975.

Privacy Protection Study Commission. *Personal privacy in an information society*. Washington, D.C.: Government Printing Office, 1977.

Raines, J. C. *Attack on privacy*. Valley Forge, Pa.: Judson, 1974.

Vatican Council II. W. M. Abbott (S.J.) (Ed.). *The documents of Vatican II*. New York: Herder & Herder, 1966.

Westin, A. F. *Privacy and freedom*. New York: Atheneum, 1967.